GERALD MASSEY'S LECTURES

BY
GERALD MASSEY

THE BOOK TREE
San Diego, California

Originally published
1900

New material, revisions and cover
© 2008
The Book Tree
All rights reserved

ISBN 978-1-58509-322-9

Cover layout and design
by Toni Villalas

Published by
The Book Tree
P O Box 16476
San Diego, CA 92176
www.thebooktree.com

We provide fascinating and educational products to help awaken the public to new ideas and information that would not be available otherwise.
Call 1 (800) 700-8733 for our *FREE BOOK TREE CATALOG*.

TABLE OF CONTENTS

The Historical (Jewish) Jesus and the Mythical (Egyptian) Christ 1

Paul as a Gnostic Opponent, not the Apostle of Historic Christianity 27

The Logia of the Lord; or the Pre-Christian Sayings ascribed to Jesus the Christ. 49

Gnostic and Historic Christianity 73

The Hebrew and other Creations fundamentally explained 105

The Devil of Darkness; or Evil in the Light of Evolution 141

Luniolatry: Ancient and Modern 165

Man in search of his Soul, during Fifty Thousand Years, and how he found it 193

The Seven Souls of Man, and their Culmination in the Christ 219

The Coming Religion 261

THE
HISTORICAL JESUS
AND
MYTHICAL CHRIST.

(All necessary references to the original authorities may be found in the Author's "Natural Genesis.")

IN presenting my readers with some of the data which show that much of the Christian History was pre-extant as Egyptian Mythology, I have to ask you to bear in mind that the facts, like other foundations, have been buried out of sight for thousands of years in a hieroglyphical language, that was never really read by Greek or Roman, and could not be read until the lost clue was discovered by Champollion, almost the other day! In this way the original sources of our Mytholatry and Christology remained as hidden as those of the Nile, until the century in which we live. The mystical matter enshrouded in this language was sacredly entrusted to the keeping of the buried dead, who have faithfully preserved it as their Book of Life, which was placed beneath their pillows, or clasped to their bosoms, in their coffins and their tombs.

Secondly, although I am able to read the hieroglyphics, nothing offered to you is based on my translation. I work too warily for that! The transcription and literal rendering of the hieroglyphic texts herein employed are by scholars of indisputable authority. There is no loop-hole of escape that way. I lectured upon the subject of Jesus many years ago. At that time I did not know how we had been misled, or that the "Christian scheme" (as it is aptly called) in the New Testament is a fraud, founded on a fable in the Old!

I then accepted the Canonical Gospels as containing a veritable human history, and assumed, as others do, that the history proved itself. Finding that Jesus, or Jehoshua Ben-Pandira, *was* an historical character, known to the Talmud, I made the common mistake of supposing that this proved the personal existence of the Jesus found portrayed in the Canonical Gospels. But after you have heard my story, and weighed the evidence now for the first time collected and presented to the public, you will not wonder that I should have changed my views, or that I should be impelled to tell the truth to others, as it now appears to myself; although I am only able to summarise here, in the briefest manner possible, a few of the facts that I have dealt with exhaustively elsewhere.

The personal existence of Jesus as Jehoshua Ben-Pandira can be established beyond a doubt. One account affirms that, according to a genuine Jewish tradition, "that man (who is not to be named) was a disciple of Jehoshua Ben-Perachia." It also says, "He was born in the fourth year of the reign of the Jewish King Alexander Jannæus, notwithstanding the assertions of his followers that he was born in the reign of Herod." That would be more than a century earlier than the date of birth assigned to the Jesus of the Gospels! But it can be further shown that Jehoshua Ben-Pandira may have been born considerably earlier even than the year 102 B.C., although the point is not of much consequence here. Jehoshua, son of Perachia, was a president of the Sanhedrin—the fifth, reckoning from Ezra as the first: one of those who in the line of descent received and transmitted the oral law, as it was said, direct from Sinai. There could not be two of that name. This Ben-Perachia had begun to teach as a Rabbi in the year 154 B.C. We may therefore reckon that he was *not born* later than 180-170 B.C., and that it could hardly be later than 100 B.C. when he went down into Egypt with his pupil. For it is related that he fled there in consequence of a persecution of the Rabbis, feasibly conjectured to refer to the civil war in which the Pharisees revolted against King Alexander Jannæus, and consequently about 105 B.C. If we put the age of his pupil, Jehoshua Ben-Pandira, at fifteen years, that will give us an approximate date, extracted without pressure, which shows that Jehoshua Ben-Pandira may have been born about the year 120 B.C. But twenty years are a matter of little moment here.

According to the Babylonian Gemara to the Mishna of Tract "Shabbath," this Jehoshua, the son of Pandira and Stada, was stoned to death as a wizard, in the city of Lud, or Lydda, and afterwards crucified by being hanged on a tree, on the eve of the Passover. This is the manner of death assigned to Jesus in the Book of Acts. The Gemara says there exists a tradition that on the rest-day before the Sabbath they crucified Jehoshua, on the rest-day of the Passah (the day before the Passover). The year of his death, however, is not given in that account; but there are reasons for thinking it could not have been much earlier nor later than B.C. 70, because this Jewish King Jannæus reigned from the year 106 to 79 B.C. He was succeeded in the government by his widow Salomè, whom the Greeks called Alexandra, and who reigned for some nine years. Now the traditions, especially of the first "Toledoth Jehoshua," relate that the Queen of Jannæus, and the mother of Hyrcanus, who must therefore be Salomè, in spite of her being called by another name, showed favour to Jehoshua and his teaching; that she was a witness of his wonderful works and powers of healing, and tried to save him from the hands of his sacerdotal enemies, because he was related to her; but that during her reign, which ended in the year 71 B.C., he was put to death. The Jewish writers and Rabbis with whom I have talked always deny the identity of the Talmudic Jehoshua and the Jesus of the Gospels. "This," observes Rabbi Jechiels, "which has been related of Jehoshua Ben-Perachia and his pupil, contains no reference whatever to him whom the Christians honour as God!" Another Rabbi, Salman Zevi, produced ten reasons for concluding that the Jehoshua of the Talmud was *not* he who was afterwards called Jesus of Nazareth. Jesus of Nazareth (and of the Canonical Gospels) was unknown to Justus, to the Jew of Celsus, and to Josephus, the supposed reference to him by the latter being an undoubted forgery.

The "blasphemous writings of the Jews about Jesus," as Justin Martyr calls them, always refer to Jehoshua Ben-Pandira, and not to the Jesus of the Gospels. It is Ben-Pandira they mean when they say they have another and a truer account of the birth and life, the wonder-working and death of Jehoshua, or Jesus. This repudiation is perfectly honest and soundly based. The only Jesus known to the Jews was Jehoshua Ben-Pandira, who had learnt the arts of magic in Egypt, and who was put to death by them as a sorcerer. This was likewise the only Jesus known to Celsus, the writer of the "True Logos," a work which the Christians managed to get rid of altogether, with so many other of the anti-Christian evidences.

Celsus observes that he was not a pure Word, not a true Logos, but a man who had learned the arts of sorcery in Egypt. So, in the Clementines, it is in the character of Ben-Pandira that Jesus is said to rise again as the magician. But here is the conclusive fact: The Jews know nothing of Jesus, the Christ of the Gospels, as an historical character; and when the Christians of the fourth century trace his pedigree, by the hand of Epiphanius, they are forced to derive their Jesus from Pandira! Epiphanius gives the genealogy of the Canonical Jesus in this wise:—

Jacob, called Pandira, Mary = Joseph—Cleopas, Jesus.

This proves that in the fourth century the pedigree of Jesus was traced to Pandira, the father of that Jehoshua who was the pupil of Ben-Perachia, and who became one of the magicians in Egypt, and who was crucified as a magician on the eve of the Passover by the Jews, in the time of Queen Alexandra, who had ceased to reign in the year 70 B.C.—the Jesus, therefore, who lived and died more than a century too soon.

Thus, the Jews do not identify Jehoshua Ben-Pandira with the Gospel Jesus, of whom they, his supposed contemporaries, know nothing, but protest against the assumption as an impossibility; whereas the Christians *do* identify their Jesus as the descendant of Pandira. It was he or nobody; yet he was neither the son of Joseph nor the Virgin Mary, nor was he crucified at Jerusalem. It is not the Jews, then, but the Christians, who fuse two supposed historic characters into one! There being but one history acknowledged or known on either side, it follows that the Jesus of the Gospels is the Jehoshua of the Talmud, or is not at all, as a Person. This shifts the historic basis altogether; it antedates the human history by more than a hundred years, and it at once destroys the historic character of the Gospels, together with that of any other personal Jesus than Ben-Pandira. In short, the Jewish history of the matter will be found to corroborate the mythical. As Epiphanius knew of no other historical Jesus than the descendant of Pandira, it is possible that this is the Jesus whose tradition is reported by Irenæus.

Irenæus was born in the early part of the second century, between 120 and 140 A.D. He was Bishop of Lyons, France, and a personal acquaintance of Polycarp; and he repeats a tradition testified to by the elders, which he alleges was directly derived from John, the "disciple of the Lord," to the effect that Jesus was not crucified at 33 years of age, but that he passed through every age, and lived on to be an oldish man. Now, in accordance with the dates given, Jehoshua Ben-Pandira may have been between 50 and 60 years of age when put to death, and his tradition alone furnishes a clue to the Nihilistic statement of Irenæus.

When the true tradition of Ben-Pandira is recovered, it shows that he was the sole historical Jesus who was hung on a tree by the Jews, not crucified in the Roman fashion, and authenticates the claim now to be made on behalf of the astronomical allegory to the dispensational Jesus, the Kronian Christ, the mythical Messiah of the Canonical Gospels, and the Jesus of Paul, who was not the carnalised Christ. For I hold that the Jesus of the "other Gospel," according to the Apostles Cephas and James, who was utterly repudiated by Paul, was none other than Ben-Pandira, the Nazarene, of whom James was a follower, according to a comment on him found in the Book Abodazura. Anyway, there are two Jesuses, or Jesus and the Christ, one of whom is repudiated by Paul.

But Jehoshua, the son of Pandira, can never be converted into Jesus Christ, the son of a virgin mother, as an historic character. Nor can the dates given ever be reconciled with contemporary history. The historical Herod, who sought to slay the young child Jesus, is known to have died four years before the date of the Christian era, assigned for the birth of Jesus.

So much for the historic Jesus. And now for the mythical Christ. Here we can tread on firmer ground.

The mythical Messiah was always born of a Virgin Mother—a factor unknown in natural phenomena, and one that cannot be historical, one that can only be explained by means of the Mythos, and those conditions of primitive sociology which are mirrored in mythology and preserved in theology. The virgin mother had been represented in Egypt by the maiden Queen, Mut-em-ua, the future mother of Amenhept III.

some 16 centuries B.C., who impersonated the eternal virgin that produced the eternal child.

Four consecutive scenes reproduced in my book are found portrayed upon the innermost walls of the *Holy of Holies* in the Temple of Luxor, which was built by Amenhept III., a Pharoah of the 17th dynasty. The first scene on the left hand shows the God Taht, the Lunar Mercury, the Annunciator of the Gods, in the act of hailing the Virgin Queen, and announcing to her that she is to give birth to the coming Son. In the next scene the God Kneph (in conjunction with Hathor) gives the new life. This is the Holy Ghost or Spirit that causes the Immaculate Conception, Kneph being the spirit by name in Egyptian. The natural effects are made apparent in the virgin's swelling form.

Next the mother is seated on the midwife's stool, and the new-born child is supported in the hands of one of the nurses. The fourth scene is that of the Adoration. Here the child is enthroned, receiving homage from the Gods and gifts from men. Behind the deity Kneph, on the right, three spirits—the Three Magi, or Kings of the Legend, are kneeling and offering presents with their right hand, and life with their left. The child thus announced, incarnated, born, and worshipped, was the Pharaonic representative of the Aten Sun in Egypt, the God Adon of Syria, and Hebrew Adonai; the child-Christ of the Aten Cult; the miraculous conception of the ever-virgin mother, personated by Mut-em-ua, as mother of the "only one," and representative of the divine mother of the youthful Sun-God.

These scenes, which were mythical in Egypt, have been copied or reproduced as historical in the Canonical Gospels, where they stand like four corner-stones to the Historic Structure, and prove that the foundations are mythical.

Jesus was not only born of the mythical motherhood; his descent on the maternal side is traced in accordance with this origin of the mythical Christ. The virgin was also called the harlot, because she represented the pre-monogamic stage of intercourse; and Jesus descends from four forms of the harlot—Thamar, Rahab, Ruth and Bathsheba—each of whom is a form of the "stranger in Israel," and is not a Hebrew woman. Such history, however, does not show that illicit intercourse was the natural mode of the divine descent; nor does it imply unparalleled human profligacy. It only proves the Mythos.

In human sociology the son of the mother preceded the father, as son of the woman who was a mother, but not a wife. This character is likewise claimed for Jesus, who is made to declare that he was earlier than Abraham, who was the typical Great Father of the Jews; whether considered to be mythical or historical. Jesus states emphatically that he existed before Abraham was. This is only possible to the mythical Christ, who preceded the father as son of the virgin mother; and we shall find it so throughout. All that is non-natural and impossible as human history, is possible, natural and explicable as Mythos.

It can be explained by the Mythos, because it originated in that which alone accounts for it. For it comes to this at last: the more hidden the meaning in the Gospel history, the more satisfactorily is it explained by the Mythos; and the more mystical the Christian doctrine, the more easily can it be proved to be mythical.

The birth of Christ is astronomical. The birthday is determined by the full moon of Easter. This can only occur once every 19 years, as we have it illustrated by the Epact or Golden Number of the Prayer Book. Understand me! Jesus, the Christ, can only have a birthday, or resurrection, once in 19 years, in accordance with the Metonic Cycle, because his parents are the sun and moon; and those appear in the earliest known representation of the Man upon the Cross! This proves the astronomical and non-human nature of the birth itself, which is identical with that of the full moon of Easter in Egypt.

Casini, the Italian Astronomer, has demonstrated the fact that the date assigned for the birth of the Christ is an Astronomical epoch in which the middle conjunction of the moon with the sun happened on the 24th March, at half-past one o'clock in the morning, at the meridian of Jerusalem, the very day of the middle equinox. The following day (the 25th) was the day of the Incarnation, according to Augustine, but the date of the Birth, according to Clement Alexander. For two birth days are assigned to Jesus by the Christian Fathers, one at the Winter Solstice, the other at the Vernal Equinox. These, which cannot both be historical, are based on the two birthdays of the double Horus in Egypt. Plutarch tells us that Isis was delivered of Horus, the child, about the time of the winter Solstice, and that the festival of the second or adult Horus followed the Vernal Equinox. Hence, the Solstice and spring Equinox were both assigned to the one birth of Jesus by the Christolators; and again, that which is impossible as human history is the natural fact in relation to the two Horuses, the dual form of the Solar God in Egypt.

And here, in passing, we may point out the astronomical nature of the Crucifixion. The Gospel according to John brings on a tradition so different from that of the Synoptics as to invalidate the human history of both. The Synoptics say that Jesus was crucified on the 15th of the month Nisan. John affirms that it was on the 14th of the month. This serious rift runs through the very foundation! As human history it cannot be explained. But there is an explanation possible, which, if accepted, proves the Mythos. The Crucifixion (or Crossing) was, and still is, determined by the full moon of Easter. This, in the lunar reckoning, would be on the 14th in a month of 28 days; in the solar month of 30 days it was reckoned to occur on the 15th of the month. Both unite, and the rift closes in proving the Crucifixion to have been Astronomical, just as it was in Egypt, where the two dates can be identified.

Plutarch also tells us how the Mithraic Cult had been particularly established in Rome about the year 70 B.C. And Mithras was fabled as having been born in a cave. Wherever Mithras was worshipped the cave was consecrated as his birthplace. The cave can be identified, and the birth of the Messiah in that cave, no matter under what name he was born, can be definitely dated. The "Cave of Mithras" was the birthplace of the Sun in the Winter Solstice, when this occurred on the 25th of December in the sign of the Sea-Goat, with the Vernal Equinox in the sign of the Ram. Now the Akkadian name of the tenth month, that of the Sea-Goat, which answers roughly to our December, the tenth by name, is *Abba Uddu*, that is, the "Cave of Light;" the cave of re-birth for the Sun in the lowest depth at the Solstice, figured as the Cave of Light. This cave was continued as the birthplace of the Christ. You will find it in all the Gospels of the Infancy, and Justin Martyr says, "Christ was born in the Stable, and afterwards took refuge in the Cave." He likewise vouches for the fact that Christ was born on the same day that the Sun was re-born in *Stabulo Augiæ*, or, in the Stable of Augias. Now the cleansing of this Stable was the sixth labour of Herakles, his first being in the sign of the Lion; and Justin was right; the Stable and Cave are both figured in the same Celestial Sign. But mark this! The Cave was the birthplace of the Solar Messiah from the year 2410 to the year 255 B.C.; at which latter date the Solstice passed out of the Sea-Goat into the sign of the Archer; and no Messiah, whether called Mithras, Adon, Tammuz, Horus or Christ, could have been born in the Cave of *Abba Uddu* or the Stable of Augias on the 25th of December after the year 255 B.C., therefore, Justin had nothing but the Mithraic tradition of the by-gone birthday to prove the birth of the Historical Christ 255 years later!

In their mysteries the Sarraceni celebrated the Birth of the babe in the Cave or Subterranean Sanctuary, from which the Priest issued, and cried:—"The Virgin hath brought forth: The Light is about to begin to grow again!"—on the Mother-night of the year. And the Sarraceni were *not* supporters of Historic Christianity.

The birthplace of the Egyptian Messiah at the Vernal Equinox was figured in Apt, or Apta, the corner; but Apta is also the name of the Crib and the Manger; hence the Child born in Apta, was said to be born in a manger; and this Apta as Crib or Manger is the hieroglyphic sign of the Solar birthplace. Hence the Egyptians exhibited the Babe in the Crib or Manger in the streets of Alexandria. The birthplace was indicated by the colure of the Equinox, as it passed from sign to sign. It was also pointed out by the Star in the East. When the birthplace was in the sign of the Bull, Orion was the Star that rose in the East to tell where the young Sun-God was re-born. Hence it is called the "Star of Horus." That was then the Star of the "Three Kings" who greeted the Babe; for the "Three Kings" is still a name of the three stars in Orion's Belt. Here we learn that the legend of the "Three Kings" is at least 6,000 years old.

In the course of Precession, about 255 B.C., the vernal birthplace passed into the sign of the Fishes, and the Messiah who had been represented for 2155 years by the Ram or Lamb, and previously for other

2155 years by the Apis Bull, was now imaged as the Fish, or the "Fish-man," called Ichthys in Greek. The original Fish-man—the An of Egypt, and the Oan of Chaldea—probably dates from the previous cycle of precession, or 26,000 years earlier; and about 255 B.C. the Messiah, as the Fish-man, was to come up once more as the Manifestor from the celestial waters. The coming Messiah is called Dag, the Fish, in the Talmud; and the Jews at one time connected his coming with some conjunction, or occurrence, in the sign of the Fishes! This shows the Jews were not only in possession of the astronomical allegory, but also of the tradition by which it could be interpreted. It was the Mythical and Kronian Messiah alone who was, or could be, the subject of prophecy that might be fulfilled—prophecy that was fulfilled as it is in the Book of Revelation—when the Equinox entered, the cross was re-erected, and the foundations of a new heaven were laid in the sign of the Ram, 2410 B.C.; and, again, when the Equinox entered the sign of the Fishes, 255 B.C. Prophecy that will be *again* fulfilled when the Equinox enters the sign of the Waterman about the end of this century, to which the Samaritans are still looking forward for the coming of their Messiah, who has not yet arrived for them. The Christians alone ate the oyster; the Jews and Samaritans only got an equal share of the empty shells! The uninstructed Jews, the *idiotai*, at one time thought the prophecy which was astronomical, and solely related to the cycles of time, was to have its fulfilment in human history. But they found out their error, and bequeathed it unexplained to the still more ignorant Christians. The same tradition of the Coming One is extant amongst the Millenarians and Adventists, as amongst the Moslems. It is the tradition of El-Mahdi, the prophet who is to come in the last days of the world to conquer all the world, and who was lately descending the Soudan with the old announcement the "Day of the Lord is at hand," which shows that the astronomical allegory has left some relics of the true tradition among the Arabs, who were at one time learned in astronomical lore.

The Messiah, as the Fish-man, is foreseen by Esdras ascending out of the sea as the "same whom God the highest hath kept a great season, which by his own self shall deliver the creature." The ancient Fish-man only came up out of the sea to converse with men and teach them in the daytime. "When the sun set," says Berosus, "it was the custom of this Being to plunge again into the sea, and abide all night in the deep." So the man foreseen by Esdras is only visible by day.

As it is said, "E'en so can no man upon earth see my son, or those that be with him, but in the daytime." This is parodied or fulfilled in the account of Ichthys, the Fish, the Christ who instructs men by day, but retires to the lake of Galilee, where he demonstrates his solar nature by walking the waters at night, or at the dawn of day.

We are told that his disciples being on board a ship, "when even was come, in the fourth watch of the night, Jesus went unto them walking upon the sea." Now the fourth watch began at three o'clock, and ended at six o'clock. Therefore, this was about the proper time for a solar God to appear walking upon the waters, or coming up out of them as the Oannes. Oannes is said to have taken no food whilst he was with men : "In the daytime he used to converse with men, but took no food at that season." So Jesus, when his disciples prayed him, saying "Master, eat," said unto them, "I have meat to eat that you know not of. My meat is to do the will of Him that sent me."

This is the perfect likeness of the character of Oannes, who took no food, but whose time was wholly spent in teaching men. Moreover, the mythical Fish-man is made to identify himself. When the Pharisees sought a "sign from heaven," Jesus said, "There shall no sign be given but the sign of Jonas. For as Jonas became a sign unto the Ninevites, so shall also the son of man be to this generation."

The sign of Jonas is that of the Oan, or Fish-man of Nineveh, whether we take it direct from the monuments, or from the Hebrew history of Jonah, or from the Zodiac.

The voice of the secret wisdom here says truly that those who are looking for signs, can have no other than that of the returning Fish-man, Ichthys, Oannes, or Jonah; and assuredly, there was no other sign or date—than those of Ichthys, the Fish who was re-born of the fish-goddess, Atergatis, in the sign of the Fishes, 255 B.C. After whom the primitive Christians were called little fishes, or Pisciculi.

This date of 255 B.C. was the true day of birth, or rather of re-birth for the celestial Christ, and there was no valid reason for changing the time of the world.

The Gospels contain a confused and confusing record of early Christian belief: things most truly believed (Luke) concerning certain mythical matters, which were ignorantly mistaken for human and historical. The Jesus of our Gospels is but little of a human reality, in spite of all attempts to naturalize the Mythical Christ, and make the story look rational.

The Christian religion was not founded on a man, but on a divinity; that is, a mythical character. So far from being derived from the model man, the typical Christ was made up from the features of various Gods, after a fashion somewhat like those "pictorial averages" portrayed by Mr. Galton, in which the traits of several persons are photographed and fused in a portrait of a dozen different persons, merged into one that is not anybody. And as fast as the composite Christ falls to pieces, each feature is claimed, each character is gathered up by the original owner, as with the grasp of gravitation.

It is not I that deny the divinity of Jesus the Christ; I assert it! He never was, and never could be, any other than a divinity; that is, a character non-human, and entirely mythical, who had been the pagan divinity of various pagan myths, that had been pagan during thousands of years before our Era.

Nothing is more certain, according to honest evidence, than that the Christian scheme of redemption is founded on a fable misinterpreted; that the prophecy of fulfilment was solely astronomical, and the Coming One as the Christ who came in the end of an age, or of the world, was but a metaphorical figure, a type of time, from the first, which never could take form in historic personality, any more than Time in Person could come out of a clock-case when the hour strikes; that no Jesus could become a Nazarene by being born at, or taken to, Nazareth; and that the history in our Gospels is from beginning to end the identifiable story of the Sun-God, and the Gnostic Christ who never could be made flesh. When we did not know the one it was possible to believe the other; but when once we truly know, then the false belief is no longer possible.

The mythical Messiah was Horus in the Osirian Mythos; Har-Khuti in the Sut-Typhonian; Khunsu in that of Amen-Ra; Iu in the cult of Atum-Ra; and the Christ of the Gospels is an amalgam of all these characters.

>The Christ is the Good Shepherd!
>So was Horus.
>Christ is the Lamb of God!
>So was Horus.
>Christ is the Bread of Life!
>So was Horus.
>Christ is the Truth and the Life!
>So was Horus.
>Christ is the Fan-bearer!
>So was Horus.
>Christ is the Lord!
>So was Horus.

Christ is the Way and the Door of Life!
Horus was the path by which they travelled out of the Sepulchre. He is the God whose name is written with the hieroglyphic sign of the Road or Way.

Jesus is he that should come; and Iu, the root of the name in Egyptian, means "to come." Iu-em-hept, as the Su, the Son of Atum, or of Ptah, was the "Ever-Coming One," who is always portrayed as the marching youngster, in the act and attitude of coming. Horus included both sexes. The Child (or the soul) is of either sex, and potentially, of both. Hence the hermaphrodital Deity; and Jesus, in Revelation, is the Young Man who has the female paps.

Iu-em-hept signifies he who comes with peace. This is the character in which Jesus is announced by the Angels! And when Jesus comes to his disciples after the resurrection it is as the bringer of peace. "Learn of me and ye shall find rest," says the Christ. Khunsu-Nefer-Hept is the Good Rest, Peace in Person! The Egyptian Jesus, Iu-em-hept, was the second Atum; Paul's Jesus is the second Adam. In one rendition of John's Gospel, instead of the "only-begotten Son of God," a variant reading gives the "only-begotten God," which has been declared an impossible rendering. But the "only-begotten God" was an especial type in Egyptian Mythology, and the phrase re-identifies the divinity whose emblem is the beetle. Hor-Apollo says, "To denote the only-begotten or a father, the Egyptians delineate a scarabæus!

By this they symbolize an only-begotten, because the creature is self-produced, being unconceived by a female." Now the youthful manifestor of the Beetle-God was this Iu-em-hept, the Egyptian Jesus. The very phraseology of John is common to the Inscriptions, which tell of him who was the Beginner of Becoming from the first, and who made all things, but who himself was not made. I quote verbatim. And not only was the Beetle-God continued in the "only-begotten God"; the beetle-type was also brought on as a symbol of the Christ. Ambrose and Augustine, amongst the Christian Fathers, identified Jesus with, and as, the "good Scarabæus," which further identifies the Jesus of John's Gospel with the Jesus of Egypt, who was the Ever-Coming One, and the Bringer of Peace, whom I have elsewhere shown to be the Jesus to whom the Book of Ecclesiasticus is inscribed, and ascribed in the Apocrypha.

In accordance with this continuation of the Kamite symbols, it was also maintained by some sectaries that Jesus was a potter, and not a carpenter; and the fact is that this only-begotten Beetle-God, who is portrayed sitting at the potter's wheel forming the Egg, or shaping the vase-symbol of creation, was the Potter personified, as well as the only-begotten God in Egypt.

The character and teachings of the Canonical Christ are composed of contradictions which cannot be harmonised as those of a human being, whereas they are always true to the Mythos.

He is the Prince of Peace, and yet he asserts that he came not to bring peace: "I came not to send peace, but a sword," and not only is Iu-em-hept the Bringer of Peace by name in one character; he is the Sword personified in the other. In this he says, "I am the living image of Atum, proceeding from him as a sword." Both characters belong to the mythical Messiah in the Ritual, who also calls himself the "Great Disturber," and the "Great Tranquilizer"—the "God Contention," and the "God Peace." The Christ of the Canonical Gospels has several prototypes, and sometimes the copy is derived or the trait is caught from one original, and sometimes from the other. The Christ of Luke's Gospel has a character entirely distinct from that of John's Gospel. Here he is the Great Exorciser, and caster-out of demons. John's Gospel contains no case of possession or obsession: no certain man who "had devils this long time"; no child possessed with a devil; no blind and dumb man possessed with a devil.

Other miracles are performed by the Christ of John, but not these; because John's is a different type of the Christ. And the original of the Great Healer in Luke's Gospel may be found in the God Khunsu, who was the Divine Healer, the supreme one amongst all the other healers and saviours, especially as the caster-out of demons, and the expeller of possessing spirits. He is called in the texts the "Great God, the driver away of possession."

In the Stele of the "Possessed Princess," this God in his effigy is sent for by the chief of Bakhten, that he may come and cast out a possessing spirit from the king's daughter, who has an evil movement in her limbs. The demon recognises the divinity just as the devil recognises Jesus, the expeller of evil spirits. Also the God Khunsu is Lord over the pig—a type of Typhon. He is portrayed in the disk of the full moon of Easter, in the act of offering the pig as a sacrifice. Moreover, in the judgment scenes, when the wicked spirits are condemned and sent back into the abyss, their mode of return to the lake of primordial matter is by entering the bodies of swine. Says Horus to the Gods, speaking of the condemned one: "When I sent him to his place he went, and he has been transformed into a black pig." So when the Exorcist in Luke's Gospel casts out Legion, the devils ask permission of the Lord of the pig to be allowed to enter the swine, and he gives them leave. This, and much more that might be adduced, tends to differentiate the Christ of Luke, and to identify him with Khunsu, rather than with Iu-em-hept, the Egyptian Jesus, who is reproduced in the Gospel according to John. In this way it can be proved that the history of Christ in the Gospels is one long and complete catalogue of likenesses to the Mythical Messiah, the Solar or Luni-Solar God.

The "Litany of Ra," for example, is addressed to the Sun-God in a variety of characters, many of which are assigned to the Christ of the Gospels. Ra is the Supreme Power, the Beetle that rests in the Empyrean, who is born as his own son. This, as already said, is the God in John's Gospel, who says:—"I and the Father are one," and who *is* the father born as his own son; for he says, in knowing and seeing the son, "from henceforth ye know him and have seen him"; *i.e.*, the Father.

Ra is designated the "Soul that speaks." Christ is the Word. Ra is the destroyer of venom. Jesus says:—"In my name they shall take up serpents, and if they drink any deadly thing it shall not hurt them." In one character Ra is the outcast. So Jesus had not where to lay his head.

Ra is the "timid one who sheds tears in the form of the Afflicted." He is called Remi, the Weeper. This weeping God passes through "Rem-Rem," the place of weeping, and there conquers on behalf of his followers. In the Ritual the God says:—"I have desolated the place of Rem-Rem." This character is sustained by Jesus in the mourning over Jerusalem that was to be desolated. The words of John, "Jesus wept," are like a carven statue of the "Afflicted One," as Remi, the Weeper. Ra is also the God who "makes the mummy come forth." Jesus makes the mummy come forth in the shape of Lazarus; and in the Roman Catacombs the risen Lazarus is not only represented as a mummy, but is an Egyptian mummy which has been eviscerated and swathed for the eternal abode. Ra says to the mummy: "Come forth!" and Jesus cries: "Lazarus, come forth!" Ra manifests as "the burning one, he who sends destruction," or "sends his fire into the place of destruction." "He sends fire upon the rebels," his form is that of the "God of the furnace." Christ also comes in the person of this "burning one"; the sender of destruction by fire. He is proclaimed by Matthew to be the Baptiser with fire. He says, "I am come to send fire on the earth."

He is portrayed as "God of the furnace," which shall "burn up the chaff with unquenchable fire." He is to cast the rebellious into a "furnace of fire," and send the condemned ones into everlasting fire. All this was natural when applied to the Solar-God, and it is supposed to become supernatural when misapplied to a supposed human being to whom it never could apply. The Solar fire was the primary African fount of theological hell-fire and hell.

The "Litany" of Ra collects the manifold characters that make up the total God (termed Teb-temt), and the Gospels have gathered up the mythical remains; thus the result is in each case identical, or entirely similar. From beginning to end the Canonical Gospels contain the Drama of the Mysteries of the Luni-Solar God, narrated as a human history. The scene on the Mount of Transfiguration is obviously derived from the ascent of Osiris into the Mount of Transfiguration in the Moon. The sixth day was celebrated as that of the change and transformation of the Solar God in the lunar orb, which he re-entered on that day as the regenerator of its light. With this we may compare the statement made by Matthew, that "after six days Jesus went up into a high mountain apart, and he was transfigured, and his face did shine as the sun (of course!), and his garments became white as the light."

In Egypt the year began just after the Summer Solstice, when the sun descended from its midsummer height, lost its force, and lessened in its size. This represented Osiris, who was born of the Virgin Mother as the child Horus, the diminished infantile sun of Autumn; the suffering, wounded, bleeding Messiah, as he was represented. He descended into hell, or hades, where he was transformed into the virile Horus, and rose again as the sun of the resurrection at Easter. In these two characters of Horus on the two horizons, Osiris furnished the dual type for the Canonical Christ, which shows very satisfactorily HOW the mythical prescribes the boundaries beyond which the historical does not, dare not, go. The first was the child Horus, who always remained a child. In Egypt the boy or girl wore the Horus-lock of childhood until 12 years of age. Thus childhood ended about the twelfth year. But although adultship was then entered upon by the youth, and the transformation of the boy into manhood began, the full adultship was not attained until 30 years of age. The man of 30 years was the typical adult. The age of adultship was 30 years, as it was in Rome under the *Lex Pappia*. The *homme fait* is the man whose years are triaded by tens, and who is *Khemt*. As with the man, so it is with the God; and the second Horus, the same God in his second character, is the *Khemt* or *Khem-Horus*, the typical adult of 30 years. The God up to twelve years was Horus, the child of Isis, the mother's child, the weakling. The virile Horus (the sun in its vernal strength), the adult of 30 years, was representative of the Fatherhood, and this Horus is the anointed son of Osiris. These two characters of Horus the child, and Horus the adult of 30 years, are reproduced in the only two phases of the life of Jesus in the Gospels. John furnishes no historic dates for the time when the *Word* was incarnated and became flesh; nor for the childhood of Jesus; nor for the transformation into the Messiah. But Luke tells us that *the child of twelve years* was the wonderful youth, and that he increased in wisdom and stature. This is the length of years assigned to Horus the child; and this phase of the child-Christ's life is followed by the baptism and anointing, the descent of the pubescent spirit with the consecration of the Messiah in Jordan, when Jesus "*began to be about 30 years of age.*"

The earliest anointing was the consecration of puberty; and here at the full age of the typical adult, the Christ, who was previously a child, the child of the Virgin Mother, is suddenly made into the Messiah, as the Lord's anointed. And just as the second Horus was regenerated, and this time begotten of the father, so in the transformation scene of the baptism in Jordan, the father authenticates the change into full adultship, with the voice from heaven saying:—"This is my beloved son, in whom I am well pleased;" the spirit of pubescence, or the *Ruach*, being represented by the descending dove, called the spirit of God. Thus from the time when the child-Christ was about twelve years of age, until that of the typical *homme fait* of Egypt, which was the age assigned to Horus when he became the adult God, there is no history. This is in exact accordance with the Kamite allegory of the double-Horus. And the Mythos alone will account for the chasm which is wide and deep enough to engulf a supposed history of 18 years. Childhood cannot be carried beyond the 12th year, and the child-Horus always remained a child; just as the child-Christ does in Italy, and in German folk-tales. The mythical record founded on nature went no further, and there the history consequently halts within the prescribed limits, to rebegin with the anointed and re-generated Christ at the age of Khem-Horus, the adult of 30 years.

And these two characters of Horus necessitated a double form of the mother, who divides into the two divine sisters, Isis and Nephthys. Jesus also was bi-mater, or dual-mothered; and the two sisters reappear in the Gospels as the two Marys, both of whom are the mothers of Jesus. This again, which is impossible as human history, is perfect according to the Mythos that explains it.

As the child-Horus, Osiris comes down to earth; he enters matter, and becomes mortal. He is born like the Logos, or "as a Word." His father is Seb, the earth, whose consort is Nu, the heaven, one of whose names is MERI, the Lady of Heaven; and these two are the prototypes of Joseph and Mary. He is said to cross the earth a substitute, and to suffer vicariously as the Saviour, Redeemer, and Justifier of men. In these two characters there was constant conflict between Osiris and Typhon, the Evil Power, or Horus and Sut, the Egyptian Satan. At the Autumn Equinox, the devil of darkness began to dominate; this was the Egyptian Judas, who betrayed Osiris to his death at the last supper. On the day of the Great Battle at the Vernal Equinox, Osiris conquered as the ascending God, the Lord of the growing light. Both these struggles are portrayed in the Gospels. In the one Jesus is betrayed to his death by Judas; in the other he rises superior to Satan. The latter conflict followed immediately after the baptism. In this way:—When the sun was half-way round, from the Lion sign, it crossed the River of the Waterman, the Egyptian Iarutana, Hebrew Jordan, Greek Eridanus. In this water the baptism occurred, and the transformation of the child-Horus into the virile adult, the conqueror of the evil power, took place. Horus becomes hawk-headed, just where the dove ascended and abode on Jesus. Both birds represented the virile soul that constituted the anointed one at puberty. By this added power Horus vanquished Sut, and Jesus overcame Satan. Both the baptism and the contest are referred to in the Ritual. "I am washed with the same water in which the Good Opener (Un-Nefer) washes when he disputes with Satan, that justification should be made to Un-Nefer, the Word made Truth," or the Word that is Law.

The scene between the Christ and the Woman at the Well may likewise be found in the Ritual. Here the woman is the lady with the long hair, that is Nu, the consort of Seb—and the five husbands can be paralleled by her five star-gods born of Seb. Osiris drinks out of the well "to take away his thirst." He also says: "I am creating the water. I make way in the valley, in the Pool of the Great One. Make-road (or road-maker) expresses what I am." "I am the Path by which they traverse out of the sepulchre of Osiris."

So the Messiah reveals himself as the source of living water, "that springeth up unto Everlasting Life." Later on he says, "I am the way, the truth, the life." "I am creating the water, discriminating the seat," says Horus. Jesus says, "The hour cometh when ye shall neither in this mountain nor yet at Jerusalem worship the Father." Jesus claims that this well of life was given to him by the Father. In the Ritual it says, "He is thine, O Osiris! A well, or flow, comes out of thy mouth to him!" Also, the paternal source is acknowledged in another text. "I am the Father, inundating when there is thirst, guarding the water. Behold me at it." Moreover, in another chapter the well of living water becomes the Pool of Peace. The speaker says, "The well has come through me. I wash in the Pool of Peace."

In Hebrew, the Pool of Peace is the Pool of Salem, or Siloam. And here, not only is the pool described at which the Osirified are made pure and healed; not only does the Angel or God descend to the waters—the "certain times" are actually dated. "The Gods of the pure waters are there on the fourth hour of the night, and the eighth hour of the day, saying, 'Pass away hence,' to him who has been cured."

In the margin, the Pool of Siloam is said to be the Pool of "Sent," and the word "Sennt" is an Egyptian name for a medicated or healing bath!

An epitome of a considerable portion of John's Gospel may be found in another brief chapter of the Ritual—" Ye Gods come to be my servants, I am the son of your Lord. Ye are mine through my Father, who gave you to me. I have been among the servants of Hathor or Meri. I have been washed by thee, O attendant!" Compare the washing of Jesus' feet by Mary.

The Osiris exclaims, "I have welcomed the chief spirits in the service of the Lord of things! I am the Lord of the fields when they are white," *i.e.*, for the reapers and the harvest. So the Christ now says to the disciples, "Behold, I say unto you, Lift up your eyes and look on the fields, that are white already unto the harvest."

"Then said he unto his disciples, The harvest truly is plenteous, but the labourers are few. Pray ye, therefore, the Lord of the harvest that he send forth labourers into his harvest. And he called unto him his twelve disciples.' Now, if we turn to the Egyptian "Book of Hades," the harvest, the Lord of the harvest, and the reapers of the harvest are all portrayed : the twelve are also there. In one scene they are preceded by a God leaning on a staff, who is designated the Master of Joy—a surname of the Messiah Horus when assimilated to the Soli-Lunar Khunsu; the twelve are "they who labour at the harvest in the plains of Neter-Kar." A bearer of a sickle shows the inscription: "These are the Reapers." The twelve are divided into two groups of five and seven—the original seven of the Aahenru; these seven are the reapers. The other five are bending towards an enormous ear of corn, the image of the harvest, ripe and ready for the sickles of the seven. The total twelve are called the "Happy Ones," the bearers of food. Another title of the twelve is that of the "Just Ones." The God says to the reapers, "Take your sickles! Reap your grain! Honour to you, reapers." Offerings are made to them on earth, as bearers of sickles in the fields of Hades. On the other hand, the tares or the wicked are to be cast out and destroyed for ever. These twelve are the apostles in their Egyptian phase.

In the chapters on "Celestial Diet" in the Ritual, Osiris eats under the sycamore tree of Hathor. He says, "Let him come from the earth. Thou hast brought these seven loaves for me to live by, bringing the bread that Horus (the Christ) makes. Thou hast placed, thou hast eaten rations. Let him call to the Gods for them, or the Gods come with them to him."

This is reproduced as miracle in the Gospels, performed when the multitude were fed upon seven loaves. The seven loaves are found here, together with the calling upon the Gods, or working the miracle of multiplying the bread.

In the next chapter there is a scene of eating and drinking. The speaker, who impersonates the Lord, says:—"I am the Lord of Bread in Annu. My bread at the heaven was that of Ra; my bread on earth was that of Seb." The seven loaves represent the bread of Ra. Elsewhere the number prescribed to be set on one table, as an offering, is five loaves. These are also carried on the heads of five different persons in the scenes of the under-world. Five loaves are the bread of Seb. Thus five loaves represent the bread of earth, and seven the bread of heaven Both five and seven are sacred regulation numbers in the Egyptian Ritual. And in the Gospel of Matthew the miracles are wrought with five loaves in the one case, and seven in the other, when the multitudes are fed on celestial diet. This will explain the two different numbers in one and the same Gospel miracle. In the Canonical narrative there is a lad with five barley loaves and two fishes. In the next chapter of the Ritual we possibly meet with the lad himself, as the miracle-worker says:—"I have given breath to the said youth."

The Gnostics asserted truly that celestial persons and celestial scenes had been transferred to earth in our Gospels; and it is only within the Pleroma (the heaven) or in the Zodiac that we can at times identify the originals of both. And it is there we must look for the "two fishes."

As the latest form of the Manifestor was in the heaven of the twelve signs, that probably determined the number of twelve basketsful of food remaining when the multitude had all been fed. "They that ate the loaves were five thousand men;" and five thousand was the exact number of the Celestials or Gods in the Assyrian Paradise, before the revolt and fall from heaven. The scene of the miracle of the loaves and fishes is followed by an attempt to take Jesus by force, but he withdrew himself; and this is succeeded by the miracle of his walking on the waters, and conquering the wind and waves. So is it in the Ritual. Chap. 57 is that of the breath prevailing over the water in Hades. The speaker, having to cross over, says: "O Hapi! let the Osiris prevail over the waters, like as the Osiris prevailed against the taking by stealth, the night of the great struggle." The Solar God was betrayed to his death by the Egyptian Judas, on the "night of the taking by stealth," which was the night of the last supper. The God is "waylaid by the conspirators, who have watched very much." They are said to smell him out "by the eating of his bread." So the Christ is waylaid by Judas, who "knew the place, for Jesus often resorted thither," and by the Jews who had long watched to take him.

The smelling of Osiris by the eating of his bread is remarkably rendered by John at the eating of the last supper. The Ritual has it: —"They smell Osiris by the eating of his bread, transporting the evil of Osiris."

"And when he had dipped the sop he gave it to Judas Iscariot, and after the sop Satan entered into him." Then said Jesus to him into whom the evil or devil had been transported, "That thou doest, do quickly." Osiris was the same, beseeching burial. Here it is demonstrable that the non-historical Herod is a form of the Apophis Serpent, called the enemy of the Sun. In Syriac, Herod is a red dragon. Herod, in Hebrew, signifies a terror. Heru (Eg.) is to terrify, and Herrut (Eg.) is the Snake, the typical reptile. The blood of the divine victim that is poured forth by the Apophis Serpent at the sixth hour, on "the night of smiting the profane," is literally shed by Herod, as the Herrut or Typhonian Serpent.

The speaker, in the Ritual, asks: "Who art thou then, Lord of the Silent Body? I have come to see him who is in the serpent, eye to eye, and face to face." "Lord of the Silent Body" is a title of the Osiris. "Who art thou then, Lord of the Silent Body?" is asked and left unanswered. This character is also assigned to the Christ. The High Priest said unto him, "Answerest thou nothing?" "But Jesus held his peace." Herod questioned him in many words, but he answered him nothing. He acts the prescribed character of "Lord of the Silent Body."

The transaction in the sixth hour of the night of the Crucifixion is expressly inexplicable. In the Gospel we read:—"Now from the sixth hour there was darkness over all the land unto the ninth hour." The sixth hour being midnight, that shows the solar nature of the mystery, which has been transferred to the sixth hour of the day in the Gospel.

It is in the seventh hour the mortal struggle takes place between the Osiris and the deadly Apophis, or the great serpent, Haber, 450 cubits long, that fills the whole heaven with its vast enveloping folds. The name of this seventh hour is "that which wounds the serpent Haber." In this conflict with the evil power thus portrayed the Sun-God is designated the "Conqueror of the Grave," and is said to make his advance through the influence of Isis, who aids him in repelling the serpent or devil of darkness. In the Gospel, Christ is likewise set forth in the supreme struggle as "Conqueror of the Grave," for "the graves were opened, and many bodies of the saints which slept arose;" and Mary represents Isis, the mother, at the cross. It is said of the great serpent, "There are those on earth who do not drink of the waters of this serpent, Haber," which may be paralleled with the refusal of the Christ to drink of the vinegar mingled with gall.

When the God has overcome the Apophis Serpent, his old nightly, annual, and eternal enemy, he exclaims, "I come! I have made my way! I have come like the sun, through the gate of the one who likes to deceive and destroy, otherwise called the 'viper.' I have made my way! I have bruised the serpent, I have passed."

But the more express representation in the mysteries was that of the annual sun as the Elder Horus, or Atum. As Julius Firmicus says: "In the solemn celebration of the mysteries, all things in order had to be done which the youth either did or suffered in his death."

Diodorus Siculus rightly identified the "whole fable of the underworld," that was dramatised in Greece, as having been copied "from the ceremonies of the Egyptian funerals," and so brought on from Egypt into Greece and Rome. One part of this mystery was the portrayal of the suffering Sun-God in a feminine phase. When the suffering sun was ailing and ill, he became female, such being a primitive mode of expression. Luke describes the Lord in the Garden of Gethsemane as being in a great agony, "and his sweat was, as it were, great drops of blood, falling to the ground." This experience the

Gnostics identified with the suffering of their own hemorrhoidal Sophia, whose passion is the original of that which is celebrated during Passion week, the "week of weeping in Abtu," and which constitutes the fundamental mystery of the Rosy Cross, and the Rose of Silence.

In this agony and bloody sweat the Christ simply fulfils the character of Osiris Tesh-Tesh, the red sun, the Sun-God that suffers his agony and bloody sweat in Smen, whence Gethsmen, or Gethsemane. Tesh means the bleeding, red, gory, separate, cut, and wounded; tesh-tesh is the inert form of the God whose suffering, like that of Adonis, was represented as feminine, which alone reaches a natural origin for the type. He was also called Ans-Ra, or the sun bound up in linen.

So natural were the primitive mysteries!

My attention has just been called to a passage in Lycophron, who lived under Ptolemy Philadelphus between 310 and 246 B.C. In this Heracles is referred to as

> "That three-nighted lion, whom of old
> Triton's fierce dog with furious jaws devoured,
> Within whose bowels, tearing of his liver,
> He rolled, burning with heat, though without fire,
> His head with drops of sweat bedewed all o'er."

This describes the God suffering his agony and sweat, which is called the "bloody flux" of Osiris. Here the nights are three in number. So the Son of Man was to be three nights as well as three days in the "heart of the earth." In the Gospels this prophecy is *not* fulfilled; but if we include the night of the bloody sweat, we have the necessary three nights, and the Mythos becomes perfect. In this phase the suffering Sun was the Red Sun, whence the typical Red Lion.

As Atum, the red sun is described as setting from the Land of Life in all the colours of crimson, or Pant, the red pool. This clothing of colours is represented as a "gorgeous robe" by Luke; a purple robe by Mark; and a robe of scarlet by Matthew. As he goes down at the Autumn Equinox, he is the crucified. His mother, Nu, or Meri, the heaven, seeing her son, the Lord of Terror, greatest of the terrible, setting from the Land of Life, with his hands drooping, she becomes obscure, and there is great darkness over all the land, as at the crucifixion described by Matthew, in which the passing of the Lord of Terror is rendered by the terrible or "loud cry" of the Synoptic version. The Sun-God causes the dead, or those in the earth, to live as he passes down into the under-world, because, as he entered the earth, the tombs were opened, *i.e.*, figuratively. But it is reproduced literally by Matthew.

The death of Osiris, in the Ritual, is followed by the "Night of the Mystery of the Great Shapes," and it is explained that the night of the mystery of the Great Shapes is when there has been made the embalming of the body of Osiris, "the Good Being, justified for ever." In the chapter on "the night of the laying-out" of the dead body of Osiris, it is said that "Isis rises on the night of the laying-out of the dead body, to lament over her brother Osiris." And again: "The night of the laying-out" (of the dead Osiris) is mentioned, and again it is described as that on which Isis had risen "to make a wail for her brother."

But this is also the night on which he conquers his enemies, and "receives the birthplace of the Gods." "He tramples on the bandages they make for their burial. He raises his soul, and conceals his body." So the Christ is found to have unwound the linen bandages of burial, and they saw the linen in one place, and the napkin in another. He too conceals his body!

This is closely reproduced, or paralleled, in John's Gospel, where it is Mary Magdalene who rises in the night and comes to the sepulchre, "while it was yet dark," to find the Christ arisen, as the conqueror of death and the grave. In John's version, after the body is embalmed in a hundred pounds weight of spice, consisting of myrrh and aloes, we have the "night of the mystery of the shapes": "For while it was yet dark, Mary Magdalene coming to the sepulchre, and peering in, sees the two angels in white sitting, the one at the head and the other at the feet, where the body had lately lain." And in the chapter of "How a living being is not destroyed in hell, or the hour of life ends not in Hades," there are two youthful Gods—"two youths of light, who prevail as those who see the light," and the vignette shows the deceased walking off. He has risen!

Matthew has only one angel or splendid presence, whose appearance was as lightning, which agrees with Shepi, the Splendid One, who "lights the sarcophagus," as a representative of the divinity, Ra. The risen Christ, who is first seen and recognised by Mary, says to her, "Touch me not, for I am not yet ascended to my Father." The same scene is described by the Gnostics: when Sophia rushes forward to embrace the Christ, who restrains her by exclaiming that he must not be touched.

In the last chapter of the "Preservation of the Body in Hades," there is much mystical matter that looks plainer when written out in John's Gospel. It is said of the regerminated or risen God—"*May the Osirian speak to thee?*" The Osirian does not know. He (Osiris) knows him. "*Let him not grasp him.*" The Osirified "comes out sound, Immortal is his name." "He has passed along the upper roads" (that is, as a risen spirit).

"*He it is who grasps with his hand,*" and gives the palpable proof of continued personality, as does the Christ, who says, "See my hands and my feet, that it is I myself."

The Sun-God re-arises on the horizon, where he issues forth, "saying to those who belong to his race, Give me your arm." Says the Osirified deceased, "I am made as ye are." "Let him explain it!" At his reappearance the Christ demonstrates that he is made as they are; "See my hands and feet, that it is I myself; handle me and see. And when he had said this he showed them his hands and feet. Then he said to Thomas, Reach hither thy finger, and see my hands, and reach hither thy hand and put it into my side." These descriptions correspond to that of the cut, wounded, and bleeding Sun-God, who says to his companions, "Give me your arm; I am made as ye are."

In the Gospel of the Hebrews he is made to exclaim, "For I am not a bodiless ghost." But in the original, when the risen one says to his companions, "Give me your arm, I am made as ye are," he speaks as a spirit to spirits. Whereas in the Gospels, the Christ has to demonstrate that he is *not* a spirit, because the scene has been transferred into the earth-life.

The Gnostics truly declared that all the supernatural transactions asserted in the Christian Gospel "were counterparts (or representations) of what took place above." That is, they affirmed the history to be mythical; the celestial allegory made mundane; and they were in the right, as the Egyptian Gospel proves. There are Healers, and Jehoshua Ben-Pandira may have been one. But, because that is possible, we must not allow it to vouch for the impossible! Thus, in the Gospels, the mythical is, and has to be, continually reproduced as miracle. That which naturally pertains to the character of the Sun-God becomes supernatural in appearance when brought down to earth. The Solar God descended into the nether world as the restorer of the bound to liberty, the dead to life. In this region the miracles were wrought, and the transformations took place. The evil spirits and destroying powers were exorcised from the mummies; the halt and the maimed were enabled to get up and go; the dead were raised, a mouth was given to the dumb, and the blind were made to see.

This "reconstitution of the deceased" is transferred to the earth-life, whereupon "the blind receive their sight, and the lame walk, the lepers are cleansed, the deaf hear, and the dead are raised up" at the coming of the Christ, who performed the miracles. The drama, which the Idiotai mistook for human history, was performed by the Sun-God in another world.

I could keep on all day, and all night, or give a dozen lectures, without exhausting my evidence that the Canonical Gospels are only a later literalised réchauffé of the Egyptian writings; the representations in the Mysteries, and the oral teachings of the Gnostics which passed out of Egypt into Greece and Rome—for there is plenty more proof where this comes from. I can but offer a specimen brick of that which is elsewhere a building set four-square, and sound against every blast that blows.

The Christian dispensation is believed to have been ushered in by the birth of a child, and the portrait of that child in the Roman Catacombs as the child of Mary is the youthful Sun-God in the Mummy Image of the child-king, the Egyptian Karast, or Christ. The alleged facts of our Lord's life as Jesus the Christ, were equally the alleged facts of our Lord's life as the Horus of Egypt, whose very name signifies the Lord.

The Christian legends were first related of Horus the Messiah, the Solar Hero, the greatest hero that ever lived in the mind of man—not in the flesh—the only hero to whom the miracles were natural, because he was not human.

From beginning to end the history is not human but divine, and the divine is the mythical. From the descent of the Holy Ghost to overshadow Mary, to the ascension of the risen Christ at the end of forty days, according to the drama of the pre-Christian Mysteries, the subject-matter, the characters, occurrences, events, acts, and sayings bear the impress of the mythical mould instead of the stamp of human history. Right through, the ideas which shape the history were pre-extant, and are identifiably pre-Christian; and so we see the strange sight to-day in Europe of 100,000,000 of Pagans masquerading as Christians.

Whether you believe it or not does not matter, the fatal fact remains that every trait and feature which go to make up the Christ as Divinity, and every event or circumstance taken to establish the human personality were pre-extant, and pre-applied to the Egyptian and Gnostic Christ, who never could become flesh. The Jesus Christ with female paps, who is the Alpha and Omega of Revelation, was the IU of Egypt, and the Iao of the Chaldeans. Jesus as the Lamb of God, and Ichthys the Fish, was Egyptian. Jesus as the Coming One; Jesus born of the Virgin Mother, who was overshadowed by the Holy Ghost; Jesus born of two mothers, both of whose names are Mary; Jesus born in the manger—at Christmas, and again at Easter; Jesus saluted by the three kings, or Magi; Jesus of the transfiguration on the Mount; Jesus whose symbol in the Catacombs is the eight-rayed Star—the Star of the East; Jesus as the eternal Child; Jesus as God the Father, re-born as his own Son; Jesus as the Child of twelve years; Jesus as the Anointed One of thirty years; Jesus in his Baptism; Jesus walking on the Waters, or working his Miracles; Jesus as the Caster-out of demons; Jesus as a Substitute, who suffered in a vicarious atonement for sinful men; Jesus whose followers are the two brethren, the four fishers, the seven fishers, the twelve apostles, the seventy (or seventy-two in some texts) whose names were written in Heaven; Jesus who was administered to by seven women; Jesus in his bloody sweat; Jesus betrayed by Judas; Jesus as conqueror of the grave; Jesus the Resurrection and the Life; Jesus before Herod; in the Hades, and in his re-appearance to the women, and to the seven fishers; Jesus who was crucified both on the 14th and 15th of the month Nisan; Jesus who was also crucified in Egypt (as it is written in Revelation); Jesus as judge of the dead, with the sheep on the right hand, and the goats on the left, is Egyptian from first to last, in every phase, from the beginning to the end—

MAKE WHATSOEVER YOU CAN OF JEHOSHUA BEN-PANDIRA.

In some of the ancient Egyptian Temples the Christian iconoclasts, when tired of hacking and hewing at the symbolic figures incised in the chambers of imagery, and defacing the most prominent features of the monuments, found they could not dig out the hieroglyphics, and took to covering them over with plaster or tempera; and this plaster, intended to hide the meaning and stop the mouth of the stone Word, has served to preserve the ancient writings, as fresh in hue and sharp in outline as when they were first cut and coloured.

In a similar manner the Temple of the ancient religion was invaded, and possession gradually gained by connivance of Roman power; and that enduring fortress, not built, but quarried out of the solid rock, was stuccoed all over the front, and made white awhile with its look of brand-newness, and re-opened under the sign of another name—that of the carnalised Christ. And all the time each nook and corner were darkly alive with the presence and the proofs of the earlier gods, and the pre-Christian origines, even though the hieroglyphics remained unread until the time of Champollion! But stucco is not for lasting wear, it cracks and crumbles; sloughs off and slinks away into its natal insignificance; the rock is the sole true foundation; the rock is the only record in which we can reach reality at last!

Wilkinson, the Egyptologist, has actually said of Osiris on earth:— "Some may be disposed to think that the Egyptians, being aware of the promises of the *real saviour*, had anticipated that event, regarding it as though it had already happened, and introduced that mystery into their religious system!" This is what obstetrists term a *false presentation;* a birth feet-foremost. We are also told by writers on the Catacombs, and the Christian Iconography, that this figure is Osiris, as a type of Christ. This is Pan, Apollo, Aristeus, as a type of Christ. This is Harpocrates, as a type of Christ. This is Mercury, but as a type of Christ; this is the devil (for Sut-Mercury was the devil), as a type of Christ; until long hearing of the facts reversed, perverted and falsified, makes one feel as if under a nightmare which has lasted for eighteen centuries, knowing the Truth to have been buried alive and made dumb all that time; and believing that it has only to get voice and make itself heard to end the lying once for all, and bring down the curtain of oblivion at last upon the most pitiful drama of delusion ever witnessed on the human stage.

And here the worst foes of the truth have ever been, and still are, the rationalisers of the Mythos, such as the Unitarians. They have assumed the human history as the starting point, and accepted the existence of a personal founder of Christianity as the one initial and fundamental fact. They have done their best to humanise the divinity of the Mythos, by discharging the supernatural and miraculous element, in order that the narrative might be accepted as history. Thus they have lost the battle from the beginning, by fighting it on the wrong ground.

The Christ is a popular lay-figure that never lived, and a lay-figure of Pagan origin; a lay-figure that was once the Ram, and afterwards the Fish; a lay-figure that in human form was the portrait and image of a dozen different gods. The imagery of the Catacombs shows that the types there represented are not the ideal figures of the human reality! They are the sole reality for six or seven centuries after A.D., because they had been so in the centuries long before. There is no man upon the cross in the Catacombs of Rome for seven hundred years! The symbolism, the allegories, the figures, and types, brought on by the Gnostics, remained there just what they had been to the Romans, Greeks, Persians, and Egyptians. Yet, the dummy ideal of Paganism is supposed to have become doubly real as the God who was made flesh, to save mankind from the impossible "fall!" Remember that the primary foundation-stone for a history in the New Testament is dependent upon the Fall of Man being a fact in the Old; whereas it was only a fable, which had its own mythical and unhistorical meaning.

When we try over again that first step once taken in the dark, we find no foothold for us, because there was no stair. The Fall is absolutely non-historical, and, consequently, the first bit of standing-ground for an actual Christ, the redeemer, is missing in the very beginning. Any one who set up, or was set up, for an historical Saviour from a non-historical Fall, could only be an historical impostor. But the Christ of the Gospels is not even that! He is in *no* sense an historical personage. It is impossible to establish the existence of an historical character, even as an impostor. For such an one the two witnesses—Astronomical Mythology and Gnosticism—completely prove an alibi for ever! From the first supposed catastrophe to the final one, the figures of the celestial allegory were ignorantly mistaken for matters of fact, and thus the orthodox Christolator is left at last to climb to heaven with one foot resting on the ground of a fall that is fictitious, and the other foot on the ground of a redemption that must be fallacious. It is a fraud founded on a fable!

Every time the Christian turns to the East to bow his obeisance to he Christ, it is a confession that the cult is Solar, the admission being all the more fatal because it is unconscious. Every picture of the Christ, with the halo of glory, and the accompanying Cross of the Equinox, proffers proof.

The Christian doctrine of a resurrection furnishes evidence, absolutely conclusive, of the Astronomical and Kronian nature of the origines! This is to occur, as it always did, at the end of a cycle; or at the end of the world! Christian Revelation knows nothing of immortality, except in the form of periodic renewal, dependent on the "Coming One;" and the resurrection of the dead still depends on the day of judgment and the last day, at the end of the world! They have no other world. Their only other world is at the end of this.

Now there are no fools living who would be fools big enough to cross the Atlantic Ocean in a barque so rotten and unseaworthy as this in which they hope to cross the dark River of Death, and, on a pier of cloud, be landed safe in Heaven. The Christian Theology was responsible for substituting faith instead of knowledge; and the European mind is only just beginning to recover from the mental paralysis induced by that doctrine which came to its natural culmination in the Dark Ages.

The Christian religion is responsible for enthroning the cross of death in heaven, with a deity on it, doing public penance for a private failure in the commencement of creation. It has taught men to believe that the vilest spirit may be washed white, in the atoning blood of the purest, offered up as a bribe to an avenging God. It has divinized a figure of helpless human suffering, and a face of pitiful pain; as if there were naught but a great heartache at the core of all things; or the vast Infinite were but a veiled and sad-eyed sorrow that brings visibly to birth in the miseries of human life. But "in the old Pagan world men deified the beautiful, the glad;" as they will again, upon a loftier pedestal, when the fable of this fictitious fall of man, and false redemption by the cloud-begotten God, has passed away like a phantasm of the night, and men awake to learn that they are here to wage ceaseless war upon sordid suffering, remediable wrong, and preventable pain; here to put an end to them, not to apotheosize an effigy of Sorrow to be adored as a type of the Eternal. For the most beneficent is the most beautiful; the happiest are the healthiest; the most Godlike is most glad. The Christian Cult has fanatically fought for its false theory, and waged incessant warfare against Nature and Evolution—Nature's intention made somewhat visible—and against some of the noblest instincts, during eighteen centuries. Seas of human blood have been spilt to keep the barque of Peter afloat. Earth has been honeycombed with the graves of the martyrs of Freethought. Heaven has been filled with a horror of great darkness in the name of God.

Eighteen centuries are a long while in the life-time of a lie, but a brief span in the eternity of Truth. The Fiction is sure to be found out, and the Lie will fall at last! At last!! At last!!!

> No matter though it towers to the sky,
> And darkens earth, you cannot make the lie
> Immortal; though stupendously enshrined
> By art in every perfect mould of mind:
> Angelo, Rafael, Milton, Handel, all
> Its pillars, cannot stay it from the fall.
>
> The Pyramid of Imposture reared by R. me,
> All of cement, for an eternal home,
> Must crumble back to earth, and every gust
> Shall revel in the desert of its dust;
> And when the prison of the Immortal, Mind,
> Hath fallen to set free the bound and blind,
> No more shall life be one long dread of death;
> Humanity shall breathe with ampler breath,
> Expand in spirit, and in stature rise,
> To match its birthplace of the earth and skies.

PAUL THE GNOSTIC OPPONENT OF PETER,

NOT AN

APOSTLE OF HISTORIC CHRISTIANITY.

(Fuller Egyptian and Gnostic Data, with references to the authorities, may be found in the Author's "Natural Genesis."

IT has been shown in previous lectures that the matter of our Canonical Gospels is, to a large extent, mythical, and that the Gnosis of Ancient Egypt was carried into other lands by the underground passage of the Mysteries, to emerge at last as the literalised legend of Historic Christianity.

The mythical Christ was as surely continued from Egypt as were the mythical types of the Christ on the Gnostic Stones and in the Catacombs of Rome! Once this ground is felt to be firm underfoot it emboldens and warrants us in cutting the Gordian knot that has been so deftly complicated for us in the Epistles of Paul. To-day we have to face a problem that is one of the most difficult; it is my object to prove that Paul was the opponent and not the apostle of Historic Christianity. It is well known to all serious students of the subject that there was an original rent or rift of difference between the preacher Paul and the other founders of Christianity, whom he first met in Jerusalem— namely, Cephas (or Peter), James, and John. He did not think much of them personally, but scoffs a little at their pretensions to being Pillars of the Church. Those men had nothing in common with him from the first, and never forgave him for his independence and opposition to the last. But the depth of that visible rift has not yet been fathomed in consequence of false assumptions; and my own researches and determination to look and think for myself have led me to the inevitable conclusion that there is but one way in which it can be bottomed for the first time.

It is likewise more or less apprehended that two voices are heard contending in Paul's Epistles, to the confounding of the writer's sense and the confusion of the reader's. They utter different doctrines, so fundamentally opposed as to be for ever irreconcilable; and this duplicity of doctrine makes Paul, who is the one distinct and single-minded personality of the "New Testament," look like the most double-faced of men; double-tongued as the serpent. The two doctrines are those of the Gnostic, or Spiritual Christ, and the historic Jesus. Both cannot be true to Paul; and my contention is that both voices did not proceed from him personally.

We know that Paul and the other Apostles did not preach the same gospel; and it is my present purpose to show that they did not set forth or celebrate the same Christ. My thesis is, that Paul was not a supporter of the system known as Historical Christianity, which was founded on a belief in the Christ carnalised; an assumption that the Christ had been made flesh; but that he was its unceasing and deadly opponent during his lifetime; and that after his death his writings were tampered with, interpolated, and re-indoctrinated by his old enemies, the forgers and falsifiers, who first began to weave the web of the Papacy in Rome. In this way there was added a fourth pillar or corner-stone to the original three in Jerusalem, which was turned into the chief support of the whole structure; the firmest foundation of the fallacious faith.

The supreme feat, performed in secret by the managers of the Mysteries in Rome, was this conversion of the Epistles of Paul into the main support of Historic Christianity! It was the very pivot on which the total imposture turned! In his lifetime he had fought tooth and nail, with tongue and pen, against the men who founded the faith of the Christ made flesh, and damned eternally all disbelievers; and after his death they reared the Church of the *Sarkolatræ* above his tomb, and for eighteen centuries have, with a forged warrant, claimed him as being the first and foremost among the founders. They cleverly dammed the course of the natural river that flowed forth from its own independent source in the Epistles of Paul, and turned its waters into their own artificial canal, so that Paul's living force should be made to float the bark of Peter. Nevertheless, those who care to look closely will see that the two waters, like those of the river Rhone, will not mingle in one colour! And it appears to me that, whether Paul was mad or not in this life, such nefarious treatment of his writings was bad enough to drive him frantic in the next, and make him insane there until the wrong is righted.

It is the universal assumption that Paul, the persecutor of the early Christians, was converted by a vision of the risen Jesus, who proved his historic nature and identity by appearing to Paul in person. So it is recorded in the Acts of the Apostles. The account, however, is entirely opposed to that which is given by Paul himself in his Epistle to the Galatians. He tells how the change occurred, which has been called his conversion. It was by revelation of the Christ within, but not by an objective vision of a personal Jesus, who demonstrated in spirit world the reality and identity of an historic Jesus of Nazareth, who had lately lived on earth. Such a version as that is rigorously impossible, according to Paul's own words. His account of the matter is totally antipodal. He received his commission to preach the Christ, as he declares, "*when it was the good pleasure of God to reveal his Son in me*," and therefore not by an apparition of Jesus of Nazareth outside of him! His Christ within was not the *Corpus* of Christian belief, but the Christ of the Gnosis. He heard no voice external to himself, which could be converted into the audible voice of an historic Jesus; and nothing can be more instructive to begin with, than a comparative study of these two versions, for showing how the matter has been manipulated, and the facts perverted, for the purpose of establishing or supporting an orthodox history. What he did hear when caught up in the spirit he tells us was unspeakable; words which it is not lawful for a man to utter! He makes no mention of a Jesus of Nazareth. Indeed, Jesus of Nazareth is unknown to Paul! His name never once appears in the Epistles; and the significance of the fact in favour of the present view can hardly be exaggerated. So, Jesus of Nazareth does not appear in the Gospel of Marcion; or, as it was represented by some of the Christian Fathers, Marcion had removed the name of Jesus of Nazareth from his particular Gospel— being so virulent a heretic! Here we find Paul in agreement with Marcion, the Gnostic rejecter of Jesus of Nazareth, and of historic Christianity. Moreover, Paul was the only apostle of the true Christ who was recognised by Marcion. Now, as Marcion had rejected the human nature of the Christ, and left the sect which ultimately became the church of historic Christianity, it is impossible that he could have adopted or upheld the Gospel of Paul as it has come down to us in our version of the Epistles. Hence, Irenæus complains that Marcion dismembered the Epistles of Paul, and removed those passages from the prophetical writings which had been quoted to teach us that they announced beforehand the coming of the Lord! That is, Marcion, the man who knew, recognised his fellow-Gnostic in Paul, but rejected the literalisations and the spurious doctrines which had been surreptitiously interpolated by the founders, who were the forgers, of Historic Christianity. Further, with regard to the Marcionites, Irenæus says they allege that Paul alone, of all the Christian teachers, knew the truth; and that to him the Mystery was manifested by revelation. They spoke as Gnostics of a Gnostic. At the same time, as Irenæus tells us, the Gnostics, of whom Marcion was one, charged the other Apostles with hypocrisy, because they "*framed their doctrine according to the capacity of their hearers, fabling blind things for the blind according to their blindness; for the dull, according to their dulness; for those in error, according to their errors.*"

Clement Alexander asserts that Paul, before going to Rome, stated that he would bring to the Brethren (not the true Gospel history, but) the Gnosis, or Gnostic communication, the tradition of the hidden mysteries, as the fulness of the blessings of Christ, which Clement says were revealed by the Son of God, the "*teacher who trains the Gnostic by mysteries,*" i.e., by revelations made in the state of trance. He was going there as a Gnostic, and therefore as the natural opponent of Historic Christianity.

The conversion of Paul, according to the Acts, is supposed to have occurred sometime after the year 30 A.D. at the earliest; and yet if we accept the data furnished by the book of Acts and Paul's Epistle to the Galatians, he must have been converted as early as the year 27 A.D. Paul states that after his conversion he did not go up to Jerusalem for three years. Then after 14 more years he went up again to Jerusalem with Barnabas. This second visit can be dated by means of the famine, which is historic, and known to have occurred in the year 44, at which time relief was conveyed to the brethren in Judea by Barnabas and Paul. If we take 17 years from 44, the different statements go to show that Paul had been converted as early as the year 27. Thus, according to the dates and the data derived from the Acts, from Paul's epistle, and the historic fact of the famine, Paul was converted to Christianity in the year 27 of our era! This could not have been by a spiritual manifestation of the supposed personal Jesus, who was not then dead, and had not at that time been re-begotten as the Christ of the canonical history. This is usually looked upon (by Renan, for example,) as such an absurdity that no credence can be allowed to the account in the Acts. On the contrary, and notwithstanding all that has been said by those whose work it is to put a false bottom into the Unknown, I am free to maintain that nothing stands in the way of its being a possibility and a fact, except the assumption that it is an impossibility. You cannot date one event by another which never occurred, or, if it did occur, is not recorded by Paul, especially when his own account offers negative evidence of its non-occurrence. It is only using plain words justifiably to say that the concocters of the Acts falsify whenever it is convenient, and tell the truth when they cannot help it! In Paul's own account of his conversion he continues: "*Immediately, I conferred not with flesh and blood; neither went I up to Jerusalem to them who were Apostles before me; but I went away into Arabia.*" He did not seek to know anything about the personal Jesus of Nazareth, his life, his miracles, his crucifixion, resurrection, and ascension; had no anxiety to hear anything whatever from living witnesses or relatives about the human nature of this Divine Being, who is supposed to have appeared to Paul in person; completely changed the current of his life, and transformed his character; no wish even to verify the historic or possible ground-work for the reality of his alleged vision of Jesus! When he did go up to Jerusalem, three years afterwards, and again in fourteen years, he positively learned nothing whatever from those who ought to have been able to teach him and tell him all things on matters of vital importance (for *historic* Christianity), about which he should have been most desirous to know, but had no manifest desire of knowing. He saw James, Peter, and John, who were the pillars of the church, and persons of repute, but whatever they were it made no matter to him; they imparted nothing to him. He says these respectable persons, these pillars, who seemed to be somewhat, communicated nothing to him; contrariwise, it was he who had a gospel of his own, which he had received from no man, to communicate to them! He had come to bring them the Gnosis. They privately gave him the hand of fellowship, and offered to acknowledge him if he would keep out of their way with his other gospel—go to the Gentiles (or go to the Devil), and leave them alone. There was a compromise, and therefore something to compromise, though not on Paul's account; but the only point of genuine agreement between them was that they agreed to differ! On comparing notes, he found that they were preaching quite *another* gospel, and *another* Jesus. We know what their gospel was, because it has come down to us in the doctrines and dogmas of historic Christianity. It was the gospel of the literalisers of mythology; the gospel of the Christ made flesh to save mankind from an impossible fall; the gospel of salvation by the atoning blood of Christ; the gospel that would make a hell of this life, on purpose to win heaven hereafter; the gospel of flesh and physics, including the corporeal resurrection, and the immediate ending of the world; the gospel that has no other world except at the end of this. Theirs was that *other* gospel with its doctrines of delusion, against which Paul waged continual warfare. For, *another Jesus, another Spirit*, and *another gospel* were being preached by these pre-eminent apostles who were the opponents of Paul. He warns the Corinthians against those "pre-eminent apostles," whom he calls false prophets, deceitful workers, and ministers of Satan, who came among them to preach "*another Jesus*" whom he did not preach, and a different gospel from that which they had received from him. To the Galatians he says: "*If any man preacheth unto you any gospel other than that which ye received, let him be damned;*" or let him be Anathema. He chides them: "*O, foolish Galatians, who did bewitch you? Are ye so foolish: having begun in the Spirit, are ye perfected in the flesh?*" That is, in the gospel of the Christ made flesh, the gospel of those who were at enmity with him, who followed on his track like Satan sowing tares by night to choke the seed of the spiritual gospel which Paul had so painfully sown, and who, as he intimates to the Thessalonians, were quite capable of forging epistles in his name to deceive his followers. It has never yet been shown *how* fundamental was this feud between Paul and the forgers of the fleshly faith, because the real facts had not been grappled with or grasped concerning the totally different bases of belief, and the forever irreconcilable gospels of the Gnostic or spiritual Christ, and of the Christ made flesh, to be set forth as the Saviour of mankind, according to Historic Christianity. It was impossible that Paul and Peter should draw or pull together; the different grounds of their faith were in the beginning from pole to pole apart. He says: "*I made known to you, brethren, as touching the gospel which was preached by me, that it is not after man. For neither did I receive it from man (or from a man), nor was I taught it, save through revelation of the Christ revealed within.*"

He did not derive his facts from history, nor his gospel from the Apostles; he was neither taught by man nor book. He derived his gospel from direct personal revelation of the Christ within. In short, his Christ was not that Jesus of Nazareth whom he never mentions, and whom the others preached, and who may have been, and in all likelihood was, Joshua Ben Pandira, the Nazarene.

From the present standpoint there is no doctrinal difficulty, even about Paul being the writer of the Epistle to the Hebrews. I do not need to call in another author here anymore than elsewhere. The double-dealing of the interpolaters and forgers would be cause enough to account for all the difference and the difficulty. They who would have, or who had forged epistles in his own name, would not scruple to indoctrinate his writings when they got the chance; and if this epistle be not Paul's, then his name as author has been forged. Now, in this epistle, the Christ is non-historical, he is the Kronian Christ, the Æonian manifestor of mythical, that is astronomical prophecy; he is after the order of Melchizedek, who was "*without father, without mother, without genealogy, having neither beginning of days, nor end of life.*" This was the ever-coming one who could not become a human personage; and for that reason, I take it, Paul repudiates the genealogies of Christ. In advising Titus to give no heed to "*Jewish Fables,*" he tells him to "*shun foolish questionings and genealogies.*" He counsels Timothy to warn his followers against giving heed to "*fables and endless genealogies,*" such, for instance, as we now find in the canonical gospels of Matthew and Luke." These could have no application to the Christ of the Gnosis, hence their absence from the gospel according to John. Human genealogy could not indicate the Gnostic mode of the Divine Descent; could not authenticate the "*Word*" of John, or Philo; nor the Christ of Marcus, or of Paul; consequently we learn that Marcus, the Gnostic, eliminated the genealogies from the gospel of Luke, and all that was written respecting the generation of the Lord. The Docetæ who rejected the humanity of Christ had, as Epiphanius phrases it, "*Cut away the genealogies in the gospel after Matthew.*" Tatian, the pupil of Justin, who is called an "*Apostate from the Church,*" also struck out the genealogies that were intended to prove the human descent of the Christ; he who had once accepted the gospel of the Christ made flesh, but rejected it when he had learned to know better. This they did because their Christ was spiritual, not an historic Jesus; and the same reason holds good as an explanation for Paul. He repudiated the vain genealogies employed in vain by those who sought to establish a human line of descent for the Christ, because he rejected the flesh-and-blood Jesus who was preached by the advocates of Historic Christianity. This being so, it follows that the opening passage of the Epistle to the Romans, which now looks like Paul's first utterance to all the world, begins the tale of the interpolations, and thus appears in the right place, for it stands nearly alone in the writings of Paul, with its frank or forced acknowledgment of the humanity of Jesus, by admitting the Word made flesh to be of the seed of David. But the Christ of Paul could not, at one and the same time, have been "*without genealogy*" and yet be of the seed of Abraham or David. That would be a complete reversal of his teaching, who, in rejecting the genealogies, had already repudiated the descent from David. Moreover, Barnabas, the most intimate friend of Paul and fellow-teacher with him, who, as a Gnostic, denied the human nature of the Christ, and, like Paul, spoke disrespectfully of the other Apostles—Barnabas assures us it was according to the error of the wicked that Christ was called the Son of David. Paul also tells us that no "man can say that Jesus is the Lord, but by the Holy Spirit" (1 Cor. xii. 3), and therefore not through the facts of an external history, or human pedigree.

The Christ of the Gnosis was not connected with *place* any more than personality, or line of human descent. His only birthplace was in the mind of man. Consequently, in his gospel, Marcion, who was a Gnostic Christian, does not connect his Christ with Nazareth. His Christ is not Jesus of Nazareth. And this note of the Gnosis is apparent in the writings of Paul. His Christ is nowhere called Jesus of Nazareth, nor is he born at Bethlehem, either of the Virgin Mary, or of Mary the wife of Cleopas, who was not the Virgin. Of course, either an historic Jesus could become the Christ, as Saviour of the world, or he could not; and, as the world never was lost in any such sense as the ignorant have derived from a fable misinterpreted, why he could not, and as he could not, then he did not, and Paul who was an Adept in the mysteries, a Master of the Hidden Wisdom, could never have mistaken the fable for a fact on which to build his system of Christology; nor could he accept it from others. When once we have got the Gnostic clue to the Hidden Wisdom, we find an universal argument amongst the Gnostics concerning their tenets. Wherever we meet with them they give us the Masonic grip; and by the same sign we know that Paul was a Gnostic. This is further corroborated by his own claim to have been an Adept, a wise master-builder, one who spoke wisdom amongst the Perfected. He was a Gnostic in the supreme degree, and all Gnostics agree that the Christ of the Gnosis could not be made flesh, and therefore all are, and must be opposed to Historic Christianity, Paul included. It was as a Gnostic, a wise master-builder, that Paul laid the foundations which others built upon; and the superstructure they reared became the Church of Historic Christianity. The Gnostics were Christians in an esoteric sense, but not because they explained a human history esoterically. There was no history to explain until the myth had been made exoteric by those who were ignorant, or who cunningly converted the Gnosis into history. It was the work of Peter to make the mysteries exoteric in a human history. It was the work of Paul to prevent this being effected by explaining the Gnosis. Hints of this appear in the Epistles when he speaks of *his gospel*, and the revelation of his mystery concerning the Christ, and warns his disciples against the preaching of that "*other gospel*" and "*other Jesus,*" which are opposed to his own truer teaching. As when he tells Timothy to "*remember Jesus Christ according to my gospel,*" and says to the Romans, "*establish you according to my gospel;*" that was the gospel of the *Gnosis* which he had brought to them.

We are also able to watch the interpolators of his writings at their work. The tampering with the text of Paul's Epistles is still made apparent by a comparison of the various recensions, as the marginal notes in the Revised version yet suffice to show; and if this remains so palpable in the latest transcript, what must it have been in the earlier and nearest to the author's original? In some instances, instead of a perfect join, there is a gaping gulf of doctrinal difference, too deep for the interpolators themselves. There is a ludicrous mixture of the historical Jesus and spiritual Christ in the First Epistle of Paul to Timothy, where Christ Jesus is spoken of as he "*who, before Pontius Pilate, witnessed the good confession;*" and half a dozen lines later on Paul's Jesus is the "*lord of lords dwelling in light unapproachable, whom no man hath seen, nor can see.*" That is the Christ of the Gnosis who could not be made flesh to stand in the presence of Pontius Pilate. Again, Paul speaks as a spiritualist of our transformation in death and the continuity of consciousness, when he says: "*Behold, I tell you a mystery, we shall not entirely sleep, but shall all be changed in a moment, in the twinkling of an eye.*" This was the mystery of the Gnosis and the transformation revealed by spiritual phenomena. Then follows the interpolated doctrine of the resurrection at the last day: "*For the trumpet shall sound and the dead shall be raised*" physically, which was impossible to Paul. These are as opposite as yes and no, or day and night. Once more, we know how emphatically Paul insists on the *originality* of his gospel. It was his very own, personally received by revelation. He derived nothing from the supposed apostles of an historic Jesus; they imparted nothing to him, and he received nothing from any man. Yet in face of this fatal evidence the writer of the Epistle to the Hebrews, which is assigned to Paul, is made to say, that the "*salvation first spoken through the Lord was confirmed unto us by them that heard!*" And in his Epistle to the Corinthians he is made to declare that he first of all delivered to them *that which he had received (*not by subjective revelation, but according to the history externalised), "*How that Christ died for our sins, according to the Scriptures; and that he was buried; and that he hath been raised on the third day, according to the Scriptures, and that he appeared to Cephas, then to the twelve, then he appeared to above five hundred of the brethren at once* [this is piling it up!] *then he appeared to James, then to all the apostles, and last of all, as unto one born out of due time, he appeared to me also, for I am the least of the apostles, that am not meet to be called an apostle.*" But James and Cephas were those whom he saw in Jerusalem, and who, as he expressly tells us, had imparted nothing to him! The passage belies what Paul has elsewhere said, and is at war with all he was! So far from lowering himself in that way, he asserts in the very same epistle: "*In nothing was I behind these pre-eminent apostles*"—therefore he was not behind in time! "Let me speak proudly!" that was his attitude when he compared himself with Cephas, James, and John. And if Paul ever did call himself an abortion (the true rendering of the sense), we may be sure that he did not apply such a figure of that which is *premature* to the *lateness* of his birth as an apostle. It cannot be made to apply. The Gnostics tell us what he did mean. They alone could understand the allusion, which carries the Christ of the Gnosis with it. The Christ appears to Paul, as to an abortion, just as did Horus the Christ to Sophia (or Achamoth), when she forlornly lay outside of the pleroma as an amorphous abortion, and the Christ came and extended himself cross-wise and gave her flowing substance form! Here the Gnostic doctrine involves the Christ of the Gnosis, and not of the human history. Paul applies the figure to himself. If these statements had been true, Paul must have been taught by men. This *was* to receive his information from Scriptures (whatsoever they may have been!), and was not to receive his revelation solely from the Christ, who came within, as he declares. In this way it becomes apparent how Paul's writings were made orthodox by the men who preached another gospel than his; with whom he was at war during his lifetime, and who took a bitter-sweet revenge on his writings by suppression and addition, after he was dead and gone.

The Christ proclaimed by Paul is frequently designated the "*firstborn.*" He is the "*first-born of all creation*" (Col. i. 16), "*the first-born from the dead*" (Col. i. 18), the "*first-born among many brethren.*" "*Now hath Christ been raised from the dead, the first-fruits of them that slept!*" But in what sense? It is impossible to apply such descriptions to any historical character. No Historical Jesus *could* be the First-born from the dead.

If continuity be a natural fact, as was held by the Gnostics (and Paul was a Gnostic!), and is maintained by all Spiritualists (and Paul was a Spiritualist!), we shall live on by a law of nature, not by some jugglery with natural law, called a miracle, performed once upon a time! The first-born from the dead could not have waited for the resurrection until *Anno Domini;* nor could our spiritual continuity have been demonstrated at that or any previous period by a physical resurrection, such as forms the foundation of the Christian faith! The doctrine enunciated by Paul was Egyptian, Chaldean, Kabbalist, and Gnostic, and, as such, it can be explained.

In the Ritual the soul that rises again from the dead exults and exclaims, "*I am the only one that comes forth from the body!*" that is, as the supreme soul of all the seven; the one representative of the pleroma of powers, or as Paul has it, "*the first-born of many brethren;*" the first-born from the dead, because the only one that attained immortality, as the spiritual man, or the Christ, called the Second Adam by Paul; that celestial man referred to by Philo when he says: "*There* is the man whose name is East. A strange appellation if it had been intended to speak of a man composed of soul and body. But if it be the Incorporeal man, who comprehends in himself the divine Idea, it must be admitted that East is the name that suits him best;" i.e., the re-orient man of the resurrection, or re-arising. It is the same Gnostic typology employed by Paul when he speaks of *"building up the body of Christ; till we all attain unto the unity of faith, and of the knowledge* (or Gnosis) *of the Son of God; unto a full-grown man; unto the measure of the stature of the fulness of Christ."* The fulness of the Christ being the Egyptian, Buddhist, and Gnostic pleroma of all the seven preceding powers that culminated in the Christhood.

One title of the Gnostic Christ is *"All things."* He is called Totum, or *"All things."* Nothing short of the Gnosis can tell us why. The Christian world is without the Gnosis, and therefore without the means of understanding Paul! Concerning the formation or creation of the Gnostic Christ in the character of *"All things,"* or Totum, we are told that *"The whole pleroma of the Æons, with one design and desire, brought together whatever each one had in himself of the greatest beauty and preciousness, and uniting all these contributions, so as to skilfully blend the whole, they produced a being of most perfect beauty, the very star of the pleroma, and the perfect fruit of it, namely, Jesus, or the Saviour Christ."* This *"All things,"* who was the consummate flower of the fulness or pleroma of the previous seven powers, is the Christ of Paul, who, himself, is *"All things,"* because in *"him are all things,"* and in *"all things"* he has the pre-eminence. *"All things are summed up in Christ"* (Eph. i. 10). *"Of him, through him, and unto him, are all things"* (Rom. xi. 36). *"In him dwelleth all the fulness of the Godhead bodily"* (Col. ii. 9). That is as the Gnostic Totum!—the All—the Christ—the eternal Soul or Spirit, in *"whom all the treasures of wisdom and knowledge"* are hidden! He warns his followers against a certain false teacher, whom he knows personally, and might name, and whose teaching is after the *"tradition of men, after the rudiments of the world, and not after the Christ"* of the pleroma. The Gnostic Christ was also called *Eudocetos*, because the whole pleroma of the Godhead was well pleased with him as glorifier of the Father. This is Paul's Christ, in whom the whole fulness (pleroma) was pleased to dwell. The text in Paul's Epistle to the Colossians should be *"for the whole fulness was pleased to dwell in him."* There is neither *"God"* nor *"Father"* in the case. It is the whole Gnostic pleroma of powers which made up the immortal soul, or came to the consummate flower of soul in man, and the Godhead in the Christ, as sum total of the powers. The Ancient Gnosis comes first. Paul repeats it; and then we have an adaptation of it to the later gospel history, in which we hear the voice of the Father in heaven saying: *"This is my beloved Son in whom I am well pleased."* The Gnostics did not derive their knowledge from the history, any more than Paul did, and therefore it follows that the history was derived from an adaptation of the Gnosis.

The founders of Historic Christianity taught and enforced the doctrine that their Jesus the Christ had risen from the dead, body, bones, and all, and that he demonstrated the fact to his followers when he declared that he was *not* a spirit! The resurrection, therefore, was physical from the first! In a confession found in the Apostolic Creed, in the year 600, the convert has to say, "*I believe in the resurrection of the flesh*"; and only the other day Canon Gregory declared in St. Paul's Cathedral, that if you took away the physical resurrection of Jesus, the one foundation of their spiritual life was gone! If the Christ did not rise corporeally from his tomb, then that tomb would be the grave of Christianity. But Paul's doctrine of the resurrection is totally opposed to this cardinal doctrine of the Christian creed, the resurrection of the body. He does not expect to rise corporeally because of any physical resurrection of the Christ. His doctrine is that of the Gnostics, and consequently identifiable by the comparative process. It is also entirely opposed to that which was proclaimed by his contemporaries, Hymenœus and Philetus, who taught that the resurrection was past already, and who had overthrown the faith of some in the doctrine preached by Paul. He says "*they are in error*," and "*their word will eat as doth a gangrene*." Now, the sole way in which the resurrection could be set forth as *already past* was the same then as it is to-day—namely, as the resurrection once for all of a personal and historical Saviour, who there and then arose from the dead for the first time and instituted the resurrection. Paul's own resurrection from the dead was not assured by any such miraculous, non-natural, or impossible means! On the contrary, in a passage which shows a cleavage in the context, he breathes an aspiration thus: "*If by any means I may attain unto the resurrection from the dead*"—therefore, not the means set forth by Historical Christianity—and he continues: "*Not that I have already attained, or am already made perfect, but I press on.*" Again, this is pure Gnostic doctrine. The Perfect were those who had reached the octave, or height of attainment, in a sense which can only be understood by the Gnosis. It was his endeavour to reach the Christhood of the Gnosis on which the continuity in death depended—a glimpse of which had been obtained by him in abnormal vision. This kind of working out of one's own salvation, and earning one's own eternal living in this life, is absolutely opposed to the Christian doctrine of the Atonement! The old Jewish doctrine of Atonement by blood, continued into historic Christianity, is provably impossible to a Gnostic and a spiritualist like Paul. But this *was* the doctrine promulgated by those who preached that "*other gospel*" which he repudiated. Therefore I infer that texts like these are a part of the matter interpolated: "*Without shedding of blood is no remission of sin*" (Heb. ix. 22). "*Having made peace through the blood of his cross*" (Col. i. 20). "*In whom we have our redemption through his blood*" (Eph. i. 7). Such doctrine being impossible to the Gnostic, I hold these texts to have been falsely fathered upon Paul. The two doctrines cannot co-exist in one mind, or system of thought; and we have to ascertain which of the two is the genuine Pauline doctrine before we can determine the nature of his Christology. Again he says, "*wherefore let us cease to speak of the first principles of Christ, and press on unto perfection, not laying again a foundation of repentance from dead works, and of faith towards God, of the teaching of baptisms, and of laying on of hands, and of resurrection from the dead, and of eternal judgment, and this will we do!*" Here we find a complete repudiation by Paul of certain cardinal doctrines of Historic Christianity elsewhere ascribed to him! These are called first principles, or those belonging to an exoteric or exterior interpretation of the Gnosis, which is looked upon as a pernicious and deadly heresy. They were a part of those "beggarly rudiments" which kept men in bondage to the Petrine gospel of the flesh. Paul positively repudiates, and most distinctly denies, salvation by means of these Christian Sacraments! Those who have taken up with this teaching are treated as backsliders from the true faith, which is that of Paul's own gospel, and of the esoteric interpretation. "*For as touching those who were once enlightened, and tasted of the heavenly gift, and were made partakers of the Holy Ghost, and tasted the good word of God, and the powers of the age to come, and then fell away, it is impossible to renew them again.*" Every special phrase reveals the Gnostic and the Gnosis. Those who fell away have lapsed from the interior teaching of Paul, and gone over to those who now preach the externalised history, the "*other gospel*" of the "*other Jesus*," with its corporeal resurrection. Having been fed on solid food they have become such as have need of milk. This repudiation of dogmas culminates in his banishing the resurrection of the dead, and the Eternal Judgment or punishment at the Last Day. Here the resurrection of the dead must include that of the historic Jesus, if there had been one, and therefore this also is denied. He rejects any foundation laid on that, and says, "let us cease to speak of it." Paul, like all Gnostics, taught the resurrection *from* the dead in *this* life; not the resurrection OF the Dead in the life hereafter. Now, it is quite certain that these Gnostic doctrines could not have been interpolated in Paul's writings by the founders of the Fleshly Faith. Therefore, it is the physical dogmas that have been foisted into the Epistles of Paul.

I have never yet seen a sign in the works of Christian writers that they knew anything whatever of the real nature of these doctrinal mysteries. All alike are ignorant of the Tradition or Gnosis on which a true explanation depended. They assume the human history as the initial point of a new beginning, and ignore, or are ignorant of, that which lies beyond. When called upon to face the facts in broad daylight they themselves will be all in the dark, and will have to fight against them blindfold. But it is impossible to enter within range of understanding Paul's teaching until we do know something of the doctrines that were unfolded in the mysteries. It is impossible to comprehend the mystery of Paul's Christ without a fundamental knowledge of the Messianic mystery that had been from the Beginning. This was his mystery, which he would not make so much of if he had started with what are held to be plain historical gospel truths. He spoke the "*Wisdom of God in a mystery that hath been hidden; which God foreordained before the worlds unto our glory.*" The "*mystery of Christ which in other generations was not made known.*" The "*mystery which is Christ in you.*" His was the "*revelation of the mystery which hath been kept in silence through times eternal.*" The fact is that Paul was a publisher of the ancient mysteries; that was why his enemies strove to kill him! He openly promulgated the Gnosis which had always been kept secret. But to comprehend him we must have some knowledge of the Messianic mystery, which had an origin in phenomena that are both natural and explicable. When one has worked at the subject for years, it can be explained in a few hours. The root of the Messiah's name is *Mesi* in Egyptian. One meaning, like that of the Christ in Greek and Messiach in Hebrew, is to anoint. But the fundamental signification is *re-birth*. The month, *Mes-ore*, was so named from the re-birth of the Inundation. The mam-*mesi* was the re-birth-place of the mam or mummy. The evening meal on the first day of the New Year was the *Mesiu*, or festival of its re-birth. *Cf.* Sanskrit *masa*, for a moon or month, and *masala* for a year.

This *re-birth* could be very various in phenomena, and so was the typical Messiah or re-born one. The serpent called *Mesi*, the Sacred Word, was the Messiah by name, because the reptile sloughed its skin, and renewed itself. Hence the Serpent was a symbol of the Gnostic Christ. *Re-birth* was the manifestation and the personified Manifestor was the Messiah, under whichever type or in whatever phase of the phenomena. *Re-birth* of the Nile, of the light in the moon, of the time-cycle, or of the Dead, could have its Messiah! Hence the Messiah had a monthly re-birth in the lunar orb, and a solar one every year—with re-birth from the virgin mother in the Zodiac. But there was a more mysterious manifestation when the girl or boy attained pubescence, or re-birth, into womanhood and manhood. Here the Messiah is both male and female—Charis as well as Christ; Wisdom as well as the Word! According to the natural facts, at that period of re-birth was born the procreative power for further ensuring the future re-birth of the race. Men and women could reproduce themselves in this life. Hence the re-birth of the Anointed One, the Messiah of Adultship. But beyond these natural re-births, it was demonstrated in the spiritual mysteries of abnormal mediumship, that there was a spirit in man, or, at least, in some men, that could repro-duce itself, or, by alliance with the power above, could be reproduced, or re-born, for the next life. This was the Christ of the Gnosis, the Messianic Manifestor in a psychial or spiritual phase; the Revealer, according to the mystery of Paul. That which he had received from no man, was communicated to him by this revelation of the Christ. But mark; in no one of these phases, elemental, Kronian, or human, could the Messiah, the Christ of the manifestation, become any *one* historic personage. Also, in the human phase, there is but one sense in which the Christ could be born of a virgin mother, and that can only be understood by taking the Christ as the Immortal in man, and supplementing it with the knowledge that the mother was the first recognised inspirer of the soul. When typified and made doctrinal, this mother, as quickener of the soul, this mother of the Horus, or Christ, may be said to be virgin in a region beyond that of physical contact in the fleshly human phase. In a final form, the Messiah was the immortal spirit in man, or the Christ within, according to the language of Paul. Those who understood these things could not take to, or be taken in by, historic Christianity; could only think of it as did Celsus when he says of the Christians: "*Certain most impious errors are committed by them, which are due to their extreme ignorance, in which they have wandered away from the meaning of the divine enigmas*"; and as did Porphyry, who denounced the Christian religion as a "*blasphemy, barbarously bold.*" The Christian doctrine of being *born again* was derived without knowledge from this Gnostic *re-birth*, which was the conversion of the total man, and his seven lower souls, into a likeness of his supreme or divine self, with the eighth one, the Christ-spirit, as the reproducer for eternal life. Paul sometimes claims that he possesses this Christ-nature, this Revelator within, because, according to the Gnosis, humanity could attain to the divine altitude, and demonstrate upon the Mount of Transfiguration the immortal element in the nature of man. The Christian world let go, and lost this basis that Paul found in natural, though supra-normal fact, when it ignorantly substituted the *modus operandi* of miracle applied to a physical resurrection.

But, as we have seen, this manifestor of the re-birth might be feminine as well as masculine. In fact, the female announcer was first, and there are mystical reasons for this in nature. In Hebrew, the Holy Spirit, or *ruach*, is of a feminine gender. The soul is female. Some of the Gnostic sects assigned the soul to the female nature, and made their Charis not only anterior, but superior, to the Christ. In the Book of Wisdom it is Sophia herself who is the pre-Christian *Saviour* of mankind. It was Wisdom, not the Christ, who had brought Adam out of his Fall. It is by Wisdom that men are taught, and she is the Saviour through knowledge and good works. Whereas the Christ was turned into a Saviour through faith. The same Tree of Knowledge that supplied the fruit which damned the primal pair in the Genesis, is the Tree of Wisdom in the Apocrypha, where Wisdom, personified as the Tree, exclaims, "*I am the mother of fair love, and fear, and knowledge, and holy hope. Come unto me all ye that be desirous of me, and fill yourselves with my fruits. For my memorial is sweeter than honey, and mine inheritance than the honey-comb. He that obeyeth me shall never be confounded.*" This complete reversal of the Christian belief is to be found in the Hidden Wisdom! Such was the interpretation, by the men who knew, of that Fable on which the Fall of Man was based by those who have imposed on us with their ignorance, and made us blind with their belief. Wisdom is the **renewer** and renovator of all things, and it is she who confers immortality on man; she who is the Christ as bringer to re-birth. The Gnostic Marcus maintained that Charis was superior to "all things" or Totum; and Charis, the female Christ, was the illuminating spirit of his teaching, as when he is made to say to his mediums:— "*Behold, Charis has descended upon thee; open thy mouth and prophesy; open thy mouth and thou shalt prophesy.*" Apply this to the Spirit as male, instead of female, and you have the Christ, or illuminating spirit of Paul. It was a question of priority in the type, and belonged to a mystical interpretation of natural phenomena. The blood of Charis preceded the blood of Christ, and but for the purification by the blood of Charis, there would have been no doctrine of the purification of souls by the blood of Christ. The Eucharist was a celebration of Charis before it was assigned to the Christ.

Again, Paul's Christ is identified with the angel Metatron, as the Messiah who followed the Israelites in the wilderness. Thus he makes the angel masculine. But in the Targumists' traditions the Well of Miriam takes the place of this sustaining Christ, who was the spiritual rock according to Paul. In the gospel of the Egyptians, quoted by Clement Alexander, the Lord says: "*I am come to destroy the works of the Woman.*" The two manifestors, male and female, are continued by the "*Shepherd of Hermas*," which some of the Fathers regarded as a divinely inspired scripture. Here the spirit, or Logos, who is an old woman—*i.e.*, the ancient Wisdom—in one vision, becomes the son of God in another! Of her it is said: "*She is an old woman, because she was the first of all creation, and the world was made by her.*" Wisdom, the woman, was first; she was the mother of God. Christ, the son, was second; then he superseded the female in one representation; in another he was blended with her, and consequently portrayed in the image of both sexes, as a spiritual type. The Wisdom or Sophia of the Gnostics was first at the head of the seven pre-planetary powers, and was called "*Ogdoas*," as mother of the first and inferior Hebdomad; next the Christ was made the head as manifestor of the seven later planetary powers, called by them the superior Hebdomad, he being the outcome of a later creation, and representative of the Fatherhood in heaven, which followed the fatherhood established on earth; and that same Gnostic manifestor of the seven powers or Gods had been *Iu* in Egypt, *Iao* in Phoenicia, *Assur* in Assyria, and the *Buddha* or *Agni* in India, ages on ages earlier.

Now Paul was opposed to those Gnostics who exalted the feminine type of the soul—the female as bringer to re-birth hereafter. He repudiated it, and proclaimed his Christ. His Word, Logos or Messiah, is strictly masculine. In India his type would be *lingaic* versus the *Yonian*. He maintains that the "*World by Wisdom knew not God.*" This is exactly the same as saying that at one time men only recognised the motherhood in heaven, and did not know who were their own fathers on earth. The Lord is the spirit, the Christ is the spirit, he declares; not Sophia, not the wisdom of a feminine nature. Christ, he affirms, is both the "*power and the wisdom of God.*" He proclaims all the treasures of Sophia and of the Gnosis to be contained in the Christ, and says the Christ has been "*made unto us Wisdom.*" The Christ has taken her place. Again, his glorifying is not in *fleshly Wisdom*, not in the female *Charis*, but in the *grace* of God (2 Cor. i. 12). For the female Wisdom *had been* according to the flesh, the woman or mother being of the flesh fleshly; and Paul, as Gnostic or Kabbalist, had been acquainted with the fleshly Wisdom, one of whose mysteries appertained to feminine periodicity, which he now repudiates when he says: "*Even though we have known Christ* (or the manifestor) *after the flesh, yet now we know so no more.*" Here it cannot be pretended that Paul ever knew the personal Christ in the flesh, and therefore some other fact has to be encountered. However interpreted, he is speaking doctrinally, and not of *two historic characters*. Paul's is the Gnostic Christ as the Second Adam; the man from heaven, whose type superseded the man of earth. Paul knew well enough that Adam was not a man in the literal sense; he was the typical man of the flesh; the son of the woman; and as was the type, such was the antitype, when he calls his Christ the second Adam, the later spiritual type of man, and of the Father above. Neither were, or could be, historic personages. To use his own words, "*These things are an allegory.*" In her most occult phase the feminine messenger was a Word that could be made flesh; for she was the flesh-maker, the mother of Matter. But this was on physiological grounds alone. Hence she was superseded by the masculine messenger; the spirit that never could be made flesh. None but the initiated in these matters could possibly know what was meant by this transfer of type, and substitution of the Lord for the Lady, the Christ for Wisdom, the second Adam for the first. But there it is truth-like at the bottom of the well; the source of so much difficulty found in the depths of Paul's writings. And *this contention of Paul on behalf of one Gnostic dogma against another has been made to look as if he were fervently fighting for an Historic Jesus.*

This transfer of type is not limited to Paul! For instance, the Vine was a feminine symbol. Wisdom says, "*As the Vine brought I forth*" (Ecc. xxiv. 17); and in the Book of Proverbs Sophia cries, "*Come eat of my bread, and drink of the wine I have mingled.*" The Fig-Tree in Egypt was a figure of the Lady of Heaven, who is pourtrayed *as* the Tree of Life and Knowledge, in the act of feeding souls. She literally gives her body as the Bread and her blood as the Wine of Life! In the later Ptolemeian times this Tree was assigned to Sophia or Wisdom! which shows the link between Egypt and Greece. The superseding of Sophia is also illustrated in the cursing of the fruitless Fig-tree by the Cánonical Christ, where the Parable of Mythology is represented as a human history. In John's Gospel the type has been transferred, just as the sayings were, to the masculine nature, and the Christ becomes the bread and wine of life. In the Apocrypha it is Sophia who is "*The brightness of the everlasting light, the unspotted mirror of the power of God, and the image of his goodness!*" (Wisdom vii. 26.) In the Epistle to the

Hebrews the Christ takes the place of Sophia. He is called the *"effulgence of the glory" of God,* the *"very image of his substance."* Nevertheless, the male Christ *could no more be made flesh in a man than Sophia or Charis could have previously been incarnated in an historical woman.* You cannot understand one half without the other. Both must be taken together. The doctrine is doubly and wholly opposed to any and all historic personality.

But, we have not yet completely mastered the entire Mystery of Paul for modern use; and it is not possible for any one but the phenomenal Spiritualist, who knows that the conditions of trance and clairvoyance are facts in nature; only those who have evidence that the other world can open and lighten with revelations, and prove its palpable presence, visibly and audibly; only those who accept the teaching that the human consciousness continues in death, and emerges in a personality that persists beyond the grave; only such, I say, are qualified to comprehend the mystery, or receive the message, once truly delivered to men by the Spiritualist Paul, but which was thoroughly perverted by the *Sarkolators,* the founders of the fleshly faith. In the first place he was an Initiate in the Gnostic Mysteries, called Kabbalist in Hebrew. He tells us how exceedingly jealous for the traditions he had been, which must have included the traditional interpretation of the mysteries and of the Gnosis or hidden Wisdom. He was a perfected Adept. He knew the nature of the Kronian Christ, and of the Spiritual Christ, according to the Gnosis. Beyond that, Paul, on his own testimony, was an abnormal Seer, subject to the conditions of trance. He could not remember if certain experiences occurred to him in the body or out of it! This trance condition was the origin and source of his revelations, the heart of his mystery, his infirmity in which he gloried—in short, his *"thorn in the flesh."* He shows the Corinthians that his abnormal condition, ecstacy, illness, madness (or what not), was a phase of spiritual intercourse in which he was divinely insane— insane on behalf of God—but that he was rational enough in his relationship to them. He says: *"I will come to visions and revelations of the Lord. I knew a man in Christ fourteen years ago (whether in the body I know not; or whether out of the body I know not; God knoweth), such an one caught up even to the third heaven"*—on behalf of that man he will glory. *"And by reason of the exceeding greatness of the revelations, wherefore that I should not be exalted over much, there was given me a thorn in the flesh, a messenger of Satan to buffet me, that I should not be exalted over much."* Paul's Thorn in the Flesh has been attributed to lechery, and to sore eyes; but no Christian commentator known to me has ever connected it with abnormal phenomena, except as miracle. The Marcionites said the Mystery was manifested to Paul by revelation. Paul says the same. By this abnormal mode the Mystery was revealed to him in person. His eyes were opened, so that he could see for himself the truth that was taught in the Mysteries. If a Spirit appeared in vision to Paul, that would positively prove the *re-birth* for a future life, and constitute the revelation of his Messianic mystery. Paul's Christ, the Lord, is *the* spirit ; his gospel is that of spiritual revelation, the chief mode of manifestation being abnormal, as it was, and had been, in the Gnostic mysteries.

The Gnostic Christ was the Immortal Spirit in man, which first demonstrated its existence by means of abnormal or spiritualistic phenomena. It did not and could not depend on any single manifestation in one historic personality. And when Paul says, "*I knew a man in Christ*," we see that to be in Christ is to be in the condition of trance, *in the spirit*, as they phrased it, in the state that is common to what is now termed mediumship.

Being in the trance condition, or in Christ, as he calls it, he was caught up to the third heaven, and could not determine whether he was in the body or out of the body. Here he identifies his Christ with a condition of being, and that condition with the abnormal phenomena known to some of us who have studied Modern Spiritualism. This is the Gnostic Christ, not the Christ of any special historic personality, who is supposed to have manifested only once upon a time, and once for all. The Christ of the Gnosis, of Philo and of Paul preceded Christianity, and is sure to supersede it, because it is based upon facts known in nature and verifiable to-day. It was those who were entirely ignorant of those subtle and obscure facts, unfolded in the Mysteries, who became Christians in the modern sense, and believed, because they were blind. Paul was both a Seer and a Knower. He became one of the public demonstrators of the facts, just like any itinerant medium of our time. He says to the Galatians : "*Ye know that because of an infirmity of the flesh, I preached the gospel unto you the first time, and that which was a temptation to you in my flesh, ye despised not nor rejected* (or spat out) ; *but ye received me as an angel of God, as Christ Jesus!*" This infirmity of the flesh was his tendency to fall into trance. When it first occurred, at a given date, he received his revelation and began to preach his own gospel. He talked and taught as do the mediums in trance to-day. He received his revelations—visions and revelations of the Lord—and gave proofs of the Christ, or spirit, speaking within him, speaking through him, when he was in trance. And on this ground they received him as an angel of God—they received him *as the Christ*. This Christ, personated by Paul as the revealer in trance, was of necessity the Gnostic Christ, the Spirit of God, as he often calls it, the Christ that spoke through him, founded on what is now termed spirit control, but not based on the spirit of any Jesus of Nazareth. His Christ is the spirit which revealed itself abnormally in, and through him, so that he "spoke the wisdom and the words which the spirit teacheth ; he spoke mysteries in the spirit." His Christ was the same spirit that "*hath a diversity of workings*" in various spirit manifestations. "*To one it gives the word of wisdom; to another, the word of knowledge; to another, faith; to another, gifts of healing; to another, miraculous powers; to another, prophecy; to another, seeing of spirits; to another, the gift of tongues, and to another, their interpretation.*" And as this was *the* Christ, that always had been so manifested, nothing depended upon any historical character. All that was real, that is, spiritual, would be the same afterwards as it had been before. Nothing *did* depend on it, and historical Christianity itself is but a vast interpolation, the greatest of all obstacles to mental development and the unity of the human race.

One more illustration that Paul was outside the ring of conspirators who were the founders, as forgers, of Historic Christianity in Rome, and I shall have done.

The Christ proclaimed by Peter and James was the mythical Messiah of the Time-cycles, the *ever-coming one*, converted into an historical character; hence he who was supposed to have just come still remained the Coming One. He himself is made to say that he is coming before the then present generation shall have passed away.

Apart from the mythos and its meaning, there was no other coming, or end of the Times, of the age, Æon, or world! The Kronian allegory can only apply to the Kronian Christ, as the metaphorical manifestor of the Eternal in the sphere of time, who could neither be made flesh nor assume historic personality. This was known to Paul as an Adept. Such things *were* an Allegory; but it was not known to those who preached that " *other gospel.*" James asserts that " *the coming of the Lord is at hand.*" John declares that it is the Last Hour. In the Second Epistle of Peter we find the writer mentions Paul by name, and replies to his Epistles. He is covertly trying to counteract the influence of Paul's teaching on a matter of such importance as the second coming of Christ, and the immediate ending of the world. In the first chapter he proclaims that the *end of all things is at hand.* Here he says the mockers are asking, " *Where is the promise of his coming?*" They forget the cataclysms and deluges by which the previous heavens and earth have perished. This time the end will come with a universal conflagration, and, according to promise, " *We look for new heavens and a new earth.*" . . . " *Our beloved brother, Paul, has been speaking of these things. . . . According to the wisdom given to him he wrote unto you; as also in his Epistles, speaking in them of these things; wherein are some things hard to understand, which the ignorant and unsteadfast wrest (as also the other scriptures) unto their own destruction.*" The subject-matter here is the nature of the time-cycles, and the mythical destruction by flood and fire, which Paul as an Adept knew to be typical and allegorical. Peter mistakes them for literal realities. Being an outsider, he did not understand the Wisdom or Gnosis of Paul, but says it is misleading, inasmuch as the ignorant wrest it unto their own destruction. Peter had also said the day of the Lord will come as a thief. To this we have direct replies from Paul. " *Concerning the times and the seasons, brethren, ye have no need that aught be written unto you. For yourselves know perfectly well that the day of the Lord so cometh as a thief in the night. But ye, brethren, are not in darkness, that that day should overtake you as a thief; for ye are all sons of light and sons of the day; we are not of the night nor of the darkness*" — as were those foolish Physicalists, the Petrine A-Gnostics. And again he says to the Thessalonians—"*Now we beseech you, brethren, touching the coming of our Lord Jesus Christ, and our gathering together unto him, that ye be not quickly shaken from your mind, nor yet be troubled either by spirit, or by word, or by epistle as from us! as that the day of the Lord is present at hand. Let no man beguile you in any wise;*" give no heed to that ignoramus' *gobemoucherie!* Then follows a break in the sense. But a falling away is to come first, and the *Man of Sin* must be revealed or exposed; the *son of perdition*, "*he that opposeth and exalteth himself against all that is called God, or that is worshipped; so that he sitteth in the Temple of God setting himself forth as God.*" That, I say, is St. Paul's opposer, Peter, who was set up in the Church of Rome. "*Remember ye not that when I was with you I told you these things. And now ye know that which restraineth to the end that he may be revealed in his own season. For the mystery of lawlessness doth already work only until he that restraineth now shall be taken out of the way. And then shall be revealed the Lawless one whom the Lord Jesus shall slay with the breath of his mouth, and bring to nought by the manifestation of his coming,* (him) *whose 'coming' is according to the working of Satan, with all power and signs and lying wonders, and with all deceit of unrighteousness for them that are perishing, because they received not the love of truth that they might be saved; and for this cause God sendeth them a working of error that they should believe a lie.*" In both quotations the subject-matter identifies Peter as palpably as if Paul had named him. He is replying to the teaching of one particular man who is proclaiming the " Coming" of the Christ and the day of the Lord, or end of the world, as being close at hand. He says in effect—Do not be troubled or beguiled by any such ignorant trash. The Lord will not come in his sense, and cannot come in mine, except that man of sin be revealed. No one has ever dared to dream that this "Man of Sin" is Peter himself! But the person aimed at is considered capable of forging epistles in the name of Paul; thus attributing this kind of teaching to him, and making him father it whilst Paul was yet living. This " man of sin " and " son of perdition" has set himself up in the temple of God, *setting himself forth as God.* This is no emperor Nero, but a portrait of Peter, the life-long enemy of Paul; he whose preaching is concerning signs and lying wonders, such as the stories about the end of the world, the passing away of the heavens with a great noise, the dissolution of the elements with fervent heat, and the burning up of the earth with all the works therein, and other teachings of this cataclysmalist, which Paul denounces as delusive, and knows to be a lie! This misleader of men is restrained for the time being by Paul himself, but when he departs Peter will reveal himself or be revealed in his true colours, and the Thessalonians will then see what Paul has known all along, and against which he had warned them once before, *i.e.*, against that *working of error and belief in a lie,* which we now know by name as *Historic Christianity.*

It is here, then, that we can peer right down into the deep, dark gulf that divided Peter from Paul, of which we get such a lightning glimpse in the Clementine Homilies. These writings were inspired by the faction of Peter. By them Paul is designated the "*Hostile Man*"; his own epithet, *Anomas*, the Lawless, is there flung back at him by Peter, who denounces the puerile preaching of the man that is his enemy, and who says: "*Thou hast opposed thyself as an Adversary against me, the firm rock, the foundation of the Church.*" Paul's conversion, by means of abnormal vision, is attributed to the false Christ, the Gnostic and Spiritualist opposed to an Historic Christ. In Homily 17, Peter is obviously hitting at Paul and his visions when he asks: "*Can anyone be instituted to the office of a teacher through visions?*" Paul is treated as the arch-enemy of the Christ crucified— he is the very Anti-Christ. He will be the author of some great heresy which is expected to break out in the future. Peter is said to have declared that Christ instructed the disciples not to publish the only true and genuine gospel for the present, because the false teacher must arise, who would publicly proclaim the false gospel of the Anti-Christ that was the Christ of the Gnostics. "*As the true Prophet has told us, the false gospel must come from a certain misleader;*" and so they were to go on secretly promulgating the true gospel, until this false preacher had passed away. This true gospel was confessedly "*held in reserve, to be secretly transmitted for the rectification of future heresies.*" They knew well enough what had to come out, if Paul's preaching, proclaimed in his original Epistles, got vent more and more. It was Paul whom they had reason to fear. Hence those who were the followers of Peter and James anathematized him as the great apostate, and rejected his Epistles. Justin Martyr never once mentions this founder of Christianity, never once refers to the writings of Paul. Strangest thing of all is it that the book of the Acts, which is mainly the history of Paul, should contain no account of his martyrdom or death in Rome! The gulf, however, cannot be completely fathomed, except on the grounds that there was no personal Christ, and that Paul was the natural opponent of the men who were setting up the Christ made flesh for the salvation of a world that never was lost. My conclusion is, that fabricated evidence is the sole support of Historic Christianity which can be derived from the Epistles of Paul; that the manipulation for an ulterior purpose, which is so obvious in the book of Acts, was far more subtly and fundamentally applied to his Epistles and doctrines; that they have been worked over as thieves manipulate stolen linen when they pick out the marks of ownership to escape from detection; that false doctrines have been foisted into the original text, which seems to have been withheld for a century after the writer's death, until the leaven of falsehood had done its fatal work. The problem of the plotters and forgers in Rome was how to convert the mythical Christology into historic Christianity, and when Paul's Epistles were permitted to emerge from obscurity in a collection, what had occurred was the *restoration* of the carnalised Christ, that *"other Jesus"* who was repudiated by Paul in his own lifetime. Paul felt or feared, and foretold that this would be the case when once he was removed out of the way. He saw the mystery of lawlessness already at work—the falsifiers sending forth letters as if from himself—and we have seen what Paul foresaw! the problem of the plotters who forged the foundations of the Church in Rome was how to successfully blend the Christ Jesus of the Gnostics, of the pre-Christian Apocrypha, of Philo, and of Paul, with that *Corporeal Christ* and impossible personality, in whom they ignorantly believed, through a blind literalisation of mythology, so as to make the historic look like the true starting-point, and the Gnostic interpretation become a later heresy. This was finally effected when the declaration of John—that *"the Word was made flesh, and dwelt amongst us"*—had been accepted as the genuine Gospel, and that which had been an impossibility for the Gnostics was an accomplished fact for those who knew no better than to believe. The Gospel, according to John, was concocted and calculated to serve as a harmonising amalgam of doctrines that were fundamentally opposed. In this Amalgam they tried to mix the "gall and honey," so that, if "well shaken before taken," it might be swallowed by the followers on both sides. But there was a great gulf forever fixed between the Gnostic Christology and Historic Christianity. It was a gulf that never could be soundly bridged, and never has been plumbed, or bottomed, or filled in. The bodies of two million martyrs of free-thought, put to death as heretics, in Europe alone, and all the blood that has ever been shed in Christian wars, have failed to fill that gulf, which waits as ever wide-jawed for its prey. Across that gulf the Christian Church was erected upon supports on either side. On one side stood those pillars of the Church which were seen by Paul in Jerusalem. On the other was Paul himself, the pillar that stood alone. A difference the most radical and profound divided him from the other apostles, Cephas, John, and James. From the first they were on two sides of the chasm that could not be closed; and the *Prædicatio Petri* declares that Peter and Paul remained unreconciled till death. The great work of the first centuries was how to bridge the chasm over, or at least how to conceal it from the eyes of the world in later times. This could only be done by resting on Paul as a prop and buttress on the one side and Peter on the other, which had to be done by converting or perverting the Epistles of the Gnostic Paul into a support for Historic Christianity. In that way the Church was founded. It was built as a bridge across the gulf, and the Pope of Rome appointed and aptly designated *Pontifex Maximus*. It was reared above the chasm lying darkly lurking like an open grave below, and to-day, as ever, the Christian world is horribly haunted with the fear that a breath or two of larger intellectual life, a too audible utterance of free-er thought, a dose of mental dynamite may bring the edifice of error down in wreck and ruin to fill that gulf at last, over which it was so perilously founded from the first.

THE "LOGIA OF THE LORD;"
OR,
PRE-HISTORIC SAYINGS
ASCRIBED TO
JESUS THE CHRIST.

(References to Authorities may be found in the Author's "NATURAL GENESIS.")

IT would take almost a life-time of original research to fathom or approximately gauge the depths of ignorance in which the beginnings of Historic Christianity lie sunken out of sight.

The current ignorance of those pre-Christian evidences that have been preserved by the petrifying past must be well-nigh invincible, when a man like Professor Jowett could say, as if with the voice of superstition in its dotage, "*To us the preaching of the Gospel is a New Beginning, from which we date all things; beyond which we neither desire, nor are able, to inquire.*"

It is the commonly accepted orthodox belief that Christianity originated with the life, miracles, sayings, and teachings; the birth, death, resurrection, and ascension of an historic Jesus the Christ at the commencement of our era, called Christian; whereas, the origins were manifold, but mostly concealed. It is impossible to determine anything fundamental by an appeal to the documents which, alone out of a hundred Gospels, were made Canonical. And when Eusebius recorded his memorable boast that he had virtually made "all square" for the Christians, it was an ominous announcement of what had been done to keep out of sight the mythical and mystical rootage of historic Christianity. The Gnostics had been muzzled, and their extant evidences, as far as possible, masked. He and his co-conspirators did their worst in destroying documents and effacing the tell-tale records of the past, to prevent the future from learning what the bygone ages could have said directly for themselves. They made dumb all Pagan voices that would have cried aloud their testimony against the unparalleled imposture then being perfected in Rome. They had almost reduced the first four centuries to silence on all matters of the most vital importance for any proper understanding of the true origins of the Christian Superstition. The mythos having been at last published as a human history everything else was suppressed or forced to support the fraud. Christolatry is founded on the Christ, who is mythical in one phase and mystical in the other; Egyptian (and Gnostic) in both, but historical in neither. The Christ was a type and a title that could not become a person. As such, the Christ of the Gnostics was the Horus continued from Egypt and Chaldea; and that which was original as mythos ages earlier cannot be also original as a later personal history. We who commence with our canonical Gospels are three or four centuries too late to learn anything fundamental concerning the real beginnings of Christianity. You have only to turn to the second Book of Esdras to learn that Jesus the Christ of our canonical history was both pre-historic and, pre-Christian. This is one of the books of the hidden wisdom which have been rejected and set apart as the Apocrypha—considered to be spurious, because they are opposed to the received history; whereas, they contain the secret Gnosis by which alone we can identify the genuine Scripture. In this book it is said, "*My son Jesus shall be revealed with those that are with him . . . . and they that remain shall rejoice within four hundred years; and after these years shall my son Christ die, and all men shall have life.*" And this was to be even as it had been in the former judgments at the end of the particular cycles of time, and the renewal of the world, which was to occur according to date! Now, if an historic Jesus Christ of prophecy is to be found anywhere it is here,—foretold even as the prediction is supposed to have been fulfilled. Yet these books are not included among the canonical Scriptures, because they prove too much; because they are historical in the wrong sense,—*i.e.*, they are not and could not be made humanly historical; their Jesus Christ is entirely mythical,—is the Kronian Christ; and his future coming therein announced was only the subject of astronomical prophecy. The true Christ, whether mythical or mystical, astronomical or spiritual, never could become an historical personage, and never did originate in any human history. The types of themselves suffice to prove that the Christ was, and could only be, typical, and never could have taken form in historic personality. For one thing, the mystical Christ of the Gnosis and of the pre-Christian types was a being of both sexes, as was the Egyptian Horus and other of the Messiahs; because the mystical Christ typified the spirit or soul which belongs to the female as well as to the male, and represents that which could only be a human reality in the spiritual domain or the Pleroma of the Gnostics. This is the Christ who appears as both male and female in the Book of Revelation. And the same biune type was continued in the Christian portraits of the Christ. In Didron's Iconography you will see that Jesus Christ is pourtrayed as a female with the beard of a male, and is called Jesus Christ as Saint Sophia,—*i.e.*, the Wisdom, or the Spirit of both sexes. The early Christians were ignorant of this typology; but the types still remain to be interpreted by the Gnosis and to bear witness against the History. Both the type and doctrine combine to show there could be no one personal Christ in this world or any other. Howsoever the written word may lie, the truth is visibly engraved upon the stones, and still survives in the Icons, symbols, and doctrines of the Gnostics, which remain to prove that they preserved the truer tradition of the *origines*. And so this particular pre-Christian type was continued as a portrait of the historic Christ. It can be proved that the earliest Christians known were Gnostics—the men who knew, and who never did or could accept Historic Christianity.

The Essenes were Christians in the Gnostic sense, and according to Pliny the elder, they were a Hermetic Society that had existed for ages on ages of time. Their name is best explained as Egyptian. They were known as the Eshai, the healers or Therapeutae, the physicians in Egypt ; and Esha or Usha means to doctor or heal, in Egyptian. The Sutites, the Mandaites, the Nazarites well as the Docetae and Elkesites, were all Gnostic Christians ; they all preceded, and were all opposed to, the cult of the carnalised Christ. The followers of Simon, the Samaritan, were Gnostic Christians, and they were of the Church at Antioch, where it is said the name of Christian was primarily applied. Cerinthus was a Gnostic Christian, who, according to Epiphanius, denied that Christ had come in the flesh. The same writter informs us that; at the end of the fourth century there were Ebionite Christians, whose Christ was the mythical fulfiller of the time-cycles, not an historic Jesus. Even Clement Alexander confesses that his Christ was of a nature that did not require the nourishment of corporeal food.

Now, from the time of Irenæus to that of Mansell, it has been confidently asserted that Gnosticism was a heresy of the second century, a backsliding and apostacy from the true faith of historic Christianity. This is simply a delusion of the ignorant, founded on the original lie of the falsifiers ! Later teachers of Gnosticism, such as Basilides and Saturninus, did arise during the second century; but these were not the founders of any fresh doctrines, nor did they make any new departure. They were Revivalists ! The Christian Fathers only knew of the Gnostics of their time ; they never troubled to trace the roots of Gnosticism in the remoter past.

The Christian report respecting the Gnostics, Docetae, and others, always assumes the human reality of the supposed history, and then explains the non-human interpretation of the Gnostics themselves as an heretic denial, or perversion of the alleged facts. Hence the Gnostics are charged by Irenæus with falsifying the oracles of God, and trying to discredit the word of revelation with their own wicked inventions.

We learn from Origen that, during the third century, there were various different versions of Matthew's gospel in circulation, and this he attributes partly to the forgers of gospels. Jerome, at the end of the fourth century, asserts the same thing; and of the Latin versions he says, there were as many different texts as manuscripts. The Gnostics, who had brought on the original and pre-Christian matter of the mysteries that were taught orally, no sooner placed it on record than they were said to be forging the Scriptures of Anti-Christ, whereas it was the Gnosis of the Ante-Christ of whom they, the Christians, were ignorant.

Theirs is altogether a false mode of describing the position of those who always and utterly denied that the Christ could be made flesh, to suffer and die upon a veritable cross. Here is a specimen of the way in which the Gnostic doctrines had been turned to historic account:—The true light which lighteth every man coming into the world was Gnostic, and had been Gnostic ages before the prologue of John was written; and as Gnostic doctrine it has to be read. This Light of the world, born, as the Gnostics held, with every one coming into the world, is the immortal principle in man! Hyppolytus, referring to the teaching of Basilides, a Gnostic teacher of the second century, shows us how the doctrine of the Gnostics was falsified. "*And this*," says he, "*it is which is said in the Gospels, 'The true light which lighteth every man was coming into the world!'*" "Was coming" is an interpolation of the believers in the fact of historic fulfilment applied to that eternal light which lighted every man coming into the world; the light that dawned within, and could not come without in any form of flesh or historic personality. The Emperor Julian also remarks on the monstrous doings and fraudulent machinations of the fabricators of Historic Christianity. We may look upon the Gnostics as Inside Christians; the others as Christians Without.

Never were mortals more perplexed, bewildered, and taken back, than the Christians of the second, third, and fourth centuries, who had started from their own new beginning, warranted to be solely historic, when they found that an apparition of their faith was following them one way and confronting them in another—a faith not founded on their alleged facts, claiming to be the original religion, and ages on ages earlier in the world—a shadow that threatened to steal away their substance, mocking them with its aerial unreality—the hollow ghost of that body of truth which they had embraced as a solid and eternal possession! It was horrible. It was devilish. It was the devil, they said; and so they sought to account for Gnosticism, and fight down their fears of the phantom terrifying them in front and rear: the Gnostic ante-Christ who had now become their anti-Christ. The only primitive Christians then apart from, or preceding, the Christianised pagan church of Rome, were the various sects of Gnostics, not one of which was founded on an historical Christ. One and all they based upon the mystical Christ of the Gnosis, and the mythical Messiah,—Him who should come because he was the Ever-Coming One, as a type of the Eternal, manifesting figuratively in time. Historic Christianity can furnish no sufficient reason why the biography of its personal founder should have been held back; why the facts of its origin should have been kept dark; and why there should have been no authorised record made known earlier. The conversion of the mythos, and of the Docetic doctrines of the Gnosis into human history, alone will account for the fatal fact. The truth is, the earliest gospels are the furthest removed from the supposed human history. That came last; and only when the spiritual Christ of the Gnosis had been rendered concrete in the density of Christian ignorance! Christianity began as Gnosticism continued, by means of a conversion and perversion, that were opposed in vain by Paul. The mysteries of the Gnostics were continued, with a difference, as Christian. The newly-christened re-beginnings were not only shrouded in mystery, they were the same mysteries at root as those that were pre-extant. The first Christians founded on secret doctrines that were only explained to initiates during a long course of years. These mysteries were never to be divulged or promulgated until the belief in historic Christianity had taken permanent root. We are told how it was held by some that the Apocrypha ought only to be read by those who were perfected, and that these writings were reserved exclusively for the Christian adepts. It must be obvious that the doctrine or knowledge that was forced to be kept so sacredly secret as that, could have had no relation to the human history, personality, or teachings of an inspired founder of that primitive Christianity supposed to have had so simple an origin. True history is not established in that way, although the false may be—as it has been. Nobody was allowed by Peter to interpret anything except in accordance with "*our tradition!*" Nobody, says Justin Martyr, is permitted to partake of the Eucharist "*unless he accepts as true that which is taught by us*"—and unless he received the bread and wine as the very flesh and blood of that Jesus who was made flesh. In this we see the forgers fighting against the Gnostic Christ. There were many sects of so-called Christians, and various versions of the Christ; whether Kronian, mythical, or mystical. But the Church of Rome was the Christian church with foundations in Egypt; hence the deities of Egypt which have been discovered at the foundations of Rome; and when historic Christianity hasn't a bit of ground left to stand upon, the Church of Rome will be able and prepared to say, "*We never did really stand on that ground, and now we alone can stand without it. We are the one true church with foundations in an illimitable past.*"

According to the unquestioned tradition of the Christian Fathers, which has always been accepted by the Church, the primary nucleus of our canonical gospels was not a life of Jesus at all, but a collection of the Logia, oracles, or sayings, the Logia Kuriaka, which were written down in Hebrew or Aramaic, by one Matthew, as the scribe of the Lord. Clement Alexander, Origen, and Irenæus agree in stating that Matthew's was the primary gospel. This tradition rests upon the testimony of Papias, Bishop of Hieropolis, and friend of Polycarp, who is said to have suffered martyrdom for his faith during the reign of Marcus Aurelius, about 165-167 A.D. Papias is named with Pantœus, Clement, and Ammonius as one of the ancient interpreters who agreed to understand the Hexæmeron as referring to an historic Christ and the Church. He was a believer in the millenium, and the second coming of the Lord, and therefore a literaliser of mythology. But there is no reason to suspect the trustworthiness of his testimony, as he no doubt believed these "*sayings*" to have been the spoken words of an historic Jesus, written down in Hebrew by a personal follower named Matthew. He wrote a work on the subject, entitled *Logion Kuriakon Exegesis*, a commentary on the sayings of the Lord. A surviving fragment of this last work, quoted by Eusebius, tells us that Matthew wrote the sayings in the Hebrew dialect, and each one of the believers interpreted them as he was best able. Thus, the beginning of the earliest gospel was not biographical. It was no record of the life and doings of Jesus; it contained no actual historic element, nothing more than the Sayings of the Lord.

It is not pretended that our gospel, according to Matthew, is the identical work of the scribe who first wrote down the logia, but the statement of Papias is so far corroborated inasmuch as the sayings ascribed to Jesus are the basis of the Book. We read "*When Jesus had finished these sayings*," or parables, several times over. Now, there is plenty of evidence to show that these sayings, which are the admitted foundations of the canonical gospels, were not first uttered by a personal Founder of Christianity, nor invented afterwards by any of his followers. Many of them were pre-extant, pre-historic, and pre-christian. And if it can be proved that these oracles of God and Logia of the Lord are not original, if they can be identified as a collection, an *olla podrida* of Egyptian, Hebrew, and Gnostic sayings, they can afford no evidence that the Jesus of the Gospels ever lived as an historic teacher. To begin with, two of the sayings assigned by Matthew to Jesus as the personal teacher of men are these:—"*Lay not up for yourselves treasure upon earth*," etc., and, "*If ye forgive men their trespasses your heavenly Father will also forgive you*"! But these sayings had already been uttered by the feminine Logos called Wisdom, in the Apocrypha. We find them in the Book of Ecclesiasticus; "*Lay up thy treasure according to the Commandments of the Most High, and it shall bring thee more profit than gold*," and "*Forgive thy neighbour the hurt that he hath done thee, so shall thy sins also be forgiven when thou prayest*"! Wisdom was the Sayer personified long anterior to the Christ. But it has never been pretended or admitted by mankind that wisdom was ever incarnated on this earth as a woman! Yet Wisdom, or Charis, had the primary right to incarnation, for she preceded the Christ. Luke also quotes a saying of Wisdom—"*Therefore also said the Wisdom of God, 'I will send them prophets and apostles, and some of them they shall slay and persecute*';" "*that the blood of all the prophets which was shed from the foundation of the world may be required of this generation."* This also is quoted or adapted from the words of Wisdom recorded in a Book of Wisdom (Esdras 2nd), where we read "*I sent unto you my servants, the prophets, whom ye have taken and slain, and torn their bodies in pieces, whose blood I will require of your hands, saith the Lord. Thus saith the Almighty Lord, your house is desolate*"! In the verses immediately preceding, the speaker in the Book of Esdras had said, "*Thus saith the Almighty Lord, Have I not prayed you as a Father his sons, as a mother her daughters, and a nurse her young babes, that ye would be my people, and I should be your God; that ye would be my children, and I should be your Father? I gathered you together as a hen gathereth her chickens under her wings; but now what shall I do unto you? I will cast you out.*" This is in one of the Books of Wisdom hidden away in our Apocrypha. Now, if we turn to the gospels of Luke and Matthew we shall find that they have quoted these words of Wisdom: but we now see that Wisdom is not credited with her own sayings concerning the Father God! On the contrary, they are given to an historic Christ, as a personal teacher and a prophet. That which was said of the house of Israel by Wisdom in Esdras is now applied to the city of Jerusalem by the Christ; and if you re-date a saying like that by a few hundred years there is little wonder if it dislocates the history. Paul likewise quotes the saying from the Book of Esdras when he says, "*I will receive you and will be to you a Father, and ye shall be to me Sons and Daughters saith the Lord Almighty.*" But he does not refer or re-apply it to Jesus as is done in the Gospels! Here we see that the current coinage of Wisdom has been defaced by the Gospel compilers—not by Paul— and then re-issued under the sign and superscription of another name, that of Jesus the Christ; and historic evidence of a nature like that is as futile as the negro's non-effective charge of gunpowder which he shrewdly suspected of having been fired off before. Paul likewise quotes or refers to one of the sayings found in Matthew. "*Faithful is the saying,*" he writes to Timothy. But although he is speaking of the Christ, he does not say *his* saying, nor refer it to an historic teacher.

It was one of *the* sayings, or true words, called the "Logia," which had been the dark sayings and parables of the pre-christian mysteries from of old, and which in Egypt were the sayings of Truth herself. The Hebrew Psalmist says, "*I will utter dark sayings of old.*" The Proverbs of Solomon are the sayings. The Jewish Haggadah were the sayings. The Commandments were sayings, as is shown by Paul, Rom. xiii. 9. Peter, in the Clementine Recognitions, does not pretend to "*pronounce the sayings of the Lord as spoken by himself*" (or profess that they were spoken by himself in person, as I read the passage), he admits that it is not in their commission to say this. But they are to teach and to show from the sayings how every one of them is based upon truth. This is in reply to

Simon Magus, who has pointed out the contradictory nature of the sayings. I hold it only to be a matter of time and research to prove that the sayings in general assigned to Jesus, which are taken to demonstrate his historic existence as a personal teacher, were pre-extant, pre-historic, and pre-christian. One of the sayings in the Mysteries reported by Plato was, "*Many are the Thyrsus-bearers but few are the Mystics,*" which is echoed twice over by Matthew in the saying, "*Many are called but few are chosen.*" "*It is more blessed to give than to receive,*" is one of the Logia of the Lord quoted in the book of Acts, but not found in the Gospels. Two of the sayings are identified as Essenic by Josephus, who says the Essenes swear not at all, but whatsoever they say is firmer than an oath; and when Jesus says, "*A new commandment I give unto you, that ye love one another,*" there was certainly nothing new in that which had been a command and a practice of the Essenes ages before. Men knew who were the Essenes by their love for one another. Some of the parables appear in the Talmud, amongst them are those of the Wise and Unwise Builders and that of the Marriage Feast. Various sayings are collected from the Talmud, such as the golden rule, "*Do unto others as ye would they should do unto you.*" "*Love thy neighbour as thyself.*" "*With the measure we mete we shall be measured again.*" "*Let thy yea be just and thy nay be likewise just.*" "*Whoso looketh upon the wife of another with a lustful eye is considered as if he had committed adultery.*" "*Be of them that are persecuted, not of them that persecute.*" But as Deutsch has said, to assume that the Talmud borrowed these from the New Testament would be like assuming that Sanskrit sprang from Latin.

The nature of the "Sayings" is acknowledged by Irenæus when he says, "*According to no one Saying of the heretics is the word of God made flesh.*" That is the Sayings which were current among the Gnostics as Knowers. Marcion knew and quoted the Gnostic saying which was afterwards amplified and quoted in John's Gospel—"*No one knew the father save the son, nor the son save the father, and he to whom he will reveal him.*" This is a Gnostic saying, and it involves the Gnostic doctrine which cannot be understood independently of the Gnosis. It is quoted as one of the sayings before it was reproduced in the Gospel according to John.

Such sayings were the Oral teachings in all the mysteries ages before they were written down. Some of them are so ancient as to be the common property of several nations. Prescott gives a few Mexican sayings; one of these, also found in the Talmud and the New Testament, is called the "*the old proverb.*" "*As the old proverb says*—'*Whoso regards a woman with curiosity commits adultery with his eyes.*'" And the third commandment according to Buddha is—"*Commit no adultery, the law is broken by even looking at the wife of another man with lust in the mind.*" Amongst other sayings assigned to Buddha we find the one respecting the wheat and the tares.

Another is the parable of the sower. Buddha likewise told of the hidden treasure which may be laid up by a man and kept securely where a thief cannot break in and steal; the treasure that a man may carry away with him when he goes. The story of the rich young man who was commanded to sell all he had and give to the poor is told of Buddha. It is reported that he also said—" *You may remove from their base the snowy mountains, you may exhaust the waters of the ocean, the firmament may fall to earth, but my words in the end will be accomplished.*"

Some of Buddha's sayings are uttered in the same character as that of the canonical Christ. For example, when speaking of his departure Buddha, like the Christ, promises to send the Paraclete, even the spirit of truth, who shall bear witness of him and lead his followers to the truth. The Gnostic Horus says the same things in the same character, and these sayings, by whomsoever uttered, carry the mythical character with them. The sayings of Krishna as well as those of the Buddha are frequently identical with those of the Christ. I am the letter A, cries the one. I am the Alpha and Omega (or the A.O.), exclaims the other. I am the beginning, the middle, and the end, says Krishna—"*I am the Light, I am the Life, I am the Sacrifice.*" Speaking of his disciples, he affirms that they dwell in him and he dwells in them.

The attitude of the Sayer as the personal revealer, the veritable and visible image of the hidden God in the Gospels, is that of the mythical Horus, the representative of Osiris—of Iu as manifestor of Atum, and of Khunsu as the son of Amen-Ra, who was the hidden God by name. The status had been attained, and the stand was occupied by the mythical divinity, and no room was left for a human Claimant many centuries later. If we take the transfiguration on the Mount, Buddha ascended the mountain in Ceylon called Pandava or Yellow-White. There the heaven opened, and a great light was in full flood around him, and the glory of his person shone forth with "*double power.*" He "*shone as the brightness of Sun and Moon.*" This was the transfiguration of Buddha, identical with that of the Christ, and both are the same as that of Osiris in his ascent of the Mount of the Moon. The same scene of the temptation on the Mount was previously pourtrayed in the Persian account of the Devil tempting Zarathustra, and inviting him to curse the Good Belief. But these several forms of the one character do not meet, and did not originate in any human history—lived either in Egypt, India, Persia, or Judea. They only meet in the Mythos, which may be traced to a common origin in Egypt, where we can delve down to the real root of the matter. Astronomical mythology claims, and Egypt can account for, at least 30,000 years of time; and that alone will explain these relationships and likenesses found on the surface by an original identity at root. The myths of Christianity and Buddhism had a common origin, and branched from the same root in the soil of Egypt, whence emanated several dogmas, like that of the Immaculate virgin motherhood, and the divine child who is the ancestral soul self-reproduced. And in company with the doctrines we naturally find a few of the sayings of the Buddha, which have often been paralleled with some of those assigned to the Christ.

The Logia or sayings are the *mythoi* in Greek. They were mythical sayings assigned to Sayers, who were also mythical in that mythology which preceded and accounts for our Theology and Christology. The sayings were the oral wisdom, and, as the name implies, that wisdom was uttered by word of mouth alone. They existed before writing, and were not allowed to be written afterwards. The mode of communicating them in the Mysteries, as in Masonry, was from mouth to ear; and, in passing, it may be remarked that the war of the Papacy against Masonry is because it is a survival of the pre-Christian Mysteries, and a living, however imperfect, witness against Historic Christianity! Mythos or myth denotes anything delivered by word of mouth, myth and mouth being identical at root. Now, as the mouth of utterance preceded the word that was uttered, it follows that the first form of the sayer or Logos was female, and that the feminine wisdom was first, although she has not yet been made flesh. The mother was primordial, and the earliest soul or spirit was attributed to her; she was the mouth, utterer, or sayer, long before the sayings were assigned to the male Logos or Christ. Thus in the Apocrypha, as in other Gnostic books, the sayings of Wisdom are found which have been made counterfeit in the mouth of the Christ made historic. She was the primal type of Wisdom, who built her house with the Seven Pillars, and who was set in the heavens as Kefa, later Sefekh, and latest Sophia. She is called the Living Word or Logos at Ombos, because as her constellation, the Great Bear, turned round annually, it told the time of the year. She is pourtrayed in the planisphere with her tongue hanging out to show that she is the mouthpiece of time who utters the Word. Wisdom was also the earliest teller of human time. In her mystical phase she told the time for the sexes to come together. Thus, on the ground of natural phenomena, the Logia were first uttered by the Lady, and not by the Lord. This is the woman who has been so badly abused by those who desired to dethrone her; the primitive protestants who set up the male image in her place and on her pedestal. In Egypt the Sayings were assigned to various divinities, that is mythical characters. One of these was the Solar God Iu-em-hept, the Egyptian Jesus, who was the son of Atum, and who is called "*the Eternal Word*" in the "*Book of the Dead.*" After these sayings had been recorded it is said of them in a text at least 5000 years old, "*I have heard the words of Iu-em-hept and Har-ta-tef as it is said in their sayings!*" The Osirian form of the "*the Lord*" who utters the Logia in the Egyptian Ritual is Horus, he whose name signifies the Lord.

I cannot prove that sets of the sayings of the Lord, as Horus, were continued intact up to the time of Papias. Nor is that necessary. For, according to the nature of the hidden wisdom they remained oral and were not intended to be written down. They were not collected to be published as historic until the mysteries had come to an end or, on one line of their descent, were merged in Christianity. But a few most significant ones may be found in the Book of the Dead. In one particular passage the speaker says he has given food to the hungry, drink to the thirsty, clothes to the naked, and a boat to the shipwrecked; and, as the Osirified has done these things, the Judges say to him, " *Come, come in peace,*" and he is welcomed to the festival which is called " *Come thou to me.*" Those who have done these things on earth are held to have done them to Horus, the Lord; and they are invited to come to him as the blessed ones of his father Osiris. In this passage we have not only the sayings reproduced by Matthew, but also the drama and the scenes of the Last Judgment represented in the Great Hall of Justice, where a person is separated from his sins, and those who have sided with Sut against Horus are transformed into goats. Here it is noticeable that Matthew only of the four Evangelists represents this drama of the Egyptian Ritual! Among the sayings of Jesus, or Logia of the Lord, is the saying that *"the very hairs of your head are numbered;"* and in the Ritual every hair is weighed; also the night of the judgment-day is designated that of " *weighing a hair.*" Various chapters of the Ritual are the "*sayings.*" They are preceded by the formula, "*said by the deceased,*" or "*said to the deceased.*" Horus, the Lord, is the divine Sayer. "*Says Horus*" is a common statement; and the souls repeat his sayings. He is the Lord by name, and therefore his are the original sayings, or Logia of the Lord. These sayings, or Logia of the Lord, were written by Hermes or Taht, the Scribe of the Gods, and they constituted the original Hermean or inspired Scriptures, which the Book of the Dead declares were written in Hieroglyphics by the finger of Hermes himself. This Recorder of the sayings is said to have power to grant the Makheru to the Solar God—that is, the gift of speaking the Truth by means of the Word, because he is the Registrar of the " *sayings* "—the scribe of the wisdom uttered orally, the means, therefore, by which the Word was made Truth to men; not flesh in human form. This is the part assigned to Matthew, the called one, the Evangelist and Scribe, who first wrote down the Logia, or sayings of the Lord. Now, the special name or title of Hermes in the particular character of the Recorder and Registrar in the Hall of the Double Truth, or Justice, is Matthew in Egyptian—that is, Matiu. And my claim is not only that the primary Logia of the Lord were the sayings of Horus, whose name means " *the lord,*" but also that *the* Matthew who, according to the testimony of Papias, first wrote down the Logia of the Lord, was none other than Matiu, or Hermes, the recorder of the sayings in the Egyptian Ritual, who has been made an historic personage in the Canonical Gospel in exact accordance with the humanising of the Mythical Christ.

One mode of manipulating the sayings, and making out a history is apparent, and can be followed. This was by looking it out in the alleged Hebrew prophecies, and inserting it piecemeal between the groups of sayings. There is proof that, with the sayings as primary data, the history in the Canonical Gospel, according to Matthew, was written on the principle of fulfilling the supposed prophecies found in the Old Testament, or elsewhere. The compiler was too uninstructed to know that the prophecies themselves belonged entirely to the Astronomical Allegory, and never did or could relate to forthcoming events that were to be fulfilled in human history; and never were supposed to do so, except by the ignorant, who knew no better, and who, in fact, thought the zodiacal Virgin had brought forth her child on earth; which could only be born, and that figuratively, in heaven. Those who did know better, whether Jews, Samaritans, Essenes, or Gnostics, entirely repudiated the historic interpretation, and did not become Christians. They could no more join the ignorant, fanatical Salvation Army in the first century than we can in the nineteenth. The so-called prophecies not only supply a *raison d'être* for the history in the gospels, the events and circumstances themselves are manufactured one after another from the prophecies and sayings—that is, from the mythos which was pre-extant, in the course of the literalisation into a human life, and the localisation in Judea, under the pretext, or in the blind belief, that the impossible had come to pass. Justin Martyr's great appeal for historical proofs is made to the Old Testament prophecies; and so is Matthew's. According to him, Jesus was born at Bethlehem in order that it might be fulfilled which was said by Micah that a Governor and Shepherd for Israel should come out of Bethlehem in Judea. That was in the Celestial Bethlehem or House of Bread-Corn, the zodiacal sign of the Fishes, where the mythical Messiah was to be reborn about the year 255 B.C.

Again, the young child was only taken to Nazareth that it might be fulfilled which was spoken by the prophets, that he should be called a Nazarene. And yet he would no more become a Nazarene in that way than a man could become a horse by being born in a stable. Jesus came to dwell in Capernaum, on the borders of Zebulun and Naphtali, that a saying of Isaiah's might be fulfilled!

He cast out the spirits with a word, and healed all that were sick, that it might be fulfilled which was spoken by Isaiah the prophet. For the same impotent reason he charged his followers not to make him known to men *as* the Christ! He taught the multitude in parables only that it might be fulfilled which had been spoken by the prophet. Although Jesus wrought his miracles, and did so many wonderful works, *yet* the people believed not on him, because Isaiah had previously said : "*Lord! who hath believed our report? and to whom hath the arm of the Lord been revealed?"* For this cause (or on this account) they could not believe! And where, then, was the sense in expecting them to believe? Jesus only sent the two disciples to steal the ass and colt, that it might be fulfilled which was spoken by the prophet Zechariah. The choosing of Judas as one of the disciples, and his consequent treachery, do but occur in the Gospels, because it had been written by the Psalmist: *" Yea, mine own familiar friend, in whom I trusted, which did eat of my bread, hath lifted up his heel against me!"* which refers to an identifiably Egyptian Mythos. In another Psalm assigned to David, the speaker cries: *" My God! my God! why hast thou forsaken me! They part my garments among them, and cast lots upon my vesture."* And in another he exclaims: *" They gave me also gall for meat; and in my thirst they gave me vinegar to drink."* And these sayings, which were pre-extant and pre-applied, constitute the Christian record of the historic crucifixion! It cannot be pretended that they are prophecies. The transactions and sayings in the Psalms are personal to the speaker there and then, whether Mythical or Historical, and *not* to any future sufferer; and the tremendous transactions pourtrayed in the Gospels are actually based upon a repetition of that which had already occurred! When Jesus is represented by John as being in his death-agony, he only said, *" I thirst,"* in order that the Scripture might be fulfilled—and not because he was thirsty!—the Scripture being these Sayings previously attributed to the psalmist David. The earlier sayings are repeated as the later doings, and the non-historical is finally the sole evidence for the Historical. When the Roman soldiers had crucified Jesus they took the vesture that was without a seam, and said: *" Let us not rend it, but cast lots for it,"* that the Scripture might be fulfiled which saith: *" They parted my garments among them, and upon my vesture did they cast lots."* Such was the familiarity of the Roman soldiers with the Jewish Scriptures, and such their respect for them, that they could do nothing that was not laid down in the Hebrew Writings to be interpreted as prophecy! And in such a desperate way the prophecies had to be fulfilled in order that the History might be written. In the first place the sayings are not original, not personal to any historical Jesus, and yet they are the acknowledged foundations of the four gospels. Therefore in them we have the foundations laid independently of any supposed Founder of Christianity. Next, we have more or less seen *how* a part of the history superimposed on the sayings first collected by Matthew was extracted piecemeal from the parables, oracles, alleged prophecies, and un-alleged Mythos of the Old Testament; and thus we get upon the track of the compilers, and can trace their method of working from the matter of the Mythos. Now, when we find, and can identify, the skeleton of some particular person, we have got the foundation of the man, no matter where the rest of him may be—recoverable or not. So is it with the Christ of our Canonical Gospels. The mythical Christ is the skeleton, and that is identifiably Egyptian. This mythical Christ, as Horus, was continued in the more mystical phase as the Horus of the Gnostics. The Gnostic Rituals repeat the matter, names, symbols, and doctrines found in some later chapters of the Egyptian Book of the Dead. The Gnostics supply the missing links between the oral sayings and the written Word; between the Egyptian and the Canonical Gospels; between the Matthew who wrote down the sayings of the Lord in Hebrew or Aramaic, and the Matiu who is said to have written the Ritual in hieroglyphics with the very finger of Hermes himself. The Gnostics were the knowers by name; their artists perpetuated the Egyptian types; and the original myths, symbols, and doctrines now recovered from the buried land of Egypt vouch for their knowledge of the mysteries which lurk in the sayings, parables, events, and characters that have been gathered up in our Gospels, to be naturalised and re-issued in an historic narrative as the fulfilment of prophecy. They inherited the Gnosis of Egypt, which remained unwritten, and therefore was unknown to the Christians in general; the mysteries that were performed in secret, and the science kept concealed. The Gnostics complained, and truly maintained, that their mysteries had been made mundane in the Christian Gospels; that celestial persons and celestial scenes, which could only belong to the pleroma—could only be explained by the secret wisdom or gnosis—had been transferred to earth and translated into a human history; that their Christ, who could not be made flesh, had been converted into an historical character; that their Anthropos was turned into the Son of Man—according to Matthew—Monogenes into the Only-begotten, according to John, their Hemorrhoidal Sophia into the woman who suffered from the issue of blood, the mother of the seven inferior powers into Mary Magdalene possessed by her seven devils, and the twelve Æons into the twelve Apostles. Thus, the Gnostics enable us to double the proof which can be derived directly and independently from Egypt. They claim that the miracle of the man who was born blind, and whose sight was restored by Jesus, was their mystery of the Æon, who was produced by the Only-begotten as the sightless creature of a soulless Creator. Irenæus, in reporting this, makes great fun of the Word that was born blind! He did not know that this Gnostic mystery was a survival of the Egyptian myth of the two Horuses, one of whom was the blind Horus, who exclaims in his blindness—"*I come to search for mine eyes*," and has his sight restored at the coming of the Second Horus—the light of the world. Nor did he dream that the two-fold Horus would explain why the blind man in our Gospels should be single in one version and two-fold in another account of the same miracle. The Gnostic Horus came to seek and to save the poor lost mother, Sophia, who had wandered out of the pleroma, and the Gnostics identified this myth with the statement assigned to Jesus when he said he had only come after that lost sheep which was gone astray. For, as Irenæus says, they explain the wandering sheep to mean their mother. This shows how the character of the Christ was limited to the mould of the Mythos and the likeness of Horus. But the lost sheep of the House of Israel has not yet found Jesus.

The very same transactions and teachings ascribed to Jesus in the Gospels are assigned to the Gnostic Christ, who, like the Egyptian Horus, is the Sayer in heaven, or within the pleroma, and not upon our earth. And, in the Gospel according to John, we have Jesus identifying himself as the Son of Man which is in heaven, whilst at the same time he is represented as talking and teaching the Gnosis of the mysteries on earth. He tells Nicodemus, who came to him by night, that "*No man hath ascended into heaven but he that descended out of heaven, even the Son of Man which is in heaven,*" as was Anthropos when he taught the twelve according to the Gnostic account of the transactions within the pleroma. Also, the twelve Æons are addressed in the language of the Gnosis when Jesus says to the twelve—"*Ye also shall bear witness, because ye have been with me from the beginning.*" They tell us, says Irenæus, that the knowledge communicated by the Christ to the Æons within the pleroma has not been openly divulged, because all are not capable of receiving it; but it was mystically made known, by means of parables, to those who were qualified for receiving it. The Gnostic Christ reveals the mysteries of the kingdom of heaven to the twelve Æons in parables. And in the Gospel the Christ speaks to the twelve in parables only, and to them alone is it given to know the mysteries of the kingdom of heaven. In this process of converting the mythical into the historical we are told that Jesus, the very Son of God, was sent into the world to teach and enlighten and save mankind, and yet he spoke his teaching in parables which the people could not, and were not intended to, understand. "*All these things spake Jesus in parables to the multitude; and without a parable spake he nothing unto them,*" in order that it might be fulfilled which was spoken by the prophet, saying, "*I will open my mouth in parables; I will utter things hidden from the foundation of the world!*" He spoke to the multitudes in this wise, so that they might not understand. Yet in the chapter following it is said—"*He called to him the multitude* (not the disciples) *and said unto them, Hear and understand,*" and immediately uttered a dark saying. We are also told that the common people heard him gladly! In another instance, as crucial as it is interesting—illustrative of the way in which the mythical, the Kronian Christ, was made human as the instructor of man—it is said as Jesus sat on the Mount of Olives the disciples came to him privately, and asked him to tell them about his coming in the clouds at the end of the world. And amongst other things they are to do, he says,—Let them that are in Judea flee unto the mountains. Let him that is on the house-tops not go down. But what sense is there in advising any such mode of escape from the great tribulation and catastrophe which involved the end of the world? There would not be much advantage on the house-top or even the hill-top if the stars were falling from heaven, with the firmanent raining all round with flames, and the end of all things had indeed come. We might just as well seek refuge at the top of a fire-escape. And they are to pray that their flight may not be in winter, or on the Sabbath, as if it could possibly matter to any mortal in what season of the year, or day of the week, such a catastrophe should occur. The final explanation of all such foolishness is that the matter is mythical, and, of course, it refuses to be realised in any such literal way. The parable never meant the end of this world; the literalisers of the mythos thought it did. That was only a false inference of ignorant belief. But such are the foundations of the faith. Such desperate dilemmas as these are the inevitable result of representing the Mythical Sayer in heaven as an historical teacher on earth.

The two chief abiding places to which the peripatetic Christ retires are called "*the Mountain*" and "*the Desert.*" These localities in the Egyptian mythos are the upper and lower heavens, otherwise the mount of the equinox and the wilderness of the underworld; and where John cries in the wilderness, Aan or Anup howled in the desert. Now, according to Egyptian thought and mode of expression the dead are those who are on the mountain; the living are those who are in the valley or on the earth. Horus on earth, or in the valley, is mortal, the child of the immaculate mother Isis alone. Horus on the mountain is spiritualised as the son of the Father Osiris, in whose power he overcomes the devil. Sut or Satan has the best of it down in the wilderness, and Horus conquers up on the mount, in the day of their Great Battle. Jesus undergoes the same change as Horus does in his baptism. He likewise becomes the son of the Father, and in the strength of his adultship he ascends the mountain and becomes the vanquisher of Satan. This typical mountain is a pivot on which a good deal may be said to turn. The contest between Jesus and Satan, called the temptation on the Mount, is pourtrayed upon the monuments in a scene where Horus and Sut contend for supremacy, and at last agree to divide the whole world between them. Horus takes the south, and Sut the north, called the hinder part, where Jesus says,—"*Get thee behind me, Satan!*" The devil's long tail is an extant sign of this hinder part, which was typified in Egypt by the tail. If the Christ had been historical in this transaction, the devil must be historical too. Both stand on the same footing of fact or fable. According to the record, Satan must have been as real as the Christ, or Christ as mythical as the devil. Was Satan also incarnated for life in the flesh? If so, when did he die? where was the place of *his* burial? and did *he* also rise again? Nobody seems to care what became of the poor devil after he was told to get behind, or take a back seat, that of the hinder part. The scene in the Mount of Transfiguration is obviously derived from the ascent of Osiris (or Horus), and his transfiguration in the Mount of the Moon. The sixth day was celebrated as that of the change and transfiguration of the solar god in the lunar orb, which he re-entered as the regenerator of its light. With this we may compare the statement made by Matthew that *"After six days Jesus"* went *"up into a high mountain apart, and he was transfigured." "And his face did shine as the sun"* (of course!), *"and his garments became white as the light."*

The natural phenomena on which these Egyptian legends or myths were founded are the contentions of light and darkness at the time of the equinox, or in the waxing and waning of the light in the lunar orb. *"He must increase, but I must decrease,"* says John, who plays the part of Sut-Aan to Jesus as the Light of the World. This was the battle between Horus and Satan. In one legend it is said that Sut was seven days fleeing on the back of an ass from his battle with Horus. That means the seven days of the second quarter of the moon, during which Horus triumphs as Lord of the growing light. And here we can point to a curious survival! The Unicorn was a type of Sut, and the Lion of Horus; and their conflict is described in our legend—

"The Lion and the Unicorn
Were fighting for a farthing,
The Lion beat the Unicorn
Up and down the garden!
The Lion and the Unicorn
Were fighting for a crown,
The Lion beat the Unicorn
Up and down the town!"

The farthing is a fourth; and they fought for a fourthing, or a quarter of the moon; equal to the seven days during which darkness was put to flight; and the crown is the full, round disk of the moon. Thus, as the Egyptian imagery proves, the arms of England illustrate the same subject-matter as the contest of Horus and Sut, of Angro-Mainyus and Zarathustra, and of the Christ and Satan. And now, if you will have the patience, I will show a scene in which the Christ of the Gospels is restored to his proper place and station in the heavens, as the Teacher on the Mount, and as such can be identified. Jesus goes up into the mythical mountain when he appoints the twelve disciples, that they might be with him, and have authority to cast out devils (Mark iii. 14).

In Matthew's compilation Jesus calls the twelve, and gives them authority to cast out devils. It is here that he says *"the harvest is plenteous, but the labourers are few."* Luke describes the same scene in the same words, and the same commission is granted, the same powers are given to the disciples! But now the seventy have taken the place of the twelve. *"And the Seventy returned with joy, saying, Lord, even the devils are subject unto us in thy name!"* The *"Seventy in the Mount"* are an ancient pre-Christian institution. They were once the "*Seventy Elders*" who received their instructions from Moses in the Mount. But in many ancient authorities these Seventy with Christ are Seventy-two. The two different numbers are identifiably astronomical, and they go to double my proof. Previous to the heaven of twelve divisions, and seventy-two sub-divisions, or duo-decans of the zodiac, there was a heaven of ten divisions and seventy sub-divisions; and we find the same mixture of the seventy with the seventy-two, and of the ten with the twelve, in the Astronomical Book of Enoch. Here, in the Canonical Version, we have the twelve, and the complementary seventy-two, but no ten to account for the seventy! This missing factor we shall find in the Divine Pymander, or fragments of Hermes. There we meet with the ten in the mount, and the ten are the expellers of devils or torments, just as the twelve and the seventy are in the gospels. All these parts belong to one system of mythological representation, and wherever they are separately found can be identified, as certainly as the scattered pieces of a puzzle by those who know the subject-matter of the total picture. As before said, the scene on the mount of transfiguration reproduces the ascent of Buddha into Mount Pandava or Yellow-White, and of Osiris into the Moon! Now, this Mount of the Moon was a seat of the eight great gods of Egypt. And in the Divine Pymander it is called the Octonary of Tat, who is Lord in Smen, the region of the eight, at the north celestial pole. Lower down it was the mount of the four quarters, or of the Moon, and of the four with Horus in the Mount; and, still lower down, it becomes the heaven of the twelve signs, the zodiacal circle; and here the fragments of Hermes, or the Divine Pymander, have brought on matter of very special importance. One of the chapters is entitled "*The Secret Sermon on the Mount of Regeneration.*" Regeneration is the mystical form of the transfiguration of Osiris in the Mount of the Moon. This Mount, also called the Tabernacle, is said to consist of the Zodiacal circle, the signs of which are the twelve belonging to the Mount—the Zodiac being the lowest of three heavens, or stories to the Mount, Stellar, Lunar, and Solar. Now, let us see how the Mount, together with the Sayer and the Sermon on the Mount, have been reproduced in the Gospels. In the account furnished by Matthew we find but four companions with Christ in the Mount. These are the two pairs of the brethren, who answer to the four brothers of Osiris, who are the gods of the four quarters. But in Luke's Gospel the Mount of the four has become the Mount of the twelve. Accordingly the sermon is here delivered lower down, at the bottom of the Mount! In fact, Jesus, instead of being seated with the four on the Mount, is said to stand with the twelve in the plain below! This shows the Mount to be astronomical as well as mythical. Further, in the same scene, where the disciples are twelve in number, as lords of the harvest—according to Matthew's Gospel—they are seventy or seventy-two according to Luke, the number of duo-decans into which the twelve signs of the Zodiac were finally sub-divided. In the Divine Pymander the title of the "*Mount of Regeneration*' serves to show the nature of the sermon. It is the "*Secret Sermon.* "*Oh, son,*" says Hermes, "*this wisdom is to be understood in silence;*" that is, the knowledge or experience of the Regeneration taught by the Secret Sermon on the Mount. Hermes had said that *No man can be saved before regeneration;* and Tat desires to understand the nature of this regeneration. He says to Hermes, "*I do humbly entreat thee, at the going up to the mountain!*"—just as the Twelve besought Jesus privately in the Mount. And Hermes shows him how the mortal man while in the flesh can transform into the immortal mind. In the mysteries this was figured as the rising from the dead, and it was so taught by the Gnostics. The process was illustrated by transformation, or entering into the state of trance, whereby (as was held) the mortal was changed into the immortal in this life; and it is evident that in the scene of the transfiguration described by Matthew, the vision of the three witnesses belongs to the trance condition, for they had a vision which they were to tell to no man! In the Canonical Gospels the mythical Mount has been made mundane; the divine speakers have been made human; the mystical teaching has been literalised by the endeavour to make the total transaction historical. After the "*Secret Sermon* (or spiritual representation) *in the Mount of Regeneration, and the profession of silence,*" Hermes tells Tat to keep silence—these things are neither to be taught nor told: they are to be hid in silence! In the gospels Jesus charges the disciples that they shall tell no man what things they have witnessed, save when the Son of Man shall have risen again from the dead. And the disciples, who are said to have just seen a resurrection from the dead performed before them, are described as questioning among themselves what the rising again from the dead should mean! (Mark ix. 9.) In the Osirian myth the rising from the dead was the re-birth of the Lord of light in the orb of the New Moon. That was the transfiguration of Osiris in the Mount of the Moon, on the sixth day of the month. In the mystical phase the rising from the dead in the Mount of Regeneration, as pourtrayed by Hermes, was a transformation into the spiritual or abnormal state, which demonstrated immortality. Thus we have the rising from the dead in two phases—astronomical and spiritual; both Egyptian, both able to explain their own meaning, and both pre-Christian! In the gospels we have the same Mount, the same Mythos, the same matter, the same Numbers, the same characters, rendered historically. You can't help seeing the bones of the Mythos staring through its skin! You are positively present at the transformation of the mythical into the historical. The soli-lunar god and the Gnostic Christ have both contributed obviously to the make-up of the humanised Christ on the "*Mount of Regeneration and the profession of silence!*" No wonder the disciples could not understand what this rising from the dead should mean! In this manner the Mythos can be followed, as it goes on eating its way through the history, like the larvæ of the *Anobium pertinax*, of which it is recorded by Peiquot that one specimen perforated twenty-seven folio volumes in a line so straight that a cord could be passed through the hole, and the twenty-seven volumes slung up altogether.

It is claimed by Christian teachers that the Christ was incarnated as the especial revealer of the father who is in heaven, and that the revelation culminated on the Mount when he taught the fatherhood of God in the Lord's prayer. But the Lord's prayer is no more original than is the Lord to whom it was last assigned. In the Jewish "Kadish" we have the following pre-Christian form of it, which is almost word for word the same:—"*Our father which art in heaven! Be gracious to us, O Lord our God! Hallowed be thy name! And let the remembrance of thee be glorified in heaven above and upon earth below! Let thy kingdom reign over us now and for ever! Thy holy men of old said, 'Remit and forgive unto all men whatsoever they have done against me!' And lead us not into temptation! But deliver us from the evil thing! For thine is the kingdom, and thou shalt reign in glory for ever and for ever.*"

If such a revelation had ever been historical, if the divine son had once been incarnated to reveal the fatherhood, it could not have remained until the Christian era for this to be done. It did not need any Deity to descend from heaven to reveal that which had been common doctrine in Egypt at least 4,000 years earlier. And this prayer was prayed by the one particular people who rejected the Son of God when he had come down. But the matter is mythical and mystical,—it can only be understood doctrinally by means of the Gnosis. The initial point of the teaching is this,— there could be no fatherhood in heaven until the human fatherhood was individualized on earth. Previously there was only the divine mother and the fathers in general. Hence the first Messiah was called the Son of the Woman, as he is in the book of Enoch; the later is the Son of Man—the Gnostic Anthropos, and the only-begotten of the Father, the Gnostic Monogenes. This is he who was the last of the Æons, and who came at the end of the world. He instructed the Æons who had preceded him, and "*taught them that those who had a comprehension of the unbegotten were sufficient for themselves, or needed no higher knowledge than that proclaimed by him.*" He first announced among them what related to the knowledge of the father, but that was within the Pleroma, not on the earth. This was the great and abstruse mystery of the Gnostics, says Irenæus, that the Proarche, the Power which is above all others and contains all, is termed Anthropos; hence the manifester is styled the "*Son of Man.*" This title of the Christ occurs nearly eighty times over in the Gospel according to Matthew, where he is identical with the Gnostic Anthropos—Son of Anthropos. That is, the Son of the God who was now imaged in the likeness of the individualized Father, which was the latest institution in heaven, because it had been last on earth. Here, it may be observed in passing, is a fact that is forever fatal to the theory that the Christology of the Gospels was derived from Buddhism. There is no divine fatherhood proclaimed by the Son in Buddhism. But the teaching was Egyptian.

The most important sayings assigned to Jesus by the writer of John's Gospel are not recorded or referred to by the Synoptics —Matthew, Mark, and Luke. These contain the secret wisdom of the Gnostics; they are the Logia of the Gnostic Christ, who was Horus, the Lord, in Egypt. They are spoken by the Son of Man, who is in heaven (John iii. 13), and who taught the twelve Æons there with the same doctrinal sayings that are here assigned to the Teacher of the twelve on earth, or on the Mount. Moreover, in John's gospel we meet with the Seven Fishers on board the boat. These correspond to the seven who are followers of Horus in the Egyptian Ritual, and who are said to fish for Horus. They go a-fishing with Horus in his boat; and they are also called the "*Seven planks in the boat of souls.*" The miraculous draught of fishes occurs in both. Now, it is noticeable that this miraculous take of fishes is described by Luke as occurring during the life-time of Jesus, but according to the Johanine gospel, the transaction takes place in a region beyond the tomb, or at least, after the death and resurrection of Jesus,—and therefore in the very region where the Gnostics declared these things had occurred. Which, think ye, was first,—the assuredly mythical, or the alleged historical?

The gospel according to John is the link of connection between the true Gnosis and the false history of the other gospels. It shows the very ground on which the mythos alighted to be made mundane, and that is why it was kept secret, and withheld until the middle of the second century or so, by which time the doctrine of the Christ made flesh was considered safe, and sure to supersede the teachings of the Gnostics with the gospel of historic Christianity.

An identifiable personal founder and historical teacher of Christianity is the least of all the various factors! The Church of Rome did not derive its secret dogmas and doctrines from the canonical gospels in which his teachings are believed to be enshrined. Various Egyptian doctrines, not to be found in our canonical gospels, survived in the Church of Rome; these were taught esoterically according to an unwritten tradition, and only allowed to become exoteric as time and opportunity permitted. Take for example the worship of the "*Sacred Heart.*" That is no recent invention of Rome or the Ritualists. The doctrine is Egyptian, and of the remotest antiquity. The heart, on account of its relation to the blood, was held to be the house of life, and also the mother of life. The heart was the shrine of the soul. Its Egyptian name of Hat, and Hor, the soul, or divine child, compose the name of Hathor, the mother of Horus, the Christ. And as the heart or habitation is the mother of life, it was adopted as a type of the birth-place. And so in the Ritual the soul, speaking as Horus, says, "*My heart is (or was) my mother*," in a chapter (30) which contains the doctrine of the "*Sacred Heart*." For this reason the heart-shaped fruit of the Persea tree of life was an emblem of Hathor and her child. The stone of it was shown through a cleft in the fruit to denote the seed of the woman.

Now, as previously said, one name of Hathor is Meri. Horus was the Child-Christ of the Sacred Heart of Meri, who was the goddess of love in Egypt, as well as the abode or dwelling of life, before she became the Madonna Mary in Rome. This is not only the source of the Sacred Heart as a Christian doctrine, it is also the origin of Cupid, the child-god of love, and the typical heart still sacred to lovers on Valentine's day.

Possibly the nearest we can get to Jesus ben Pandira as a teacher, if he makes any appearance whatever in the Gospels, is in the gloomy ascetic, the anti-naturalist, who mistook the non-natural for the divine; who would have had men to save their protoplasmal souls by becoming eunuchs for the Kingdom of heaven's sake! and whose model for heaven itself was a monastery, as when he says, "*In my father's house are many monai*," or monasterion,—with no women there to cause a second fall from heaven! He might possibly have been the self-tormenting teacher of a creed of monkery, only that institution was already established, and no place was left for him to be the founder even there. It is just possible that Joshua ben Pandira may have brought out of Egypt a version of the Sayings of the original Matiu or Matthew, together with a form of the Horus-myth. If so, these would be manipulated by his followers, one of whom, James, is said, in the book Abadazurah, to have been a follower of Jehoshua the Nazarene, and so by degrees the historic Joshua would be confused with, and finally converted into, Jesus the Christ of Nazareth, and the mystical Sayer into the Word made flesh: the Jesus of that "other Gospel" which was opposed by Paul. The sayings themselves, selected in a last assortment, have not even the consistency of a kaleidoscope. They will not fall into any set form of themselves, or reflect any mental unity anywhere. And so each sect or system of interpretation has to take them and construct its own kaleidoscope, and determine its own views, doing all it can to impose them upon others. Texts may be quoted on all sides for purposes the most antagonistic. Diversity radiates outwardly from them because there was no unity of origin, no individual life at the heart of them all.

When our missionaries first made the sayings known to the Arawaks of Guiana, they remarked, "*The word is good but we knew most of it before.*" Most of the true sayings were known before! As we have them they are so various—good, bad, and indifferent—as to constitute that hybrid mixture which is certain to entail sterility. Some of the sayings are no more appropriate to our human wants than was the old lady's tract on the sin of dancing, which she offered to a poor fellow who had to hobble about on two wooden legs and crutches! "*If thy right eye offend thee, pluck it out!*" Of what value is such advice as that? Also, it is impossible for us to love our enemies, if it were right to do so; and, as has been said, it would be wrong to do it if it were possible. "*Blessed are they who have not seen yet have believed.*" Why, tyranny could devise no doctrine that could be turned to more fatal account! "*Blessed are the poor in spirit, for their's is the kingdom of heaven.*" Do you call the teaching of that saying divine? I think it would be false and fraudulent if uttered by a voice from the Infinite with all heaven for its mouthpiece! The poor in spirit are the accursed, the outcasts, and pariahs of the earth; those who sink into the squalor and crawl in the filthy dens of poverty, to become the natural victims of all its parasites of prey. The poor in spirit are the prematurely old men, weary, worn-out women, and wizened children, all bleaching into a ghastly white in the chilling shadow of daily want! The poor in spirit are those who crouch and offer their backs to the whip, who remain bowed just as they were bent, and allow their hands to be fettered and held fast in the attitude of prayer, when they ought to be up and striking. They who are content to crawl like caterpillars, and be trodden as caterpillars underfoot. Poverty of spirit is the very devil; the source of half the evil extant; most of the meannesses in human nature may be traced to poverty of spirit! It dwarfs the mental stature of men, makes them bow the neck, and creep and grovel for a little gain, or go down on all fours in the dirt, as beasts in human form, from lack of spirit enough to stand erect! The poor in spirit dare not think for themselves, or utter what they think! They only wonder what other folk will think! They who are only mere preliminary people that go monkeying round under the pretence of being women and men! In this world of struggle, this scene of survival for the fittest, the poor in spirit stand no chance, and find no place; there is no victory for those who fight no battle. And as to heaven—do you really think heaven is a harbour of refuge for the poor in spirit and the area-sneaks of earth? The poor and needy, the hungry and suffering, are not the blessed, and no assumption of divine authority on the part of the sayer will ever make them so. These beatitudes are not divine revelations, they are only the false promises of the priests, who were the crafty founders of the faith made conformable to Roman rule.

One very striking note of the want of human personality and historic verity in the Christ of the canonical Gospels is the absence of all recognition of Rome. There is no shadow of Rome to be seen on the face of the Christ; no word of rebuke for her inhuman and non-natural crimes; no sign of anything contemporary: except the counselling of submission to Cæsar. The slave would look in vain to the sayings of Jesus for any denunciation of slavery. There is not one word of condemnation for the oppressors, nor of comfort for the oppressed. No vision of the better day on earth for them. Nothing but the mythical Day of the Lord.

Yet the existence of slavery was endorsed by the Roman law, was practised with all its evils, and enforced by all her legions. Jesus, however, makes no attack on the institution; and the fact was quoted and emphatically emphasised by the ministers of the Gospel of Christ against the persecuted Abolitionists of America. Nor is there a single word uttered on behalf of subjugated, down-trodden womankind. Not a saying that will aid in lifting woman to an equality with man—not a rebuke to the bigoted Jew who thanked his God each morning that he was *not* a woman. Nor is he credited with uttering one word against cruelty to animals; he gives no voice to the dumb creation. No quickening of conscience in these matters can be attributed to him. Neither the mother, the wife, nor the sister, owes any gratitude to his alleged teaching, who exclaimed, "*Woman, what have I to do with thee?*" Neither the slaves, nor the women, nor the children, nor the animals, owe their deliverance from inhuman thraldom to him. He had nothing to say about these pitifully-human interests. And it is a foolish farce to go on attributing the emancipation of humanity to the teachings of Jesus the Great Reformer. As a human history nothing can be made of it. It does not even begin to be—however much you believe. The contradictions are such as make history impossible. Amidst the dissolution of dogmas and the universal wreck of creeds, vain is the endeavour to prop the falling structure with the personality of the Canonical Christ, which evades us and vanishes in proportion as we seek for it in the Gospels. The common assumption is that the historic element was the kernel of the whole, and that the fable accreted around it. But, if you will try it over again this other way, you will find the mythos which was fundamental will explain all. The mythos being pre-extant, shows that the core of the matter was mythical, and it follows that the alleged history is incremental. And when at last we do get to the bottom of the abyss we learn that the historic grounds have been formed from the sunken *débris* or dregs of the ancient mythology.

> That pyramid of imposture reared by Rome,
> All of cement, for an eternal home,
> Must crumble back to earth; and every gust
> Shall revel in the desert of its dust;
> And when the prison of the Immortal, Mind,
> Hath fallen to set free the bound and blind,
> No more shall life be one long dread of death,
> Humanity shall breathe with fuller breath;
> Expand in spirit and in stature rise,
> To match its birth-place of the earth and skies.

GNOSTIC AND HISTORIC CHRISTIANITY.

My purpose in the present lectures is to enforce with further evidence, and sustain with ampler detail, the interpretation of facts, which has been already outlined in the "Natural Genesis." My contention is, that the original mythos and *gnosis* of Christianity were primarily derived from Egypt on various lines of descent, Hebrew, Persian, and Greek, Alexandrian, Essenian, and Nazarene, and that these converged in Rome, where the History was manufactured mainly from the identifiable matter of the Mythos recorded in the ancient Books of Wisdom, illustrated by Gnostic Art, and orally preserved amongst the secrets of the Mysteries.

My stand-point had not previously been taken. It was not until this, the Era of Excavation, that we were able to dig down far enough to recover the fundamental facts that were most essential for the Student of Survivals and development to know anything certain concerning the remoter origins and evolution of the Christian System; the most ancient evidences having been neglected until now.

Instead of the Roman Church being a crucible for purging the truth from the dross of error, to give it forth pure gold, we shall have to look upon it rather as the melting-pot, in which the beautiful and noble mental coinage of Greece and Egypt was fused down and made featureless, to be run into another mould, stamped with a newer name, and re-issued under a later date.

In the course of establishing Apostolic Christianity upon historical foundations, there was such a reversal of cause and outcome that the substance and the shadow had to change places, and the husk and kernel lost their natural relationship and value. All that was first in time and in originality has been put latest, in order that the prophecy might be fulfilled, and the last become first. All that preceded Christianity in the religion of knowledge, or the Gnostics, has come to be looked back upon as if it were like that representation in the German play where Adam is seen crossing the stage in the act of going to be created!

Historic Christianity has gathered in the crops that were not of its kind, but were garnered from the seed already in the soil. Whosoever tilled and sowed, it has assumed the credit, and been permitted to reap the harvest, as undisputed master of the field. It claimed, and was gradually allowed, to be the source of almost every true word and perfect work that was previously extant; and these were assigned to a personal Christ as the veritable Author and Finisher of the Faith. Every good thing was re-dated, re-warranted, declared, and guaranteed to be the blessed result of Historic Christianity, as established by Jesus and his personal disciples. It can be demonstrated that Christianity pre-existed without the Personal Christ, that it was continued by Christians who entirely rejected the historical character in the second century, and that the supposed historic portraiture in the Canonical Gospels was extant as mythical and mystical before the Gospels themselves existed. In short, the mythical theory can be proved by recovering the Mythos and the Gnosis.

The picture of the New Beginning commonly presented is Rembrandt-like in tone. The whole world around Judea lay in the shadow of outer darkness, when suddenly there was a great light seen at the centre of all, and the face of the startled universe was illuminated by an apparition of the child-Christ lying in the lap of Mary. Such was the dawn of Christianity, in which the Light of the World had come to it at last! That explanation is beautifully simple for the simple-minded; but the picture is purely ideal—or, in sterner words, it is entirely false.

When the fountain-heads of the Nile were reached at last, it was perceived that the great river did not rise from any single source in one particular place, but from a vast concourse of many tributary springs. So when we come to examine for ourselves the vast complex that passes under the vague name of Christianity, we learn that it can be traced to no one single source or locality. So far from its being an original system as product of the life, character, work, and teachings of a personal founder, we have to acknowledge sooner or later that it is more like a unique specimen of what school-boys profanely call a "Resurrection pie."

Another popular delusion most ignorantly cherished is, that there was a golden age of *primitive Christianity*, which *followed* the preaching of the Founder and the practice of his apostles; and that there was a falling away from this paradisiacal state of primordial perfection when the Catholic Church in Rome lapsed into idolatry, Paganised and perverted the original religion, and poisoned the springs of the faith at the very fountain-head of their flowing purity. Such is the pious opinion of those orthodox Protestants who are always clamouring to *get back beyond* the Roman Church to that ideal of primitive perfection supposed to be found in the simple teachings of Jesus, and the lives of his personal followers, as recorded in the four canonical gospels and in the Acts of the Apostles. But when we do penetrate far enough into the past to see somewhat clearly through and beyond the cloud of dust that was the cause of a great obscuration in the first two centuries of our era, we find that there was no such new beginning, that the earliest days of the purest Christianity were pre-historic, and that the real golden age of knowledge and simple morality preceded, and did not follow, the Apostolic Roman Church, or the Deification of its Founder, or the humanising of the "Lamb of God," whom Lucian calls the "Impaled One of Palestine."

In an interesting book just published, entitled "Buddhism in

Christendom," Mr. Lillie thinks he has found Jesus, the author of Christianity, as one of the Essenes, and a Buddhist! But there is no need of craning one's neck out of joint in looking to India, or straining in that direction at all, for the origin of that which was Egyptian born and Gnostic bred! Essenism was no new birth of Hindu Buddhism, brought to Alexandria about two centuries before our era; and Christianity, whether considered to be mystical or historical, was not derived from Buddhism at any time. They have some things in common, because there is a Beyond to both. The crucial test, however, is to be found on the threshold, at the first step we take, in the doctrine of the divine Fatherhood. The supreme rôle assigned to the Christ of the Gospels, as of the Gnostics, is that of Manifestor and Revealer of the Father in heaven. His sign-manual is the seal of the Father. A dozen times, according to Matthew, he calls God, "My Father." In John's Gospel, he says, "I and my Father are one." "I am come in my Father's name." "My Father hath sent me." "My Father hath taught me." "I am in my Father." "The word ye hear is my Father's." Buddha makes no revelation of the Fatherhood. This doctrinal difficulty can only be bottomed in mythology. The Buddha is the veiled God unveiled, the un-manifested made manifest, but not by the line of descent from Father to Son! Buddha, like Putha (or Khepr-Ptah), was begotten by his own becoming, before the time of the divine paternity. There being no real Father-God in Buddhism, the Buddha has none to make known on earth. The doctrine was Egyptian, as when it is proclaimed in the Texts that Horus is "the son who proceeds from his father," and Osiris is the "father who proceeds from his son."

Again, in the Hindu myth of the ascent and transfiguration on the Mount, the Six Glories of the Buddha's head are represented as shining out with a brilliance that was blinding to mortal sight. These Six Glories are equivalent to the six manifestations of the Moon-God in the six Upper Signs, or, as it was set forth, in the Lunar Mount. During six months, the Horus, or Buddha, as Lord of Light in the Moon, did battle with the Powers of Darkness by night, whilst the Sun itself was fighting his way through the Six Lower Signs. Now, in the Gospel according to John, there is no contest with Satan, and no Transfiguration on the Mount! Instead, we have the "Light of the world," which is in heaven, warring with the Darkness, and manifesting His glory in six miracles—no more, no less—answering to the Six Glories of the Buddha's head on the Mount, or the six manifestations in the luminous hemisphere of the superior signs. The "beginning of his signs," by which Jesus "manifested his glory," was the turning of water into wine. The sixth, and last, of these, was the raising of Lazarus, which corresponds exactly with the rising of the Mummy-constellation (Sahu) of Orion, which ascended as the star of the Resurrection, when the solar god returned from the dark hemisphere of the under-world, or the sun re-entered the sign of the Bull at the vernal equinox. The source of all is the identifiable astronomical allegory in the Soli-Lunar phase, but the fable followed in the Gospel is Egyptian, not Buddhist. The Christ is one with Horus as Lord of the Lunar light, who manifested the glory (or the Six Glories) of his father, in the six upper signs, as his only-begotten Son. The claim now made is that the common Mythos determined the number of the six Glories, or six Miracles, and the history was moulded accordingly.

I also think that Jesus—or Joshua-ben-Pandira—*was* an Essene. That is, he was a Nazarite, and the Nazarites were one with the Essenes. And these, for example, are amongst the "sayings" in the Book of the Nazarenes. "Blessed are the peacemakers, the just, and 'faithful.'" "Feed the hungry; give drink to the thirsty; clothe the naked." "When thou makest a gift, seek no witness whereof, to mar thy bounty. Let thy right hand be ignorant of the gifts of thy left." Such were common to all the Gnostic Scriptures, going back to the Egyptian. This is a Nazarene saying from the Book of Adam :—"No poor sculpture of earth has fashioned his throne. The palace of the King was not built up by earthly masons." And this is from an Egyptian hymn:—"He is not graven in marble, nor adored in sanctuaries. There is no building that can contain him." In the ancient Egyptian "Maxims of Ani" we read:—"The sanctuary of God abhors noisy demonstrations. Pray humbly with a loving heart, all the words of which are uttered in secret. He will listen to thy words; He will accept thy offerings. Exaggerate not the liturgical prescriptions; it is forbidden to offer more than is prescribed. Thou shalt make adorations in his name." These contain the essence of the early verses in the 6th chapter of Matthew, where the injunctions given are:—" Sound not a trumpet before thee, etc. Pray in secret to thy Father, which is in secret, and he shall recompense thee. And in praying use not vain repetitions." Ani denotes one of the names of Taht who, as Mati = Matthew, wrote down the Sayings of the Lord, some of which are amongst these Maxims. But, unfortunately, you cannot prove anything, or, still more unfortunately, you *can* prove anything from the Gospels! You must first catch your Jesus, before you pretend to tell us what he was personally, and what were his own individual teachings. These " sayings of mine," cannot be judged as *his* if they were pre-extant, and can be proved to be anyone's sayings, or may be identified as ancient sayings, whether Buddhist, Nazarene, Apocryphal, or Egyptian. Also, there are different versions of the same sayings in the Gospels! In Matthew, we read: "Blessed are they that hunger and thirst after righteousness." In Luke it is :—"Blessed are ye that hunger now." In Matthew:— "Blessed are the poor in spirit." In Luke :—" Blessed be ye poor. Woe unto you that are rich!" Which, then, is the version that is personal to Jesus, the Nazarene? or where is the sense of claiming that the personal Jesus was an Essene or Nazarite—one of those who never touched wine, or strong drink—when one of the inspired writers testifies that he was described as a glutton, and a wine-bibber; and, according to another, his very first miracle was the turning of water into wine for a marriage feast? Suppose we admit that you have laid hold of Joshua, the Essene, the Nazarite, the reputed Great Healer, the Comforter, what can you make of a character so unhuman as this?

A poor Canaanitish woman comes to him from a long distance and beseeches him to cure her daughter who is grievously obsessed. "Have mercy on me, O Lord," she pleads. But he answered her not a word. The disciples, brutes as they were, if the scene were real, besought him to send her away because she cried after them. Jesus answered, and said :—" I was only sent to the lost sheep of the House of Israel." She worships him, and he calls her one of the dogs. And it is only her extreme deference that wins a kindly word from him at last. The Essenes and Gnostics absolutely denied the physical resurrection, because they were Spiritualists; therefore, it was impossible for an Essene to have taught the resurrection of the dead at the Last Day as Jesus is made to do. (John vi. 39, 40, and xi. 24.)

Again, if the pupil of Ben Perachia was an Essene, or, as reputed, an initiate in Egyptian mysteries, he never could have endorsed the mistakes attributed to Moses; never would have died for the reality of a parable, which he must have known to be astronomical. As one of the Magi or an Essene, he would understand the "Doctrine of Angels," *i.e.*, of the cycles of time, the character of the Kronian Messiah and the Coming in 400 years, according to the prophecy of Esdras. He would know the celestial nature of the Seventy-two whose names were written in Heaven as servants of the Lord of Light, and who had been with him "from the beginning" as the opponents of the Seventy-two *Sami* who served Sut-Typhon, the devil of darkness. He would know that the myths were not to be fulfilled in human history, and could not have personally set up the crazy claim that he was the messenger of Hebrew prophecy in person. No. The claims are made in his name by those who naturalized the Mythos on its Hebrew-Aramaic line of descent in Matthew, Egyptian in Luke, and Greek in John. What we do hear is not the voice of the founder teaching one thing at one time and the direct opposite at another; we hear the voices of the different sections, each proclaiming its own particular doctrines and dogmas, each assigning them to the Christ as their typical teacher, in the course of making out a personal history from the Mythos, and of giving vent to their own particular prejudices. The sayings of the Lord were pre-historic, as the sayings of David (who was an earlier Christ), the sayings of Horus the Lord, of Elijah the Lord, of Mana the Lord, of Christ the Lord, as the divine directions conveyed by the ancient teachings. As the "Sayings of the Lord" they were collected in Aramaic to become the *nuclei* of the earliest Christian gospel according to Matthew. So says Papias. At a later date they were put forth as the original revelation of a personal teacher, and were made the foundation of the historical fiction concocted in the four gospels that were canonized at last. In proving that Joshua or Jesus was an Essene there would be no more rest here than anywhere else for the sole of your foot upon the ground of historic fact. You could not make him to be the Founder of the Essene, Nazarite or Gnostic Brotherhoods, and communities of the genuine primitive Christians that were extant in various countries a very long while before the Era called Christian.

Nor is there any need to go to India for the original healers, called Essenes or Therapeutæ. The dawn of civilisation arose in Egypt, with healing on its wings. Egypt was the land of physicians through all her monumental history. Amongst the nations of antiquity she stands a head and shoulders above the rest; first in time and pre-eminent in attainment. Egypt was the great physician of the human race, and she sent out her medical missionaries from the earliest times. The Essenes were the same as the Therapeutæ or Healers, and they are the healers by name in Egyptian. Philo farther identifies their name with Essa in Hebrew, for healing. But Egypt had given birth to the Essenic name, and, therefore, to the persons named, before the letter E existed; that was previous to the middle empire (which ended over 4,000 years ago). In old Egyptian, the word Usha means to doctor. Whence the Ushai, later, Eshai, or Essenes, are the healers and physicians Josephus has compared the Pythagoreans with the Egyptian Therapeutæ or Alexandrian Essenes; and attempts have been made to shov the derivation of Buddhist doctrines from India through Pythagoras whose name has been derived from Put=Buddha and Guru, a teacher with intent to prove that he was a teacher of the religion of Buddha. But the Egyptian Putha (the original of Buddha as I suggest) is indefinitely older than any known Buddha in India; therefore, as Pythagoras was learned in the wisdom of Egypt and was a teacher of it, I should derive his name from Putha (Ptah) and Khuru (Eg.), the Voice or Word of; as a teacher of the Cult of Putha or Ptah, the Opener and "Lord of Life."

Also, when he entered the first stage of the Essenic mysteries as a student of divinity, the Initiate was presented with an axe; that is the Egyptian hieroglyphic of divinity, called the Nuter; the sign with which the name of the priest, prophet, or Holy Father, was written. Philo informs us that the Jewish lawgiver (Moses) had trained into fellowship a large number of those who bore the name of Essenes. There were both Egyptian and Jewish communities of the healers preceding those that were known by the Christian or Gnostic names. Jerome calls the Essenes or Therapeuts "The monks of the old law," and Evagrius Ponticus speaks of "A monk of great renown who belonged to a sect of the Gnostics" that dwelt near Alexandria, and were known by name as the "Christian Gnostics." Clement of Alexandria also claimed to be a Gnostic Christian. As M. Renan points out, the life of the so-called Christian hermits was first commenced in Egypt. Ages earlier there had been Egyptian communities of recluses, both male and female, near the Serapæum of Memphis, which were supported by the State. In Philo's letter to Hephæstion, he says the cells of the Egyptian healers are scattered about the region on the farther shore of Lake Mareotis, in Egypt. Pliny speaks of the "Ages on ages' during which the Essenes had existed, and Epiphanius, about the year 400, says,—"The Essenes continue in their first position, and have not changed at all." Such permanency, of course, demands a long period of induration. But it is enough for the present argument to know they were extant for at least 150 years before the Christian era. Epiphanius also admits that the Christians were at first called Therapeutæ and Jesseans, an equivalent name, as he explains, for the Essenes. They were all healers or doctors. As the Ushai or Jesseans they were already extant as the healers by name, independently of any personal Jesus or Joshua the Healer. Also, in Greek the verb for healing comes from the same root as the name of Jesus. The Essenes were healers, not because they were the workers of mythical miracles like Jesus, but because they were profound students of Nature's secret powers; because they were masters of the science of mental medicine, consciously able to draw on the spirit-world for healing influences!

They had discovered that health was infectious as well as disease, and that the capacity for receiving and giving, as a medium of the higher life, depended on conditions that could be cultivated in this life. Hence the stress they laid on personal purity and its eight stages of attainment. They were healers by virtue of the Christ within. Again, we learn from pseudo-Dionysius, the Areopagite, that the name of healer, *i.e.*, the "Essene" or Therapeut, whom Eusebius calls the Curate, was employed in the early Church to denote the perfected Adept, who had attained the highest standing, just as it was with the earlier Essenes. The current expression,—"A Cure of Souls," or a "Curacy," still shows the Christian line of descent from the pre-Christian healers.

We sometimes hear of early Christian Communities in which there was no private property, but all things were held in common, as we read in the Book of Acts; although in that case the Twelve would but constitute a *late* community. The members of these brotherhoods are said to have dwelt together in perfect equality; in fact, to have lived according to those principles of liberty, equality, and fraternity which were formulated as an aim of the French Revolution! But such societies *did not first originate* as the result of establishing "*Historic Christianity.*" They did not come from the Twelve Apostles, nor from the church at Jerusalem, nor from Rome. They were founded by the prehistoric Christians, who were primitive enough to practise their creed instead of merely preaching it as a faith. But such primitive Christians were quietly at work in various parts of the world, giving health to the sick, peace to the troubled, freedom to the slave, and knowledge to the ignorant, long before the existence of Papal or Apostolic Christianity.

Philo-Judæus, who was one of the Essenes—but does not seem to have met with the Gospel Jesus amongst them, or heard of him—Philo says of them,—"Three things regulate all they learn and do—viz., love to God, love of virtue, love for man. A proof of the first is the matchless sanctity of their entire life, their fear of oaths and lies, and the conviction that God is only the originator of good, never of evil. They show their love of virtue by their indifference to gain, glory, and pleasure; by their temperance, perseverance, simplicity, absence of wants, humility, faithfulness, and straightforwardness. They exemplify their love for their fellow-creatures by kindness, absence of pretensions, and lastly by the community of goods." There you have what is termed an Ideal Christian Community! but this was a Reality, and it was not founded by any personal Jesus; nor was it a result of his personal teachings being reduced to practice. It preceded, and was not a birth of, Historic Christianity.

Philo tells us that those who retired from the turmoil of public life to dwell apart in solitary places (these being the precursors of the monks and nuns in the Roman Church) handed over their private property to others, and left their parents, brothers and sisters, wife and child, and gave up all to the mysteries of a dedicated life. This, which was a common reality with the Essenes, is set forth as an Ideal when the Canonical Teacher says—"If any man cometh unto me, and hateth not his own father and mother and wife and children and brethren and sisters, yea, and his own life also, he cannot be my disciple." Here the ideal is perhaps a trifle overdone. The Essenes did not express or inculcate any such spirit of hatred to all one's relations. They were no such rabid anti-naturalists as that! The peaceful Essenic spirit is not present, but rather the spirit of Christian persecution that lighted the fires of martyrdom.

Of those Essenes who moved about in the world Josephus tells us (he also was an Essene in early life who did not find Jesus), "They have no one certain city, but many of them dwell in every city; and if any of them come from other places, what they have lies open for the strangers, just as if it were their own—for which reason they carry nothing at all with them on their travels; nor do they buy or sell anything one to another, but every one of those who have gives to him that requires it."

The Essenes were phenomenal Spiritualists, in the current sense, who walked with open sight, and could never become the blind followers of the shut-eyed faith of the Historicisers, who banned the "malignant spirit of free inquiry." As Spiritualists they could not, and did not, believe in the resurrection of the body, consequently a corporeal resurrection of the Christ was a fundamental fallacy upon which no Essene or Gnostic could found at any time. So Anti-Christian were they in the Catholic sense, and so opposed to the Messiah of pubescence, the Christ according to the flesh, that they repudiated anointing with oil, and considered it to be a filthy defilement. Therefore their Christ did not depend upon any external anointing in baptism at the age of thirty years, and they never could become Christians as the anointed ones. They were the opponents of all blood-sacrifice, animal or human. The only sacrifice upheld by them was that of self. Therefore they did not accept the bloody sacrifice of the incarnate Son of God when it was proclaimed. The Essenes as Gnostics held that every man must be his own Christ. Their Christ came within—the Christ that could not become historical without. In the minds of those who knew, Historic Christianity was repudiated beforehand; and it was as impossible after the facts were forged, the falsehood established, and the dogma was founded, as it was before; consequently those Gnostics who had been Ante-Christians beforehand were of necessity Anti-Christians afterwards.

The Essenes discarded the Pentateuch and repudiated most of the later prophets—that is, they rejected the ground-work of the future redemption of mankind, together with the Fall that never was a fact, and the fulfilment of prophecy which never could be human. The Essenes and other Gnostics are constantly charged by the ignorant Christians with turning very plain matters of fact into fantastical parables. M. Renan talks of Simon's and Philo's allegorising exegesis as if the ancient fables had been historic facts which the Gnostics perverted into myths. They were nothing of the kind. They were fables and allegories from the first—the mysteries that were taught in parables—and all Gnostics rejected the historic explanation from beginning to end, because they preserved the true interpretation of the supposed history. Philo tells us—" They regard the letter of each utterance as the symbol of that which was concealed from sight, but was revealed in the hidden meaning "—not by its being rationalised into history. Mythology is, in its way, as real as mathematics, but its way is not that of the literalisers, who have made the symbolism false on the face of it to the underlying natural facts.

The fall of man, the temptation of the serpent and the coming of a Messiah were not historic realities, which the Gnostics converted into their allegories. It is altogether misleading to speak of the allegorizing Essenic and Docetic methods of exegesis, as if the Gnosis consisted in whittling away and attenuating the solid facts of history! That is merely echoing the language of those who were at war with the Gnostic interpretation, on behalf of the supposed history by which we have been misled. The allegories were first; and they are final; the his-history had no deeper foundations. The Essenes knew the hidden nature of these representations and taught it "through symbols, with time honoured zeal," being in possession of the books of wisdom and other scriptures than ours. They were the jealous preservers of the hidden Gnosis, and qualified expounders of the ancient mysteries by means of the secret tradition. The initiate was sworn to keep secret the scriptures of the hidden wisdom and not to communicate the Gnosis to others, not even to a new member except in the same way in which it had been communicated to him. But it was especially prescribed that the "Doctrine of the Angels," *i. e.*, of the time cycles, was not to be revealed to any non-Essene. Unfortunately that secresy in the mode of communication became the fatal curse of all the ancient knowledge by allowing the false to come first in being publicly proclaimed.

De Quincy, in his essay on the Essenes, has remarked on the monstrosity of the omission when the Christians are not even mentioned by the Jewish historian, Josephus. There is the same portentous omission when the Essenes are never mentioned in the Christian Gospels. They are there in fact, though not by name; nor as any new-born brotherhood. They are only there in disguise, because historic Christianity has drawn the mask over the features of primitive Christianity. The existence of primitive and pre-historic Christians is acknowledged in the Gospel according to Mark when John says,—"Master, we saw one casting out devils in thy name, and he followeth not us." That, as the context shows, was done in the name of the Christ, and, consequently, such were Christians. According to the account in Matthew, before ever a disciple had gone forth or could have begun to preach historic Christianity, there was a widespread secret organization ready to receive and bound to succour those who were sent out in every city of Israel. Who, then, are these? They are called "The Worthy." That is, as with the Essenes, those who have stood the tests, proved faithful, and been found worthy. According to the canonical account these were the pre-historic Christians, whether called Essenes or Nazarenes; the worthy, the faithful, or the Brethren of the Lord. "Peace be with you!" was the greeting or pass-word of the Essenes, and also of the Nazarenes, to judge from its appearing in the book of Adam. And in the instructions given to the Seventy (Luke x. 5) it is said:—" Into whatsoever house ye enter first say, 'Peace be to this house.'"

After the resurrection the mystic pass-word is employed three times over by the risen Christ. And "He who comes with peace" is the name of the Egyptian god, Iu-em-hept, the son of Atum, who, as the coming son, is Iu-su = Jesus. We also learn from the Clementine Homilies (3, 19) that the "Mystery of the Scriptures" which was taught by (or ascribed to) Christ was identical with that which *from the first* had been communicated to *those who were the Worthy.* We may learn from the Gospel according to Luke that the "Worthy" were those who had been initiated into the Mysteries of the Gnosis, and who were "accounted Worthy" to attain that "resurrection from the dead" in this life, which Paul was not altogether sure about—"those who knew that they could die no more, being equal to the angels as sons of God and sons of the Resurrection." Such were then extant as pre-Historic Christians (ch. xx. 35-6).

These communities of the primitive Christians had long been accustomed to send forth their bare-footed apostles into all the known world, to inculcate the common brotherhood of man, founded on the common fatherhood of God, and to labour for the family of the human race. That had been the practice in the past which was afterwards made a matter of precept in the present, and a prospect for the future! For this ancient practice of the Essenes is reduced to the precept of the teacher made personal, who says, " Go your way; carry neither purse, nor scrip, nor shoes;" and gives instructions to do the very things the Essenes had always done! The supposed personal teacher and historic founder of primitive Christianity is made to say to his followers, "A new commandment I give unto you that ye love one another." But the statement is entirely untrue. There was nothing new in it! This was a primary commandment of the Essenic communities who had practised the principles they professed, and had lived for ages according to the golden rule which is afterwards laid down as a divine command, a direct revelation from God, in the Gospels. No matter who the plagiarist may be, the teaching now held to be divine was drawn from older human sources, and palmed off under false pretensions. Josephus declares in his account of the Essenes, that " Whatever they say is firmer than oath; but swearing is entirely avoided by them. They consider it worse than perjury." And such is the original revelation in the Gospel. But I was sorry to find, in the Clementine Homilies, that the same speaker breaks the Essenic pledge, for it is there written,—"And Christ said (with an oath), Verily I say unto you, unless ye be born again of the water of life, ye cannot enter in the kingdom of heaven." Thus we have an Essene who swears as well as tipples and plays the part of Bacchus. Again, Jesus is presented as the original revealer of the mysteries and author of the Gnosis. He says to his disciples,—"It is given you to know the mysteries of heaven;" but the Essenic Communities always had been composed of those who were in possession of the Gnosis, and had already obtained and sacredly preserved the knowledge of the mysteries of the kingdom of heaven, which they had taught only in parables.

The divine morality inculcated in the Sayings ascribed to Jesus had been completely forestalled by the Essenes in their lives and works, their individual characters, common practices, and societary conditions. His words are but a later echo of their very human deeds. We are told that Jesus taught mankind to pray,—"Thy kingdom come, thy will be done on earth as it is in heaven." But this was exactly what the pre-historic Christians had been working out in life. They strove to found the kingdom there and then, and realise the world to come in this. Everything noble and ennobling, unselfish and spiritual, in the ethics of Jesus, or rather in the sayings assigned to him as a teacher of men, had been anticipated by the Egyptians, the Essenes, and the primitive Christians of the Gnostic religion. Nothing new remained to be inculcated by the Gospel of the new teacher, who is merely made to repeat the old sayings with a pretentious air of supernatural authority; the result being that the true sayings of old are, of necessity, conveyed to later times in a delusive manner. The commandments are not new. Life and immortality were not brought to light by any personal Jesus, but by the Christ of the Gnosis. The most important proclamations assigned to Jesus turned out to be false. The kingdom of God was not at hand; the world was not nearing its end; the catastrophe foretold never occurred; the second coming was no more actual than the first; the lost sheep of Israel are not yet saved. And the supposed Divine Truth in very person remains exposed as the genuine false prophet to this day, or rather as the mere mouthpiece of the most ignorant beliefs of that day.

It may be said more justly of Historic Christianity, than of anything else within the compass of my knowledge, that what is true in it was not new, and that which was new in it is not true! It is not new, because it represents the ancient Mythos under an intended disguise. It is not true, because it is not a genuine history. The supposed human original, set forth in the Gospels, is but the mundane shadow of the Gnostic Christ.

Christianity began as Gnosticism, refaced with falsehoods concerning a series of facts alleged to have been historical, but which are demonstrably mythical. By which I do not mean mythical as exaggerations or perversions of historic truth, but belonging to the pre-extant Mythos. Of course, the setting-up of this vast falsehood made all truth a blasphemy. "The Gnostics," says Irenæus, "have no gospel which is not full of blasphemy." Their crime was that they denied the Christ carnalised, and they were denounced as being Anti-Christian, because they were *Ante*-Christian!

We are told in the Book of Acts that the name of the *Christiani* was first given at Antioch; but so late as the year 200 A.D. no canonical New Testament was known at Antioch, the alleged birth-place of the Christian name. There was no special reason why "the disciples" should first have been named as Christians at Antioch, except that this was a great centre of the Gnostic Christians, who were previously identified with the teachings and works of the mage Simon of Samaria. Simon had taught the people of Antioch for a "long time" before, and had been accepted by them "from the least to the greatest" (Acts). Simon was the great Anti-Christ in the eyes of the founders of the belief in Historic Christianity, for whom the Ante-Christ was always, and everywhere, the Anti-Christ; and it was necessary to account for there being Christians, other, and earlier, than the believers in a carnalized Christ. This was clumsily attempted in the "Acts," by making Simon become a baptised convert to the new superstition, and then back-sliding—a common mode of accounting for Gnostic heretics, but false on the face of it. Irenæus shall furnish us with a crucial instance of the orthodox lying on this subject. He tells us that the Gnostics, such as those who followed Valentinus and Marcion, in the second century, had no existence before these later teachers (B. III. ch. 4, 3); whereas he had already stated in his first book, that Simon of Samaria was the first and foremost of all the founders of Gnosticism, and the father of all its heresies; and he was a century earlier. Simon had brought on the Gnosis from Alexandria. He taught his doctrines, and wrought his wonders long anterior to the apostles of the later creed. Epiphanius acknowledges that all the heretical forms of Christianity were derived from the Pagan Mythology—that is, they were survivals of the original pre-historic Gnostic religion.

It is obvious that the Roman Church remained Gnostic at the beginning of the second century, and for some time afterwards. Marcion, the great Gnostic, did not separate from it until about the year 136 A.D Tatian did not break with it until long after that. In each case the cause of quarrel was the same. They left the Church that was setting up the fraud of Historic Christianity. They left it as Gnostic Christians, who were anathematised as heretics, because they rejected the Christ made flesh and the new foundations of religion in a spurious Jewish history.

The Church in Jerusalem, at the head of which was James, called the "brother of the Lord," was one of the Essenic or Therapeutic communities that were founded by the Gnostic Nazarenes. James was reputed to have been a follower of Joshua, the Nazarene—*i.e.*, Ben Pandira—who was converted more or less into the later Jesus of Nazareth. The Jewish legends show that he was of the Nazarene sect. But no *Nazarene* brotherhood could have been founded on any supposed Jesus of Nazareth. They also show that James was a Nazarene of the ancient ascetic type—one of those who were set apart and consecrated from the mother's womb—one who never shaved or cut his hair, who drank neither wine nor strong drink, nor ate of any animal food; he would not anoint himself with oil, nor wear woollen garments. Bishop Lightfoot admits that the members of the early Church at Jerusalem were Gnostics, like the other Essenes: only, for him, they were heretics. He cannot make out the hiatus, which was not then filled in with the Gospel history.

Now, whether it be called Christian or pre-Christian, the Gospel of James is good, as far as it goes. It was undoubtedly the same Gospel of the Essenes that opened the poor man's door to heaven. It teaches their doctrines in their own language, and without the Historic apparatus. It puts certain things which have been disestablished on their original foothold. In the Lord's prayer we are taught to ask the Divine Father not to lead us, his children, into temptation. But James declares emphatically that " no man should say he is tempted of God, for God cannot be tempted with evil, and he himself tempteth no man." The epistle of James is of Supreme importance.

Esebius, the suspected forger and falsifier, when he made his fatal admission, must have known that the Scriptures of the Essenes had been utilised as *ground-work* for the Epistles and the later Canonical history. He claims the Essenes themselves as Christians when he tells us that Philo "describes with the closest accuracy the lives of our ascetics" —that is, of the Therapeutæ. He confesses "it is highly probable that the ancient commentaries, which Philo says they have, are the very gospels and writings of the apostles, and probably some expositions of the ancient prophets, such as are contained in the Epistle to the Hebrews and many other of Paul's epistles." He might have said, including the Ebionite Epistle of James, only that was to be denounced as spurious. But it is impossible to claim the Essenic Scriptures as being identical with the Canonical records, without, at the same time, admitting their pre-historic existence, their non-historical nature, and their anti-historical testimony. They could only be the same in the time of Eusebius by the non-historical having been falsely converted into the historical. This was what had been done, and that alone will explain why the earliest scriptures, which ought to have contained the historical record, have not been preserved, but were got rid of altogether when the Council of Nice "suppressed all the devices of the heretics."

I have previously shown that the real root of the whole matter can be delved down to and identified in the mythology and mysteries of Egypt. When we see the Child-Horus emerging from the lily-lotus, or holding the forefinger to his mouth, as portrayed upon the Gnostic stones and in the Catacombs of Rome, absolutely the same as on the Egyptian monuments, we know that it is the identical divinity, no matter how it came to represent the Christian Christ. But identification is more difficult when the mythical type has passed into the more mystical phase. That is, the portraits of deities are more recognisable than the hidden doctrines and veiled features of the Gnosis. Yet, the Egyptian doctrines were as surely continued by the Gnostics and the Christians as the personal likenesses of Egyptian deities were reproduced by Gnostic Art in Rome. And by aid of the Gnosis, we can recover much that has been dislimned and made indefinite in the doctrinal stage, to be left as an unfathomable mystery! For example, the Child-Horus, with finger to mouth, wherever found, indicates the divine Word or Logos in a particular way. He was the child of the Virgin mother alone, and always remained the child. He, therefore, was not the *True Voice*, or *Voice of Truth*, only the Imperfect Word, the Inarticulate Discourse, as Plutarch calls the first Horus. But, just as the voice of the boy changes and becomes manly at puberty, so in his second or virile character Horus, as representative of the Father, becomes a True Voice, and is the "Word of Truth" personified! In this character he was designated Har-Makheru, *i.e.*, Horus, the "Word of Truth," from Ma, Truth ; Kheru, the Word. In the Egyptian texts the Word of Horus *is* Truth ; the function confided to him by the Father! He vanquishes his enemies with the Word of Truth. It is said of the Osirified deceased, He goes forth with the Word of Truth. To make the Truth by means of the Word is synonymous with the giving of life here or hereafter. In a prayer to the Pharaoh it is said, "Grant us breath by the gift which is in thee of the 'Word of Truth.'" Moreover, men conquer their sins by means of this "Word of Truth" within, the Makheru conferred on them by the Deity!

This title of Makheru, the Word of Truth, was translated the *Justified* by Dr. Birch, which M. Pierret says is "unfortunate." But there is a Christian sense in which that is a correct rendering. With the Egyptians, the Christians (οἱ χρηστοί), the faithful Departed, were actually *called* by this title of Makheru or the Justified. They were those who always had been saved by the "Word-of-Truth!" in Egypt long Ages before the *Christian* Era!

Now, let us return for a moment to the Epistle of James canonised in the New Testament, and called by Luther "an Epistle of Straw," because it had not a grain of Historic Christianity in it. James was the head of the Church in Jerusalem. He was titled a brother of the Lord—no doubt in relation to the Nazarite Brotherhood; the Lord being a typical character like Horus, Mana, or Elias, who was ignorantly assumed by the literalizers of legends to have been a Judean peasant named Jesus or Joshua. Hence the imposition of certain family details in the Canonical Gospels, which will be traced hereafter. James is believed to have died about A.D. 60. But in the whole seven chapters of this Epistle of James, excepting an opening salutation, there is not one single sign of Historic Christianity! It recognises no Jesus of Nazareth, and it announces no salvation through the atoning blood, the death, resurrection and ascension of a personal Christ.

Nothing whatever begins with or is based on the history which was afterwards made canonical, nor on the Christ that was localized at a later stage of development. Everything is absent that was and still is essential to the physical faith. Instead, we find the exact opposite of all that was made historic in the Gospels. The doctrine of salvation is Gnostic, Essenic and Egyptian. Salvation, according to James, cometh of the "Word of Truth." Speaking of the "Father of Lights" (Lord of Lights being a title of Horus) he says:—"Of his own will begat he us with the 'Word of Truth' that we should be a kind of first fruits of his creatures." "Wherefore receive ye with meekness the implanted Word which is able to save your souls." The transaction is direct between the divine father and the human soul. The Christ within is the only saviour! The total teaching of the Epistle of James is based on this ancient Egyptian Word of Truth; the implanted Word which confers the Makheru on man, which never could be represented by an historical Christ. The "Word of Truth" as rendered by James is the best possible translation of the Egyptian "Ma-Kheru." Moreover, the context shows that the Word of Truth is the Egyptian Makheru by the exhortation, "Be ye doers of the Word," which renders good Egyptian doctrine in perfect accordance with exact Egyptian phraseology.

Just as Horus Makheru was the Word of Truth; or that which was said was fulfilled indeed, so men are re-begotten in the divine likeness by the Word of Truth; and as livers or doers of that Word they are to be saved—as it was taught in Egypt thousands of years previously without the Word of Truth becoming incarnate in Horus as a human person. This Word of Truth, the Christ of James and Paul, which alone was able to save, is identical with that made known aforetime, which needed not to be brought down from heaven for any personal incarnation; needed not to be brought up from the dead by any physical resurrection; needed not to be sent from over the sea, because, as was said by the Mosaic mouthpiece of Egypt's Wisdom, "that Word is in thy heart that thou mayest do it!" And this is the position re-occupied; this is the teaching re-echoed by Paul, in whose mouth the Word of Truth becomes doubly anti-historic (*cf.* Deut. xxx. 12-14, with Romans x. 6, 7).

There is also a reference to the "Word of Truth" in Paul's Epistle to Timothy, which still further identifies the Makheru. The word Ma, for that which is true, originally means to hold out straight before one. And Paul exhorts Timothy, as a workman, to hold a straight course according to the Ma-kheru, or "Word of Truth." This True Voice or Word of Truth is, I take it, that living and abiding voice which is appealed to by Papias as evidence for his Christ, who was the Lord of the Logia; and, if so, his testimony thus far does not make for, but tends to invalidate, the history. Of course, he is supposed to mean the voice of contemporaries when he decries what would be the more certain voice of written records; but that is not what he means. He prefers, in reality, the traditions of the oral wisdom, and may be claimed as another witness for the non-Historical Christ. Also, the epistle to Diognetus, supposed to have been written by Marcion, contains the same doctrine as the epistle of James. Speaking of the Gnostic Christians, he says:—"They are put to death and they come to life again," and the reason of this is that "God the Invisible hath himself from Heaven planted the truth and the holy incomprehensible Word and established him in their hearts." This epistle of James is indefinitely older than the Canonical history. James is believed to have died about the year 60 of our era, and in this, one of the earliest utterances of the Church, instead of the History, we find the divine Makheru of the Egyptian mythos in a mystical and doctrinal phase.

Instead of an original gospel based on the life, character, and teachings of his own human brother, James presents us with the translated Word-of-truth—the Horus of Egypt, and the Christ of the Gnostics, who could not become historical. This beginning, then, is doctrinal, and the doctrine, like the portrait, is Egyptian. The same mythos was visibly continued in the Gnostic phase. In the Gospels, which were being compiled at least one hundred years later, we find this same Word of Truth, which was personated by Horus-Makheru and by Iu-em-hept in Egypt some 3,000 years earlier, is now represented in a personal character as Jesus the Christ.

This Word of Truth, which is doctrinal and non-historical, according to James, is the Word of Truth made flesh according to John. Also, the Christ is the Horus continued in his two characters. Hence the Word, or Spirit of Truth, which proceedeth from the Father, is to come as the mystic Paraclete who shall testify to the reality of an historic Jesus.

These two characters, as the Sayer and Doer, constitute the double foundation of the Christ in the other Gospels. The Christ of Matthew is chiefly the Sayer. The Christ of Luke is mainly the Doer. He is mighty in deed and word! He is the Healer or Doer with the Word. "What a Word is this"! exclaim the multitude, who are amazed at the miracles. Both characters had been blended in one as Horus-Makheru, the Word of Truth, who was mythical in Egypt, and who is mythical in the teaching of James before the Word was described as being made flesh, to become an historical personage in the later Gospel according to John. This is the fatal kind of fact that turns the canonical history into fiction, and brands the falsifiers full in the face. There is no room left here for any historic fulfilment, and no need of any personal Saviour or vicarious victim. The Word of Truth is the Spirit of God, the Begetter of Souls, the Christ within, the Bringer of Immortality to Man, as it is in the teaching of Hermes, of Zarathustra, of Philo, and of Paul, as well as James; as it was in Egypt, in Chaldea, in India, in all the Mysteries, no matter where the Gnosis or Kabalah may be found. In presence of the Gnosis, here as elsewhere, there is no place, no significance, in the alleged facts of a human history, lived for us by a carnalised Christ. And yet such a history was made out, and we are now able to get a glimpse of the forgers engaged in the process of making it out!

Our Canonical Gospels are a Palimpsest, with one writing so elaborated over another that the first is almost crossed out, and the rest are thoroughly confused. Yet, the whole of them have to be seen through before the matter can be really read. By holding this Palimpsest up to the light, and looking at it long and closely, we can trace the large outline, the water-mark, of the Egyptian mythos, with its virgin-mother, who was Hathor-Meri—the Madonna—its child-Christ of 12 years, and the virile adult of 30 years, who was Horus, the anointed son of that Father in heaven whom he came to reveal. This is the earliest and most fundamental of the *nuclei*. Next we find a collection of Sayings as the nucleus of the Gospel of Matthew. These sayings were attributed to the Lord, and that Lord is supposed to have been a Judean peasant, as the original author! It is noticeable, though, that the title of the Lord is not once applied to Jesus by Matthew in the earth-life, but after the resurrection he is called the "Lord." Now, it is well known to scholars that the Gospel according to Luke is based upon, or concocted, with suitable alterations, from an earlier "Gospel of the Lord." That is, the latest gospel according to the Gnostics, preceded the earliest of those that were made canonical. This was called the "Gospel of the Lord"—the *kurios*—and it is commonly referred to as the gospel of Marcion, the great Gnostic. But the Lord, as known to the Gnostics, was not a character that could become historical. As Irenæus declares, according to no one gospel of the heretics could the Christ become flesh; consequently the gospel of Marcion, who was the arch-heretic and very Anti-Christ of the second century, in the sight of the incipient Catholic Church, could not have been a gospel of the Christ made historical; and we have now the means of proving that it was not. When once we know that the origins were mythical, that the Christ was mystical, and the teachings in the mysteries were typical, we shall be able to utilise the gospel of Marcion as a connecting link between the Egyptian Mythos, the epistle of the Word of Truth, and the canonical history according to Luke.

"The Lord" had been Horus by name in Egypt, and the Greek kuriou, or kurios, agrees with the Egyptian kheru, for the Word, Voice, or Logos, as in Ma-kheru (earlier, Ma-khuru). This was the Lord continued as the Gnostic manifestor, their Horus, or Christ.

Marcion assigned his gospel to the Christ, in the same way that the Egyptian Ritual is ascribed to Hermes. Later on, the sayings of the Lord were also called the writings, as we see by pseudo-Dionysius, who charges the Gnostics with having falsified the Writings of the Lord.

Marcion claimed that his was the one true Gospel—the one—and he pointed to the multiplicity of the Catholic Gospels, full as they were of discrepancies, in proof that they could not be genuine. In the fourth century even, there were as many different gospels as texts. As transmitted to us by the Christian copyists, who were nothing if not historicisers, Marcion's gospel opens with the statement, that " In the fifteenth year of the reign of Tiberius Cæsar, Pontius Pilate ruling in Judea, Jesus came down to Capernaum, a city of Galilee," or " into Judea," as reported by Irenæus.

Tertullian says,—" According to the gospel of Marcion, in the fifteenth year of Tiberius, Christ Jesus *deigned to emanate from heaven, a salutary spirit.*" But, he also says, according to this " Great Anti-Christian," the Christ was a phantom, who appeared suddenly at the synagogue of Capernaum in the likeness of a full-grown man for the purpose of protesting against the law and the prophets! It would be difficult to date the descent of a phantom Christ, and impossible to date the descent of the Gnostic Christ at all, except as Lord of the æon in relation to an astronomical period! But it is certain that the Lord or Christ of Marcion is entirely non-historical. He has no genealogy or Jewish line of descent; no earthly mother, no father, no mundane birthplace or human birth. The Gnostic nature of this Christ is further and fully corroborated by both Irenæus and Tertullian. Clearly then nothing can be made of the statement on behalf of the Canonical history. This statement in Marcion's gospel takes the place of the baptism and descent of the holy spirit in Luke's; and this same date is quoted by Luke for the time when the Word of God came to John in the wilderness, which is followed by the baptism of Jesus and the transformation into the Christ or Horus of 30 years, whose unpronounceable name contained 30 letters, according to the Gnosis. Such a beginning is entirely unhistorical, and applicable solely to the mythical Christ, who became the virile adult, the anointed son of the father at 30 years of age. Of course Christian apologists like Irenæus and Tertullian maintained that Marcion had mutilated their version of Luke; and they managed to get rid of the " Gospel of the Lord," and to suppress the writings of Marcion in proof to save us the trouble of judging for ourselves. But that was only another Christian lie, as we have now the means of knowing. The Gnostics were not the falsifiers of the historic scriptures; it was not they who had anything to falsify! Hitherto the forgers and falsifiers have been believed, and now the accusers and accused are about to change places in the witness-box and the dock. Everywhere the Gnosis was first; the history was last. You are only asked to take this view tentatively, and then let us watch the process and see how the compilers and forgers of our Luke put in the touches by which the mythos was rationalized and the human history was added to the Gnostic "Gospel of the Lord." The "Sayings of the Lord" were first, and they were not personal. The "Gospel of the Lord" was first, and the Lord was not historical.

The Jesus of Marcion like the Jesus of Esdras, of Paul, and other Gnostics, is no Jesus of Nazareth. This title has been added by Luke. Marcion's Jesus being mythical and not historical, he has no Jewish father and mother; consequently we find the test question:—"Is not this Joseph's son?" does not appear in the "Gospel of the Lord." It has been added by Luke. Again, the statement, "there came to him his mother and brethren; and they could not get at him for the crowd" (Luke viii. 9), is not to be found in Marcion's gospel; it has been added by Luke. And for what? but to manufacture and make out that human history which was at last believed in, but which had no place in any gospel according to the Gnostics or true primitive Christians! It can be proved how passage after passage has been added to the earlier gospel, in the course of manufacturing the later history. For example, the mourning over Jerusalem (Luke xiii. 29-35) is taken verbatim from the 2nd Esdras (i. 28-33) without acknowledgment, and the words previously uttered by the "Almighty Lord" are here assigned to Jesus as the original speaker. The account of Pilate's shedding the blood of the Galileans and mingling it with their sacrifices (Luke xiii. 1) has been added by some one so ignorant of Hebrew history, that he has ascribed to Pilate an act which was committed when Quirinus was governor, twenty-four years earlier than the alleged appearance of Jesus. Again, the anti-Nazarene, anti-Gnostic passage about the publicans being baptised with water, and the Son of Man coming eating and drinking as a glutton and a wine-bibber, has been added.

In the scene on the Mount of Transfiguration, which is purely mythical, and therefore common to Osiris, Buddha, and Zarathustra, we are witness to the forging of another historical nexus in the statement that "Moses and Elijah appeared in glory and spake of his decease which he was about to accomplish at Jerusalem" (Luke ix. 31). This passage does not appear in the "Gospel of the Lord." Nor does the statement (Luke xviii. 31-34), "And he took unto him the Twelve, and said unto them, 'Behold, we go up to Jerusalem, and all things that are written by the prophets shall be accomplished by the Son of Man.'" This mode of making out the history in the New Testament by fulfilment of prophecy found in the Old was *not* adopted by the compilers of Marcion's "Gospel of the Lord." The story of the colt and the riding into Jerusalem in triumph, to turn all the Jews out of their sacred Stock Exchange, are additions to the earlier Gospel! In the scene of the Last Supper almost the whole of the text is missing from Marcion's Gospel. Twelve verses of Luke 22 have been added!

In Marcion's Gospel there is no distribution of the Paschal Cup amongst the disciples; no promise is given that the Apostles shall eat and drink and judge the twelve tribes of Israel in the kingdom of

Christ; nor is there any appointment made with the dying thief on the Cross to meet him that day in Paradise! *These have been added.* Now, this is no mere matter of a difference in doctrine! We are witnessing the very forgery of the human foundations and the insertion of the manufactured facts upon which the history was established.

The Primitive Christiani, the so-called *heretics*, who preceded the historic Christians, were all of them spiritualists in the modern sense.

In the sight of Bishop Lightfoot the Gnostic Spiritualism was "a shadowy mysticism which loses itself in the contemplation of an unseen world." *This* he looks upon as the *false* teaching and the *heresy* of the Gnostics! He knows nothing of any *underlying* natural verities, or *phenomenal* facts; only sees a refining, a mysticising and a whittling away of the Gospel histories.

But as practical Spiritualists, the Essenes had eight stages in the evolution of perfect personal purity and the attainment of the highest spiritual powers :—

1. Purity of baptism.
2. Purity from animal desire.
3. Spiritual purity.
4. The purity of a meek and gentle spirit.
5. The purity of holiness.
6. The purity by which the body became a temple of the Holy Ghost.
7. The purity which gave the power of healing the sick and of raising the dead; *i.e.*, the spirits of the dead!
8. They attained the mystic state of Elias, who was the Essenic Christ! And in the middle of the Nineteenth Century, Bishop Lightfoot rises to explain that the Essenes were Fortune-tellers!

Orthodox Christianity knows nothing of Spiritualism to-day, and consequently can know nothing of Spiritualism in the past, because it is fact alone that can prove the fact. They reject it because it was repudiated by the founders of the historic faith; because it offers no facts to prove, whereas it does offer facts that furnish us with disproof of a physical resurrection. But it is absolutely necessary to be a phenomenal Spiritualist, or at least to know that phenomenal Spiritualism is founded upon facts of possible human experience, before we can take the first step toward really understanding this matter of the beginnings, or gauge the impassable gulf of difference that lies between the Gnostic Religion and Historic Christianity. With the Gnostics knowledge was the foundation of their faith; but the Historic Christians made faith the basis of knowledge, and the first demand of the new faith was for the convert to believe that all the mythical typology of the past had been made literally true in the present. By faith the fable was crystallised into the dogma of historic fact.

The Gnostic doctrines of the pre-Historic religion were formulated as being those of knowledge, faith, and immortality. Knowledge was fundamental. On this their faith was founded by means of a firsthand acquaintanceship with those facts which gave them their faith for the present, and sustained it with something more than the hope or promise of continuity for the future. Knowledge, Faith, and Immortality! Historic Christianity was based upon faith without that knowledge, and those who knew the least were actually considered and designated the better believers, just as it is in the Salvation Army of to-day. Lord Bacon, in a most unworthy utterance, affirmed that "the more irrational and incredible any divine mystery is the greater the honour we do God in believing it, and so much the more noble is the victory of faith." Such, however, was the teaching of the Church whose divine mysteries were manufactured from misinterpreted mythology. Nor was it very difficult to literalise the mystical representation when a man like Origen could maintain that the planets were animated bodies and rational beings.

All the secrets of the great knowledge of the interior and mystical life, which M. Renan calls the "Most glorious creation of Christendom," were in possession of the Gnostics of various lands long ages earlier, whilst their *modus operandi* of ascertaining the truth was now to be rejected and denounced as damnable by the corporeal Christians, or carnalisers of the Christ. They not only let go, they anathematised the knowledge that was already won from nature, and prohibited the means of continuing it or of recovering it again.

The Gnostics, as Irenæus shows, pointed out the very serious error that was committed by those who imagined that the Christ had arisen in a mundane body, not knowing that "flesh and blood do not attain to the Kingdom of God!"

The Christ of the Gnostics was a mystical type continued from mythology to portray a spiritual reality of the interior life. Hence the Christ in this human phase could be female as well as male; Sophia as well as Jesus; the spirit of both sexes. It was impossible for such to become historical, or be made so, except by ignorantly mistaking a mythical Impersonation for a Hermaphrodite in Person!

What, for example, is the actual base of the "Great Renunciation" ascribed to the Buddha or the Christ in the doctrinal, mythical, or spiritual phase? It is this:—When the soul of man came to be considered as a divine principle of celestial origin, it was figured as being entirely opposed to the evil nature of matter; therefore, birth or manifestation in matter was a descent of the soul from the heaven of a pristine condition into a lower state of impurity and impermanence; of disease, decay, and death, where it was bound to bear or struggle to get out of it again as soon as possible.

This soul, personified as the Divine Man in Buddha or the Christ, is afterwards represented as being consciously able to renounce the pleasures of Paradise, and of its own free will and choice come down to earth as the Saviour of the World, by giving lessons in divinity and living a life so lowly that this life should be conquered by rejecting it on behalf of the other thus revealed to men! The mode of glorifying such a being is simply that of the infantile mind. The proof of his supernatural character is shown through his power of suspending the known laws of nature by miraculous means, such as are humanly impossible. As the Lord of Life he raises the dead! The tree bends down and bows its acknowledgment to him in the womb of his mother; or the wild beasts grow tame in presence of the radiant child that lights the darkness of the cave when born. As a mere babe he becomes a teacher to the teachers. In youth he surpasses all competitors, conquers in every trial. All nature is turned into an elastic vesture that will fit this figure of the impossible—the *false* Ideal that makes our common everyday world a scene of phantasmal unrealities. In certain respects the Buddhist portrait of this divine Ideal, believed to have been realised in Gautama, transcends the Christian—in the depths of its tenderness, the range of its sympathies, and the embrace of its compassion. All true lovers of animals are naturally Buddhistic rather than Christian. For, it is upon the down-trodden beasts which perish that the Christian sets his foot for the first step upward as the possessor of an immortal soul. His brutalising belief, and baseless assumption, that animals have no souls, are guilty before God and responsible for most of the cruelties suffered by them throughout all Christendom to-day!

In his large love for the dumb things this Hindu Ideal Redeemer is greater, and stoops lower than the would-be Saviour of human beings alone, and only the Jewish part of them, who is portrayed as the Canonical Christ. But *cui bono?* when it is only an Ideal and that Ideal takes the place of possible reality. These false Ideals are forever fatal to human verity. What has the worship of Mary ever done for woman in the character of wife? You cannot live by a Lay figure. When once we know it to be unreal, whether as the Christ, or Buddha, or Madonna, it becomes a type that we cannot print from any longer, because it fails to impress deeply enough.

Whether considered as the God made human, or as man made divine, this character never existed as a person. That pre-historic Ideal Christ of the Gnosis had always personated the divine in human form, the Immortal incarnated, the Majesty within superior to all the physical conditions without, with power to bear and serve, to serenely suffer the ills of flesh, become a sacrifice and glory in the Cross of its earthly suffering.

Spiritual mediums were considered to be a kind of intermediate beings, because they first demonstrated the existence of a living link betwixt the divine mind and matter in the human form. But the original intermediate being was the spiritual nature itself, called the Son of God, the Christ within, which constituted that living link in whomsoever it existed. No human medium could become the Christ of the Gnosis, who represented a principle which could only become a person in a future state of being—never in this world. So was it before the history alleged to have been lived, and so the fact remains to-day, and for ever. The historical was an impossible mode of realising that which could only be a spiritual possibility; and thus the truth according to the Gnosis has been refracted in the falsehood according to the History.

The Gnostic Christ was the real founder of Christianity! This was the Christ of the first Christians, and this was their model man, the Ideal meek and lowly one, which the writers of the Gospels have sought to realise in the form of historic personality. This lunar, solar, mystical, or spiritual type could not be made historical in the creed of those who knew, *i.e.*, the Gnostics. But it was humanized; it was turned into a one person, who became the one Christ in this world, and the one spirit of all others, for those who did not know. For the earliest appeal of the new faith was made to men who were so ignorant, according to the record, that when they had just witnessed a rising from the dead of certain historic characters, they did not comprehend what this rising again from the dead should mean!

Historic Christianity has retained possession of a dead Christ, the mere husk of the grub, together with a vague belief in the butterfly; and if you, likewise, believe in its one dead grub, you may cultivate the hope of some day, also, becoming a butterfly. But, for the Gnostics, the transformation from the chrysalis condition of matter to the spiritual was a natural fact of which they had an ever-present vitalising consciousness. They were transforming and seeking attainment all their life through; and their Christ was the representative type of that transformation of the mortal into an immortal.

Historic Christianity abolished the Gnostic spiritualism for all who accepted the false belief! Henceforth there was but one spirit, that of the historic Bringer of Immortality to Light; and, if any apparition appeared to the abnormal or normal vision, it would be the historic Christ for ever after! It was so with the vision of Paul, which was reported and perverted in the Book of Acts. When his inner eyes were opened he saw spirits—as Swedenborg and many others are reported to have done—whereupon they avowed he had seen the risen Jesus, their only witness for a spirit-world! So has it been with the non-Spiritualists ever since, for whom an apparition must be the Christ. In an island near Rotterdam, says Renan, the peasants believe that Christ comes to the bed of death to assure the elect of their justification. In point of fact many see him! On the other hand, the Buddhist "Lotus" declares that thousands of Buddhas show their faces to the virtuous man at the moment of his decease, which proves the Buddhas to be spirits. So has it been with the ecstatics and mediums in all the religious sects. Whenever they saw a spirit they saw Jesus the Christ their Saviour, because they knew of no other spirit or name—the history being established for the other world as well as in this—and so one delusion was bound to support the other; the true vision was made untrue; and all the facts of spiritualism have been falsified and turned into lying witnesses, to substantiate the truth of the Gospel history. All such manifestations as had previously occurred and had been attributed to the spirits of the departed, were now ascribed to the power of Christ, in whose name the prophesying was performed, the healing effected, and the mental medicine dispensed. Henceforth there was to be no other name under heaven but this. In this name only were the Gentiles to have hope. Redemption was made dependent on this name; cripples were cured, the blind made to see, devils were cast out, the dead raised, sins remitted, souls saved, and eternal life ensured by belief on this name supposed to be New. At the mention of this name the dead arose up out of their graves, and, according to the testimony of Irenæus, they survived amongst the living many years! So much more potent was faith than fact. The earlier spiritualism was founded upon facts in nature, which did not need the desperate expedient of a miracle to explain. But in the later cult the more the miracle the larger loomed the supernatural, and the broader were the foundations for the belief that was based on faith instead of facts, and on Materialism plus Miracle.

They accounted for the spiritual phenomena of the Gnostics by declaring, as Justin Martyr did, that when the devil and the demons knew that Christ was believed on, and that he was expected "in every race," they put forth Simon, Menander, and the other Gnostics to deceive the multitude with magic. Because Spiritualism was naturally and for ever at war with the historical misinterpretation, Justin asserts that after the ascension of Christ into Heaven, the demons put forward certain men like Simon to declare that they were the Gods. Whereas, historic Christianity proclaimed them to be devils; and devils they have remained ever since, according to the false belief.

The founders of the Catholic Church were the de-Spiritualizers of primitive Christianity, and the destroyers of the Gnostic religion as such, by placing their ban upon all Spiritualistic phenomena! The foundations of the ancient cult were to be built upon no longer.

In the recently discovered Didaché or the "Teaching of the Apostles," the facts of Spiritualism are admitted, and the practices of the prophets are recognized. They are spoken of as "ordering a table in the spirit," and of "assembling together for a Cosmic mystery." But those are the true mediums alone who have the "manners of the Lord;" and the law as laid down in these Didaché is:—"Thou shalt not play the mage! Thou shalt not practise witchcraft"—or spirit-intercourse. No prophet that speaks as one of the possessed is to be tried or tolerated. "Every sin shall be forgiven, but this sin shall not be forgiven." It was now and henceforth to be Spiritualism without spirits, abstract and ideal, not tangible or real, an article of faith versus fact. We see from the Epistle of John how mortally afraid of Gnostic Spiritualism were the founders of the historical fraud. "Many deceivers are gone forth into the world that confess not that Jesus Christ cometh in the flesh." These words of John state the Gnostic position. Their Christ had not so come, and could not be carnalized. These Gnostics were in the world long before they heard of such a doctrine; but when they did they denied and opposed it. This, says

John, is the anti-Christ. But, "every spirit which confesseth that Jesus Christ is come in the flesh is of God; and every spirit which annulleth Jesus is not of God. And this is the spirit of the anti-Christ whereof ye have heard that it cometh, and now it is in the world already."

A story is told of two early English saints, one of whom was supposed to have died. They were about to bury him, when, as he was being lowered into the grave, face upward and uncovered, he opened wide his ghostly staring eyes and told them he had only fallen into a trance. He had been into the other world, and found that what they were preaching about it in this was not true. There was no "Fall of Man," he said. "There is no hell," he cried; "no personal Christ—no Redeemer." But here his fellow-saint outside the grave interposed— "For God's sake fill in the earth and stop the blasphemer's mouth!" They did so, and the rest of his revelation remained unknown. That was how the Catholic Christians dealt with the Gnostic Spiritualists when they had the power. They would shut up the living mouth of the Spirit-world, because the reports from the other side were fatal to the Historic fiction. They broke down the bridge between the two worlds, and proclaimed a great gulf fixed forever, which could only be crossed by faith in the Historic Jesus. Here the movement of Historic Christianity was a direct and deliberate shunting of the human mind from off the main line, the highway of its natural development, and running it head first into all sorts of bye-ways and blind alleys, from which we have had to turn back and grope out again as best we could for any progress to be made.

Historic Christianity originated with turning the Gnostic and Esoteric teachings inside out and externalising the mythical allegory in a personal human history. All that was interior with the knowers was made objective; all that was spiritual in significance was embodied to be made palpable for the ignorant. A corporeal Christ was substituted for the trans-corporeal man—a Christ whose advent was without, instead of the one that must be evolved within—a personal Saviour who died for all, instead of the Christ that was the living Spirit working within all. It was remarked by Augustine (de Civ. Dei, 7, 24) that the Gnostics "promised eternal life to anybody"—that is, with them the soul of man was an eternal principle, and the resurrection was not cunningly reserved for the elect who accepted the Historic belief. The Gnostic claimed to be illuminated by the presence of the Christ within; the Christian, according to Justin, by the name of the Christ without. And a very curious mental link of connection between the genuine Gnostic and the counterfeit Historic Christ is apparent in the Ignatian Epistle to the Smyrneans. The writer says—"I know that even after his resurrection he was in the flesh, and I believe that he is so still." Now this combines both, after a fashion.

The writer is seeking to establish the history against those who denied that the Christ could be made a man. In doing this, he has recourse to the Gnostic Christ, who always was in the flesh, or matter, as the salt of soul, and the only spiritual Saviour from death and dissolution. Speaking from his Gnostic standpoint, Paul declared to the historic Christians who followed John and Peter, that God had sent them a working of error, that they should believe a lie, because they rejected the truth as it was according to his spiritual Gospel! The lie was established by externalising the Christ that can only dwell within—by successfully falsifying for a time that truth which is true for ever. In this way, you see, that the coming of the Holy Spirit, which always had been within, was henceforth to be without. Thus, the descent of the Holy Ghost upon Jesus, in Jordan, is an external transaction. The Holy Spirit that comes from heaven in the form of a dove—a Gnostic type of the Spirit; that is, of both sexes—or, later on, as a whirlwind, in which the Gust and Ghost are one. In the course of this conversion of the inner to the outer, we are told that the Holy Ghost, which always had been extant with the Gnostics, was not yet given, because the Historical Jesus was not yet glorified; but after he had risen from the grave, and returned bodily to the disciples, he breathed upon them, and said, "Receive ye the Holy Ghost." And again: the Holy Ghost, as an external effusion, could not be given until after forty days; whereas, in the Essenic Mysteries, the body of the disciple became the temple of the Holy Ghost when he had reached the sixth stage of interior progress. This shows the literalisers of the legend, the rationalisers of the mythos, the anti-mystics, the Exoterists, externalising the Gnosis, and converting the matter of it into human history. There was to be neither Spirit within nor Spirit-world without for the ignorant Christians, until the resurrection and ascension of Jesus had historically established both.

Two distinct charges are brought against the Carnalizers by Tatian in the second century. He cries out shame upon the Catholic Church, and exclaims, "You have given the Nazarite wine to drink, and commanded the prophets, saying, 'Prophesy not.'" They were debauching the Christian community and destroying the primitive Nazarite purity which Tertullian claimed for the Christians when he said, "We are they of whom it is written, 'Their Nazarites are whiter than snow.'" Next, they have determined to put an end to practical spiritualism on behalf of the new faith; and this is treated by Tatian as part of a subtle scheme for destroying the purity and spirituality of that Christianity which was primitive and non-historic, too!

The transformations of the Pagan cult into the Christian, and of the Gnostic into the historical representation, were effected behind the veil identifiable as the "Discipline of the Secret," the strictness of which was only relaxed after the fourth century, when the Truth had been hidden in a fog of falsehood; the inner mysteries turned to an outer mist, that made confusion cunningly complete.

The Gnostic Spiritualism was declared illegal and impious. The objective realities of the phenomenal Spiritualists, which had heretofore furnished the one bit of foothold in natural fact for a belief in the future life, were now discarded on behalf of the more subjective idealities derived from a faith that was founded by means of a fraudulent history mis-translated from a mystical fable.

The Roman Church adopted the Angels and Archangels of the Celestial Allegory as its Saints, including Saint Bacchus and Saint Satan in place of Guardian Spirits that were once human beings.

A dogma of the Real Presence of the Historic Christ was now substituted for the Real Presence of Spirit Friends in the earlier communion.

The mysteries in which the early Christian Neophytes had been initiated into a lawful communion with the dead were gradually suppressed; and in the sixth century we find the doctrine of a communion with the saints was substituted for the practical intercourse with spirits. It happens that the time when the doctrine was inserted in the Creed coincides almost exactly with the suppression of the mysteries which were connected with the so-called Agapæ of the early Christians! The Agapæ were only a continuation of the ancient Pagan funeral feasts and Eucharistic rites in honour of the departed. Hence they were held in the cemeteries and catacombs in presence of the dead, where the mummy-type or the Karest was the Christ, as the image of rising again; the image that was carried round and pointed to as a cause for festive rejoicing at the Egyptian feast! In this way we can watch the false faith taking the place of the facts. And as the Gnostic sects and brotherhoods gave up the ghost, Historic Christianity assumed their glory. In this strange scene of transformation and dramatic illusion by some Satanic sleight of hand and turn of head, the afterglow of the ancient religions was changed into the dawn of the superseding faith, which was then proclaimed to be the fountain-head of all future enlightenment! or rather the waning light of ancient knowledge has been mistaken for the dawning of the New Belief; a dawn that was followed by the grey twilight that deepened into the thousand-years-long intellectual night of the Dark Ages.

It matters not what may be the relative share of responsibility attributable to knavery on the one hand and ignorance on the other, the fact remains that a huge and hideous mistake has been made, an irretrievable error committed in the name of Historic Christianity. For ages past the false faith did feed the flames of martyrdom with the fires of hell on pretext of giving light to them that it had covered with its smoke of torment and pall of darkness. And now the sun of a better day has arisen to put out the fires infernal, to disperse the clouds of human sighs, that have obscured the heavens so long, and to aid in drying the tears from our afflicted earth at last. Revelation, by means of Evolution, has now made known for ever that the fall of man was not historic fact. Humanity has not to bear the penalty eternally for a divine failure in the beginning of time. This world is not a prison-house of fallen beings. Consequently, the promised redemption and proffered mode of salvation are a vain delusion, and all in vain has the spirit of the living Christ within been compelled to drag the dead body of the corporeal Christ from the grave for the purpose of proving the history for the ignorant, until its corruption is a sickening stench in the nostrils of the nations, and there is a clamour for the burial that shall get rid of both together. The history of Christ as our impersonated Saviour on earth, equally with the story of Adam's fall from Eden, is mythology misbelieved. The Old Testament was read backwards to be re-written as the New. The only original elements in this interpolation between the ancient Gnosis and modern science are those that prove false to the governing laws of the universe, and those facts of nature which make the sole true revelation. Theory avails nothing in the presence of the fact that Historic Christianity was founded on the "Resurrection of the Flesh," and that it has left the world where it was itself, after putting out the Gnostic Light, all in the dark concerning our spiritual continuity in death! Canon Gregory said only the other day if Jesus did not rise corporeally from the tomb, then that tomb must be the grave of Christianity. And the "Spectator" for August 13, 1887, speaking of the Greeks who died before the Resurrection was thus historically established, says:—"In the nature of things the Greeks could have had no sure hope of a glorious resurrection." Such was and is, when honestly confessed, the genuine Christian creed. It does seem to me as if those arch-forgers in Rome had subtly succeeded in converting that which was true in the old religion into a secret support for all that was false in the new. Gnostic Christianity was absolutely, fundamentally, and for ever opposed to the historic rendering, and yet the Gnostic doctrines of the fourth Gospel, and of Paul's and James' Epistles, have been allowed to remain under cover and control as spiritual forces artfully tethered to draw for the physical and anti-Gnostic Faith. I am sometimes compelled to say to myself it has been most devilishly done!—and so have we!

We have Spiritualists to-day who lay hold of the Scriptures, or can be laid hold of, by means of the Gnosis that remains there as a lure, and turn it to the account intended, that is, as a decoy towards accepting the history. And so when the risen Christ reappears in the actual body that is missing from the grave, they are prepared to explain away the physical fact by means of the spiritual Gnosis. In that way nothing is bottomed, and nothing can be really understood; but,—the purpose of the promoters, who were the founders of the falsehood, and who founded it well-nigh unfathomably,—their purpose continues to be fulfilled.

In writing to a Christian spiritualist the other day, I said, "I know no better way of waging the battle for Truth than arraying the facts face to face on either side and letting them fight it out." His reply was, "I do not believe in your facts because I do not know." Now, that is good firm ground to stand upon, however late in life we take the position. But, to be of any real service, we must apply the same reason all round! As an adherent of Historic Christianity, that writer has all along been a Believer in what he did not know to be facts; and a believer just because he did not know; and now he finds it too late, perhaps, to correct his early belief by means of later knowledge! All I ask is that people shall no longer believe because they do not know. No matter what they may call themselves—they are traitors to the Truth who will not face the facts or examine for themselves, but will go on repeating ignorantly, or in pious pig-headedness, the orthodox assumptions, and applying the hypotheses of accommodation to the Christian documents. You might as well expect to reach the next world by going round and round this, as to think of making ends meet by unifying the Gnostic religion with Historic Christianity. Phenomenal Spiritualists who go on philandering with the fallacies of the Christian faith, and want to make out that it is identical with Modern Spiritualism, have at last to face the great, indubitable fact that Historic Christianity was established as a non-Spiritualist and an anti-Spiritualistic religion! Its primary fact, its initial point of departure, its first bit of foothold for a new departure, was the acknowledgment of the physical resurrection of the dead Historic Christ. It is useless to try to wriggle out of that. The reappearance of the Corpus Christi is the fundamental fact of the Faith! The strings are pulled so that the Marionette Messiah may be forced to exclaim that he is not a bodiless ghost; not a boneless phantom; not a spirit anyway; and he offers the proof palpable that he is none of your Spiritualistic or Gnostic Christs, or the spirit of anybody! Moreover, this is the veritable dead body that is missing from the tomb! And still further, the passage in Luke has been altered from Marcion's "Gospel of the Lord" on purpose to substitute the Corporeal Christ of Historic Christianity for the Spiritual representation of the Gnostics. In Marcion's version the word *phantasma* is used, and this has not only been omitted by Luke; the phantom is made to protest very emphatically that he is not in anywise phantasmal, but is a being of flesh and blood even as they are; and after demonstrating the fact, clinches it by asking if they have got anything there for him to eat! The entire fabric of the new faith rested upon the reality of a physical resurrection; and it is too late now to shift the basis of the edifice by trying to lift it bodily, like the city of Chicago, on to the higher and surer ground of Spiritualism, so as to find a firmer basis for it and all its weight of errors! We can trace the very bifurcation and fresh starting-point of the new faith in the account given of the resurrection in the Canonical Gospels. They proclaimed the resurrection of the dead in Jesus and through him only! The historic Jesus who alone had power to open the gateways of the grave, and who had personally left with Peter the keys that lock up heaven and open hell. There was nothing to constitute a new faith in a spiritual resurrection. That was already the common property of the Gnostics, whether called Pagans or Christians. That was according to the natural fact, and here only was the miracle, in the dead body rising again to prove the presence and the power of the divinity. Such is the religious foundation, for which the Christians are responsible Trustees!

As a Spiritualist, then, I assert that the new Christian dispensation was founded upon the death and burial of the ancient spiritualism; or upon the gagging of it and getting it underground dead or alive! And the tomb out of which a corporeal Christ was believed to have emerged as the Saviour of the World, and brought immortality to light by a physical resurrection from the dead, has been the burial-place of genuine Spiritualism for 1800 years. For this reason the defenders of the faith were bound to make war upon the facts of phenomenal spiritualism, and persecute and put the psychical demonstrators to death, which they did with a consuming fury so long as they were allowed.

The terrible craze that was caused by this perversion of the ancient wisdom has sown the germs of insanity broadcast, and half-filled the world with pious lunatics for whom it offers no cure, and who are still told to look forward for an asylum in the world to come. But such pernicious teaching will make people as insane for another life as for this! Here, or hereafter, falsehood must be fraudulent, though it may be found out too late! What of the myriads of suffering souls who have been forced to wear the blinkers of ignorance all through this life for fear they should learn to see for themselves—who were drugged and deceived from birth till death with the nostrums of a false deluding faith. What of them when they awake from their stupor in death to find out that they have been foully, cruelly hocussed with a creed that was an illusion for this life and a delusion for the next.

   Delusion that is perfectly complete
   For those who die to find out the deceit!

If the teachers of the fleshly cult could but see *how* their fallacies dissolve in death—how the false ideal set up in this life dislimns and fades as the terrible light of reality whitens in the next; if they could but see that mournful multitude of the helplessly deceived who staked their all upon the truth of what they had been taught and find they have lost because the teaching was false! If you could see them wander up and down on the other side of the dark river and wring their hands over their blighted hopes and broken hearts; hear the pitiful wailings for the Christ that is no more objective there than he was here—for the visionary glory that they may not grasp, the distant rainbows, never reached, that weep themselves away in tears—for the lifeboat gone to wreck on the wrong shore because of the false beacon-lights. If you could only dream how these poor souls desire to have the deception made known on this side of life—how they want to send some word of warning to their friends—how they will almost hiss at me through the mouths of mediums whenever they have the chance, as if their fierce feelings had turned into tongues of flame, praying for us to work on faster and cry louder against the established lie, for time is getting short and the helpers are few, and the atmosphere around each live soul is so deathly dense with indifference! This would be unbearable but for those calm other voices of the Gnostics who in this life walked our world lords of themselves with "inward glory crowned," and who lived on after the Gnosis was suppressed and the ancient oracles made dumb—who live on yet, and are working with us still—who fill and inflate us at times with their influence, as if each single soul of us were a hundred thousand ("*cent mille*," as his men used to call Napoleon). It is they who are joining hands with us to-day to bridge over that dark gulf betwixt two worlds which the historic and fleshly faith first excavated, and has been deepening and widening now for eighteen centuries.

This is the Resurrection Day of the pre-Christian Gnosticism, as shown by the recent revival of Spiritualism, by the restoration of the Tree of Knowledge, by the elevation of Womankind, instead of the Fall of man; and we are living witnesses of the fact that

> "Truth, crushed to earth, *shall* rise again,
> The eternal years of God are hers;
> But Error, wounded, writhes with pain,
> And dies among his worshippers!'"

NOTE.

I HAVE been asked whether I am able to explain by means of the Egyptian Mythos, the two diverse statements in the Gospel according to Luke and the Book of Acts concerning the ascension of Jesus into Heaven. In Luke the risen Christ is "carried up into Heaven" on the third day following the crucifixion. In the Acts he is not "taken up" into Heaven until the fortieth day, or after forty days! Such serious discrepancies as these are forever irreconcilable as history, but they are found to contain the very facts that reconstitute the Mythos.

The resurrection of Osiris at the Autumn equinox was lunar; at the vernal equinox it was solar. After he was betrayed to his death, when the sun was in the sign of Scorpio, he rose again on the third day as Lord of Light in the moon, or as Horus, the child of the mother-moon. The solar resurrection was at the vernal equinox when the sun entered the first of the upper signs and Orion rose. This time it was in the character of the second Horus, the adult of 30 years; and this second resurrection followed the forty days of mourning for the suffering God which were celebrated in the Mysteries, and survive in a Christianized form as our Lent. And just as the myth of the double Horus in the two characters of the child of 12 years, and the adult Horus of 30 years, has been continued in the Gospels to furnish the two phases in the life of Jesus, so have the two different resurrections with their correct dates been applied to the Christ made historical.

Thus interpreted by means of the Mythos these two versions of one alleged fact tend to corroborate my explanation already made that the two different dates for the crucifixion given in the otherwise irreconcilable accounts belong to the luni-solar reckoning in the same luni-solar myth. In Egyptian the signs of a half-moon and fourteen days are identical; and in the dark half of the moon Osiris was torn into fourteen parts. Therefore the 14th of the lunar month was the day of full moon. Whereas in the soli-lunar month of thirty days the 15th was the middle of the month. Now the crucifixion or the crossing at Easter was and still is determined by the day of full moon. This will be on the 14th of the month of twenty-eight days in the reckoning by the moon only, but on the 15th of the month according to the soli-lunar reckoning. The 14th of the month would be the lunar reckoning of Anup=John, and the 15th that of Taht-Mati=Mathew in the two forms of the Egyptian Mythos. Both reckonings were extant in two different cults and both were separately continued by the Eastern and Western Churches for the one day of the crucifixion. Both cannot be historically correct, but they *are* both astronomically true. Both could be made to meet at a given point in the total combination which was determined by the conjunction of the sun and moon at the equinox as *the* day of full moon. But the two different dates for the mid-month remained, and these are represented by the traditions of two different dates for the crucifixion. Both the lunar and the solar dates could be utilised by the Mythos, in which there were two crucifixions and two resurrections, though these will not bear witness for the single fact of the historical crucifixion. As we have seen, the two ascensions of Osiris on the third day and at the end of forty days, have been preserved, and are repeated as historical transactions. Two different Crosses were also continued in the Christian Iconography as the cross of Autumn and of Easter; and although we may not be able to show two crucifixions in the Canonical Gospels, nevertheless the total matter of the Mythos is there. When Jesus was led up into the wilderness to be tempted of the devil, and to suffer during forty days, we have the parallel to the struggle between Osiris and Sut, which was celebrated during the forty days of mourning in the mysteries. Moreover, there were two days of death or crucifixion kept in Rome until the present century, when the dead Christ used to be laid out and exhibited on the Thursday before Good Friday; and two days of resurrection were also celebrated in the two Sabbaths on Saturday and Sunday. As the Apostolic Constitutions show, both of these days were continued for the two weekly holidays of the Christians, Saturday being the day of rising again on the 7th day of the week in the lunar cult; Sunday, the Sabbath of the 8th day, according to the solar resurrection. Such are the fundamental facts; and, to my thinking, they are of sufficient force to cleave the Canonical history right in two, each half being then claimed by the Mythos. Here, as elsewhere, the Mythos does explain the fact, but only by abolishing the history. From beginning to end the ascertainable facts are astronomical, and interpretable solely by means of the Gnostic explanation of the Egyptian Mythos, which always denied, because it disproved, the alleged human history.

The same correspondent desires to know whether I would exclude the Bible from our children's schools. Most certainly. I would have the Bible-basis superseded for all future teaching as unscientific, immoral, and false to the facts in nature. The mass of people who are Bible-taught never get free from the erroneous impressions stamped on their minds in their infancy, so that their manhood or womanhood can have no intellectual fulfilment, and millions of them only attain mentally to a sort of second childhood.

THE
HEBREW AND OTHER CREATIONS
FUNDAMENTALLY EXPLAINED.

"*If you would correct my false view of facts,*" says Emerson, "*hold up to me the same facts in the true order of thought.*"

That is the process attempted in these lectures of mine; and the true order and sequence of the facts can only be ascertained by delving down to the foundations in the physical genesis; can only be stated by means of the evolutionary method; can only be proved by the Wisdom of Egypt. I claim that on each line of research my interpretation is derived from the facts themselves, and is *not* arbitrarily imposed upon them, or read into them by my own theoretic speculation. I do but flesh the skeleton of facts.

It is *not* the ancient legends that tell us lies! The men who created them did not deal falsely by us or by nature. All the falsity lies in their having been falsified through ignorantly mistaking mythology for divine revelation and allegory for historic truth. Geology was not taught among the mysteries of ancient knowledge, floating fragments of which have drifted down to us in the Book of Genesis. The Christian world assumed that it was—or, at least, some sort of globe-making—and therefore it was found to be entirely opposed to scientific geology.

Mythology never did inculcate the historic fall of man. Theologists have ignorantly supposed that it did, and as a result they were bitterly opposed to the ascent of man, made known by means of evolution!

Such doctrines as the Fall of Man, the failure of God, and all that bankrupt business in the commencement of creation, the consequent genesis of evil and original sin, the depravity of matter, the filthy nature of the flesh, have no other basis or beginning than in the perversion of ancient typology, and the literalisation of mythology.

According to the Hebrew Genesis the first man was born without a mother or a female of any kind. If that be fact according to revelation, it cannot be according to nature! But there is nothing gained by calling it "*Revelation.*" By doing so "Revelation" has come to be a name applied to anything which we may not, for the time being, understand. "Revelation" has come to mean a series of confounding lies, warranted by God to be true! By making this a revelation direct from deity you destroy the character of the divine intelligence, which did not know the facts, processes, or order, of its own works; or, if it did, it must have palmed off a lying version on the medium of communication to the world as a divine revelation made to man!

But Adam never denoted a first man who was produced witnout a mother, nor Eve a first woman formed from an actual rib of Adam. That is but the literalisation of a symbolical mode of representation, the key to which has been *long mislaid*.

Speaking of the matter found in the Pentateuch, Philo, the learned Jew, told his countrymen the truth when he said: "*The literal statement is a fabulous one, and it is in the mythical we shall find the true.*" On the other hand, he asserts of the myths found in the Hebrew form: "These things are not mere fabulous inventions, in which the race of poets and sophists delight, but are types shadowing forth an allegorical truth according to some mystical explanation;" not a history. The literal version *is* the false; and it *is* in the mythical that we shall find the true, but only when it is truly interpreted. Mythology is not to be understood by literalisation, *even though the Christian creed has been founded on that fatal method!* It is not to be made *real* by modern rationalising, though that is the basis of Unitarianism; nor is it to be utilised by each one furnishing their own system of Hermeneutical interpretation. Mythology is an ancient system of knowledge, with its own mode of expression, which enshrined the science of the past in what looks to us at times like foolish and unmeaning fables. It is entirely useless to speculate on such a subject, or try to read one's own interpretation into the myths, with no clue whatever to their primordial meaning. Anybody can make an allegory go on all-fours, and read some sort of history into a myth. And, of course, he that hides can find; if you put your own meaning into what you read, you can discover it there. You may *say* it *is* so; any one can *say*, and possibly get a few others to hearken and believe, but no amount of mere assertion will establish the truth by means of a false interpretation of the fable. Some persons will tell us that if the "Fall of Man" be not a fact once for all, better still, it is true for ever, because men and women are always falling; therefore the allegory is over true, and, in point of fact, a divine revelation. I have heard preachers resolve the nocturnal wrestling-match between Jacob and the angel into an exquisite allegory, made to run on all-fours for very simple people to ride on, an allegory full of light and leading, and lovely in its moral and spiritual significance, for sorely tempted men. The night of the struggle is made internal. The angel is transformed into the devil, and we have the wrestle of the soul with the tempter, and a man on his knees all night in prayer. It is the conflict of Christian and Apollyon humanised, and fought out in a bedroom, in place of the dark valley of the shadow of death. It is in this wise that such stories are to be saved from absurdity, orthodoxy is to regain its lost supremacy, and science and religion are to be reconciled for ever. But *there is no truth in it all.* The history was *not* human at first, and this subjective mode of treatment does but re-face it with another sort of falsehood. If we would ascertain what these old stories originally meant we must go to mythology. In this case the Hottentots can enlighten us. They have a myth or fable of Tsuni-Goam and Gaunab, the twins, who personate the presence of light and darkness, the powers of good and evil. These two contend in mortal conflict night after night, the good one getting the better of the bad one by degrees, and growing stronger with every battle fought. At last Tsuni-Goam grew mighty enough to give his enemy a blow at the back of his ear, which put an end to Gaunab. But just as he was expiring and falling back into his own abyss of darkness, Gaunab gave his opponent a blow in the hollow of his leg, that made him go limping for life. In consequence he was called " Tsuni-Goam," the meaning of which name is " wounded knee." The struggle was that of light and darkness in the orb of the moon, or the sun of night fighting his way through the valley of the shadow of death in the underworld, during the winter, when his movement was slower; and he was represented as being lame in one knee, or maimed in his lower member. A wounded knee with a knife thrust through it is the Egyptian hieroglyphic sign for being overcome. Hence, although he conquers the powers of darkness, Tsuni-Goam is said to have been wounded in one knee. The myth is found in many lands, and is identical with that of Jacob wrestling all night with the power called an angel, who maimed him in the hollow of his thigh, and made him a form of the "wounded knee."

Also, it is worse than useless, because misleading, to begin by applying a modern mystical system of subjective interpretation to the fragments of ancient wisdom found in the Hebrew Book of Genesis, after the manner of Swedenborg. According to him the account of the Creation in Genesis is not a real history, but a narrative written in the style of the Ancient Churches, signifying spiritual and divine things.

The general subject of the first chapter is not the generation, but the regeneration, of man! In his version the old first creation becomes the new creation; the genesis becomes the re-genesis; the perverted mythos is an intentional spiritual allegory; the six days are six states in the re-creation of man; the seventh day represents the celestial man, and he is the garden of Eden, and also the most ancient Church! Adam's nakedness denotes the purity of the internal man, or the state of innocence of the celestial Church! Eve also signifies the Church. Cain is the name of those who falsified the doctrine of the most ancient Church. The serpent going on its belly denotes the grovelling of the sensual principle seeking after corporeal things. The flood or deluge was a total immersion of mankind in evil and falsehood! Everything in the Word relates to the heavenly and spiritual, and is falsified if transferred to a lower level. *But* spiritual significations are not *primary!* The natural or physical must come first, because they were first; the eschatological is last. Man was no more *re*-made than he was made on the sixth day. Swedenborg knows or acknowledges nothing of the origin in natural phenomena; nothing of the true mythical mode of representation; nothing of an astronomical basis for the Garden of Eden, the tree of knowledge, the serpent, or the primal pair, whose figures are pourtrayed and whose story can still be read as it was first written in the stars of heaven! The imagery and types of mythology can, of course, be used as a mode of expression for later ideas, and for moral or spiritual significations,—just as we continue to say the moon rises, or the sun sets, after we know better; but, from the mundane standpoint, the natural, the physical, the external alone were primal. Hence primitive Mythology is no more moral or immoral than it is obscene, senseless, or insane, simply because the *phenomena were not human*. Before the Egyptian hieroglyphics were understood Swedenborg undertook to vouch for the fact that they represented spiritual ideas by means of natural objects, according to his own doctrine of correspondences; which is no more true than his interpretation of the Hebrew Genesis. This can be proved. The hieroglyphics began as direct object-pictures, which became symbolical in a later phase. The three Water-Signs of the Zodiac do not represent a spiritual experience in this "Vale of Tears," but the three months' Inundation which is annual in the Valley of the Nile. The fact is that we cannot translate the thought of primitive or pre-historic men without first learning the language in which it was expressed. The wisdom, or gnosis, so carefully hidden and jealously guarded in the past, is *not* to be recovered with any certitude by clairvoyant insight or intuitional memory, whosoever sets up the claim! You may have the vision to see the hidden treasure lying buried at the bottom of the ocean, but you will not be able to bring it back to men by merely dredging for it in your dreams. There were Illuminati in the mysteries of old, but they did not trust to the intuitional faculty for that information, which took them seven or ten years to acquire. They were no mere *self*-illuminati! They knew that intuition could not take the place of research, and were careful to communicate all the exact knowledge they possessed to those whom they instructed. "*Add to your faith knowledge,*" is the counsel of Paul. In vain we read our own thought into the primitive types of expression, and then say the ancients meant *that!* Subtilised interpretation will not read the riddle to the root. Nor did such things originate in riddles or intentional enigmas. You may believe me when I affirm, and you can prove it for yourselves, that mythology was a primitive method of teaching natural facts, and not an esoteric mode of misinterpreting them!

What we need to know is the primary meaning of the myth-makers; and this can only be recovered by collecting and comparing all the extant versions of the original mythos.

There is no beginning with the mystical or metaphysical in the past before we have mastered the mythical; that can only lead to a maze, or to being lost in a mist of mystification, as soon as we are out of the wood of literalisation!

Cardinal Baronius has said that the intention of Holy Scripture is to teach us how to go to heaven, and not how the heavens go! But the earliest Scripture *did* teach *how* the heavens go, and it became sacred because it was celestial.

The first creation of heaven and earth was but the division into upper and lower, by whatsoever means expressed, answering to the discreting of light from darkness. This was also rendered by the dividing of an Egg or Calabash, and by the cutting of the heaven, the Cow of Heaven, or the Heifer of the Morning and Evening Star, in two. It was neither earth-making nor heaven-making in any cosmical sense—nothing more than distinguishing the light from the darkness; the vault above from the void below. This is illustrated by the creation-legend found on the Assyrian tablets, which commences—"At that time the Heaven above had not announced, nor the Earth beneath recorded, a name." The *word* first uttered in heaven related to times and seasons, and the earliest *word* was uttered by the appointed time-keepers! The account of creation given in the second chapter of Genesis is that "these are the generations of the heaven and the earth when they were created." And the generations of the heaven *were* astronomical!

We learn from the cuneiform legends of creation how in the beginning God created the heavens:—" Bel prepared the Seven Mansions of the Gods. He fixed the Stars, even the Twin Stars, to correspond to them; he ordained the year, appointing the Signs of the Zodiac over it. He illuminated the Moon-God that he might watch over the night" (Sayce). (This version, however, is comparatively late, because the fatherhood had then been founded!)

Then, as Hermes says in the Divine Pymander, the heaven was seen in seven circles, and the gods were visible in the stars with all their signs, and the stars were numbered with the gods in them, the gods being seven in number; when the old Genetrix is excluded.

From the first, our theology, based on the Old Testament records, has never been anything else than a dead branch of the ancient mythology; and just when all men, free to think, were finding out this fact, Mr. Gladstone came forward and made another effort to rehabilitate the old book so generally discredited, and chivalrously led one more forlorn hope for a cause that is hopelessly lost. Surely no Christian martyr of an earlier time could have made a more pathetic or pitiable appeal to human sympathies than this man of intellect,—who is so much larger than his creed,—holding on to his pious opinion in the face of facts the most fatal to his faith. For, with the literal interpretation of the book of Genesis, the Fall of Man remains a historic transaction, and the ascent made known by evolution is a stupendous delusion. It is a sad sight to see a man like Mr. Gladstone, who by his position and powers can attract a world's attention to his words, cheerfully content to become a leader in misleading; still fondly believing that the creations in the book of Genesis contain a veritable history that could not have been written unless it had been divinely inspired; still trying to make out that it is in accordance with geology, and the scientific interpretation of nature. In his case the child is not only father to the man, but a terrible tyrant over him as well.

Mr. Gladstone still maintains the opinion that the man who wrote the account of the creations in Genesis was "gifted with faculties passing all human experience, or else his knowledge was divine." The order of development presented, he says, is first the water population; second, the air population; third, the land population of animals; and fourth, the land population consummated in man. And Mr. Gladstone says this same four-fold order is understood to have been so affirmed in our time by natural science, that it may be taken as a demonstrated conclusion and established fact. The reply of science is a point-blank denial. It admits nothing of the kind. It knows better. This is *not* the order in which the various populations made their first appearance on the globe; and it was only by classing these populations according to the notion of distinct creations, which were produced at the rate of one a day or so, that any such definition or distinction could ever have been made. Whatsoever the order of succession, that succession was gradual, with a good deal of parallelism and lapping over on various lines of development. In short, the account is not geological, is not true, when judged by the earth's record itself! Besides, when the ancients placed water before earth, in their series of elements, they had no particular thought whether water or earth was first in existence. They were only concerned with water being *their* first recognised necessary and essential element of life. And if we were teaching our children without any pretence of revelation or assumption of divine knowledge; if we limited ourselves to the natural facts, we should have to point out that the water population as a whole did *not* exist before there was any land population. There was no such thing as a completion of creation No. 1, before the beginning of creation No. 2. No such thing as creation in that sense at all; neither as the act of one day, nor of a million years We know that many forms of life on land preceded various forms which are found in the waters, and that life was proceeding on its special lines of variation in several elements at once. Moreover, though man is the crowning out-come of the animal world, it is not necessary to assume any sudden or complete ending to the animal creation before *he* could appear,—as if *all* lines of descent had to converge and culminate in him! It is very likely that man was earlier than the horse, and almost certain that he was before the dog, as we know that animal. Man had probably put in an appearance as head of his line before various other species had reached the last term of their series. It is certain there never were four or three definite and successive periods of time (and no other) in which three or four distinct populations could have originated. That which is wrong as scientific matter-of-fact cannot be made right as trustworthy matter of faith; not even by the specious dialectic of Mr. Gladstone or any other non-evolutionist. Nor is there any loop-hole of escape in supposing that the day and night of each creation were not intended by the compiler of Genesis to mean a day and night of 24 hours! We are not allowed to wriggle out of that conclusion. The six days might have meant vastly indefinite periods (after we had heard of the geological series and sequence), but for that fatal Seventh Day which completes the week of seven days. The reason why we keep the Sabbath every seventh day is because this was the day of rest for the Lord after his six days' hard labour. "And God blessed the seventh day and hallowed it, because that in it he rested." This was the accepted origin of keeping holy the seventh day every week, and not at the end of æons of time, or six ages. The plain meaning of the compiler is not to be evaded or got away from. The writer of the Hebrew Genesis says positively that all things were made and finished in one week, and for that reason we celebrate the Sabbath day. Seven days in one week are also shown by the dedication of each day to one of the seven planetary gods. And seven days in one week cannot be geological periods any more than they can apply to the subjective experience of the soul!

Mr. Gladstone says the question is "whether natural science in the patient exercise of its high calling to examine facts finds that the works of God cry out against what we have fondly believed to be his work, and tell another tale." The answer is, they *do cry* out, and give the lie to that authority so foolishly supposed to be divine. The Word of God says that the act of Adam brought death into the world. The older record shows, leaf after leaf or stratum beneath stratum, that death had been at work tens of millions of years before man appeared on the earth.

In all these orthodox attempts to rationalise mythology, writers and preachers are dealing with matters which they have not yet understood, and which never can be understood on their plane of thought, or within their narrow limits. In Æsop's fable the wolf overhears the nurse threaten to throw the child to him, and he believes her; but, after long waiting for the fulfilment of prophecy to bring him his supper, he finds that she did not mean what she said. So is it with the myths; they never meant what they said when literally interpreted. And the literalisation of mythology is the fountain-head of all our false belief, mystification being the secondary source. From my point of view, this is merely slaying the slain over again. And yet this literalisation of mythology is continued to be taught as God's truth to the men and women of the future in their ignorant and confiding childhood. And some eight or ten millions of pounds are annually filched from our national revenues for the benefit of a Church and clergy established and legally empowered to make the people believe that these falsified fables are a true divine revelation, received direct from God; and if they doubt and deny it they will be doomed to suffer atrocious tortures through all eternity. Mr. Gladstone says he is persuaded that the belief of Christians and Jews concerning the inspiration of the Book is impregnable. He believes the Genesis to be a revelation for the Christians, made by God to the Jews, such as presents to the rejecter of that belief a problem which demands solution at his hands, and which he has not been able to solve. For himself, Mr. Gladstone is so simple and profound a believer in revelation, if biblical, and in the inspiration of the Mosaic writer in particular, that he is lost in astonishment at the phenomenon it presents to him. He asks, How can these things be, and not overcome us with wonder? How came they to be, "not among Akkadians, or Assyrians, or Egyptians, who monopolised the stores of human knowledge when this wonderful tradition was born, but among the obscure records of a people who, dwelling in Palestine for twelve hundred years from their sojourn in the valley of the Nile, hardly had force to stamp even so much as a name on the history of the world at large, and only then began to be admitted to the general communion of mankind when their scriptures assumed the dress which a Gentile tongue was needed to supply? It is more rational, I contend, to say that these astonishing anticipations were a God-given supply than to think that this race should here have entirely transcended in kind, even more than in degree, all known exercise of human faculties." The answer is, that it does not do to begin with wonder in matters which demand inquiry and research—the answer is, that this matter of the Creations did not originate with the Jewish race at all. Mr. Gladstone's assumption is the sheerest fallacy. The wonderful tradition was *not* born among them! It was wholly and far more perfectly pre-extant amongst the Persians, the Akkadians, and Egyptians. The Book of Genesis is assigned to a man who was learned in all the wisdom of the Egyptians. I cannot answer for the man, but I can for some of the matter. To begin with, the legend of Eden is one of those primeval traditions that must have been the common property of the undivided human race, carried out into all lands as they dispersed in various directions from one centre, which I hold to have been African. As Sharpe, an early English Egyptologist, and a translator of the Hebrew Scriptures, asserts correctly—"The whole history of the fall of man is of Egyptian origin. The temptation of the woman by the serpent, and of man by the woman, the sacred tree of knowledge, the cherubs guarding with flaming swords the door of the garden, the warfare declared between the woman and the serpent, may all be seen upon the Egyptian sculptured monuments."

The French Egyptologist, M. Lefébure, who has lately identified Adam with the Egyptian Atum, as I had done seven years earlier in my Book of Beginnings, refers to a scene on the coffin of Penpii in the Louvre, which is similar to the history of Adam in the terrestrial paradise, where a naked and ithyphallique personage called "the Lord of food" (Neb-tefa), is standing before a serpent with two legs and two arms, and the reptile is offering him a red fruit, or at least a little round object painted red. The same scene is again found on the tomb of Rameses VI. And on a statue relatively recent in the Museum at Turin it is to Atum=Adam that the serpent, as Tempter, is offering the round object, or fruit of the tree !

The same writer says—"The Tree of life and knowledge was well known in Egypt."

And " whether the scene of Neb-tefa can be identified with the history of Adam or not, we can see that the greater number of the peculiar features of this history existed in Egypt—the tree of life and knowledge, the serpent of Paradise, Eve thinking of appropriating divinity to herself, and in short Adam himself, are all there." (Trans. S. Bib. Arch. v. 9, pt. i., p. 180.)

These and other matters pertaining to the astronomical allegory and the natural genesis of mythology were pre-extant in Egypt, and had been carried out over the world untold ages before a Palestinian Jew had ever trod the earth. And yet, incredible as it may sound, Mr. Gladstone has the reckless confidence to declare that the Hebrew account of creation has no Egyptian marks upon it! That would indeed be strange if it had been written by a man who was a master of the wisdom of Egypt.

Mr. Gladstone may have been misled by the Hibbert lecturer, Mr. Renouf, who has said (p. 243), "It may be confidently asserted that neither the Hebrews nor Greeks learned any of their ideas from Egypt." A statement which reveals a congenital deficiency of the comparative faculty. The same may be said of Professor Sayce, when he asserts that "the Theology and the Astronomy of Egypt and Babylonia show no vestiges of a common source."

The Creation of the Woman from the Man in the second chapter of Genesis is likewise found in the Magical Texts, where it is said of the Seven Spirits—"They bring forth the Woman from the Loins of the Man" (Sayce, Hib. Lect. 395).

This also has an Egyptian mark upon it. Such a creation is alluded to in the Book of the Dead, where the speaker says, "I know the mystery of the Woman who was made from the Man." Professor Sayce also asserts that there is "no trace in the Book of Genesis" of the great struggle between the God of Light and the Dragon of Darkness, who in one form are Merodach and Tiamat. The conflict is there, however, but from the original Egyptian source. It is represented as the enmity between the Woman and the Serpent, and also between her Seed and the Serpent. The Roman Church renders the passage (Gen. iii. 15) addressed to the Serpent—" She shall bruise thy head and thou shalt bruise her heel." Both versions are Egyptian. Horus is the Son and Seed of Isis. Sometimes he is pourtrayed as bruiser of the Apap Serpent's head; at others it is she who conquers. Both are combined in the Imagery which the Egyptians set in the Planisphere, where Isis in the shape of Virgo bears the Seed in her hands, and bruises the Serpent's head beneath her feet. This Seed in one form was sown in Egypt immediately after the Inundation, and in this way (as I have shown) the Zodiacal representation reflects the Seasons of Egypt all round the year.

The Serpent itself in the Hebrew Genesis is neither an original nor a true type. Two opposite characters have been fused and confused in it for the sake of a false moral. Serpent and Dragon were primarily identical as emblems of evil in physical phenomena; each was the representative of Darkness, and as such the Deluder of Men. Afterwards the Serpent was made a type of Time, of Renewal, and, therefore, of Life; the Dragon-Crocodile a zoötype of intelligence. Both Crocodile and Serpent were combined in Sevekh-Ra. Both were combined in the Polar Dragon; and in the Book of Revelation the Dragon remains that old Serpent, considered to be the Deluder of Mankind. Both were combined in the Chnubis Serpent-Dragon of the Gnostics, which was a survival of Kneph as the Agatho-Demon or Good Serpent of Egypt. The Akkadian type as Ea, is the Good Serpent, the Serpent of Life, the God of Wisdom. Now it was the Serpent of Wisdom that first offered the fruit of the Tree of Knowledge for the Enlightenment of Mankind; whether this be Egyptian, Akkadian, or Gnostic, it is the Good Serpent. And as Guardian of the Tree set in Heaven it was the Good Serpent, or intelligent Dragon, as keeper of the treasures of Astral knowledge. It was the later Theology, Persian and Hebrew, that gave the character of the Evil One to the Serpent of Wisdom, and perverted the original meaning, both of the temptation and the Tempter who protected the Tree; which has been supplemented by the theology of the Vitriol-throwers who have scarified and blasted the face of nature on earth, and defiled and degraded the starry Intelligencers in heaven.

Professor Sayce's statements are no more correct than Mr. Renouf's, and Mr. Renouf's is no more true than Mr. Gladstone's. Further evidence may be found in my "Natural Genesis." But no non-Evolutionist can understand or interpret the Past. He is too ready to accept the re-beginning, where there can be at most a new point of departure.

Mr. Gladstone has been too much wrapt up in the One Book! He does not know that the story of Genesis is to be found written n the Bible above, and that the Happy Garden, the primal pair, the war of the serpent, and the first mother, together with the Tree of Knowledge, are all constellated in the stars of heaven, according to Egyptian mythology, and are all verifiable on the monuments. When he does learn that such *is* the fact, he cannot claim that the history inscribed upon the starry walls was written there by the Jews, or copied from the Hebrew record! But let us see whether we cannot discover a few more Egyptian marks on the Genesis!

A Paradise or Garden that is watered without rain by a mist that went up from the earth to fall upon it in refreshing dew is certainly suggestive of an Egyptian origin, as that was the one way in which Egypt was watered from above. This was not so in the Eden at the head of the Persian Gulf. Besides which the Eight Primary Powers or Gods of Egypt were the dwellers in Eden or " Am-Smen," the *Paradise of the Eight*, who comprised the Genetrix and her Seven Children. The original Genesis and all the chief Types are identifiably Egyptian to begin with. But the Hebrew version was more directly derived from the Persian, as the Evil Serpent proves.

Water was the first element of life recognised by the primitive perception. Water was considered to be the mother, or Maternal Source, personified. In Egypt the Mother of Life pours out the Water of Life from the Tree of Life! She is the first form of the Celestial Waterer. In the mystical sense, Blood is the Water of Life, and therefore the Mother of Life. This beginning on earth with and from the water was Egyptian, Babylonian, Mexican, Indian, Chinese, Greek, British, Universal.

It is said upon an Assyrian tablet that " the heaven was made from the waters." So in the Egyptian beginning the sky was looked upon as the celestial water. This water was also entified in the river Nile, which was called the "*Way of the Gods*," when the Nature-Powers had been divinised. In that sense, as it were, heaven descended, to be continued on earth. From this water of heaven the land in Egypt was visibly deposited, and the earth was " compacted out of water and by means of water." When these were discreted there was the dry land. Here if anywhere is the primary hint of a cosmical beginning with a fact in nature, but not with a theory of nature nor a system of geology.

The second element of life was Breath, anima or air. In Egyptian, breath or spirit is Nef; and this was personated by Kneph, a form of the first god, who is said to be the breath of souls, or those who are in the firmament. Nef, for breath and spirit, explains the Hebrew Nephesh for soul, as the breath of life. Kneph, the breathing life in the firmament, is also the Sailor on the water! In the Hebrew version, Kneph becomes the Spirit moving on the face of the waters. In the Egyptian representation he sails the waters in his ark,—just as Ea does in the Akkadian version of the myth. The god Kneph is also the spirit that presides over the *Bau*, which had become the Pit-hole, or the Tomb from the Womb of the Beginning. The Egyptian Bau is the Hebrew Bohu, or the Void. In both it is a place left unpersonified. In the later phase of personification this Bau of Birth becomes the Phœnician Baev, called the Consort of Kolpia, the Wind or Spirit. The Bau was also personified in the Babylonian goddess Bohu. The Phœnician Baev points back to the Egyptian Bab (or Beb) for the hole, cave, well, source, or outrance —the original of all the Babs in later language, including Babylon.

Now, that which is performed by the Elohim *en gros* in Genesis is done by the Ali, or Seven Companions, in Egypt, most of whom can be recognised individually in relation to the Seven Elements. As the Hebrew Elohim, they may be dislimned and lose their likeness, but they are the same seven powers of eternal nature (as explained by the Gnostics or Kabalists). In one of the Egyptian creation-legends—shown by a monument which was restored in the time of Shabaka—it is said of the Creator, " A blessing was pronounced upon all things in the day when he bid them exist, and before he had yet caused gods to be made for Ptah." This, it appears to me, has left another Egyptian mark on the first chapter of Genesis in the refrain, " And the Elohim saw that it was good," which is uttered seven times over, in accordance with the sevenfold nature of the Elohim; and the blessing is pronounced—" And God blessed them!" "And God blessed the seventh day!" It would be going too far afield to show all the Egyptian marks in one lecture; but I must offer another example. The Hebrew word employed for creating, when the Elohim form the heaven and the earth, is " Bara." The essential meaning of the word is to give a manifestation in form to material previously without shape. Nothing could so perfectly realise it as the potter at work on his clay. And the Egyptian image of a Creator, as the Former, is Khepr, who, as the Beetle, formed his little globe with his hands, and who, as Khepr-Ptah, is the Potter sitting at his wheel, and shaping the egg of the sun and moon, or the vase of matter to contain life—he who was the Former or Creator " in his name of Let-the-Earth-be." The Potter, in Hebrew and Phœnician, is the Jatzer; and this word is also applied to the Hebrew God as Creator, Jatzariah being Jah the Potter. Thus the Kabalist Book of Creation, named the Sepher-Jatzirah, is the Book of Creation as the workmanship of the Former or Potter. Anyone who knows anything of the monuments will here recognise another Egyptian mark; I may say the Egyptian potter's mark on the Hebrew creations. The Creator or Former, as Khepr-Ptah the Potter, is the head of the Seven Knemmu, who are his assistants in the work of creation. He is the chief of the Ali or Elohim, as the fashioner and builder of the heavens. He is also the father of the Egyptian Adam, or Atum, the Red One; just as the Hebrew or Phœnician Elohim are the creators of Adam the Red. Jehovah-Elohim, the Lord God of the second chapter of Genesis, can be further identified with Ptah, the founder of the earth and former of men. Ptah is the father of Atum = Adam, the father of human beings. He is designated the father of the fathers, an equivalent to the title of Ialdabaoth, chief of the seven Gnostic Elohim. The name of Ptah signifies the Opener from Put to open; and the Hebrew name of פתחיה shows that Jah is Puthach = Putha, or Ptah, as the Opener (cf. Fuerst, p. 1166). These we may claim for other Egyptian marks.

But I have now learned that the account of the creations in Genesis is not so directly derived from the Egyptian as I had once thought; that is, it was re-written after the time of the captivity in Babylon, and the consequent acquaintance with the creation-legends in their latest Persian form. This can be shown by a comparison with the Parsee Bundahish or Aboriginal Creation —more literally, the Creation of the Beginning. Indeed, we may suspect that the first words of the Hebrew Genesis have to do with the title of the Bundahish. They are, "B'Rashith Elohim Bara;" and "B'Rashith," when literally translated, reads, "in the beginning of," leaving an elipsis, without stating in the beginning of what! Now the meaning of the word Bundahish is, the Creation of the Beginning. This far more perfect statement seems to have been bungled in adapting it for the Hebrew version.

The first two facts distinguishable in external phenomena by man were those of Darkness and Light. The panorama of mythological representation is drawn out from these as its opening scene, and the long procession of the Powers of Nature, which became divinities at a later stage, starts upon its march through heaven above to cast its shadows on the earth below.

By observing the alternation of Light and Darkness, a primary measure of time was first established as the creation of a night and day, marked by the Twin-Star. And "there was evening, and there was morning, one day," as the result of this earliest creation of the Beginning. In the Persian Bundahish, the deity Ahura-Mazda is the chief of the Seven Amchaspands just as the creator Ptah is of the Seven Khnemmu; and the Gnostic Ialdabaoth of the Seven Elohim. Here we learn that the God created the world in six periods, although *not* in six days. The first of Ahura-Mazda's creatures of the world was the sky, and his good thought by good procedure produced the light of the world. This is identical with the Elohim seeing the light that it was good; and with the blessing pronounced on his creations by the Egyptian deity. The light now separated and distinguished from darkness in the creation of time is quite distinct from the divine, the abstract, or the illimitable and eternal light already existing with Ahura-Mazda; it is the evening and morning, one day.

Darkness and light are personified and represented as being at ceaseless enmity with each other in the confusion of Chaos, but they come to an understanding as co-creators, and make a covenant, in appointing this primeval period of time.

And such was the first creation in the Persian series of six. "And of Ahura's creatures of the world," it is said, "the first was the sky; the second, water; the third, earth; the fourth, plants; the fifth, animals; the sixth, mankind." The creation of light in the Hebrew Genesis is the creation of the sky in the Persian; and the creation of water in the Persian Genesis, becomes the dividing of the waters in the Hebrew version. The time of this creation is called the second day.

The third Persian creation is that of earth, which is the dry land of the Hebrew—"And the Elohim called the dry land Earth."

The fourth Persian creation, or rather creature, is that of plants. This is not a separate creation in the Hebrew version; it is thrown into the third creation, that of earth. Nevertheless, the third must have included the plants because it includes every herb yielding seed and every tree that bears edible fruit. And yet in chapter 2, verse 5, when the creations are all completed, and the Elohim had finished the work which they had made, we are told that "no plant of the field was yet in the earth, and no herb of the field had yet sprung up." Which proves how mixed and muddled, as well as un-original, is the Mosaic version. In the fourth Hebrew creation the heavenly bodies become the time-keepers for signs and seasons. This is not one of the six Persian creations, which six are followed by the "formation of the luminaries." Of these it is said "Ahura-Mazda produced illumination between the sky and the earth, the constellation-stars and those not of the constellations, then the moon; and afterwards the sun." The fifth Persian creation is that of the animals. This creation is limited to the winged fowl, sea animals, and fishes, in the Hebrew account, which is considerably mixed.

Mr. Gladstone asks: "Is there the smallest inconsistency in a statement which places the emergence of our land, and its separation from the sea, and the commencement of vegetable life, before the final and full concentration of light upon the sun, and its reflection on the moon and planets? and as there would be light diffused before there was light concentrated, why may not that diffused light have been sufficient for the purposes of vegetation?" Certainly, as there was light enough to make day before there was any sun or moon, there ought to, and should, have been. In my reply I am not concerned to reconcile the literal rendering of the Hebrew Genesis with scientific fact, but I shall have to point out on behalf of the mythical original that according to the present interpretation the heaven and earth could and did exist before the stars, or the moon and the sun! There was no time kept on earth or in heaven until night and day were divided and marked by the alternation of light and darkness, or by the Twin Star of Evening and Dawn, therefore the heavenly bodies were not made use of, ergo they did not exist in any requisite sense of the Mythos.

Lastly, man is the product of the sixth creation in both renderings. If taken literally, man of the sixth Persian creation appears on the scene before the stars or moon or sun, which follow the six creations, not as mere light-givers to the earth, but as time-keepers for man. And that alone will explain why the stars are said to be in existence before the moon; and the moon before the sun! In the Persian writings the invariable order is that of stars, moon, and sun! In describing the mythical mount Alborz, the mount Meru of the Persian system of the Heavens, it is said that it grew for 200 years up to the star-station; for 200 more years up to the moon-station; for 200 more years up to the sun-station; for 200 more years up to the endless light! That is a mode of building up the heavens in accordance with the order of the Celestial timekeepers, and of the Kronian creations. Time was first told by the stars, morning and evening, and by the seven which turned round once in the circle of a year; next by means of the moon and its monthly renewal; next by means of the sun; solar time being last because the most difficult to make out.

In a papyrus at Turin it is said of Taht, the god of lunar time, in Egypt, "He hath made all that the world contains, and hath given it light when all was darkness, and there was as yet no sun!" This was figurative, and applies solely to the moon, by which time was kept earlier than it could be defined by the sun. It is well known that the lunar year and the lunar zodiac, or pathway of the moon, were earlier than the solar zodiac of 12 signs, which is too late for the mythical *Beginnings*.

In the Babylonian account of creation the moon is produced before the sun. As George Smith points out, this is in reverse order to that of the Hebrew Genesis. Evidently, he says, the Babylonians considered the moon the principal body, while the book of Genesis makes the sun the greater light. "Here, it becomes evident," says this Bibliolator, "that Genesis is truer to nature than the Chaldean text." The uninspired Babylonians, you see, did not know that the moon was the lesser, and the sun the larger light!

Professor Sayce likewise tells us that "the idea which underlay the religious belief of Akkad" was, that "the moon existed before the sun" (Hib. Lect. 165). Neither of these Assyriologists appears to have had any notion why this was so represented!

The Arkadians, the Argives, the Quichés, and other races of men claimed to be Pro-Selenes, or those who lived before the time of the moon, not *before the existence* of that luminary! Truer to nature can have no meaning for an account of the creation of light prior to the existence of the heavenly bodies—that is, if literally taken. But neither the Egyptians, Babylonians, nor Persians were talking about the cosmical creation in the modern sense, as has been ignorantly assumed, and foolishly contended for, but about the mythical beginnings of the Time-keepers. In these the mapping out of the lunar month came before the solar year. Hence the sun-god was called the child of the moon-god Sin, in Assyria, and the lunar god, Taht, or Tehuti, is called the father of Osiris, the sun-god, in Egypt; the priority being dependent on the earlier observations for the keeping of time. So the Mexicans held the planet Venus to have been created before the sun! It was earlier than the moon, they said, and properly the first light that appeared in the world. That would be as a star of morning and evening which made the first day. Hence we are told that the first man, Oannes, came up out of the Red Sea, and landed in Babylonia on the "First Day."

The Great Mother, to whom the planet Venus was dedicated, was represented by the Heifer, the pure Heifer, the sacred Heifer, the Golden Calf, as it was called. This being of either sex, it supplied a twin type for Venus, as Hathor or Ishtar, the double Star, that was male at rising and female at sunset, and therefore the Twin-Stars of the "First Day."

Any other earlier sense these creations have besides that of time-keeping was merely elemental, and relating to the order in which man recognised and represented the natural elements. Darkness, with its voice of thunder, was the first! Out of the darkness issued the light. These two were the Twins of eternal alternation in external phenomena, found in so many forms of the mythos as the two Brothers, who fought each other for the Birthright. The next two were moisture and air, or the water of life and the breath of life. These four creations, or, as the Bundahish has it, four creatures of Ahura-Mazda, were the four elements of darkness and light, water and air.

In Egypt they were typified by the Jackal of darkness, the Hawk of light, the Ape of breath, and the Hippopotamus or Dragon of the waters, which were made those Keepers of the four corners who are universal in mythology. They indicate four elements, or four seasons, four quarters of the year, or the four-fold heaven by which the circle of the whole was divided; and squared as it was in the circle of Yima.

I have followed out the various creations, or heavens, from beginning to end in the "Natural Genesis." At present we must turn once more to the Persian Bundahish where it says in Revelation— such being the formula frequently employed on matters of religion, or on the periods for the observance of religious duties—"the creatures of the world were created by me complete in three hundred and sixty-five days; that is the six periods of the festivals which are completed in a year." Here, then, we part company with the six days and one week of creation in the Hebrew book of Genesis! We can see that is but a condensed summary of an earlier account, which may lead us a little nearer to nature, and to those phenomenal facts on which mythology was founded—the Rock on which our Biblical Theology will be wrecked. In this version of the creation-legend the six creations are completed in one year of 365 days, or rather the year of 365 days had been finally completed in six stages, or seasons, or periods of time-keeping! In accordance with this sixth creation we learn from the Targum of Palestine that Adam, as the Adamic man, was created in the image of the Lord, his maker, with 365 nerves. Here the divine model of humanity was the solar god of time, or of the creations perfected at last in a year of 365 days! which figures are reflected in the 365 nerves. *Now* we can see *how* the Persian sixth day of celebration of *each* of six creations became the six days of creation in the Hebrew Genesis, in the process of condensing mythology into cosmical and human history; and *one* year into *one* week to make it more tangible at a later time! The creations include the elements identified, together with the various systems of keeping time, which culminated at last in a year of 365 and a quarter days. These systems may be roughly sketched as (1) the one day of a light and dark; (2) one turn round to a year; (3) the half-years of the solstices; (4) a lunar month of the four quarters; (5) planetary time; (6) solar time, or a year of 365 days.

When it says in the Persian Revelation—" The Creatures of the world were created by me in 365 days," it does not mean during that period, any more than it meant the six days of the Hebrew mis-rendering of the matter. It means that the concluding creation of the six different creations culminated in a year of solar time, or 365 days to the year, in the image of which Adamic man was formed with 365 nerves.

The origin of the Sabbath in Genesis is curiously paralleled, or suggested, in the Bundahish. We read " on matters of religion," it says in Revelation thus—" The creatures (or six creations) were created by me complete in 365 days. That is the six Gahanbars, which are completed in a year." And *here* the matters of religion are explained as being the periods for observance of religious duties. That is, the six festivals or Sabbaths were instituted to commemorate the six creations which were created complete, or culminated, in a year of 365 days. The Persians represented their God as resting during five days after each of the six seasons of creation; and they also celebrated a great six days' festival annually, beginning on the 1st of March and ending on the sixth day, as the greatest holiday, because in this, the sixth season (in place of the sixth day in the Hebrew Genesis) Ahura-Mazda had created the most superior things. Thus the six creations in the Hebrew version have been visibly condensed into six periods of time, and there is but one period for religious observance on the seventh day! And whereas the Persians, or Parsees, hold their six festivals and periods of rest in one whole year, we have fifty-two Sabbaths, which shows the latest rendering, as well as the development of the same mythos. The Hebrew Elohim rested on the seventh day, whereas the Persian Ahura-Mazda rested for five days at a time after each of the six creations.

Further, the six seasons or periods of creation had been reduced from the earlier Babylonian version, in which the seventh day was not a Sabbath, but the period in which the Animals and Man were created.

We are also told in the Bundahish—"It says in Revelation that before the coming of the Destroyer vegetation had no thorns upon it or bark about it; and afterwards, when the Destroyer came, it was created with bark, and things grew thorny!" And in the Avesta, an older scripture, this destroyer, the evil opponent, is a serpent—as it is in the book of Genesis.

It is too late now to advance the claim, or assume that the Persians, the Babylonians, and Egyptians borrowed their versions from that given by the inspired writer of the Hebrew Pentateuch. And these facts, I submit, furnish sufficient evidence that the Book of Genesis does not contain an original revelation made by God to the Jews; in short, it does not contain any revelation at all. We are compelled to seek elsewhere before we can really understand what it does contain! The Six Creations, Creative Acts, or Periods are Persian; but the Legends in Genesis have been derived from more than one source.

Of late years a mighty fuss has been made about the fact that two different systems, known as the Elohistic and Jahvistic, have been imperfectly blended and utilised in the Hebrew version of the Genesis, but with no application of the comparative process to the various systems of creation, according to mythology, and with no clue whatever to the natural phenomena in which the mythology was founded, or to the gnosis by which the myths were anciently interpreted.

According to the Persian reckoning, the human creature was formed as the sixth creation, or, as the Hebrew version has it, on the sixth day; whereas in the version of the Seventy man was created on the eighth day. Now, if we look closely at the first chapter of Genesis, we shall find both these reckonings combined, but not blended. Although there are no more than six days of creation mentioned in the Hebrew Genesis, there are eight distinct acts of creation or utterances of the Word. These are enumerated as follows:—

    (1) The Elohim said—"Let there be light."
    (2) The Elohim said—"Let there be a firmament."
    (3) The Elohim said—"Let the waters be gathered together,"
          * * * and—"let the dry land appear."
    (4) The Elohim said—"Let the earth put forth grass."
    (5) The Elohim said—"Let there be light in the firmament."
    (6) The Elohim said—"Let the waters bring forth."
    (7) The Elohim said—"Let the earth bring forth."
    (8) The Elohim said—"Let us make man in our image."

The Bundahish has six creations only. The eight are Egypto-Gnostic, in keeping with the Ogdoad of primary powers. According to the Gnostics, who had preserved the only true knowledge of these mythical matters, man, as the eighth creation, belongs to the mystery of the Ogdoad. Irenæus tells us how the Gnostics maintained that man was formed on the eighth day of creation : "Sometimes they say he was made on the sixth, and at others on the eighth day." (B. 1, C. 18, 2.)

These two creations of man on the sixth day and on the eighth were those of the Adamic or fleshly man and of the spiritual man, who were known to Paul and the Gnostics as the first and second Adam, the man of earth and the man from heaven. Irenæus also says they insisted that Moses began with the Ogdoad of the Seven Powers and their Mother, who is called Sophia (the old Kefa of Egypt, who is the "Living Word" at Ombos). Thus we find the two systems are run into each other, and left without the means of distinguishing the one from the other, or of knowing how they had either of them originated. So that, instead of a revelation of the beginning in the Hebrew Genesis, we have to go far beyond it to find any beginning whatever.

So it is with the Fall. Here, as before, the Genesis does not begin at the beginning. There was an earlier Fall than that of the Primal Pair. In this, the number of those who failed and fell was seven. We meet with these Seven in Egypt—(Eight with the Mother)—where they are called the "Children of Inertness," who were cast out from "Am-Smen," the Paradise of the Eight; also, in a Babylonian legend of creation, as the Seven Brethren, who were Seven Kings ; like the Seven Kings in the Book of Revelation; and the Seven Non-Sentient Powers, who became the Seven Rebel Angels that made war in Heaven. The Seven Kronidæ, described as the Seven Watchers, who, in the beginning, were formed in the interior of heaven. The heaven, like a vault, they extended or hollowed out; that which was not visible they raised, and that which had no *exit* they opened; their work of creation being exactly identical with that of the Elohim in the Book of Genesis. These are the Seven elemental powers of space, who were continued as Seven timekeepers. It is said of them, "In watching was their office, but among the stars of heaven their watch they kept not," and their failure was the Fall. In the Book of Enoch the same Seven watchers in heaven are stars which transgressed the commandment of God before their time arrived, for they came not in their proper season, therefore was he offended with them, and bound them until the period of the consummation of their crimes, at the end of the *secret*, or great year of the world—*i.e.*, the Period of Precession, when there was to be restoration and re-beginning. The Seven deposed constellations are seen by Enoch, looking like Seven great blazing mountains overthrown—the Seven mountains in Revelation, on which the Scarlet Lady sits.

The Book of Genesis tells us nothing about the nature of these Elohim, erroneously rendered God, who are the creators of the Hebrew beginning, and who are themselves pre-extant and seated when the theatre opens and the curtain ascends. It says that in the beginning the Elohim created the heaven and the earth. In thousands of books the Elohim have been discussed, but with no application of the comparative process to this and the earlier mythologies, and therefore with no conclusive result. Our bibliolators were too conceited in their insular ignorance to think there was anything worth knowing outside of their own Book. Foolishly fancying they had got a revelation all to themselves, a supernatural version of the cosmical Genesis, they did not care to seek for, did not dream of, a natural or scientific Genesis, and could not make out the mythical; consequently they have never known *what* it was they were called upon to worship in the name of God. In his paper on the Evolution of Theology, Professor Huxley assumes that the Elohim of Genesis originated as the ghosts of ancestors, in doing which he no more plumbs to the bottom than does Mr. Gladstone. The Elohim are Seven in number, whether as nature powers, gods of constellations, or planetary gods. Whereas the human ghosts are not, and never were, a septenary, although they may be, and have been, confused with the typical seven as the Pitris and Patriarchs, Manus and Fathers of earlier times. The Gnostics, however, and the Jewish Kabalah preserve an account of the Elohim of Genesis by which we are able to identify them with other forms of the seven primordial powers. They are the children of the ancient Mother called Sophia. Their names are Ialdabaoth, Jehovah (or Iao), Sabaoth, Adonai, Eloeus, Oreus and Astanphæus. Ialdabaoth signifies the Lord God of the fathers; that is the fathers who preceded the Father; and thus the Seven are identical with the Seven Pitris or Fathers in India. (Irenæus B. 1, 30, 5.) Moreover, the Hebrew Elohim were pre-extant by name and nature as Phœnician divinities or powers. Sanchoniathon mentions them by name, and describes them as the Auxiliaries of Kronus or Time. In this phase, then, the Elohim are timekeepers in heaven! In the Phœnician Mythology the Elohim are the Seven sons of Sydik, identical with the Seven Kabiri, who in Egypt are the Seven sons of Ptah, and the Seven spirits of Ra in the Book of the Dead; in Britain, with the Seven Companions of Arthur in the Ark; in Polynesia, with the Seven dwarf sons of Pinga; in America, with the Seven Hohgates; in India, with the Seven Rishis; in Persia, with the Seven Amchaspands; in Assyria, with the Seven Lumazi.

They had one common genesis in phenomena, as I have traced them by number, by nature, and by name; and also one common Kamite origin. They are always seven in number as a companionship or brotherhood, who *Kab*, that is turn round together, whence the "Kab-ari." The Egyptian Ali or Ari, gives us the root meaning; the Ari *are* the companions, guardians and watchers, who turn round together. Hence the Aluheim or Elohim. They are also the Ili or gods, in Assyrian, who were seven in number! Eight with the Mother in the beginning, or the Manifestor in the end. In their primordial phase they were seven elementary powers, warring in chaos, lawless and timeless. They were first born of the Mother in space; and then the Seven Companions passed into the sphere of time, as auxiliaries of Kronus, or Sons of the Male Parent. As Damascius says, in his "Primitive Principles," the Magi consider that space and time were the source of all; and from being powers of the air, the gods were promoted to become timekeepers for man. Seven constellations were assigned to them, and so they could be called the auxiliaries of Kronus, when *time* was established. As the seven turned round in the ark of the sphere they were designated the Seven Sailors, Companions, Rishis, or Elohim. The first "Seven Stars" are not planetary. They are the leading stars of seven constellations, which turned round with the Great Bear in describing the circle of a year. These the Assyrians called the seven Lumazi, or leaders of the flocks of stars, designated sheep. On the Hebrew line of descent or development, these Elohim are identified for us by the Kabalists and Gnostics, who retained the hidden wisdom or gnosis, the clue of which is absolutely essential to any proper understanding of mythology or theology. The creation of the Elohim as auxiliaries of Kronus was not world-making at all in our sense. The myth-makers were not geologists, and did not pretend to be. The chaos which preceded Creation was simply that of timelessness, and of the unintellectual and non-sentient Nature-Powers. Creation proper began with the first means of measuring and recording a cycle of time. Thus the primary creation in the Genesis, as in the Bundahish, *is* the creation of time, in which the morning and evening measured one day.

But the Seven Cronies, as we may now call them, were found to be telling time somewhat vaguely by the year, in accordance with the annual revolution of the starry sphere; and, being found inexact and unfaithful to their trust, they were dispossessed and superseded—or, as it was fabled, they fell from heaven. The Seven were then succeeded by a Polar Pair and a Lunar Trinity of Time-keepers. For example, it had been observed that there was a fixed centre, which was a pivot to the Starry Vast all turning round. Here there were two constellations with seven stars in each. *We* call them the Two Bears. But the seven stars of the Lesser Bear were once considered to be the seven heads of the Polar Dragon, which we meet with—as the beast with seven heads—in the Akkadian Hymns and in the Book of Revelation. The mythical dragon originated in the crocodile, which *is* the Dragon of Egypt. Plutarch tells us the Egyptians said the crocodile was the sole animal living in water which has his eyesight covered over with a film, so thin that he can see without himself being seen by others—"in which he agrees with the first god." Now, in one particular cult, the Sut-Typhonian, the first god was Sevekh, who wears the crocodile's head, as well as the serpent, and who *is* the Dragon, or whose constellation was the Dragon.

The name of Sevekh signifies the sevenfold; hence the seven heads of the Dragon, the Dragon who is of the seven and "is himself also an eighth," as we are told in Revelation. In him the Seven Powers were unified, as they were in Ea, Iao-Chnubis, and various other of the chief gods who summed up the earlier powers in the supreme *one*, when unity was attained at last. For it is certain that no one god was ever made known to man by primitive revelation. The only starting-point was in external phenomena, which assuredly manifested no oneness in personality. The group of the Totemic brotherhood preceded the fatherhood, and finally the fatherhood superseded the Totemic group in heaven, as it was on earth. One form of this god was Sut-Nub, and Nub means the golden. Thus the reign of Sut was that age of gold afterwards assigned to Saturn by the Greeks. In Egypt the Great Bear was the constellation of Typhon, or *Kepha*, the old genitrix, called the Mother of the Revolutions; and the Dragon with seven heads was assigned to her son Sevekh-Kronus, or Saturn, called the Dragon of Life. That is, the typical dragon or serpent with seven heads was female at first, and then the type was continued as male in her son Sevekh, the Sevenfold Serpent, in Ea the Sevenfold, in Num-Ra, in the Seven-headed Serpent, Iao-Chnubis, and others. We find these two in the book of Revelation. One is the Scarlet Lady, the mother of mystery, the great harlot, who sat on a scarlet-coloured beast with seven heads, which is the Red Dragon of the Pole. She held in her hand the unclean things of her fornication. That means the emblems of the male and female, imaged by the Egyptians at the Polar centre, the very uterus of creation as was indicated by the Thigh constellation, called the Khepsh of Typhon, the old dragon, in the northern birthplace of Time in heaven. The two revolved about the *pole of heaven*, or the Tree, as it was called, which was figured at the centre of the starry motion. In the book of Enoch these two constellations are identified as Leviathan and Behemoth = Bekhmut, or the Dragon and Hippopotamus = Great Bear, and they are the primal pair that were first created in the garden of Eden. So that the Egyptian first mother, Kefa, whose name signifies mystery, was the original of the Hebrew Chavah, our *Eve;* and therefore Adam is one with Sevekh, the sevenfold one, the solar dragon, in whom the powers of light and darkness were combined, and the sevenfold nature was shown in the seven rays worn by the Gnostic Iao-Chnubis, god of the number seven, who is Sevekh by name and a form of the first father as head of the seven. Another bit of evidence here may be adduced from the Rabbinical legends relating to Adam's first wife. Her name was *Lilith*, and Lilith = Rerit, is that Egyptian goddess whose constellation was the Great Bear. Thus Adam and Eve are identified at last with the Greater and Lesser Bears, and the mythical Tree of Knowledge with the celestial Northern Pole. The Hebrew Adam can be likewise shown to have been a form of the chief one of the earlier seven who fell from heaven. Not only is he the head of the first group of Patriarchs turned into historical characters in the Genesis, who are seven in number, preceding the ten, but we also learn that, *in the mysteries of Samothrace,* the name of Adam was given to the first and chief one of the Seven Kabiri, who were a form of the earliest Seven time-keepers, that failed and fell from heaven! Moreover, the Gnostics identify these primary seven by nature and by name as the Seven Mundane Dæmons who always oppose and resist the human race, because it was on their account that the father among the seven was cast down to a lower world!—not to the earth. One name of this father is Ialdabaoth. Adam is another name of the same mythical personage, and Adam at Samothrace was chief of the Seven. Adam, as the father among the Seven, is identical with the Egyptian Atum, who was the father-god in his first sovereignty, and whose other name of Adon is identical with the Hebrew Adonai. In this way the second creation in Genesis reflects and continues the later creation in the mythos, which explains it. The Fall of Adam to the lower world led to his being humanised on earth, by which process the celestial was turned into the mortal, and this, which belongs to the astronomical allegory, got literalised as the fall of Man, or descent of the soul into matter, and the conversion of the angelic into an earthly being. The Roman Church has always held that mankind were created in consequence of the fall of the rebel angels who raised a revolt in heaven, which was simply a survival of the Mythos, as it is found in the texts when Ea, the first father, is said to "grant forgiveness to the conspiring gods," for whose "redemption did he create mankind" (Sayce, Hib. Lect. 140). The subject matter is celestial solely, and solely celestial because it was astronomical. The Fall was not to the earth, nor on the earth, but to a lower heaven, called the Adamah in Genesis; nor did Adam and Eve become human realities below because they were outcast gods of constellations that were superseded above. The matter is mythical, and I am trying to show, as the result of wide research, what is the meaning of that which we call "mythical," by tracing the physical origin of the ancient gods, the Hebrew included, to natural phenomena, in accordance with data and determinatives still extant.

As nothing was known concerning the Genesis and nature of the Elohim, it has always been a moot question as to whom the speakers addressed the speech, "Let us make man in our image!" It has commonly been assumed that the "us" denoted a plural of dignity like the "we" of Royalty and Editorship. But it is not so. The Elohim are the Egyptian, Akkadian, Hebrew, and Phœnician form of the universal Seven Powers, who are Seven in Egypt, Seven in Akkad, Babylon, Persia, India, Britain, and Seven amongst the Gnostics and Kabalists. They were the Seven fathers who preceded the father in heaven, because they were earlier than the individualised fatherhood on earth. Mythology reflects the primitive sociology, as in a mirror, and we could not comprehend the reflection in the divine dynasties above until we knew something fundamental about the human relationships on the earth beneath.

The field of Babylonian Mythology is one vast battle-ground

between the early Motherhood and the later Fatherhood—that is, the Mother in space, in the stellar and lunar characters opposed to the later and solar Fatherhood, which became more especially Semite; indeed, where the Akkadians wrote the "female and the male," the Semite translators prepensely reverse it, and render it by the "male and the female." This setting up of the supreme God as solely Male, to the exclusion of the female, has often been erroneously attributed to a supposed "Monotheistic Instinct" originating with the Semites! In Egypt the solar Fatherhood had been attained in the sovereignty of Atum-Ra, when the records begin; but this same battle went on all through her monumental history, more fiercely when the Heretics, the Motherites, the Black-heads, were now and again reinforced by allies from without.

When the Elohim said, "Let us make man in our image, after our likeness," there were seven of them who represented the seven elements, powers, or souls that went to the making of the human being who came into existence before the Creator was represented anthropomorphically, or could have conferred the human likeness on the Adamic man. It was in the seven-fold image of the Elohim that man was first created, with his seven elements, principles, or souls, and therefore could not have been formed in the image of the one God. The seven Gnostic Elohim tried to make a man in their own image, but could not, from lack of virile power. Thus, their creation in earth and heaven was a failure. The Gnostics identify these seven as the Hebrew Elohim who exhorted each other, saying, "Let us make man after our image and likeness." They did so; but the man whom they made was a failure, because they themselves were lacking in the soul of the fatherhood! When the Gnostic Ialdabaoth, chief of the Seven, cried, "I am the father and God," his mother Sophia replied, "Do not tell lies, Ialdabaoth, for the first man (Anthropos Son of Anthropos) is above thee!" That is, man, who had now been created in the image of the fatherhood, was superior to the gods who were derived from the mother parent alone! For, as it had been at first on earth, so was it afterwards in heaven; and thus the primary gods were held to be soulless, like the earliest races of men, because they had not attained the soul of the individualised fatherhood. The Gnostics taught that the spirits of wickedness, the inferior Seven, derived their origin from the great mother alone, who produced without the fatherhood! It was in the image, then, of the sevenfold Elohim that the seven races were formed which we sometimes hear of as the pre-Adamite races of men, because they were earlier than the fatherhood which was individualised only in the second Hebrew creation. These were the primitive people of the past,—the old, despised, dark races of the world,—who were held to have been created *without souls, because they were born before the fatherhood was individualised on earth or in heaven;* for, there could be no God the Father recognised until the human father had been identified—nothing more than the general ancestral soul of the fathers, or the soul of the seven elemental forces. These early races were first represented by Totemic zoötypes, and were afterwards abominated as the dog-men, monkey-men, men with tails, mere preliminary people, created in the likeness of animals, reptiles, fish, or birds. Warriors with the body of a bird of the valley (?), and men with the faces of ravens, were suckled by the old dragon Tiamat; and their type may be seen in the image of the twin Sut-Horus, who has the head of a bird of light in front, and the Neh, or black vulture of darkness, behind. Ptah and his Seven Khnemmu are the Pygmies.

As the black race was first on earth, so is it in the mirror of mythology. These are the "people of the black heads," who are referred to on the tablets, and classed with reptiles, during a lunar eclipse. These typical black heads were the primeval powers of darkness, to which the old black aborigines in various lands were likened or assimilated by their despisers. In the Babylonian prayers we find the many-named mother-goddess is invoked as "the mother who has begotten the black heads." These at times were intentionally confused and confounded with their elemental prototypes. Seven such races are described in the Bundahish, or aboriginal creation, as the earth-men, the men of the water, the breast-eared, the breast-eyed, the one-legged, the bat-men, and the men with tails. These were the soulless people. They are also referred to by Esdras as the other people who are nothing, "but be like unto spittle"—that is, when compared with those who descended from the father, as Adam, or Atum, on earth, and who worshipped a father, as Atum, or Jehovah, in heaven. There were seven creations altogether; seven heavens, which were planetary in their final phase, seven creators, and seven races of men. And when the one God had been evolved he was placed at the head of the Seven. Hence Ptah in Egypt was called the Father of the fathers, who in India are known as the Seven Pitris. So Ahura-Mazda, Ialdabaoth, or Jehovah, was placed first in the later creation.

The chief of the Seven Ali = Elohim as supreme one of the group became the Semitic Al or El, designated the highest god, who was the seventh as Saturn; so that El and Jehovah - Elohim are identical in their phenomenal origin, whilst El-Shadai is the same son of the old suckler who was Typhon in Egypt and Tiamat in Assyria.

When in the second creation, and in the second chapter of Genesis, Jehovah-Elohim forms man from the dust of the ground, and woman from the bone of man, Jehovah is that one God who sums up in himself the seven previous powers, precisely as they were totalled in Atum-Ra, Sevekh-Ra, Agni, or Ahuramazda. He has been identified for us by name as one of the seven Gnostic Elohim, their Iao, or Jehovah. This God appears by name in the second chapter of the Book of Genesis, and yet in verse 26 of chapter iv, it is stated that "then began men to call upon the name of Jehovah." And again the same God, apparently, is announced by name in Exodus vi. 3, where he affirms that he has not been known previously by the name of Jah or Jehovah. But the difference between Jehovah-Elohim and Jah or Iao is a fact which can only be determined by a knowledge of the phenomena. The Jewish Kabalah and Gnosticism have never yet been grappled with or discussed in relation to mythology and the rootage in nature. The subject has only been nibbled at in a little grazing, with a go-as-you-please, modern interpretation of the doctrines concerning spirit and matter. The seven-fold one God is the same in origin, whether known by name as Jehovah, Iao-Sabaoth, Sevekh the seven-fold, Ea the fish with seven fins, Ra with seven souls, Agni with seven arms, the Gnostic Chnubis or Heptaktis with seven rays, El of the Seventh Planet, or the Dragon with seven heads.

But there is another Jah or Iao, who is the lunar divinity, and who was that Duad of the mother and child which becomes a Triad as the child grows into the consort for the same mother. It is more ancient than the divine Fatherhood, and preceded the luni-solar trinity of father, mother and son. This was the Moon-God who rode on the heavens by the name of Jah! and in this phase the zoötypes were superseded by the human likeness, and the God was imaged as one in the three-fold human character, when time was reckoned by the mother-moon, the child-moon and the virile new moon. The human family exalted to heaven as the divine father, mother and child followed the recognition of the personal fatherhood in sociology, and the knowledge that the lunar light was derived from the sun. Just as this institution superseded the mother and the brotherhood of the Totemic stage on earth, so was it in heaven. In each phase the human sociology is reflected in the mirror of mythology. One Jewish sign of this trinity, given by Bochart, is a circle containing three yod letters, the numerical value of which is 30—or ten days to each of the three phases of the Moon. Another of the lunar types is the Ass—the three-legged ass of the Bundahish. In the Egyptian hieroglyphics the head of the ass is a sign for No. 30 on the same ground; and on account of such typology the Jews were charged with being worshippers of an ass. Thus the Elohim were the Seven Powers—elemental, pre-planetary or planetary; Jehovah-Elohim was the sevenfold one as supreme amongst the planetary Gods, and Jah is the three-fold lunar Deity the trinity in unity—in the likeness of the human family; these were again combined in a totality that is ten-fold in the divine fatherhood. Hence the Hebrew letter Yod, the sign of *ten*, is a symbol of the ineffable name of Iao, Jah, or Jehovah; thus the name of the Iao can be expressed in Roman numerals by the 1 and 0, which figure the number 10: and this figure of the ten-fold totality so made up is both the heavenly man, called Adam Kadmon by the Kabalists, composed of what they term the 10

Sephiroth, and the Supreme Being worshipped by the whole of Christendom to-day as the one God, supposed to have been made known by Divine revelation to a Monotheistic race of men.

The Egyptian Aten will show us how and why the Jews could use the name of Adon as an equivalent for that of Jah or the Yod, which has the numerical value of 10. Aten as a title of *Highness* is determined by the numerical sign of 10, and therefore is an equivalent for I O, or Iao of the ten-fold nature, unified at last in Aten or Adon as the Lord, who was God of the 10 Tribes.

Such, to put briefly what I have elaborated elsewhere, was the origin in natural phenomena, and such was the unity at last attained in a tenfold totality by the Supreme One, the All, the unity not being initial but final: *E pluribus unum.*

Mr. Gladstone's last and most pathetic plea—pitiful as a flag of distress fluttering at the mast-head of a doomed vessel visibly going down—is that the tale in Genesis is beautiful if not true! He says—" If we view it as a popular narrative it is singularly vivid, forcible, and effective, if we take it as a poem it is indeed sublime!" But the question is—Is it false or true? Have we been deluded, misled, and cheated? The essence of poetry even must be truth, and not falsehood, however attractive; must not mislead us on the pretext of being a revelation. The older I grow the faster I am losing my faith in all lovely unrealities. Consider the effects of such false teaching! Only the other day a child who had been taught that God made man out of the dust of the earth was watching an eddying cloud of dust being whirled into shape by the wind, when she cried, "Oh! mother, come here! Look! I think God is creating another baby!" Our mental standpoint has been made quite as childish with regard to other Beginnings. And from every pulpit of the past we have been implored to remain as little children at the mother's knee. We have been taught and compelled to surrender our reason, doff our manhood and grovel like worms in the earth as the successful mode of wriggling our way through this world into heaven. We have been robbed by a thief in the night. Children have been cheated out of their natural senses, and the mental emasculation of men has taken the place of the physical once inculcated by the Christ (Math. xix. 12). Men who are sane on most other subjects will give up all common sense on this, and talk like intellectual lunatics. See how the teachers of the people, who ought to have learned better for themselves, continue all their life through to wear the cast-off vestments of ancient mythology.

Take Mr. Ruskin as another typical example. He is in many ways a most diligent searcher after truth, and a worshipper of all things noble and beautiful. But he was so profoundly infected by the falsehood made religious to him in childhood as to be marked by it and mentally maimed for life. In his "Modern Painters" he tells us that "man perished in seeking knowledge," and "there is not any part of our nature, nor can there be through eternity, uninfluenced or unaffected by the fall." 'Tis most painful to see such a man, so human at heart, such a seer and lover of all loveliness believing so damnable a lie, and endorsing it not only for his own lifetime, but for so long as his writings may last, because it was told to him in his own confiding childhood. It is good to waken the eyes of men to the beautiful, but still better to lead them to the enduring truth! So soon as my own eyes were opened wide enough to take in the immense imposture that has been based upon mythology, I gave up my chance of a seat upon the Mount of the Muses, and turned aside from the proffered crown of poetry as a seeker after verifiable certitude. And after all how can the picture of a divinised fool at the head of affairs with so certain a break down in the beginning be beautiful when such a representation reduces the drama of the whole universe into a most pitiful one-act farce? Any God who demands the worship of fear would be unworthy the service of love. Our modern Atheism is mainly the result of this false Theism being torn up by the root to expose its godlessness. Falsehood is always fraudulent; no matter how it may be poetized or painted; no matter how religiously we have believed it true; or how long we may have been imposed on by its fairness; and woe to the revelation that is proved to be false! woe to the sphinx when her secret is at last found out! It will then be her turn to be torn.

The Hebrew Pentateuch has not only retarded the growth of science in Europe for eighteen centuries, but the ignorant believers in it as a book of revelation have tried to strangle every science at its birth. There could be and was but little or no progress in astronomy, geology, biology, or sociology until its teachings were rejected by the more enlightened among men—the free thinkers and demonstrators of the facts. The progress has been in proportion to the repudiation; and, for myself, the nearer I draw towards death the more earnestly—nay, vengefully—do I resent the false teachings that have embittered my life—not for myself only, but more for others, and most of all for the children. Remember, the education of English children to-day is chiefly in the hands of the orthodox teachers, who still give the Bible all the preference over nature and science, and who will go on deluding the innocent little ones as long as ever they are paid or permitted to do so. But what a dastardly shame it is for us to allow the children to be taught that which we know to be false, or do not ourselves believe to be true! The present calls upon you with an appealing voice to protect the unborn future against this terrible tyranny of the past. Do not any longer let the winding-sheet of death be the swaddling-bands put on the helpless little ones for life at their intellectual birth. It is appalling to think of the populations that have already passed on victimised, the lives that have been wrecked, the brains that have been bruised, and the hearts broken of those who have dashed themselves against these barriers to human progress and the freedom of thought, which were ignorantly erected and then made sacred in the name of God, by means of this Hebrew Book of the Beginnings; in short, by a literalisation of mythology.

> *That* should inspire one effort more,
> Mightier than any made before.
> The barrier-wall at last *shall* fall;
> The future *must* be free for all!

IN REPLY TO PROFESSOR A. H. SAYCE.

As an opponent of what may be termed the Aryan school of interpretation it has been my special work to show that mythology is not a farrago of foolish fables, nor the mere raving of words that have lost their senses. I have amply demonstrated the fact that the myths were no mere products of ancient ignorance, but are the deposited results of a primitive knowledge; that they were founded upon natural phenomena and remain the register of the earliest scientific observation. Those, however, who have not yet learned that mythology contains the gnosis of the earliest science, and is the great pre-historic record, are unable to teach us anything fundamental concerning it. They cannot read the record itself or verify it by continual reference to those natural phenomena on which it is based, and by which the truth of the interpretation has to be verified and tested. Without this foothold of fact being firmly established mythology resolves itself into a bog without a bottom.

It appears to me that Professor Sayce in his lectures on the Babylonian Religions, is frequently dealing with matters which can only be fathomed by the comparative process, and that it is misleading to compare the ancient mythologies with the Egyptian omitted, whereas he rigorously rejects any light from that source. No Mythological Religion can be explained by itself alone. The comparative method is as the bringing together of flint and steel to strike the first spark for the necessary light. Without question or inquiry; without collecting and comparing the data; without presenting his evidence for the assertion, he makes the following authoritative declaration. "Apart from the general analogies which we find in all early civilizations, the Script, the Theology and the Astronomy of Egypt and Babylonia show no vestiges of a common source." (Hib. Lect. p. 136.)

There may be a pitfall intended in these delusive words as the mythology and so-called cosmology are entirely omitted. But you cannot have the Astronomy apart from the Mythology by which it was represented! The Prof. says further there is one conclusive and fatal objection to the derivation from Egypt "inasmuch as there is no traceable connection between the hieroglyphics of Egypt and the primitive pictures out of which the cuneiform characters were developed." Professor Sayce is an expert and an authority passably orthodox, whose word will be taken for gospel by those who are not qualified to question it. I am not an acknowledged authority. I can only plead that my facts may have a hearing. Without knowing the facts we cannot attain the truth, and short of the fullest truth there is no final authority. The Egyptian hieroglyphics were developed out of the same primitive pictures and natural objects as the Akkadian. Both were direct transcripts from nature at first, and there is but one origin in nature for the earliest figures. Again he says: "If Lepsius were right (in maintaining the opposite view) the primitive hieroglyphics out of which the cuneiform characters were evolved would offer resemblances to the hieroglyphics. But this is not the case. Even the idea of divinity is represented differently in them. In Chaldea it is expressed by an eight-rayed star; in Egypt, by a stone-headed axe" (p. 435).

That is true; and yet in the sole illustration adduced by him the Professor is wrong! The evidence of the first witness called is against the truth of his vaguely vast generalization. The star with eight rays is likewise an Egyptian ideograph of divinity; it is a numerical figure for the Nunu or Associate Gods. (Burton E.H. 34.) This is the sign of the pleroma of the godhead, the divine ogdoad. It was continued as a symbol of Horus-Orion, the manifestor of the Eight, the mummy-constellation of the only one who rose again! The eight-rayed sign was also a symbol of Hathor and of Taht because, like the eight-rayed or eight-looped star, it was the numerical figure of the eight gods, hence it was the sign of the Abode as Hathor, and the manifestor as Taht-Smen; as it is of Ishtar and of Assur. The Egyptians not only used this octave of divinity, they also give us the reason for using it. This numerical sign of the primary group of eight gods was not continued as the symbol of abstract divinity, and it is rare, but still it exists to refute the Professor, who has to plumb far more profoundly before he touches bottom. The five-rayed star, Seb, is likewise the hieroglyphic symbol for a god or divinity, so that the Professor's suggested inference is false twice over. It will never do to presume too much on the common ignorance concerning the buried past of Egypt, the rootage out of range, and the long development of the original ideographs. For example, the Egyptian pictograph of a soul is a human-headed bird, and that type is continued when the Babylonian dead are described as being clad like birds in a garment of feathers. Notwithstanding Mr. Sayce's offhand dicta it will be seen in the future that Egypt was as truly the parent of hieroglyphics as she is of alphabets! But to show the Professor's determination to avoid Egypt: after pointing to the fact that the statues from Telloh bear a great likeness to the Egyptian in the time of the pyramid builders; and after admitting that the Egyptian art of sculpture was infinitely superior to the Babylonian at that time,—he quietly suppresses Egypt altogether on behalf of an entirely unknown "school of sculpture in the Sinaitic peninsula!" (P. 138.) Anything rather than look Egypt honestly in the face!

The Professor is so anxious to hustle unacceptable facts out of sight and get rid of their testimony, he asserts that the existence of a "Cushite race" in Chaldea solely depends on a misinterpretation and a probable corruption of the text in the Book of Genesis. But Cush is the black. The Cushites were the Black race; and the aborigines of Babylonia were the Black men of the monuments, the "black-heads" of the Akkadian Texts. Hence the god Kus, their deity of eclipse and darkness. The Professor is all hind-before with regard (or disregard) to the origins in the black land, the primeval birthplace. He is not yet out of the Ark of the Semitic or the shadow of the Aryan beginnings, which have so darkened and deluded us; and has to advance backwards a good deal further beyond the Altaic boundaries.

As I have already shown in the "Natural Genesis," the beginnings of mythology in Egypt and Akkad are definitely identical. The Old Dragon of Chaos and the Abyss is the same whether called Tiamat, Tavthe, or Typhon. By Typhon I mean the beast that imaged the first Great Mother, hippopotamus in front and crocodile behind, who therefore is the Dragon of Egypt. Her name of Tep, Teb, or Tept is the original of Typhon. Tiamat=Tavthe represents that abyss of the beginning which is the Egyptian Tepht. This Tepht is the abyss, the source, the void, the hole of the snake, the habitat of the dragon, the outrance or uterus of birth as place which preceded personification. Another name for the abyss is Abzu, the earlier form of which is the Egyptian Khepsh in the north—that is, the Pool of Khep, the hippopotamus or Typhon=Dragon. Tept and Tavthe are one, the water-horse and dragon-horse are one. In both forms they give birth to the well-known seven primal powers, elemental energies, or demons of physical force, first recognised as warring in chaos, who were afterwards cast out and superseded, or moralised as the seven wicked spirits. When the primary powers become the seven evil spirits, it is said of them, "They are not known among the sentient gods." So in Egypt the same seven were denounced as the non-sentient "Children of inertness." And just as the Akkadian seven were continued and made the messengers and ministers of wrath to the supreme God, Anu, so did the Egyptian seven survive as the seven great spirits in the service of Ra; their station being in the region of the Great Bear, the constellation of their mother. (Rit., ch. 17.)

This mother-goddess first brought forth in space and next in time. If we take the star of evening and morning as the type of the earliest time, then the mother Tiamat passes into Ishtar, goddess of the evening and the morning star. The dragon Tiamat was called the Bis-Bis, identified by George Smith with the crocodile as the symbol of Egypt; and Ishtar=Venus, the "Lady of Dawn," was called Bis-bisi, which shows the survival of the same genetrix in her change of character out of space into time. Another proof of this continuity by transformation is furnished when Ishtar as Queen of Heaven (so rendered by Mr. Sayce) calls herself the "Unique Monster" (p. 267.) Precisely in the same way do we see the Typhonian genetrix Ta-Urt in Egypt pass into Hes-ta-Urt (whence Hestaroth or Ashtaroth) and Hathor, when the domesticated cow succeeded the water-cow as the Zoötype of Hes, As (Isis), or of Hathor, the Lunar form of the Goddess of Love, in whose person the beast was transfigured into the beauty.

According to ancient tradition, the culture of Chaldea was brought to that country by a Fish-Man, who rose up in "the first year," from that part of the Red or "Erythræan Sea which borders upon Babylonia." The original of this type can be identified in Ea the fish-god, deity of the house of the deep and divinity of wisdom. Whence came Ea, then, by the Red Sea? Lepsius says from Egypt—so says Egypt herself.

Professor Sayce had previously denied our right to compare the myths of two different nations before their relationships have been established by language, and that by grammar (which is late), in preference to the vocabulary. Thus mythology is put out of court, and words are to be accounted of no weight. Still, it is well to remember that the Professor has before now taken his stand on a false bottom that was found to be crumbling under foot day by day! It is at least suggestive to find that the name and nature of Ea, the oldest Akkadian form of the One God, may be so fully explained by the Egyptian Uâ (later Ea) for the one, the one alone, isolated as the only one; also the Thinker and the Captain of the Boat. It should be premised that the Egyptian U preceded the letter or sound of E, hence Ua=Ea. The Egyptian Ua, which passed into Ea, also appears in the Akkadian Ua for the Supreme One, the sole Lord or Chief. In one form Ea is the fish-god, and the hieroglyphic sign for Ua=Ea is fishing-tackle! Ea was the deity of the deep, and Ua=Ea is Boat and Captain both. Of course the fish was the earlier image, but the Egyptians had gone far ahead in substituting the work of their own hands for the primitive natural types. Ea is the wise god, the thinker and instructor; and *Uaua* (Eg.) means to think, consider, meditate. Ea's prototype in the indefinitely earlier mythology of Egypt is Num=Kneph, whose twofold nature is indicated by the two ways of spelling one name. As Num he is Lord of the inundation; as Kneph he is the Breath of those who are in the firmament. Nef signifies breath, and is also the name of the sailor. Ea is god of the watercourse and the atmosphere. Ea was the Antelope of the deep; Num was the bearded He-goat; the Sea-goat of the Zodiac. One type of Num is the serpent; as it is of Ea. Ea is said to represent the House, which is â in Egyptian. In a case of this kind Professor Sayce can only perceive or will only admit a "general analogy."

Egyptian also offers the likeliest original for the name of Oan or Oannes, the Greek form of Ea, the fish, seeing that Ua=Oa, and that An is the fish in Egyptian; whilst An, to appear, to show, is determined by the fish in the water-precinct, where the fish is the revealer who emerged from the waters as Ea-an, or Oannes. (Denkmäler 3, 46 C.) If the original Fish-Man came from Egypt, it would probably be as the Crocodile=Dragon, the Typhonian type of both the ancient mother and her son Sevekh. The crocodile *is* the fish that passes the day on dry land and the night in the waters. Its name of Sevekh is identical with that of the number seven; and Ea is connected with a typical fish of seven fins (?). The crocodile, as Plutarch tells us, was a supreme type of the one God, or, as the name shows, of the seven-fold powers in one image. Sevekh was the same good demon of one Cult in Egypt that Num-Ra was in the other, but indefinitely earlier.

To my apprehension, the Babylonian "House of the Seven bonds of heaven and earth," is identical with the "House of the Seven Halls and Seven stairways," assigned to Osiris; and the God Nebo as stellar, lunar, and planetary Deity; as prophet and proclaimer, is identical with Sut-Anup (later Nub and Anubis) in a dozen different aspects; whilst Nebo-Nusku=the double Anubis. Further, the same Great Mother who was Venus as Hathor became the mother-moon. Professor Sayce seems to think that where the moon is male it cannot also be female. If I am right, Ishtar must also have had a lunar character as the Mother-Goddess. But Professor Sayce makes the point-blank assertion that Ishtar was not a goddess of the moon. (P. 256.) "The moon was conceived of as a God, not as a Goddess." He assures us that Ishtar was the spirit of earth and the Goddess of Love, the dual divinity of the planet Venus. But there is no male moon without the female Goddess. It is not a question of "Conception," but of begettal. The observers were concerned with the lunar phases as natural facts, the mother or reproducing phase being first. The mother Goddess brought forth the Child of light, whether as Taht, Khunsu, Duzu, Tammuz, or Horus, and there is no lunar myth possible without the motherhood, which preceded the fatherhood. The child of the moon in one phase is her consort in the other. Thus when Ishtar makes up to Izdubar, the solar god who represents the later fatherhood, he twits her on the subject of her child-consort, the bridegroom of her youth, whom she had so long pursued, like Venus wooing Adonis. In the legend of Tammuz and Ishtar the Goddess, in descending to the underworld in search of her bridegroom, passes through seven gates. In each of these she is stripped of a part of her glory, represented as her ornaments. On her return she ascends through seven other gates, when her ornaments are restored to her, both being done according to ancient rules. These gates are the 14 lower lunar mansions in which the lunar Osiris was torn into 14 parts by Typhon, the Power of darkness, when Isis descended in search of her beloved. They likewise coincide with the 14 houses of judgment and the 14 trials in the Egyptian Book of the Dead, which will explain the tests and punishments of the Goddess as the pre-solar type of the suffering and triumphing souls who had to win their crown of justification in these 14 trials. Besides which one of Ishtar's titles is that of Goddess Fifteen, because that is the day of mid-moon in a soli-lunar month of 30 days. Professor Sayce leaves this title unnoticed, and then denies that Ishtar was a goddess of the moon! Moreover, there is another test to be applied in natural phenomena. The Goddess in her Course is credited with various infidelities. Not only is she charged with having clung year after year to her child-consort Tammuz, as the Bridegroom, amongst her victims are the Eagle (Alala) the Lion, the Horse, Tabulu the shepherd, and Isullanu, the gardener. These, as I read the Mythos, refer to certain constellations, corner-keepers or others, to be found in the lunar course, which cannot apply to the planet Venus or to the Spirit of the earth. A sign of the lunar reckoning may be read in the statement that Ishtar rode the horse with whip and spur for seven leagues galloping, or during one quarter of the moon. Another lunar sign may be seen in the statement that Ishtar had also torn out the teeth of the Lion seven by seven, or for seven nights together, in her passage through the Lion-quarter of the moon; Eagle, Horse (Pegasus?), and Lion most probably stand for three of the four quarters of a lunar zodiac. Also the Errand of Ishtar corresponds to the descent of Isis into the underworld in search of Osiris, who was torn into 14 parts, and Isis was the lunar Goddess. Moreover, Ishtar robbed her lover, Isullanu, of his eye, and in his blindness mocked him; just as Horus and Samson were each robbed of an eye. Lastly, the Bow was lunar and Ishtar was Goddess of the Bow. Here, as elsewhere, we are left utterly adrift if we cannot secure a firm anchorage in the various natural phenomena themselves, by which the types of divinity must be determined. Professor Sayce acknowledges his inability to account for the name of Ishtar. "Its true etymology was buried in the night of antiquity." "It is therefore quite useless to speculate on the subject." (P. 257.) And so, of course, there is an end of it, the last word being said. It is just possible, however, that Egypt, from which the Professor looks religiously away, has something final yet to say on these matters. Not perhaps by such interpretation as Mr. Renouf's. Professor Sayce admits that Ishtar appears as Esther in the Book of Esther. Here it is Hadassah who figures in the mythical character of Ishtar as the virgin dedicated or betrothed during twelve months. Whether the typical character is thus continued or not, it is the fact that the word "Shtar "* is the Egyptian name of the Betrothed female, and Shta denotes that which is most mystical, secret, and holy, the very mother of mystery. Ishtar was the betrothed of Tammuz; she was called the "Bridal Goddess," the goddess who was mystically betrothed to the child that grew up to become her own Consort. She remained the Mother of Mystery. Thus Ishtar=Venus, the goddess of love, was the Shtar or Betrothed, as the pre-monogamic consort or bride, *i.e.*, the "bridal goddess," who is denounced in Revelation as the Great Harlot.

Again, it appears to me that much of what I have already said of Horus, of Taht, of Khunsu, Apollo, and other forms of the soli-lunar hero is applicable not only to Mithras but to Merodach, and to an Assyrian god called Adar (provisionally). I may claim to have discovered the origin of this particular mythical character through seeking the foundations in natural phenomena. Adar is a solar hero who is especially related to night and darkness, and yet is a deity of light. He is a warrior and champion of the gods. He is the voice or supreme oracle of the divinities. He is the son, the messenger, the revealer of the Solar god hidden in the deep of the underworld. In other features he is like Taht and Khunsu, each of whom is the visible representative, the revealer, of the sun-god by night. Adar was designated "Lord of the date," just as Taht was called "Lord of the date-palm." Adar was likewise "Lord of the Pig," just as Khunsu is the personified lord over the pig of Typhon in the disk of the moon at full (Zodiac of Denderah). This is the god who, as Adonis, was slain by the pig or boar at one season of the year, but who was victor over it in the first of the six upper signs, which is the sign of Pisces in the Zodiac of Denderah.† This same character is continued in Tammuz, the deity who was first brought forth by the mother alone, to become her consort, the only one of a twofold nature; and who was made the later revealer of a Father in heaven as the child of the solar god when reborn as such of the mother-moon. The month of Tammuz in the Aramaic calendar is (roughly) our month of June. This is the month of Duzu in the Assyrian calendar. In the Egyptian it was the month Mesore, as June in the sacred year, the month of the re-birth of the river and of the child Horus, who was re-born (Mes) of the river at the re-birth of the Inundation. In the pre-Osirian Mythos the child was the representative of Tum, and to be the re-born (Mes) Tum or the child of Tum, as was Iu-em-hept, the Eternal Word, would be renderable as Tum-mus or Messu, just as Ra-messu means the child of the solar god, although I am not aware that Tum does appear under that form of name, and I am supposing that Tammuz was a development from the Egyptian Tum. For this reason! We are told in the texts ‡ that Tum is the duplicate of Aten=Adon=Adonai; and Adon= Tammuz. Aten was the child-God; Tum was the father. This child of the sun-god was always born in the moon as the solar light of the world by night, the son of the Spirit of the deep who was the hidden sun in the under-world. He is pourtrayed in the disk of the full-moon both as Horus (or Tum-mes) and

---

* Champollion. Gram: 1292. † Macrobius. Saturn. 121. ‡ Records 4.95.

Khunsu (Planisphere and Zodiacs of Denderah). Now, when the actual deluge began with the sun in the sign of the Beetle (later Crab), and in the month of Tammuz or Mesore, the moon rose at full in the sign of the sea-goat, and the child was therefore reborn of the full moon in that sign, and so on through the three water signs, which are consequently solar on one side of the Zodiac and lunar on the other! Rightly read this absolutely proves the Egyptian origin of the signs set in heaven in relation to the Inundation, the lunar zodiac being first, and identifies the child of Tum as the original of the Akkadian Dumu-zi-Apzu, and of the Semite "Timmuz (or Dimmuz) of the Flood;"* not Noah's unfortunate deluge, but the inundation of the Nile, the deluge that began in the month Mes-Horus or Tum-Mes=Tammuz, and culminated at the autumn equinox as it always has done, and did this year. The Akkadian name of the month Tammuz is Su-Kul-na, "seizer of seed," and to explain that we must go back to the sign of the Beetle set above by the Egyptians, because the beetle Khepr began to roll up his seed at that time to preserve it from the coming flood. The Beetle is the sign of Cancer in the oblong Zodiac of Denderah.

Professor Sayce's account of Tammuz and Ishtar shows neither gauge nor grip of the real subject matter. He tells us that Adonis=Tammuz was "slain by the Boar's Tusk of Winter," and his "funeral-festival" was held in June because the "bright Sun of the springtide was then slain and withered by the hot blasts of summer" (pp. 227-9). But here is the true rendering as restored according to the Egyptian myth, which was extant in the pre-monumental times of the Shus-en-Har, who are claimed to have been the Rulers for 13,000 years before the time of Menes. The Solar God as Source of Life was re-born in natural phenomena, as his own child the Horus of Light in the Moon; the Child of the Lotus in the Water; the Seed as the Bread of Life in the Corn. In each phase he was opposed by Sut-Typhon in the form of Darkness, Drought, or Death. Previous to the Inundation he was pierced by Sut in the parching Drought. Then it was the errand of Isis as of Ishtar to fetch the Water of Life. This she did as the Lunar Mistress of the Water. At the birth of the River in Mesore-Tammuz, the Moon rose at full in the first Lunar Water-sign, whither she had gone for the Water of Life in the under-world—or, astronomically, entered the lowest signs. Here is one proof. Papsukal is the Regent of Capricorn, the first water-sign, and he is the messenger that hurries off to the Sun-God (who is certainly not the dead Tammuz!) with the news of Ishtar's arrival in search of the Fountain of Life.

Isis in her search was accompanied by Anup, her golden dog; and in the Hermean Zodiac Anup is stationed in the sign of the Sea-Goat, where he is shaking the Systrum of Isis to frighten away the Typhonian influences.— (Plutarch.) Here is additional evidence. When the Moon rose at full in these three signs they represented the Waters of Life to Egypt, in accordance with the then flowing Inundation of the Nile; but when the Sun itself entered the sign of Capricorn, in winter, the passage became the "*Crossing of the Waters of Death*," for the Solar God, or the Souls in the Eschatological phase. Hence the typical "Two Waters" of the Egyptian Mythos, called the Pools of the North and South. My contention is, that the imagery thus set in heaven to reflect the seasons on earth was Egyptian from the first, and that it can only be rightly read in the original version according to time and season in Egypt.

Professor Sayce makes the perplexing assertion that "the month of Tammuz was called in the Akkadian Calendar 'the month of the Errand of Ishtar.'" But the month *Ki-Innanna* (formerly read Ki-Gingir-na), the message of Nanna or Ishtar, is *Ululu*, two months later than Tammuz; and the message of Ishtar, as Virgo, in August, is not to be converted into the legend of her descent into Hades in June, when the Sun was in Cancer and the full Moon was in Capricorn.

Merodach represents the Sun in Scorpio, as the deity of that sign, but this

---

* Sayce, p. 233.

does not mean that he is the Sun itself! In the Egyptian mythos it was as the Sun in Scorpio that Osiris was betrayed to his death by Typhon. Then his son, Horus=Merodach, was reborn of the Moon in the Bull, the first of the six upper signs, to become the avenger of his victimised father! Thus as heir-apparent of the Solar God, the Hero comes to the aid of the Moon during an eclipse, and overcomes the Dragon of Darkness.

This revealer of the father-god in natural phenomena, under whatsoever name, is supremely important as the mythical character that supplied the type to current Christology. When the scientific fact was first discovered the doctrine of a divine trinity, consisting of father, mother, and child, was then established. The child was the light of the sun, his father being the hidden source in the underworld, his mother the moon, as reproducer of that light. This reflex image of the father's glory, his light of the world by night, the representative of his power in the six upper signs, whilst the sun was in the six lower signs, is the child as Horus, as the re-born Tum=Tum-mes, Tammuz, Apollo, Merodach, the hero, the warrior against the dragon, and the powers of darkness at night or during the lunar eclipse, the Masu, the anointed, the only begotten, and lastly, the mythical Messiah and the Christ. This is the all-important fact, furnished by the past as a factor in the theology of the present, which meets with no recognition whatsoever from Professor Sayce, or from any other writers on mythology who are known to me.

Except in the technique of his scholarship, one sees but little sign that the professor has thought out his far-reaching subject fundamentally. For example, Berossos repeats a Babylonian description of nature, which he distinctly affirms to have been allegorical. The professor admits (p. 392) that these "composite creatures were really the offspring of Totemism"; that is, they were symbolical Zoötypes. And yet he can say of them, "we may see (in these) a sort of anticipation of the Darwinian hypothesis"! But men with wings, two heads, and horses' feet, centaurs, mermaids, and sphinxes, belong to a mythical mode of representing ideas, not to "imperfect, first attempts of nature," in accordance with the doctrine of development. Such confusion of thought is likely to make the truth of the matter doubly indistinguishable. Again, he tells us that "the god was a beast before he became a man," whereas he means that the primary forces recognised in nature first were represented by Zoötypes before the superhuman powers were imaged in the human likeness. He does not define what he means by "worship" or "religion" when he imports these terms into the remoter past, and thus sets up a false standard of judgment. Worship of the heavenly bodies was nothing more than the looking up to them as the tellers of time, even though they may be called oracles! The Kronian gods were only types of time in a world without clocks and watches. He speaks of theological conceptions becoming mythical, whereas the mythical representation preceded the theological phase. He can "find no trace of ancestor-worship in the early literature of Chaldea" (p. 358). But I doubt whether a man who resolves the Dæmon of Socrates into an Intuition, can know how or where to look for the proof. He tells us the earliest Babylonian religion was purely Shamanistic, only the spirits it recognised were not spirits in "our sense of the word," whichever sense that may be! Now Shamanism is the most primitive kind of Spiritualism, but it includes human spirits as well as the elementals; and as human spirits include the spirits of ancestors, and as Mul-lil is the Lord of ghost-world, and Nergal is the god of apparitions, called the Khadhi (which agrees with the Egyptian Khati for the dead), then the Shamanism of Babylonia must have included a worship of ancestors! The non-evolutionist cannot truly interpret the past for us, even when reinforced by the non-spiritualist.

It matters little to me that Professor Sayce should ignore my work, but it does matter greatly to him that he should have to ignore all the facts which are fatal to his assumptions. He cannot get rid of the facts by thus ignoring them. He cannot establish a negation by closing his eyes to all that is positively opposed to his conclusions. In trying to do so he has blindly shut out all that Egypt had to say and show and suggest. That simple policy was practised long ago by the ostrich, and the ruse is generally acknowledged to have proved a preposterous failure. As the superstructure of Assyriology is now reared and settling down securely upon fixed foundations, I am willing to discuss the matters here mooted in the press or debate with Professor Sayce upon the platform, where I will undertake to demonstrate the common origin of the mythological astronomy, and prove that the Egyptian is the primeval parent of the Babylonian. Meanwhile the foregoing pages and the following comparative list (not to say anything of the "Natural Genesis") contain a sufficient answer to his declaration that the two have nothing in common but general analogies:—

EGYPTIAN.		BABYLONIAN.
Tepht, the abyss.	=	*Tavthe*, the abyss.
Khepsh, pool of hippopotamus.	=	*Abzu*, the deep.
Bau, the hole or void.	=	*Bahu*, the void personified.
Tep, Typhon, the dragon.	=	*Tavthe* = *Tiamat*, the dragon.
Matut, Storm-God.	=	*Matu*, Storm-God.
Isis as the Scorpion.	=	*Ishtar as the Scorpion.*
Triad of Isis, Nephtys, and Horus.	=	*Triad of Ishtar, Tillil, and Tammuz.*
Ra, God of the Double House.	=	*Ea*, God of the House.
Five Celestials born of Seb.	=	*Five Aninas*, or spirits of heaven.
Seven evil spirits.	=	*Seven evil spirits.*
Seven servants of Ra.	=	*Seven servants of Anu.*
The Nunu, 8 gods or spirits.	=	*The Anúnus*, or 8 spirits of earth.
The Put Circle of 9 Spirits, or gods of heaven.	=	*The Igigi*, 9 spirits of heaven.
Num, god of the deep and inundation, and the "good wind."	=	*Ea*, god of the deep and the "good wind."
Ua = *Ea*, the captain.	=	*Ea*, god of the boat.
Hathor, the white heifer.	=	*Ishtar*, the white heifer.
Shetar, the betrothed.	=	*Ishtar*, the "bridal goddess."
Anup, the announcer.	=	*Nebo*, the announcer.
Double Anubis.	=	*Nebo and Nusku.*
Taht-Khunsu.	=	*Adar.*
Horus (luni-solar hero).	=	*Merodach.*
Tum as Aten or the Messu.	=	*Tammuz.*
Kek, god of darkness.	=	*Kus*, god of darkness.
Â, moon, lunar divinity.	=	*Â*, lunar divinity.
Khekh, a spirit.	=	*Igigi*, spirits.
Rupa, the prince.	=	*Rubu*, the prince.
Nerau, the chief, the victor.	=	*Nerra*, the victor.
Ser, chief, head.	=	*Sar*, king.
Tabu, great bear or hippopotamus.	=	*Dabu*, the great bear or hippopotamus.

GERALD MASSEY.

P.S.—By the by, is Professor Sayce equally certain that he is correct in his dates of precession? He gives the entrance of the vernal equinox into the signs of the Bull and Ram as being about the years 4,700 and 2,500 B.C. I found that Cassini and other astronomers gave the figures 4,565 and 2,410 B.C. And from data kindly supplied to me by the present Astronomer Royal from independent calculations made at Greenwich, these were the dates, corroborated and confirmed.

THE DEVIL OF DARKNESS

IN THE

LIGHT OF EVOLUTION.

(Fuller Egyptian and Gnostic Data, with references to authorities, may be found in the Author's "Natural Genesis."

THERE are two things which I have come to look upon as constituting the *unpardonable* sin of the father and mother against the helpless innocence of infancy. The one is in allowing their little children to run the risk of blood-poisoning—such as was once suffered by a child of mine—from the *filthy fraud of vaccination*. The other is in permitting the mind and soul of their children to be inoculated with the still more fatal virus of the old, false, orthodox dogmas and delusions, by allowing them to believe that the fables of ancient mythology are the sacred and solely true "Word of God," if they are found in the Hebrew Scriptures—the one book of the religiously ignorant. Generation after generation we learn, unlearn, and relearn the same lying, legendary lore, and it takes the latter half of all one's lifetime to throw off the mass of corrupting error instilled into us during the earlier half, even when we do break out and slough it off in a mental eruption, and *have to* find ourselves in utter rebellion against things as they are. Unfortunately, the mass of people never do get rid of this infection, nor of the desire to give their disease to others.

The fact of the matter is, the Christian dogmas and doctrines began as such with being unintelligible and inexplicable; they were to remain as mysteries; and any true explanation of them is death to their false pretentions. It is my method to explode by explaining them. Take the doctrine of the Trinity for example. Can any theologian throughout all Christendom to-day give us any intelligible account of its origin and primary meaning? Not one. For that we must go to mythology, which was earlier than our theology, and which alone enables us to explain its primitive mysteries. The natural genesis of the Trinity was found, and is to be refound, in lunar phenomena. The moon, in mythology and chronology, was a time-measurer of a three-fold nature. At fifteen days of age, or full-moon, it was the mother-moon. Hence Ishtar, in Akkad, is designated Goddess 15. The lessening, waning moon was her little one, the child of the moon, who became the virile one, the adult, as the horned new moon, the reproducer who was fabled to rebeget himself on the mother moon, and thus become his own father, as a natural mode of describing natural phenomena.

These three *are* eternally *one* in external nature—a Trinity always manifesting monthly, and the triple aspect was humanly, or naturally, expressed by means of the mother, child, and reproducing male, which three are also one in the total human being. In the Christian Iconography, you will sometimes see the Virgin Mary enthroned in the new moon, with the child in her arms, and these two, with the horned or phallic moon, constitute the Christian Trinity in Unity. Such was the primitive mode of thinking in things, afterwards continued in a mystical or doctrinal phase. *Such*, I affirm to be the *origin* of the Trinity in mythology, which preceded religion; and when this is applied abstractly, to the nature of deity, or to mind in nature, by means of metaphysic, the result is an imposition, and he or she who practises imposition, consciously or not, is an impostor. No such thing can be known as a triune or triangular God; but we are able to show how such types originated. When our words are examined, we shall frequently find that our metaphysic has been abstracted, or falsely filched from primitive physics, as was the Trinity by Plato, which was continued by the Christian Fathers, who tell us that but for Plato they would never have understood the doctrine of the Trinity. As with the Trinity, so it is with the origin of the theological Devil. The crucial question of the savage man, Friday, was too fundamental for the theology of Robinson Crusoe. Friday asks, "But, if God much strong, much mighty as the devil, why God no kill the devil, and so make him no more wicked?" Crusoe, imitating other theologists, not knowing what to say, "pretended not to hear him." (I am told this passage has been omitted from certain recent editions.) To give an answer to that question we shall have to go round to work. It would never do to begin a lecture on this subject like the well-known chapter headed "Snakes in Iceland," which consisted of the statement, "there are no snakes in Iceland!" If I did, my lecture might be summed up in the words, "there is no devil." But every belief, superstition, and mental type, had its natural genesis once, the devil included.

The result of 14 years' research in the Records of the Past is a personal conviction that the human mind has long suffered an eclipse, and been darkened and dwarfed in the shadow of ideas, the real meaning of which has been lost to the moderns! Myths and allegories, whose significance was once unfolded to the initiates in the ancient mysteries, have been adopted in ignorance, and re-issued as real truths divinely vouchsafed to mankind for the first and only time when found in the Hebrew writings! The earlier religions had their myths interpreted by means of the oral and unwritten Wisdom. We have ours *misinterpreted;* and a great deal of what has been imposed upon us as God's direct, true, and sole revelation to man, is a mass of *inverted myths*, under the shadow of which men have been cowering as timorously as birds in the stubble, when a kite in the shape of a hawk is held hovering overhead to keep them down; as I have seen it practised in England!

The parables and types of the primeval thinkers have been elevated to the "Sphere," as the "hawk," or "serpent," the "bull," or the "crab," that give names to certain groups of stars, and we are precisely in the same relationship to these religious parables and allegories as we should be to astronomical facts, if we thought the serpent and bull, lion, sea-goat, and ram were real animals up in heaven, instead of constellations with symbolical names. The Jews picked up various traditions of other races. Moses, they tell us, was an initiate in all the learning of the Egyptians. And these myths have been so handled as to efface their primitive features altogether. They have been so "sweated" down, by later theologies, to make capital—get gold-dust, as it were, out of them—that they can only be recognised by comparison with the earlier copies yet extant among other nations, from which the Jews derived their versions.

Fossil remains, found in the lowermost strata of human thought, have been preserved as divine patterns for the ignorant and superstitious of later ages. The simple realities of the earliest times were expressed by signs and symbols, and these have been taken and applied to later thought, and converted into theological problems and metaphysical mysteries, for which our theologians have no basis whatever, and can only wrangle over *en l'air;* they cannot touch solid earth with one foot when they want to kick opponents with the other; and when they try to bite you very viciously they find that they have only been furnished with a set of teeth that are false. The only possible way of exposing the false pretentions of theological dogmas is by explaining them from the root, and showing what they meant as mythos. The orthodox teaching which is founded on the "Fall of Man," is shattered, even as a pane of glass is fractured at a blow, when once we can apply the Doctrine of Development.

The Hebrew devil, or Satan, means the opponent or adversary, and the first great natural adversary recognised by primitive man was Darkness—simply darkness, the constant and eternal enemy of the light—that is, the power of darkness was literal before it became metaphorical, moral, or spiritual.

Hence darkness itself was the earliest devil or adversary, the obstructor and deluder of man, the eternal enemy of the sun. We speak of the "jaws of darkness;" and darkness was the vast, huge, swallower of the light, night after night. We know this was identified as the primary power, because the primitive or early man reckoned time by nights, and the years by Eclipses. This mode of reckoning was first and universal. So many darks preceded so many days. The dark power is primary in all the oldest traditions and cults of the human race. Hence sacrifice was first offered to the powers of darkness. The fore-words of universal mythology are " there was darkness." All was dark at first within the mind; and the *all was* the *darkness* that created dread without. The influence of night, the eclipse, and the black thunder-cloud being first felt, the primitive man visibly emerges from the shadow of darkness as deeply impressed and indelibly dyed in mind as was his body with its natural blackness. The black man without was negroid within, as his reflection remains in the mirror of mythology. The darkness then, in natural phenomena, was the original devil that put out the light by swallowing it incessantly, as the subtle enemy, the obstructor, deluder, and general adversary of man. The first form of the Devil was female, called the Dragon of Darkness, who was Tiamat in Akkad, and Typhon in Egypt. Typhon gave birth to Sut, who became the Egyptian devil—our Satan—and who was represented by the Black jackal, the voice of Darkness; and Sut, the black one, gives us the name of Soot, the black thing. Angro-Mainyus, the Persian devil, was the black one of the two powers of Light and Darkness.

Primitive man, however, did not imagine or personify a devil behind visible phenomena, that caused the darkness. Darkness itself was the devil, and even as late as the Parsee Bundahish (which means the aboriginal creation) external darkness is the devil.

The seven devils or seven heads of the old Dragon, in the Akkadian myths of creation, are born in the mountains of sunset, which shows the same natural genesis in physical phenomena. They had their *birth-place* where the sun went down. At the same place, in the West, the Egyptians stationed the Great Crocodile that swallowed down the lights, sun, moon, and stars, as they set each night, in its wide-open jaws of darkness. Hence the crocodile was an ideograph of the swallowing darkness—and of earth, or the waters below, called the Abyss; and the tail of the crocodile remained in the Egyptian hieroglyphics as the sign of Kam—that is, of blackness or darkness. The crocodile was the typical Dragon of the waters below, the old Typhon, as the serpent was of the waters, or overwhelming darkness, above. Hor-Apollo tells us the Egyptians represent the mouth by a serpent, because the serpent is all mouth. This was another figure of the swallower, as the Akhekh and the Apap serpent. Akhekh signifies darkness, and Apap means that which rises up vast and gigantic—in short, the monster — the typical Apap being based on the great African rock-snake. Here, then, is the reason why the mythical dragon and the old serpent are identical or interchangeable in mythology, each being a representative of the devil of darkness and of Satan, that old serpent, who imaged the evil which was first perceived in physical phenomena. Out of the darkness leapt the lightning-bolt, and in the deep waters lurked another subtle foe of life, and thus the jaws, the fang, and the sting of death were assigned to the devil of darkness, who gradually assumed the character of man's mortal enemy that brought death into the world. The course of this development can be traced from the beginning, in physical darkness, to the culmination, in a psycho-theistic phase, for everything yields to an application of the evolutionary method—and you may depend upon it that evolution has come into the world to stay; and evolution and the Hebrew genesis cannot co-exist in the same mental world.

The earliest mode of representing the eternal alternation of external phenomena called night and day, or darkness and light, the good and bad, is to be found in the universal myth of the Two Brothers, who are born twins,—very imperfect versions of which may be found in the legends of Cain and Abel, and of Esau and Jacob. In this myth, the Dark and Day are born twins of the Great Mother, and these brothers are pourtrayed as always being at enmity with each other, and in conflict before their birth, as are the darkness and the light when struggling at dawn! They fight one another in the effort of each to get born first. This becomes the well-known struggle of the birthright, which is universal in mythology. Far more perfect versions of the same mythos are extant among the blacks of Australia, the Red Indians of America, the Bushmen and Hottentots of Africa, more perfect, because simpler, nearer to nature, and less moralized. It is the myth of Sut-Horus in Egypt. Sut-Horus is the dual manifestor of dark and light, who is depicted with the double head of the black vulture of night and the golden hawk of light, upon one body. The dark one was born first, because darkness was first cognised; but they both continued to struggle for supremacy after birth, as they had done before it, because they dramatised the ceaseless and endless alternation of night and day, of dark and light, seen in the heavens at eve and dawn, in the orb of the moon, and the lengthening of darkness, or of light, in autumn and in spring! Here again the dark power is the devil, the bad dev, and the light is the good power, the bright dev.

The same conflict, based upon the alternation of light and darkness, is pourtrayed as the struggle of St. George, our solar hero, who conquers the dragon just as Horus overthrows the Apap dragon upon the monuments of Egypt. And when the devil's knell is rung annually at Horbury, in Yorkshire, England, *that* is in celebration of the death of the Dragon of Darkness; and the same custom is also continued in ringing out the old year, on the last night in December. When in New South Wales I picked up a tradition of the blacks. The Devil, called Mullion, lived in a very tall tree, at

Girra, on the Barwon river, and used to eat black fellows! They tried to burn down this vast tree, in which the Devil of darkness dwelt, but the fires were always put out by invisible spirits. Then they got a red mouse, put a lighted straw in his mouth, and started him up the tree. The loose bark caught fire, the tree blazed for weeks, the devil was burned out, and never came back again. This red mouse is also a type of Horus in Egypt. Naturally, then, the devil of darkness was the first divinity, because the dark power is primal! When it came to worshipping, or, rather, to propitiating, by offering the fruits of fear, it was the dark power that predominated, because this struck terror and elicited fear. "*Primos in orbe deos fecit timor!*" Sometimes these twins of darkness and light are called the ugly and beautiful brothers. And here the persistence of the mythical types may be noticed, for these two are not only continued as the Sut-Horus, or double Horus of Egypt, but they are likewise extant in that museum of mythical types, the Catacombs of Rome, as the Twin-Christs, one of which is pourtrayed as the beautiful youth; the other is the little, old, and ugly Christ. Just as it was in the pre-Christian times, from which these figures were a Gnostic survival.

Next, Mind becomes an element in the manifestation of phenomena; and in the American myths, the born twins are called the bad mind and the good mind. In this phase the twin-brothers are not only mental, they are also moralized on their way to becoming the dual divinity, or modern God and Devil. In the Avesta, and other Persian Scriptures, for example, the twin-brothers can be traced from the Natural Genesis in phenomena, as light and darkness, to their becoming personified as divinity and devil, in Ahura-Mazda, the God of mental light, and Angro-Mainyus, the devil of mental darkness. Here the older bogey of the night has been found out! Men had dipped into the dark, and suffered from the shadow of eclipse so long, and passed through them so often and so safely, that their essential unreality was discovered at last. Thus Angro-Mainyus, the black mind, is only accredited with the creation of all that is untrue, unreal, and utterly delusive in nature. The light had now become the enduring reality, and darkness was only its deluding shadow. They now recognised that the dark one in the physical, mental, or moral domain, was only negative and negational; the bright one, the god of light, the good mind, was the Supreme Being, the reality, therefore the author of all that was finally real and eternally true! These are the two causes of the universe—it is said;—they were united from the Beginning, and, therefore, are called the *Twins*, and the Persian "Revelation" contains the Gnosis and explanation of the doctrine concerning these twin spirits.

Such was the natural origin of that doctrine of duality, which is discussed now-a-days as a metaphysical mystery, and as if it *were* a reality from the root of it, made known to the world by direct revelation! The origin of Good and Evil in the nature of man considered as a being of flesh and spirit, as the personal embodiment of two opposite principles, assumed to have a spontaneous or automatic tendency towards good on the part of the one which is supposed to originate in the spirit, and the other to originate in the flesh, as a natural antagonist, is traceable to this most primitive interpretation of the duality called good and evil in external phenomena, which was continued in the mental and moral, and lastly in the psycho-theistic phase of thought. In its latest stage the doctrine is destructive of individual responsibility in man and of personal unity in deity, or the operating Intelligence. There was no revelation, no new point of departure in phenomena, nothing added to nature or human knowledge in these later views of the metaphysicians and theosophists! It was but the transformation of mythology into metaphysic, philosophy, or theology, in which the supposed revelation of newer truth was largely founded on a falsification of the old.

We are not only contemporaries of savage man in many of our current customs and benighting beliefs, we are also the victims of his leavings—various of our superstitions being the primitive fetishism that still survives in the last stage of perversion.

But now for a development of the Devil!

In Egypt the old Devil of darkness, as Sut-Typhon or Sevekh, the Crocodile-headed divinity, acquired a soul in the stars and a place in heaven, as Plutarch says. To him was given the Crocodile or Dragon Constellation in the planisphere, whose casting out of heaven is described in the Book of Revelation, and in the Persian Bahman Yasht, where Sut, or Sevekh the Dragon, that old serpent, is identified as Satan, the eternal adversary of souls, just as it is in the Egyptian Ritual of the Dead. Thus, the devil that first rose up in revolt, as the natural darkness, called the Dragon of the deep, the rebel against the light-god, was gradually transformed into a supposed starry or spiritual being, the vice-dieu of the dark, who, in the Christian scheme, is still considered to be the supreme power of the two, or if their dominions be equally divided, he is supreme below and the light-god above—just as it had been from the beginning. And, finally, our theology has made the primal shadow of physical phenomena substantial in the mental sphere, and from the external darkness of that beginning extracted and internalised the modern devil in the end!

I have now given you a sample of what I meant by our being in the shadow of ideas whose original signification we have not understood.

There is no devil such as Milton saw! And as you must know, much current theology has been derived from "Paradise Lost." The hawk that has been flying or flown to keep timid souls cowern g down to the ground, is not the real bird of prey after all. You may trace every motion of it to the end of the string held in the puller's hand! When you go close up to it, the devil of theology is not alive. It is a bogus bug-bear, hideous, but harmless as that scarecrow in the field, the imposture of which had been found out and despised by a small bird who had built its nest, and laid and hatched its eggs in one of the grim monster's waistcoat pockets.

We have an old saying that the devil is an ass! But, in Egypt, the devil as Sut or Satan was the ass—the ass that carried the Christ as Horus, the saviour. This was the ass that was figuratively kicked out in the Christian sport of "beating the ass," when that pastime used to be practised up and down the aisles of Christian churches, and the priest used to bray three times, and the people responded like asses!

The German devil was at one time the red-bearded thunder, the Voice of Darkness! which takes us back to Sut-Typhon, who, as Plutarch informs us, was of a reddish complexion. It is common for our giants to be endowed with a red streaming comet's tail of a beard! Our forefathers, the Norsemen, had little respect and no reverence for the devil; and as to hell, why, if you did not get to heaven, then hell was the next best place in the other world, if there were but two!

To be sure, they were badly off for firewood in the Norse hell; and spirits sat shivering in the presence of the cold, uncomfortable goddess Hela, who was blue with cold, and it was trying to think how they were keeping it up overhead—they who had climbed to the top of the tree, Ygdrasil, or secured a seat in Valhalla where the wine-cups flowed and the fagots flared, and the merry dancing flames might be reflected on the windows of a heaven that was closed against them. For the North-Men knew nothing of a hell of everlasting fire. If they had, it might have proved the more attractive place of the two; as one of our missionaries once discovered. He had gone out to Greenland to carry the Gospel of Good Tidings, and illustrate it with the aid of an eternal fire! But he found himself in the wrong latitude as regards the effect of fire. He pictured it in the warmest colours, and was surprised at the result! Instead of seeing awe and terror whitening their faces, or the tears trickling down them, as he had expected, they were blubbering in quite another fashion, for the whale's fat began to run and glisten on their relaxed faces, which he saw rounding and brightening into full moons of happiness and jollity; and instead of wringing their hands at the prospect he had pictured, they sat as if spiritually warming them at this "everlasting bonfire," that was so earnestly warranted never to go out!

If this were the gospel of good tidings, why had they not heard the glorious truth before? Such a welcome and delightful change from the life they had lived in their inclement, wintry climate! They had never dreamed of conditions so delightful! So far from shunning such a place for ever, as he desired them to do, they were quite ready and willing, all of them, to go to it at once, and stay there forever.

The mythical devil was pretty much dying out, until it was revived and sublimated by the theology of Luther, Calvin, and Milton. The Romish Church did not deify the devil as the Protestants have done. She was better acquainted with the tradition of his creation and the earthly nature of his character. It was her cue to keep dark. And the devil of the Middle Ages is a poor devil enough without grandeur or terror! A very fallen intelligence, indeed, whom Romish saints can tweak by the nose with red-hot tongs, or the simplest countrymen have cunning enough to outwit. Instead of the arch-enemy of God and man, majestic in his dark divinity, infernally inspired, as Milton pictures him, he has become a grotesque image; the story-teller's most popular figure of fun, on a par with the giants of our nursery lore, whom the clever, redoubtable, little Jack, always gets the better of! Indeed, both devil and giant, as well as the serpent and dragon, had one origin, and the orthodox Satan is, after all, the popular monster of mythology. Luther and Calvin doubled the devil, and placed one at each end of their scheme of things, the upper or bright God being rather the worse devil of the two!

They put the doctrine of dualism as perplexingly as did the negro preacher who told his congregation there were but two roads open to them—one of these led directly to destruction, and the other went straight to perdition. "Stop a bit, brudder," cried one of the congregation; "hold hard, whilst I get out ob dis!" And there are many people who desire to become followers of that negro, and "get out ob dis."

The Satan of sacerdotal belief, then, is not a being for God or man to kill, but an effigy in shoddy that only wants to be ripped up to show you that it is stuffed with sawdust!

Some people may cry out in an agony of earnestness, as Charles Lamb stammered in his fun, "But this is doing away with the devil; d-d-d-don't deprive me of my devil!" "We hope for better things. How shall we be able to force people into thinking as we do, and frighten them into *our* fold of faith, for the glory of God, if we have no devil for our ferocious shepherd-dog?" And there is no doubt but that, in giving up the orthodox Hell and ancient Devil, we are losing one of the most potent motive powers. Our difficulty is how to find a substitute for the appeal to selfish fear. The fact remains that the devil is a fundamental part of the Christian scheme! No devil, no Redeemer! And those who will yell at me, and call me a blasphemer, know that well enough. I sympathise with them. They begin to see dimly, what we see clearly, that orthodox Christianity is answerable with its life for the literal truth of these stories of the Devil, the Fall of man, and the doctrine of a dying deity's atonement. Its life is *staked* upon the stories being *true*; and its life must pay the forfeit of their being found to be false! And false they are, however their defenders may squirm and wriggle, until the backbone of all manhood is changed into caoutchouc.

I can imagine that people who are not sure of their own souls, whether they are lost or are not yet found, unless their Hebrew Genesis be true, will feel the world is a rather hollow affair without their accustomed devil. It will be like depriving them of half their heaven on earth, and the whole of it hereafter, to take away the devil. What on earth, or in another place, will they do? those who are so virulent by nature for the Calvinistic sulphur, if, after all, there is no brimstone there; and they have passed out of this life with their itch for hell red-hot upon them, and there is no Old Scratch to console them after all? One would like to believe in just a very little hell for their dear sake! They have so devoutly believed in a big one for ours.

There *is* devil enough, however—only of another kind than the one we have played with. We have talked of the devil long enough; but to a Spiritualist, for instance, the devil exists for the first time in some of the facts made known by modern Spiritualism —facts which are as much matters of personal experience and constant verification to myself and myriads of others as are those of your ordinary life! Think for a moment tentatively of there being a personal motive on the other side—a vested interest in our wrong doing—degraded spirits present with us in the enjoyment of our most secret sins—the ghosts of old dead drunkards haunting the drinker's live warm atmosphere, because in that there may pass off into spirit-world some ghostly gust of the old delirious delight, and you may get at a real, present, self-interested, manifold, tempting devil that altogether surpasses the mythological monster of theology!

The devil and hell of my creed consist in that natural Nemesis which follows on broken laws, and dogs the law breaker, in spite of any belief of his, that his sins, and their inevitable results, can be so cheaply sponged out, as he has been misled to think, through the shedding of innocent blood. Nature knows nothing of the forgiveness for sin. She has no rewards or punishments—nothing but causes and consequences. For example, if you should contract a certain disease and pass it on to your children, and their children, all the alleged forgiveness of God will be of no avail if you cannot forgive yourself. Ours is the devil of heredity, working in two worlds at once. Ours is a far more terrible way of realising the hereafter, when it is brought home to us in concrete fact, whether in this life or the life to come, than any abstract idea of hell or devil can afford. We have to face the facts beforehand. No use to whine over them impotently afterwards, when it is too late. For example—

>In the olden days when Immortals
> To earth came visibly down,
>There went a youth with an Angel
> Through the gate of an Eastern town:
>They passed a dog by the road-side,
> Where dead and rotting it lay,
>And the youth, at the ghastly odour,
> Sickened and turned away.
>He gathered his robes about him,
> And hastily hurried thence:
>But nought annoyed the Angel's
> Clear, pure, immortal sense.
>
>By came a lady, lip-luscious,
> On delicate, mincing feet:
>All the place grew glad with her presence,
> All the air about her sweet;
>For she came in fragrance floating,
> And her voice most silverly rang;
>And the youth, to embrace her beauty,
> With all his being sprang.
>A sweet, delightsome lady:
> And yet, the Legend saith,
>The Angel, while he passed her,
> Shuddered and held his breath!

Only think of a fine lady who, in this life, has been wooed and flattered, sumptuously clad, and delicately fed; for whom the pure, sweet, air of heaven had to be perfumed as incense! and the red rose of health had to fade from many young human faces to blossom in the robes she wore, and every sense had been most daintily feasted, and her whole life summed up in one long thought of self —think of her finding herself in the next life a spiritual leper, a walking pestilence, a personified disease—a sloughing sore of this life which the spirit has to get rid of—an excrement of this life's selfishness at which all good spirits stop their noses and shudder when she comes near! Don't you think if she realised that as a fact in time, it would work more effectually than much preaching? The hell of the drunkard, the libidinous, the blood-thirsty, or gold-greedy soul, they tell us, is the burning of the old devouring passion which was *not* quenched by the chills of death. The crossing of the cold, dark river even was only as the untasted water to the consuming thirst of Tantalus! In support of this, evolution shows the continuity of ourselves, our desires, passions, and characters. As the Egyptians said, Whoso is intelligent here will be intelligent there! And if we haven't mastered and disciplined our lower passions here, they will be masters of us for the time-being hereafter.

There is no such possibility as death-bed salvation! No such thing as being "*jerked to Jesus*" if you are converted on the scaffold!

These old passions of ours burn and burn, and will and must burn on till they burn out. That, they tell us, is as absolutely necessary a process in the spiritual world as in the case of a fever in the physical body, which may be fed frightfully by the impurities of the previous life. Moreover, the fever will rage so long as it is supplied with fresh fuel. So long as the infatuated spirit does not try to put out the fire, and give the spiritual nature its one chance of throwing off the infernal disease, but lusts in imagination after that which fed the flame at first, and stirs the fire that kindles with every sigh for the old flesh-pots of evil passion still; and will come back to earth to prowl in filthy places, and snuff the ill odours of the lowest animal life; seeking in vain for some gust of satisfaction in shadowy apparition, as a spirit earth-bound, and self-bound to earth. Such is the teaching inculcated by our facts, accept or reject them whosoever may!

For, where the treasure is there will the heart be also. Think of that, you treasure-seekers in the earth, who have found and laid up your treasures on the earth; whose treasures represent the life you have spent on the earth! You have put the better part of your life into them. They *are* your better part. But you cannot take them away with you! The only treasure we can carry away with us must be laid up within. Now, Spiritualism reveals the possibility of the spirit's being doomed to haunt this treasure-house of earth until every particle of that hoarded wealth has been redistributed and restored to the channels for which it was intended by the Maker, and the first stage on its way back may be that the riches so carefully gathered and miserly garnered shall be the means of sinking your spendthrift son down to the lowest range of spiritual penury. For the Creator whom we postulate will not be baulked in carrying out his purposes by any temporary obstructions like these, and if you have hindered here you will have to help hereafter, when you do at last get into line with Natural *Law*.

You have been amused with a dolly devil long enough, whilst inside of you, and outside of you, and all round about you, the real devil is living, working with a most infernal activity, and playing the very devil with this world of ours. Not an ideal devil, but a legal devil, with a purpose and a plan; *the* devil in reality!

We have been following a phantom of faith, and the actual veritable devil has been dogging us indeed! This is not a Satan of God's making. Not an archangel ruined, who, in falling, found a foothold on this earth for the purpose of dragging men down with him to that lower deep for which he is bound, but a devil to be recognised by his likeness to ourselves! the devil that *is* our worser self! the devil of our own ignorance, and the deification of self—a devil bequeathed to us by the accumulated gains of centuries of ignorant selfishness, and selfish ignorance—a devil to be grappled with and wrestled with and throttled, overthrown, and overcome, and put out of existence—not only in the struggle against all that is evil in the isolated, individual life; our devil has grown too big and is too potent for that; but by the energies of all collected and clubbed, and made co-operant to destroy the causes of evil whensoever and wheresoever these can be identified, whether as Religious, or Political, Moral, or Social. We stand in Heaven's own light and cast the evil shadow of Self, and say it is the devil. And then our theologists have the blasphemous impudence to make God the author of this dark shadow of ourselves, which we shed on his creation; and assume it to be an eclipse from another world of Being.

No doubt it may be shown that the Operative Power we postulate is responsible for certain natural conditions which inevitably result in what we recognise to be evil. Nor will he shirk his responsibility in that matter. It was a necessary part and process in the human education, in strict accordance with the laws of evolution. But we see more and more every day that such evil was good in the making. We may trace many of the healing springs of heavenly purity filtering through this dark stratum of earth. Also, we are apt to look on things at first sight as evil which we finally find to be blessings in disguise. A piercing vision will perceive the deeply underlying intention of good working upward through many a superficial appearance of evil. Seen in the light of Evolution, the existence of evil is no longer a mythological mystery to be made the most of by pious ignoramuses for preaching purposes, but a necessary concomitant of development; one of the conditions by means of which we grow into conscious human beings to attain the higher life.

Indeed, whether there be a God or not, it was impossible to discuss the matter intelligently until the doctrine of Creation, by the slow processes of evolution, had been taken into account.

This shows us that the evil for which Nature is responsible, is a means of evolving in us the very consciousness of good. The moment we recognise evil, and have acquired the consciousness of its existence, the responsibility for its existence becomes ours. Here is a problem set for us to solve by way of education. Here is a foe to fight to the death, whether as a misguided passion in the individual, or a disease in the life of a nation. Here is something to be turned into good—a devil to be converted. The moment man sees so far, *he* must accept the responsibility for the continued existence of the evil, and war against it as he would if clearing any other jungle from poisonous reptiles. Ours is not a doll to dandle, and claim divine parentage for, but a misbegotten devil of ignorance, and a miscarriage of humanity in the past.

We see that life comes into visible being according to conditions. Where these are unprepared and not humanised, the life takes the lowest forms, those of reptiles and weeds, poisonous plants, thorns, thistles, and briars, forms inimical to man, and therefore considered to be evil. Then man comes to cultivate and modify, and turn the evil into good. The whole world of natural evil has to acknowledge its master. Let me give you an illustration. Pain, for example, is a consequence of imperfect conditions. It is the signal of the sentinel that warns us of the enemy. And how those faithful sentinels stand in the outworks of the body, to guard the more vital parts from approaching danger. It is necessary to warn us, or we should do most foolish things, as a child might, but for this warning of pain, thrust his hand in the fire and have it consumed! The soul's health is continually protected by this warning sentinel of pain, mental or corporeal. Pain is necessary, then, to the development of consciousness, and the perfecting of conditions. It is the reminder that there is something wrong; therefore something to be remedied. It is a part of the process in our education. Also, the loftiest pleasures of our spiritual life continually flower from a rootage in the deepest pain. I am not here to preach a gospel of the blessedness of suffering for the poor and needy—the victims of this world's laws. But suffering, as I read the Book of Life, is an incentive to effort; and the greatest pressure from without will sometimes evolve the strongest character from within, by evoking the greater force of effort. As Shakespeare points out, the flowers of March are not so fine as the flowers of June, but the finest flower of March is finer than the finest flower of June! It has overcome more opposition, and turned it to account. Perhaps in consequence of the pressure, it has established a nearer relationship at root to the source of life. Pain is but a passing necessity, for, as it is the result of imperfect conditions, it follows that pain itself must pass away as those conditions are perfected—and *we* are here to improve and perfect them. God does not destroy the devil of pain right off, by working a miracle at a moment's notice! For God is not that Automaton of the sects—that weather-cock atop of creation which they suppose will veer round at every breath of selfish prayer. You are called upon to ascertain what is the law of the case, who is the law-breaker, and how is the law to be kept. You must look out for natural consequences, and effects that follow causes, not for rewards and punishments!

You know that a little bile in the blood may cause great mental distress! But it is perfectly absurd to ask God to save you from these blacks in your eyes and blue devils in your brain. You must look to your liver, and obey the laws of health. Eschew tobacco and take less whisky, or coffee, as the case may be. God works no immediate miracle in response to your offer of a tempting opportunity! He intends man to get rid of evil as he grows enlightened enough to deal more wisely with our human conditions in the process of—what? Of becoming manlier and womanlier.

> Our Science grasps with its transforming hand;
> Makes real half the tales of fairy land;
> It turns the deathliest fetor to perfume;
> It gives decay new life and rosy bloom;
> It changes filthy rags to virgin white,
> Makes pure in spirit what was foul to sight.

We burn the darkness and the density out of earthy matter, and transfigure it into glass, which we can see through. We are here to apply a similar process of annealing to our dense, unexcavated, earthy humanity, so that the light from heaven may shine through it purely! We are here to try and clear away these visible causes of obstruction which have been bequeathed to us by ages on ages of horrible ignorance, and not look forward helplessly to their being burned out of human souls by an eternity of hellfire, or, backwards, for a salvation supposed to have taken place some eighteen centuries ago, but which is no nearer now than it ever was, on the terms set forth by orthodox teachings.

It was impossible to see anything clearly, or get any glimpse of justice above or below, in heaven, or earth, or hell, under the old creed, which proclaims that pain and suffering constitute the curse wherewith God has unjustly afflicted *all* for the sin of one, instead of the beneficent, though stern, angel of his presence and bearer of his blessing: that it was an eternal decree, to be executed through all eternity, instead of an awakener in time, that calls to action now and at once, for the changing of the present conditions in which Humanity crawls, as it were, upon all fours, or hobbles on crutches, as if we were born mental cripples.

We all know there is an awful deal of suffering in the world that cannot be considered as a mere individual question!—sufferings that we do not individually cause, and are not personally responsible for — sufferings bequeathed to us as individuals and as members of the State; for we have to bear the accumulated burdens of centuries on centuries of ignorance, or, worse still, of wilful crime, and, worst of all, of wrong made sacred by religious sanction, and supported by Law and the Press. And the burden of the many crushes the individual to the earth; and the God of Justice appears to be blind to the case—makes no rush to the rescue, even when we suffer for the sins of others. Be sure even these can be turned to eternal account. But, he has this lesson to convey to the world—

Humanity is one. And the power that *is* has instituted certain laws—laws that operate for the species rather than the individual, an important distinction to be made in any interpretation of nature; laws that deal with the species *as one* in spite of our manifold diversities and our deified doctrine of every-one-on-his-own-hook-ism. He does not put forth his hand to take *you* off your hook when it happens to run into you particularly sharp, flesh or soul, and makes you supplicate *or* swear. Establish what private relationship you can with your Maker, and derive what spiritual succour you may whilst bearing the burden, or writhing on the iron that enters you, the laws that do deal with humanity in the aggregate, and operate for the good of the species, *will* go grinding on with their larger revolutions that subserve eternal interests whilst crushing terribly many smaller claims of individual life

For, mark this, the Eternal intends to show us that humanity is one, and the family are more than the individual member, the nation is more than the family, and the human race is more than the nation. And if we do not accept the revelation lovingly, do not take to the fact kindly, why then 'tis flashed upon us terribly, by lightning of hell, if we will not have it by light of heaven, and the poor neglected scum and *canaille* of the nations rise up mighty in the strength of disease, and prove the oneness of humanity by killing you with the same infection.

It has recently been shown how the poor of London do not live, but fester in the pestilential hovels called their homes. To get into these you have to visit courts which the sun never penetrates, which are never visited by a breath of fresh air, and which never know the virtues of a drop of cleansing water. Immorality is but the natural outcome of such a devil's spawning-ground. The poverty of many who strive to live honestly is appalling.

And this disclosure is made with the customary moan that such people attend neither church nor chapel, as if that were the panacea.

I should not wonder if these revelations result in the building of more churches and chapels, and the consecration of at least one or two more bishops.

The Bishop of Bedford said the other day—"It was highly necessary that in these times when the poor have so little earthly enjoyment, the joys of heaven should be made known to them." It is not possible to caricature an utterance so grotesque as that.

How appallingly unjust it seems that the victims of this world's laws should be handed over as ready-made victims of Nature's laws —that the most helpless poor should be the first to suffer—that they should be filthily housed where fevers are sure to breed and abound, that their intestines should be the favourite thriving ground for tape-worms—just because they are in such a poverty. This is hard, but so it is, and so it will and must be till the lesson is learned and applied—that the human family is one, and all are bound up together by certain laws willy-nilly; that we are our brother's keeper for all our Cain-like questionings of the fact. We cannot shirk our responsibility; and you are not allowed to get out of the grip of the violated law of the whole, on any pretence of individuality or limited liability. It is we who create the fevers to feed on the poor, when we allow others to get rich by permitting the filth and the poisoned air and water that are sent into the world sparkling with purity; when we allow the rights of property to over-ride the interests of humanity. It is we who breed the diseases and literally invent the hungry, hundred-mouthed tape-worms that get their living out of poverty-stricken blood and hungry stomachs, churning the slime of gnawing emptiness, because we created, or continue, the laws that doom the many to poverty and its parasites of prey.

Providence—that is a very comprehensive name—providence

does not create poverty. The cupola of heaven overhead is like the inverted horn of everlasting plenty, pouring down its blessings of abundance in sunshine and shower, in air and dew, in ripening fire and purifying frost, and the harvests never fail the world over. All round, all ways, there is plenty for all—if not in one country, there is in another. There is no failure on the part of Providence, the Creator of plenty.

This neglected garden of our world, which has in it every element of a paradise, if rightly planted and properly tended, has been left to run to weeds of sin and ignorance and crime, in the most wasteful way. Heavens of spirit-worlds around us are for ever sowing the divine seed-germs broad-cast over our earth, and they have to scatter a harvest in order that we may grow a single grain, because the human conditions are so un-receptive, the fields are so neglected, the soil so unprepared to receive their bounty! The heavens around us are ever ready to pour out blessings in a larger measure than we are to make a lap for receiving them. All they ask are the conditions under which we may receive most abundantly.

We are the manufacturers of misery! We have sedulously cultivated or permitted all manner of foul conditions, and then in the midst of some calamity, for which we are criminally responsible, that comes home to all, the praying machine of the State is set rotating with a furious forty-thousand-parson-power, and God is implored to stay his hand or work a miracle forthwith on behalf of us poor human worms, who ask the Creator to take particular notice of these our penitential writhings at his feet! The Bishop of Truro said recently that we are approaching a period of pain and peril, and the situation calls for strong words and strong prayers. You must cry aloud or the Lord won't hear you!

Standing face to face with certain facts, the result of things as they are, and have been, the atheists exclaim,—"There is no God! If there were an omnipotent God such things would not be tolerated by him!" But, by an "omnipotent God," is meant a god with power to change, at a moment's notice, all that is fixed for ever. Let me assure our free-thought friends, that Evolution necessitates a new idea altogether of the operating power! It abolishes the incompetent personal Creator of the Hebrew Genesis! But, in presence of evolution, it is useless to demand that, if there be a God, it shall prove itself to be the deity of the orthodox, which, as I said before, is a sort of eternal weather-cock on the summit of creation, that may be made to veer round as it is blown about by every breath of selfish human prayer, if people collect together in sufficient numbers to blow it round! A vain idea of divinity whosoever entertains it. The deity who is belaboured so unmercifully, and, as I think, so cheaply, by Robert Ingersol, is the god of the non-evolutionary theory of creation, the impossible monster of the past.

"Did God govern America when it had four millions of slaves?" asks Ingersol. Well, why not? in accordance with the Laws of Evolution, seeing that slavery has come to an end! If he had put an end to it, *ab extra*, Americans could not have had the credit of doing the work, and might never have evolved the consciousness that slavery was criminal.

God did not put an end to slavery as an outside Governor of Men; but who shall say that the power, the will, the perception, the affection, or whatsoever we can express by analogy with the human—that is called God—was not operant, and, therefore, governing, within the souls of the men who rose up foremost in revolt against the accursed wrong, and called upon their fellows to cast it out? Possibly the existence of God, then, does not depend upon the particular visible way of working that may be so easily indicated! Slavery only existed *pro tem.*, to come to an end, and, therefore, was consistent, like other educational forms of evil, with the divine government, according to the laws of evolution.

The argument of the non-theist is continually directed and limited to the false premises and inadequate conclusions of the orthodox, which it is as easy and cheap to pulverise as it is to pummel a sack of straw! We can know nothing of an omnipotent God who plays fast and loose with the conditions of law! Were it so, all human foothold and trust in the stability of the universe would be gone. Education would be impossible. We are first taught by means of the fixed facts, in order that we may found on solid earth, not on the ever-shifting sands—with prayers for God to catch them now and again, and keep them quiet, *for God's sake!* I rather think it would be more just to reply, there is not sufficient manhood and intelligence in you to put an end to the evils you deplore! "*I, God! gave the earth for all;*" and you permit the initial iniquity of absolute private property in land, whereby one man may clutch a county all to himself, and a few may claim a country. You allow the rights of property to over-rule and over-ride the interests of humanity!

If your national property is doubling every thirty years, so is the national pauperism! You allow the "one" to possess the soil, and the thousands to be driven off and exported as refuse, in order that game may multiply, and the human parasites of earth may pursue their savage sport! I gave the land for all; to be the property and grazing ground of each living generation brought to birth; and you allow it to be locked up by the dead hand of the past, for the benefit of the few! These few framed the laws that inevitably doom the many, sooner or later, to poverty, to man-made sufferings, to diseases and miseries innumerable, all of which get mixed up with a supposed inscrutable origin of evil and other grotesque and fallacious views, endorsed and inculcated by the current theology for the benefit of parsons and patrons, which are only fit to be made a mock of, and to be laughed into oblivion!

And here, let me say, that whilst recognising the inexorableness of the natural law in certain spheres of operation, where it works like the bound Samson of blind force for the good of the species, I find that Spiritualism introduces a consciousness akin, and, at least, equal, to the human, into the working of law in a realm beyond the immediately visible. It shows the existence of subtler forces and modes of law for dealing with man the individual, and the culminating consciousness of creation. When the mind of man had been evolved on this earth, remember, a new factor was introduced amongst the natural forces—one that was destined to greatly modify and counteract them; fetter the fire, and ride the ocean waves; guide the lightning, and train it to carry messages; bridge the planetary spaces, and outstrip Time itself. In like manner, the knowledge of an existence beyond the visible present—no matter by what means—and of intelligence operating in hidden and extraordinary ways, introduces a new factor among the forces now to be reckoned with as mental modifiers in certain domains of law. The unseen world can no longer be the same when we learn that Intelligence is there; no more than this world could remain the same after the advent of man! And when we can identify the consciousness *there* as being akin to the human *here*, we know all that is necessary for putting a conscience into the previously inexorable law, and an *eye* into the image of blind force. Here we get a margin that would take a long while to fill in with possible annotations. Man is no longer alone in the universe! There are other intelligences, affections, powers of will and work, beside his; and in relation to him this just makes all the difference in the manifestation and interpretation of the law that *is* blind and inexorable in its lower range. We begin to distinguish! Here are the means for a possible response to invocation, and to the need of mental help!

The now demonstrated fact of Thought-Transference, which was familiar enough before, in common with other kindred phenomena, to many of us, opens up a vista of immortal possibility in the mode of mental manifestation, and in the modification of supposed hard-and-fast, or immutable, law, in relation to life in its higher phases!

It seems to me that this fact alone turns the ground of mere materialism into a kind of Goodwin Sands! We extend this thought-transference upwards or round us by means of living telegraphic mental lines! The operators on which at one end can work, and only work according to the conditions at the other end. At present I do not perceive, and cannot pretend to know, when and where we can touch Conscious Source itself along these lines. Who does know anything of God, in the domain of things? or who has any right to pretend to know, or to be paid a salary for pretending to know, anything of God personally, or a personal God? To me the question as to the personality of God is altogether premature. I can wait for a few future lifetimes to find out God.

In a sense it may be "there is no God yet, but there's one coming!" and you will find the saying a profound one if you think it over for a month. We ourselves, of the race of man, are only in the condition of becoming (let us cultivate a becoming modesty!); and such is the human apprehension of the cause of becoming. The eye, as Goëthe has said, can only see what it brings with it the power of seeing; and so, in a sense, a God is not yet, but one is coming. The deity hitherto set up for worship is more or less an effigy of the God of primitive or savage man. If that be a true likeness, why, then, men ought not to become Atheists merely—they ought not to marry and propagate, but commit suicide forthwith! It is such an outrage on all human feeling, this primitive portraiture of Eternal power, that the moral revolt is certain, and the mental result is atheism. I assert that non-theism is sometimes, and in some natures, the necessary revolt of the most inner consciousness against the abortion called God! They shut their eyes altogether to get rid of a representation so unsightly and unworthy; and better is such blindness than much false seeing. I say it is the real Presence operating within that is at war with this hideous sham set up for worship without. I seldom use the name of God myself in speech or writing now, it has been so long taken in vain—so profaned by the orthodox blasphemers. It has been so degraded as a brand and hall-mark, made use of to warrant the counterfeit wares that are passed off upon the ignorant and unsuspecting, who think them genuine so long as they are stamped with that name, as to have become quite discredited.

For myself, I have come to apprehend a Conscious Source of all, working outwardly from the core of things, by means of what we term matter, and understand as the Laws of Evolution. A Conscious Source of all! I cannot state that consciousness in words, but it appears to me that this is the work of phenomena which do actually state it in the process of appealing to, or becoming, the Consciousness in us. But I am utterly unable to personify this Power! Also, I find the essence of the whole matter is sacred to privacy. The more intuition, the less blabbing—the more reverence, the more reticence. The facts of an abnormal or extraordinary nature that came under my own cognisance during many years of my life, which were continually occurring and verified, proved to me that Mind exists and operates out of sight!

By degrees these facts peopled the unknown void with life and intelligent beings; that finally gave one bit of foothold on the very first step of a ladder which will stand up for the first time when one tries to prop it against the sky! That one step bridges the dark void of death for me. I don't trouble myself, for myself, about the other world at all—that's all right, if we are! It is for this world people need to be helped. Life is not worth living if we are not doing something towards helping on the work of this world. It is only in helping others that we can truly help ourselves. And we have reason to think that myriads of those who have already left this life with false hopes of salvation are only too glad to help themselves by coming back and helping us to carry on the work of this world.

It is only when we pass out of the domain of self, that the unseen helpers can steal in upon us, and help us as Agents for those who are Agents for others, and so on and on, until the whole vast universe is filled and quick with modes and motions, and forms of being all athrob with subtly-related life; all radiating from central source to uttermost limit; all unified in one eternal consciousness, in which the soul of man, full statured and full-summed, may possibly become conscious that it touches God at last, as a presence, a power, a principle, and may then be made aware that it did so unconsciously from the first.

Our orthodox teachers in the present are responsible for playing into the hands or claws of the devil that was created for them in the past. They are the consecrators of all the ignorance, robbery, and wrong! In England the sinister army of forty thousand men in masks, as it has been truly termed, is paid from the national revenue to act the part of a secret Sunday police! Their chief representatives are the obstructives of sane and humane legislation to-day as ever. A man can't marry his wife's sister because of them.

At the debate on the Pigeon Bill in the House of Lords, some time since, not a single bishop was found to lift up his voice on behalf of the poor dumb and miserably-murdered doves. Not a man was to be found behind any one of the aprons! Every bishop present in the House voted against opening the Museums and and Picture Galleries on Sunday! They say, in effect, If you won't come to church, d—n you! you shan't go anywhere else, if we can help it! They want to stand just where they have always stood, at the end of the long dark passage through which mankind slowly emerges out of darkness into day—in the very entrance of the light, to shut out the face of heaven itself from those who are groping their way through the gloom, and bid them in God's name to go back and religiously keep to the obscurity of the cave, if they would be saved!

Each Sunday they trail the red herring across the scent of their followers, so that their attention may be drawn off from this world and all the wrongs we are sent here to remedy. They promise that those who remain sufficiently poor and wormlike in spirit during this life, shall rise erect from the grublike condition in death, full-fledged, to soar as winged angels in the next life. They have exalted the lot of Lazarus as a Scriptural Ideal for the most needy and miserable to live up to, as if the cowering outcast and diseased starveling of earth were the proper model man for the heavens. They keep up the lying farce of insisting that man is a fallen creature, and persist in preaching their doctrine of his degradation and damnation in order that people may go to them to be saved—and pay well for it.

The Secularist asserts that the orthodox cult and theology are a hopeless failure for this world, and as a Spiritualist I affirm that they are also a fraud for the other.

False beliefs are, and forever must be, opposed to all real and true doing. And these false beliefs have from the beginning been bitterly opposed to every truth revealed by science; and every advance made for humanity has had to be made in spite of them. Moreover, this doctrine they teach, of saving yourselves and "devil take the hindmost," is most miserably degrading to any true sense of real manhood or womanhood. He wouldn't be much of a hero who in the midst of the battle took it into his head that the first duty of man is to get himself saved!

They get up a horrible hullabaloo in the rear, as if all hell were let loose after you, on purpose to frighten the blind and foolish, and make them rush through the one door open in front of those who are fleeing from the wrath to come, at which they take tax and toll. But there is no hell, there is no devil, close after the hindmost of those who are furiously fleeing from the avengers of the "fall of man." Moreover, it's of no use rushing. However fast you go you carry your own heaven or hell inside of you, whether for this life or any other. All this is a bogus business, with the mythical devil for bogey. The world is not yet on fire with the final conflagration, nor can they set it on fire with the painted flames of a pictorial hell. A little girl was once asked what she must first do to be saved; and the innocent replied, "Get lost." Moreover, before we join in the stampede of self-salvation at the call of those who cry "fire" when the theatre is crammed, let us be sure that we have grown a soul that is worth saving. If we had, I doubt whether we should manifest such a consuming anxiety of utter selfishness, or be in such an infernal hurry to get it saved anyhow. Those who are truly desirous of saving or helping others, seldom trouble much about their own souls. Theirs is the burden of a nobler care. Theirs is a loftier inquietude than any sense of self can ever give. They lose all such unworthy fears for themselves in the thought of others. They are like that grand captain of the "Northfleet," of whom I proudly wrote some years ago—

> "Others he saved. He saved the name
> Unsullied, that he gave his wife,
> And, dying with so pure an aim,
> He had no need to save his life."

I also hold their other cowardly doctrine, that of vicarious sacrifice, to be the real, if indirect, cause of Vivisection. It would have been impossible for a nation of animal lovers like the English to tolerate the vivisection of the dog, for example, man's first friend in the wilderness of the early world, his ally in the work of civilisation, unless the *motor nerve* and conscience of the race had been paralysed by the *curare* of vicarious suffering. The beastly cruelties of its practitioners, which are flaunted in our faces with intent to terrorise the conscience of others, could not have been permitted by men who had not been indoctrinated by the worship of *a vivisecting deity*, whose *victim* was his own son! And these myriads of slowly murdered dogs and rabbits, cats and frogs, cannot have the consolation of knowing that vivisection is salvation, and they are saviours of the human race from the consequences of its own crimes against nature, and sins against self! It is impossible to establish the throne of Eternal Justice by the violation of all that is human, as is fruitlessly attempted on this ground of the orthodox Creed. It is impossible for you to save or serve humanity by sacrificing all that constitutes the essence of humanity, as is done in this pourtrayal of a vivisecting deity, who is the responsible operator, with his own son for suffering victim. And this victim of vicarious punishment is held forth as a lure to draw humanity toward a father in heaven of such a nature as that! We may depend upon it that this preaching of what is called Christianity, to get a Sunday sensation, or solace out of it—this plunging of the theological poker red-hot into your seventh-day dose of spiritual flip to give it a zest—this using of hell-fire as a persuader, after the manner of the furnace heated beneath the turkeys, which persuaded the poor things to dance to music played in quick time—this weekly whipping of the devil round the stump is, as the Americans say, pretty well played out; there is nothing new to be said. Suppose we go to work and try to *do* something, instead of making ourselves miserable on Sunday, doing nothing but putting ourselves through all the postures and impostures of the orthodox Sabbatical fashion? In future, mankind will not herd together, like terror-stricken cattle in a thunder-storm, to deprecate the wrath of their God, and offer him praise and presents by way of propitiation, and as a bribe for him not to lose his temper! Good God! What an idea of a God! It is precisely the elemental god of Browning's Caliban, and of the primitive savage! In future, I say, men will not look upon it as a sacred duty to herd together, on purpose to praise and glorify their God one day in seven with their psalm of conceit:

" Let all Creation hold its tongue,
 While I uplift my Sunday song;"

lest, being a jealous God, he should blight their harvest, or peradventure burst the boiler of the Excursion Train. Nor will men form leagues, religious or otherwise, on purpose to think alike and make all other people think the same. They cannot think alike if they are ever to grow. The lower the type the greater the likeness! The loftier the development the larger the diversity! *That* is the Natural law. We may co-operate to work, but *not* to *think* alike. *That* could never be free-thinking. Nor will mankind henceforth allow their arms to be paralysed for action by being fixed or "bailed up" in the posture of prayer. We say,—It is a farce, a pitiful one, not a laughable one, for you to pray for God to work a miracle for the kingdom of heaven to come, when you are doing all you can, all your lives, to prevent its coming, or doing nothing to hasten its coming. It is the sheerest mockery of God and man! You were sent here to create the kingdom, to work it out by living that law of love proclaimed as laying down the life in love for others, and the very reason why the kingdom does not come, and cannot come, is because you stand in the way of its coming. And you, and all who think and act as you do, praying for the better day to come, must be swept out of the way in order that it may come.

Get up from your knees and work for it! Take your weapon in hand and fight for it! Turn fiercely on the devil that dogs our own footsteps, and rescue those that fall by the way and succumb to the powers that make for evil. Turn on the devil—not theoretically, but practically, having ascertained the work that remains to be done. Turn on the devil, not singly, but associated together for doing, instead of believing and talking and praying for God to do! What the Eternal Worker asks of us, as I apprehend the whole matter, is that we shall become conscious co-workers with him in carrying out the divine purposes in proportion as we can make them out! He does not want us to be fear-bound and devil-driven slaves! Not beasts in blinkers, not laggers behind, forever probed by the goad of sheer and sharp necessity; not blind obeyers of his sternest laws that go grinding on willy-nilly, hauling and hurling us along with them in their incessant, vast revolution! but seers of his work, intelligent interpreters of his will, and sharers in his life and love.

In conclusion. There is no origin of evil in the moral domain that is not derivable from ignorance. "The wickedness of a soul," said Hermes, "is its ignorance;" and there is no devil in the moral domain except in the devilish determination to *do* the wrong or *permit* the wrong to be done, after we have evolved the consciousness that recognises the right!

The reason then why God does not kill the devil is because man has unconsciously created or permitted all that is the devil finally; and here or hereafter he has to consciously destroy his own work, and fight himself free from the errors of his own ignorance. Not man the individual merely, but man as part of the whole family of universal humanity. Not man as mortal simply, but as an immortal, standing up shoulder to shoulder, and marching onward step by step and side by side with those who are our elders in immortality, and who still unite with us, and lend a hand to effect in time the *not* altogether inscrutable, but slowly-unfolding, purposes of the Eternal.

LUNIOLATRY,

ANCIENT AND MODERN.

For thirty years past Professor Max Müller has been teaching in his books and lectures, in the *Times*, *Saturday Review*, and various magazines, from the platform of the Royal Institution, the pulpit of Westminster Abbey, and his chair at Oxford, that Mythology is a disease of language, and that the ancient symbolism was a result of something like a primitive mental aberration.

"We know," says Renouf, echoing Max Müller, in his Hibbert lectures, "We know that mythology *is* the disease which springs up at a peculiar stage of human culture." Such is the shallow explanation of the non-evolutionists, and such explanations are still accepted by the British public, that gets its thinking done for it by proxy. Professor Max Müller, Cox, Gubernatis and other propounders of the Solar Mythos have portrayed the primitive myth-maker for us as a sort of Germanised-Hindu metaphysician, projecting his own shadow on a mental mist, and talking ingeniously concerning smoke, or, at least, *cloud;* the sky overhead becoming like the dome of dreamland, scribbled over with the imagery of aboriginal nightmares! They conceive the early man in their own likeness, and look upon him as perversely prone to self-mystification, or, as Fontenelle has it, "subject to beholding things that are not there!" They have misrepresented primitive or archaic man as having been idiotically misled from the first by an active but untutored imagination into believing all sorts of fallacies, which were directly and constantly contradicted by his own daily experience; a fool of fancy in the midst of those grim realities that were grinding his experience into him, like the griding icebergs making their imprints upon the rocks submerged beneath the sea. It remains to be said, and will one day be acknowledged, that these accepted teachers have been no nearer to the beginnings of mythology and language than Burns's poet Willie had been near to Pegasus. My reply is, 'Tis but a dream of the metaphysical theorist that mythology was a disease of language, or anything else except his own brain. The origin and meaning of mythology have been missed altogether by these solarites and weather-mongers! Mythology was a primitive mode of *thinging* the early thought. It was founded on natural facts, and is still verifiable in phenomena. There is nothing insane, nothing irrational in it, when considered in the light of evolution, and when its mode of expression by sign-language is thoroughly understood. The insanity lies in mistaking it for human history or Divine Revelation. Mythology is the repository of man's most ancient science, and what concerns us chiefly is this—when truly interpreted once more it is destined to be the death of those false theologies to which it has unwittingly given birth!

In modern phraseology a statement is sometimes said to be mythical in proportion to its being untrue; but the ancient mythology was not a system or mode of falsifying in that sense. Its fables were the means of conveying facts; they were neither forgeries nor fictions. Nor did mythology originate in any intentional double-dealing whatever, although it did assume an aspect of duality when direct expression in words had succeeded the primitive mode of representation by means of things as signs and symbols. For example, when the Egyptians portrayed the moon as a *Cat*, they were not ignorant enough to suppose that the moon was a cat; nor did their wandering fancies see any likeness in the moon to a cat; nor was a cat-myth any *mere expansion of verbal metaphor*; nor had they any intention of making puzzles or riddles to mislead others by means of such enigmatical sign-language, at a time when they could not help themselves, having no choice in the matter. They had observed the simple fact that the cat saw in the dark, and that her eyes became full-orbed and grew most luminous by night. The moon was the seer by night in heaven, and the cat was its equivalent on the earth; and so the familiar cat was adopted as a representative, a natural sign, a living pictograph of the lunar orb! Where we should make a comparison, and say the moon saw in the dark *like* a cat, or the cat saw like the moon by night, they identified the one with the other (a mode of metaphor which still characterises the great style in poetry), and said the cat up there can see by night. And so it followed that the sun which saw down in the under-world at night, could also be called the cat, as it was, because *it also saw* in the dark. The name of the cat in Egyptian is *mau*, which denotes the seer, from *mau*, to see. One writer on mythology asserts that the Egyptians "imagined a great cat behind the sun, which is the pupil of the cat's eye." But this imagining is all modern. It is the Müllerite stock in trade! The moon *as cat was* the eye of the sun, because it reflected the solar light, and because the eye gives back the image in its mirror. In the form of the Goddess Pasht the cat keeps watch for the sun, with her paw holding down and bruising the head of the serpent of darkness, called his eternal enemy! The cat was the eye of night in the same symbolical sense that our daisy, which opens and shuts with the rising and setting of the sun, is called the *eye of day*. Moreover, the cat saw the sun, had it in its eye by night, when it was otherwise unseen by men. *We* might say the moon *mirrored* the solar light, because we have *looking glasses*. With them the cat's eye *was* the mirror.

The *hare* was another type of the eye that opened in heaven and saw in the dark. Consequently, we find the hare in the moon is a myth that gave birth to a common and wide-spread superstition. In later times the symbol is literalized, and it is supposed that primitive men were always on the look-out for likenesses, like a youthful poet in search of comparisons, and that they saw some resemblance to the form of a hare in the dark shadows of the lunar orb. Whereas in mythology things *are not* what they seem to *anybody;* that would lead to no consensus of agreement, nor establish any science of knowledge. A learned man once remarked to me on the strange fact that the ancients should have selected the least observable of all the planets, Mercury, to make so much of, as *the* messenger. He was entirely ignorant of the fact that mythology includes a system of time-keeping, and that Mercury was made the planetary messenger (in addition to his lunar character), because his revolution round the sun is performed in the shortest space of planetary time. In like manner, Max Müller will tell you that the moon was called by the name of Sasānka in Sanskrit, from *sasa*, the hare, *because* the common people in India think the black marks in the moon look like a hare! But this is mere fool's work or child's play with the surface appearances of things which has little or no relation to true myth or ancient symbolism; and all such interpretation is entirely misleading! Egypt, as I contend, has left us the means of determining the original nature and significance of these types.

When the Egyptians would denote an opening, says Hor-Apollo, they delineate a hare, because this animal always has its eyes open. The name of the hare in Egyptian is *Un*, which signifies open, to open, the opener, especially connected with periodicity, as the word also means the hour. This will explain how the wide, open-eyed hare became a type of the moon, which opens with its new light once a month, as the hare in heaven. The hare is the hieroglyphic sign of the opener, which can be variously applied to the phenomena of opening; to the sun as well as the moon. The hare is an especial emblem of the god Osiris in the character of Un-Nefer, the good opener; in later phrase, the good revealer! It is as the *seer* that both hare and cat are associated with the witch as types of abnormal seership. The hare also denoted the opening time, as the period of pubescence, when it was lawful for the sexes to come together. Hence it was the type of periodicity and legality in the human phase! For this reason, the youths among the Namaqua Hottentots are (or were) not allowed to eat the hare—which is meat for mature men only! The type of periodicity was thus utilised as a mode of distinguishing those who had come of age, the reproducers only being permitted to eat the hare. With the Chinese the rabbit takes the place of the hare as a lunar type. Its period of gestation being thirty days, that would make it an appropriate representative of the lunation, of opening anew, and of re-birth.

The Selish Indians have a myth of the frog in the moon. They tell how the wolf, in love with the frog, was pursuing her by night, when she leaped into the moon, and escaped. Amongst the superstitions of our English folk-lore, we also have one respecting the frog or toad, that is supposed to be visible in the moon. Now it can be shown how the frog got deposited there; but only as a type, not in reality, nor as a mere appearance. The frog is a natural transformer from the tadpole phase in the water to the four-legged stage on land! The moon likewise transforms, and the metamorphosis of the lunar orb could be typified by the change in the frog, and so the frog as picture-object, natural type and living demonstrator for the moon, ultimately became the frog in the moon. The moon rose up monthly from the celestial waters, renewed like the frog, and as the horned one grew full-orbed it might be thought of as losing the tail of its tad-pole condition. The frog was figured as the head of the Egyptian goddess Hekat (= Greek Hecate), the consort of Khnef, one of whose titles is the "king of frogs." Hekat being a lunar goddess and Khnef a solar god, this title would denote that he was lord of the numerous transformations of light in the moon, described as being the father, and she as the mother, of frogs, because the frog was the typical transformer, as representative of the moon. The Chinese have a three-legged frog in the moon that was an ancient beauty, named Chang Ngo, who lives there because she once drank the amrita of immortality. I have elsewhere suggested that the original Phryne of Greece was a form of the frog-goddess who transformed! The name of Phryne denotes the frog; and in the most famous statue of her, carved by Apelles, she was portrayed as Venus transfiguring from the foam, as did the frog-goddess Hekat, of Egypt, who was the frog in the moon. Only by reading these types, which preceded letters, can we at all understand the thought and intention of the primitive thingers or thinkers.

Another example: the dung-beetle in Egypt was a type of Khepr-Ptah, the creator by transformation, who is said to have been begotten by his own becoming, and to have been born without a mother, through repetition of himself. Khep, the root of the name, signifies to transform. External nature was the scene of eternal transformation and never-ending metamorphosis. And it had been observed that Khepr, the beetle, was likewise a transformer, inasmuch as it laid its eggs in dung found on the banks of the Nile, rolled it up into a ball, and buried itself deep in the dry sand along with its seed, where, *qua* beetle, it transformed, the old beetle into the young one, and so continued as the same beetle by transformation! Thus the beetle served to typify that being or existence which could not be expressed, but which was seen to continue forever by self-repetition in phenomenal manifestation. They knew nothing of beginning, and did not pretend to know, but only of becoming, and of repetition or "renewal coming of itself." So the beetle was adopted as a type of transformation, whether of the old moon into the new one, of the sun out of the lower into the upper heaven, or, in the latter times, of the dead mummy into a living soul. Hor-Apollo says the scarabæus deposits his ball of seed in the earth for the space of 28 days, the length of time during which the moon passes through the 12 signs of the zodiac, and on the 29th day it opens the ball. The day on which the conjunction of sun and moon occurred was the day of resurrection for the new life. The beetle in heaven had once more transformed, and there was another new moon!

The orb of the moon with its changes night after night, its drama longer even than any performed by the Chinese now-a-days, its drop-scene of the darkness at the end, and the transformation into the new life of light in the beginning, presented the earliest form of the primitive theatre, which offered its celestial show in heaven, gratis to all eyes that gazed up from below. This must have been one of the earliest educators in natural phenomena! There is nothing more interesting to me than to watch the nascent mind of man making its infantile clutch, and trying to catch on and lay hold of external things—to lay hold, as it were, of the skirts of the passing powers, that were held to be superior to itself: nothing more instructive than to follow the primitive ways of keeping touch with the life of external nature, and of sharing in the operations going on, so as to be on the right and safe side, and get on the true line for deriving some benefit from the way in which things were seen to be going! This is very touching in its simplicity, and will teach us more concerning the past of man than all the metaphysical interpretation hitherto attempted. The proper time for prayer, wishing or invoking aid, was at first sight of the new moon, just as it started visibly on the way to fulfilment, the mental attitude being, "May my wish be fulfilled like the light in thy orb, oh moon! May my life be renewed like thy light!" Such was the prayer of the Congo negroes. The full moon being the mother-moon, the *eye* that mirrored or reproduced the light of the sun, that will account for the day of the full moon being accounted—as it was by the Greeks, Britons, and others—the most propitious time for the marriage ceremony. The full moon was held to come forth great with good luck! Boy-children ought to be weaned when the horned moon was waxing, and girls when it was on the wane—the female being the reproducer as bringer-forth. So peas and beans were sown in the wane of the moon to rise again like the moon renewed. Corns ought to be cut during the wane of the moon if you would have them disappear quickly. In very simple ways the primitive observers had tried to set their life in time with the life going on around them, and thus get what light they could from Nature for their own guidance, and also make her language their own. Butler asks (in Hudibras):—

> "Why on a sign no painter draws
> The full moon ever but the half?"

Now, that is very good sign language, especially as the "half-moon" is a public-house symbol. It was an invitation to eat and drink to the full, or come to the full as the half-moon does; it may be, to "get fu'," in the Scottish sense. A moon already full would not have answered the purpose.

An eclipse projected the shadow of coming calamity. The renewed light of the old moon was like a promise of eternal life and everlasting youth. When personified this was the healer, the saviour, an image of very life. The first-born from the dead, the first-fruits of them that slept in the graveyard of sunken suns, and cemetery of old dead moons, was reproduced visibly in external phenomena, as the new moon which was personated by the male moon-god Taht, called the eighth, and lord of the eighth region, as the place of rising again from the dead in the orb of the moon. There was a lunar mythology extant long before it was known that the lunar orb was a reflector of the solar light. There was a time also when it was not known, and could not be divined, that the moon which dwindled and died down visibly was the same moon that rose again from the dead. Hence there were *two* different messages conveyed from heaven to men on earth, by the hare as messenger for the moon in the lunar myths of the Hottentots and other primitive races. In one of these versions the moon declared that, as it died and did not rise again from its grave, even so was it with man, who went down to the earth and came back no more. But, when it had made out that the same moon returned as the old orb renewed, the nature *of its revelation was reversed*. Its message *now* contained a doctrine of the resurrection from the dead for man as well as moon. The re-arising and transforming orb at last proclaimed that even as it did not die out altogether, but was renewed from some hidden spring or source of light, so was it with the human race, who were likewise hereafter to re-live on hereafter like the moon. In a myth of the Caroline Islanders it is said that at first men only quitted this life on the last day of the dying moon, to be revivified when the new moon appeared. But there was a dark spirit that inflicted a death from which there was no revival. This dark spirit, with its fatal message, was primary in fact, and the true assurance of survival, like the moon, depended on its being identified as the same moon which rose again. It is in this way that we can re-think the primitive thought, by getting it re-thinged in the physical realities of natural phenomena. In the Ute Mythos the task of making a moon was assigned to Whip-Poor-Will, a god of the night. The frog offered himself as a willing sacrifice for this purpose, and he was transformed by magical incantations into the New Moon. The symbolism is identical, whether derived from Egypt or not. So is it when the Buddha offers his body as a sacrifice, and transforms himself into the lunar hare.

The Maories have a tradition of the first children of earth, in which they relate that the earliest subject of human thought was the difference between light and darkness; they were always thinking what might be the difference betwixt light and darkness. Naturally, the primary conditions of existence observed by primitive men were those that were most observable, and, foremost amongst these, were the phenomena of the day and the dark, which followed each other in ceaseless change. Mythology begins with this vague and merely elemental phase of external phenomena, alternating in night and day. In a secondary stage, it was observed that the battle field of this never ending warfare of day and dark was focussed and brought to a definite point in the orb of the moon, where the struggle betwixt the two personified powers of light and darkness went on and on for ever, each power having its triumph over the other in its turn,—these being depicted in one representation as the solar light and the serpent of darkness, in another by the lion and the unicorn. These phenomena of light and darkness were at first set forth by means of animals, reptiles, birds, and other primitive types of the elemental powers; and lastly the human type was adopted, and the cunning of the crocodile, or the jackal of darkness, is represented by the Egyptian *Sut*, the Norse *Loki*, the Greek *Hermes*, or the Jewish *Jacob*, the dark deceiver; and to-day, we find the Christian Evidence Society engaged in defending such characters as that of Jacob, in the full and perfect belief that Jacob was a human being, and one of God's chosen race. Whereas, he was no more a person than was Sut-Anup in Egypt, or Reynard the fox in Europe! The human form, like that of the earlier animal type, was only representative of some power manifested in natural phenomena. This mode of representation was known when these sacred stories were first told of mythical characters; it was afterwards continued and taught in the so-called "mysteries" by means of the Gnosis. When the art or Gnosis was lost to the world outside, the ancient histories were ignorantly supposed to be human in their origin; mythology was euhemerized (that is, the ideal was mistaken for the real), and Egyptian mythology was converted into Hebrew miracles and Christian history.

Thus when the Iroquois Indians claim that the first ancestor of the red man was a hare, we do not know what that saying means until we learn the representative value of the symbol! So is it all sign-writing through.

When Herodotus went to Egypt, he recognised the originals of the gods that were adored, amplified, embellished, or laughed at in Greece. At present, however, the Müllerites dare not mention Egypt, but look askance at those who do. Here is a crucial instance of survival, evidenced by philology,—the name of Mars as Ares will serve to prove how Egyptian underlies the Greek! The planet Mars is called Har-Tesh in Egyptian, which signifies the *red lord*, or the lord of gore. Cedrenus writes the name of Arês as Hartosi, and Vettius Valens as Hartes, whence Artis, and finally Arês. Again, the name of Hera denotes the heaven, over, in Egyptian; which certainly describes the nature of the Greek goddess of that name.

When we are told by the Roman Catholic Egyptologist, Renouf, that "Neither Hebrews nor Greeks borrowed any of their ideas from Egypt," we can only think of such a dictum as an intentional blind, or as a result of putting up the glass to an eye that cannot see. It is simply impossible for the non-evolutionist, the bigotted Bibliolator, or the Müllerite, to interpret or to understand the mythology of Egypt. Its roots go too deep, and its branches spread too far, for their range of thought. And now, let me offer a remarkable example of the modes in which the Egyptians expressed or thinged their thoughts, by means of external phenomena. The sun-god Ra is represented as possessing fourteen spirits or *kaus*, the living likenesses and glorified images of himself. These are portrayed as fourteen personages at Edfu and Denderah. In one text it is said,—"Hail to thee and thy fourteen spirits fourteen times." These are also mentioned in the tablet of Ipsambul, as the fourteen *kaus* of Ra, which "Taht has added to all his ways." Taht is the moon-god, and this gives us a clue to the fourteen spirits, which, I think, no Egyptologist has yet suspected. But Taht is the god of the first fourteen days of the moon's lunation, and fourteen nights of the new moon reproduced the likeness of the solar god in light fourteen times over; these were designated his fourteen kaus, the visible images of his hidden self—in short, his *apparition* seen nightly in the moon! Indeed, the moon in its dark half was treated as the *mummy* or un-illuminated *body* of the sun-god, who is described as coming to visit, to comfort it, to beget upon it, in the under-world. This lunar body of the solar soul is represented by the ass-headed god Aai (upon which the sun-god rode), who is found mummified on the tomb of Rameses 6th. Thus, the dark orb or body of the moon was the mummy of the sun, and its fourteen days of growing light were thought of as fourteen manifestations of the solar-god in spiritual apparition, visible by night in the moon; hence the fourteen spirits assigned to the sun-god Ra. From such an origin it will be seen how natural it was that the lunar orb should be looked up to as the home of spirits, as when the Egyptian prays that his soul may ascend to heaven in the disk of the moon! Another fable of the dark half of the lunation has been preserved by Plutarch, who relates that when Typhon, the evil power, was hunting by moonlight, he by chance came upon the dead body or mummy of Osiris prepared for burial, and, knowing it again, he tore it into fourteen parts, and scattered them all about. These fourteen parts typify the fourteen days of the lessening light, during which the devil of darkness had the upper hand. The twenty-eight days made one lunar month according to Egyptian reckoning.

The earlier and simpler representation of the lunar light and dark is portrayed in the myth of the Two Brothers, who always contend for supremacy over each other. The most ancient and primitive myths are found to be the most universal; and this of the twin brothers is extant all over the world. It is the myth of Sut-Horus in Egypt; the Asvins or Krishna and Balarama in India; the Crow and the Eagle of the Australian blacks; Tsuni-Goam and Gaunab among the Hottentots; Jack and Jill, and twenty other forms that I have compared in my "Natural Genesis." It is that struggle of two brothers in the beginning which is represented in the Hebrew book of Genesis as the murderous conflict of Cain and Abel. *Cain* as the victor is the *same character* as the Egyptian *Khunsu*, Khun or Khen, meaning to *chase*, hunt, beat, be the victor, and therefore I take it that the *name* of Cain is probably one with the Egyptian *Khun*. Abel is the dark little one that fades and falls and passes away, the one who becomes a sacrificial type, because of the nature of the phenomena. The conqueror is portrayed as the killer. The Gnostic Cainites, however, maintained truly that Cain derived his being from the power above, and not from the evil power below. They knew the Mythos. The contention of Jacob and Esau for birth and for the birth-right is another form of the same myth. Esau, the *red* and *hairy*, is really the lord of light in the new moon. Jacob is the child of darkness, hence the deceiver by nature and by name. A Jewish tradition relates that Esau, when born, had the likeness of a serpent marked upon his heel. This shows he was a personification of the hero who bruised the serpent's head, and that Jacob, who laid hold of Esau's heel, was a co-type in phenomena with the serpent of darkness. There is nothing moral or immoral in mere physical phenomena themselves. No fratricide is actually committed by the conquering Cain, nor fraud by the dark and wily Jacob. But when these same phenomena are dramatised, and the characters are made human, or inhuman, as the case may be, the un-moral becomes immoral, and the human image is disfigured by the most wilful flaw, or wanton brand of degradation. Cain is made the murderer of his own brother, in the beginning, and that red stain is supposed to run through all human history, as a first result of Adam's fall, and to burn on the brow of man until it is washed out at last in the blood of a redeeming Saviour—who is *equally mythical*.

This lunar representation has several shapes in Egyptian mythology, where the Twin Brothers are Sut and Osiris, Sut and Horus, the two Horuses, Taht and Aan, or Khunsu and Typhon.

In his Hibbert lectures Mr. Renouf says curtly, the Egyptian god "Khunsu is the moon." But such Egyptology has not yet blazed the veriest surface of the mythology. Such statements teach nothing truly, because they do not put in the bottom facts. They do not help us to think in those phenomena which have been entified or divinised *in* and *as* mythology. It may be said quite as bluntly that Khunsu is not the moon. He only represents one phase of the lunar phenomena, which are triadic. Khunsu is the child of the sun and moon. His name denotes the young hero. When this deity was evolved it had been discovered that the moon derived her light from the sun. In the planisphere of Denderah the youthful God Khunsu is portrayed in the disk of the full moon of Easter, where he represents the light and force of the sun that is reborn monthly and annually of the lunar orb considered to be his mother, who thus reproduces the child of light in the disk of the moon. The same myth is likewise Osirian, as we learn from one of the hymns, where it is said, "Hail to thee, Osiris, Lord of Eternity! When thou art in heaven thou appearest as the sun, and thou renewest thyself as the moon." But this renewal of light in the moon was portrayed as the re-birth of the god in the person of his own child; hence the child Horus is also depicted like the child Khunsu in the disk of the full moon, as both may be seen in the same planisphere of Denderah. Khunsu is the Egyptian Jack the giant-killer. In the Ritual he is called the slayer of rebels and piercer of the proud. His natural genesis was in the tiny light of the new moon, which rose up with its sharp horns to pierce the powers of night, and drive them out of the darkened orb. The giants of the primitive mind *were* the powers of darkness, which forever rose up in revolt against the light, kept all life cowering in their shadow by night, took possession of the moon in the latter half of the lunation, or covered its face with the blood and dust of battle during the terrible time of an eclipse. Then the little hero, the child of light, arose and made war on the giants, and overcame them as he grew in glory and waxed greatly in the plenitude of his Hidden father's power and might. The name of Khunsu's father is Amen, the Hidden God, the child Khunsu being his visible representative re-born in the new moon.

Mythology is the ground-work of all our theology and Christology, and it is only by mastering the plan that we can learn how the superstructure has been built. This character of Khunsu is that of the mythical Messiah, or manifester in external nature, as a representative of the Eternal in the phenomena of time. In Egypt, Seb-Kronus, or Time, was designated the true Repa, or Heir-Apparent of the Gods. Later, the Repa was Heir-Apparent to the father, Osiris or Amen-Ra, and the re-birth in time, might be monthly or annually, every nineteen or twenty-five, 500 or 2155, years, according to the particular period. In the mystical or spiritual phase this representative of divinity was the Christ within, the Son of God incarnate in matter; the Christ of the Gnostics who was *not* a man; their Jesus, who could not be a Jew; their Redeemer, who was but the immortal principle in man, a Deliverer from the degradation; a Saviour solely from the dissolution of matter, which the Greek poet Linus calls the "Giver of all shameful things."

But to return to the Moon Mythos. The legend of Samson can now be read for the first time as the Hebrew version of the Egyptian myth of Khunsu, the luni-solar hero who slays the giants—or Philistines—and overcomes the powers of darkness. It was impossible to read the riddle by supposing, with Steinthal, that Samson was simply the sun-god himself; because if he were, in killing the lion he would be only slaying the reflection of himself—the lion being a solar type. The name of Shimshon denotes the luminous or shining one, as an emanation of the solar fire. Samson, like Khunsu, is the typical hero. Khunsu is the Egyptian Heracles. Samson, like Heracles, slays the lion, as his first great labour, or feat of strength. This deed is represented allegorically, and is put forth as his riddle. Out of the eater came forth meat, and out of the mighty came forth sweetness. The mighty one who devours is the lion, and the honey was found in its dead carcase. The Mithraic and Egyptian monuments will enable us to read the riddle. In the Persian we see the lion depicted with a bee in its mouth. The lion, or rather the *lioness, was* an Egyptian figure of fire—the lioness in heat. She was represented, by the goddess of the solar fire and alcoholic spirit, as Sekhet, who carries the sun's disk on the head of a lioness. The name of this she-lion, Sekhet, is also the name for the bee, which is the royal symbol of Lower Egypt; and the *bee* denotes the sweetness in the lion. Now, the fiercest solar heat was coincident with the waters of the Inundation, two-thirds of which (according to Hor-Apollo) poured down into Egypt whilst the sun was in the sign of the lion. Sekhet was also the goddess of sweetness or pleasure—we may say literally, goddess of the honey-moon. Hence the association of the lion and the bee, or the honey in the lion. The triumph over the lion may be understood in this way. Sekhet, the she-lion, impersonated the force of the sun, which was often fatal, hence she was made the punisher of the wicked with hell-fire; and this lunar hero, as Heracles, Khunsu, or Samson, *was* the *conqueror* in the cool of the night, which followed the fiery fervour of the sun by day. Further, at the time the sun was in the lion-sign, the full moon rose *vis-a-vis* in the sign of the Waterman, or Waterwoman, in the Hermean Zodiac; and we cannot read one part of the celestial imagery independently of the other. In this full moon, which brought the sweet, fresh waters to Egypt, the hero attained the height of his glory, as conqueror of the furnace-heat which culminated then and there with the sun in the sign of the lioness, as reflector of the fiercest solar fire. As the moon was the bringer of the waters, and the breath of life in the coolness and the dews of night, the lunar hero was not only credited with drawing the sting of Sekhet, but with extracting honey from the dead lion.

When the young hero as son of the sun-god, reborn of the new moon, has once more conquered in conflict with his eternal enemy, and he breaks out in triumph, free from the throttling folds of the dragon, of the Sami, or the Philistines, as he ascends aloft he is seen bearing the dark orb of the old moon as a palpable proof of his power. He had burst through the barriers of the underworld, the gates of death and darkness; and so it would be fabled that he carried the barriers away with him, and bore them visibly on high to the summit of the lunar ascent! It is so represented when Samson not only breaks out of Gaza, but tears up the city gates, and carries them away by night with their posts, bolts, and bars, to the top of the hill, or mountain of the moon, as the lunar height was called! The soli-lunar nature of the hero is shown by the number 30 (the thirty days to the month in the soli-lunar reckoning.) Samson has thirty companions. He smote thirty men at Ascalon, and spoiled them of thirty changes of raiment. The number 7 is also an all-important factor in the lunar mythos, with its twenty-eight days to the month. In the cuneiform legend of Ishtar the goddess descends and ascends through seven gates, each way in her passage to and from the netherworld, as female representative of the moon. So when Sut-Typhon, the dark one of the lunar twins, was *beaten* by Horus, he is described by Plutarch as fleeing from the battle during seven days on the back of an ass! In each case the number 7 signifies one quarter of a moon. The number 7, answering to one lunar quarter, is prominent in the legend of Samson. In one phase he tells Delilah that if he is bound with seven new bow-strings his strength will depart, and he will become weak, and be as another man. But when these are applied to him they are snapped like a string of fire-singed tow! We may suppose this phase to represent the *first* seven days of the *growing crescent* moon; hence the seven new bow-strings, which are in keeping with the seven strings of the lunar harp. In the second phase the hero is bound with new ropes, which he freed himself from as if they had been thread. Fourteen days bring us to the moon at full, and to the culmination of Samson's glory. Then he confesses to his charmer that if the seven locks of his head are shaven off his strength will assuredly depart. Now, hair is an especial, primitive type of virility, potency, and power. In the Egyptian Ritual the Osirified, as Horus, ascends the heaven with his long hair reaching down to his shoulders as a type of his growing glory. Moreover, Samson's hair, the emblem of his strength, is in seven locks. These answer to the seven nights of the quarter in which the lunar splendour comes to the full, and the opposing powers of darkness, called the Philistines, are very literally "cleared out." When this period is past, and the hero is shorn of his hair, the Philistines are upon him once more. This time the drama is to come to an end. But not without an intimation of its being continued or repeated in the next new moon, for the narrative confesses conscientiously that Samson's hair began to grow again after he was shaven. But for the present the powers of darkness prevail; and having shorn the hero of his glory during seven nights, and brought him low, they put out his sight and bind him with fetters of brass, eyeless in Gaza, pitiful and forlorn as "blind Orion hungering for the morn."

The eye of the blinded Horus being put out by Sut, who was at the head of the Typhonian powers, called the *Sami*, or conspirators, is identical in the Egyptian mythos with the putting out of Samson's eyes in the Hebrew version! In the Osirian myth, however, it is *the* eye of Horus that is wounded; the eye that is swallowed by Sut; the eye that is restored at dawn of day, and this one-eyed form of the mythos survives in the account of Samson's blindness when he prays for strength enough to avenge the loss of *one of his two eyes*, as we have it in the margin! The lunar light was *the* eye of the sun, but this becomes the two eyes of the hero when he is rendered according to the complete human likeness, which shows us how the mythos was rationalised as history. It is Delilah who causes the ruin of Samson, just as Ishtar, called goddess 15, as the moon at full, is the ruin of her lovers, in the legend of Ishtar and Izdubar, where she is charged with being an enchantress.

a prisoner, a destroyer of male potency. Izdubar, the sun god, reproaches her with witchcraft, her murderous lust, her merciless cruelty, and declines to become her lover himself! According to the myth the luni-solar male divinity was represented in the wane of the light as suffering from the evil influence of the female moon. It is very evident that the myths were made by men; as in case of a fall or catastrophe it was always *she* who *did* it. *She* tempted the poor man, or overcame the god. It was *she* who had reduced his strength, and brought him so low; *she* who had shorn him of his glory; *she* who had given him poison to drink, and betrayed him to the powers of darkness; *she* who is the cause of his impotential mood, his waning, languishing, and drooping down. And the true meaning of Delilah's name, I take it, expresses the weakened, worn-out, impotent condition of the lunar hero thus brought low—the name being derivable from a root signifying to totter, droop, and hang inertly down—Delilah being the personified cause of this emasculated condition of the reduced and wretched, bound and blinded lunar god, the mighty hero in his fallen state. The Danes have a lunar Delilah or lady of the moon, who is described as being very beautiful when seen in front, but she is hollow behind: she plays upon a harp of seven strings, and with this she lures young men to her on purpose to destroy them. The Hebrews have a Talmudic tradition that Samson was lame in both his feet. And this *was* the status or condition of the child-Horus, who was said to be maimed and halt in his lower members; the cripple deity, as he is called by Plutarch. Other scattered fragments of the true myth are to be found; for instance, in the lunar triad of the mother and the twin brothers, one of them accompanies the female moon during the *first half* of the total lunation, the other during the *latter half;* and this appears to be reflected by the Hebrew mythos when Samson's wife is "given to his companion whom he had used as a friend." Again, the *jackal* was an Egyptian type of the dark one that devoured by night, and of Sut, the thief of light in the moon, he who swallowed the Eye of Horus. Jackal and fox are co-types, and they have one name, that of Shugal, the howler, in Hebrew. This enables us to understand the story of the 300 foxes or jackals in the Jewish form of the myth. Samson being the representative of the sun-god who drives the darkness out of or away from the lunar orb, and does all the damage he can to the Typhonian powers, or Philistines, the story-teller multiplies the jackal to enhance the triumph of his hero; and instead of the struggle between Horus and the jackal-headed Sut-Anup, we have the more difficult feat of catching 300 jackals and setting fire to their tails, so that they might consume the crops of the Philistines, or, in other words, burn out the darkness from the orb of the moon.

It is probable that Mithra, son of Ahura Mazda, and natural opponent of the dark Power, is the same representative of the God of Light, reflected in the moon as the witness by night for the absent sun. It may be noted that Matra in Egyptian means the Witness, or more fully, the Witness for Ra. The scene portrayed on the Persian monuments is nocturnal, and the time of year is that of the sun's entrance into the sign of Scorpio, where it is deprived of its virility. At this time the moon rises at full in the sign of the Bull, the first of the superior signs. The Lord of Light in the moon is now the dominating power during six months. Thus Mithras slaying the Bull is equivalent to Samson killing the Lion, or overcoming the fierceness of the Solar fire; and also of Osiris doing battle with Sut-Typhon and conquering his terrors in external phenomena. Osiris dies on the 17th of the month Athor, which was at the time of the Autumn Equinox, or rather he enters the six lower signs at that time. An ark was made in the shape of a crescent moon, and on the 19th of the same month the priests proclaimed that Osiris was found, his resurrection on the third day being in the moon. Thus it was in the new moon that the Dead Osiris *first* returned to life in the form of his own son.

Our modern solarite interpreters can talk of little else but the sun, the dawn, and the dark. Mr. Renouf, in his Hibbert lectures, identifies Sut-Anubis with the twilight, or as the *dusk*. Hence, when it is said in the texts that he " swallowed his father Osiris," this on the face of it looks like the darkness of night swallowing the disappearing sun. But Egyptian mythology is by no means so simple as that. It is not to be fathomed on the face of it, nor can it be interpreted without such a knowledge of the total typology, as the Aryan School all put together do not possess. There is nothing simply solar in it anywhere! It is true that *Sut* represents the presence and the power of darkness. It is true that the nocturnal sun in the under world was called Osiris, or Atum, or Amen-Ra. Also, the setting orbs of light were represented as being swallowed down by the crocodile or some other type of the devourer. But the continual conflict and alternate victory of light and darkness were *seen* to have their most obvious, most visible, most interesting field of battle in the moon! It was *there* the watchers observed the never-ceasing struggle for the birthright of the twin brothers, who personated the opposing powers. The dark one was first born from the mother moon at full; but the light one was acknowledged to be the genuine heir-apparent! There is a myth of the blind Horus in which he is described as sitting solitary in his darkness. Sut is said to have swallowed his eye, or to have wounded it, and put out the sight. In one text Horus says, " Behold, my eye is as though Sut (Anup) had pierced it." In another he cries, " I am Horus. I come to search for mine eyes." Sut, who swallows the eye, is made to restore it again! In one account the eye is said to be restored at the dawn of day; *that* is in the vague stage of the conflict between the darkness and the light.

At one time, says Plutarch, Sut smote Orus in the Eye; this represented the diminution of the moon. At another he plucked the eye out and swallowed it, afterwards giving it back to the sun. This blinding denoted the Eclipse.

In the lunar phase of the mythos the *Eye* of light, or of the sun, is the moon. The moon at full was the mirror of light, hence it was the mother of Horus as the child of light! But the eye was the primitive mirror. So the moon was called the Eye of the sun, when it was *known* as a reflector of the solar light. Thus the lunar orb was the *consort* of the sun; his Eye by night, as the reproducer of his light when he was in the under-world; and in reproducing the light she was as the mother bringing forth his child! For instance, the cow was a type of the moon as Hathor, or as Aahti, and when the cow is portrayed with the solar disk between her horns, the imagery denotes the mother-moon as bearer of the sun, that is, as reproducer of the solar light in the lunar orb, or, as it was also said, in the Eye.

For this reason the mother of Horus, child of light, is also described as being the eye of Horus, the moon-mirror in which the father Osiris made babies in the eye, as the poets say, or was reflected as Horus, the child of light, re-born monthly of the moon as his mother. The lunar god Taht is sometimes portrayed with the eye of Horus, or the new moon in his hand. And the goddess Meri = Mary bears the eye upon her head, as typical reproducer of the child. Now this is the eye that was swallowed by Sut. When the power of darkness *had* put out the lunar light, the eye was not only pierced but swallowed, as the phenomena were rendered in the mythos. Moreover, as Osiris had become the father of all, he was also the acknowledged father of Sut; and as it was the father who was reflected by the mother-moon, or the eye, Sut may be said to have swallowed his own father when he obscured the lunar light, or swallowed it with the darkness during an eclipse. This was the symbolic eye that was full on the 14th of the month in the lunar, or on the 15th in the soli-lunar reckoning, or on the 30th Epiphi, when the eye of the year was full, according to the Egyptian Ritual. The swallowing of Osiris by Sut belongs to the soli-lunar phenomena! Plutarch tells us that some of the Egyptians held the shadow of the earth, which caused an eclipse of the moon, to be *Sut Typhon*. By aid of which we can identify the original dragon of the eclipse! The mythical and celestial dragon, as I have elsewhere demonstrated, was founded on the crocodile as the natural type of the swallowing darkness. The crocodile *is* the swallower of the lights as they go down in the west, and the tail of the crocodile reads kam, *i.e.*, black, darkness. Typhon (both male and female) is represented by the crocodile, the dragon of the waters and of darkness. Now the most thrilling and fearsome act of the lunar drama was during the period of eclipse. There is something very weird, uncanny, and unked, in the projection of the earth's shadow across the luminous face of the moon. To the primitive mind it was the crocodile above, or the dragon, swallowing the orb of light, or Sut swallowing his father Osiris. An eclipse was the meal-time of the monster. An eclipse was the scene of the great battle between Horus and Sut, or Horus and the Dragon, and the great battle was identical with that of our George and the Dragon. The same struggle between the powers of light and darkness is portrayed in the Book of Revelation when the woman clothed with the sun, and the moon under her feet, is about to bring forth her man child, and the great dragon of eclipse stands before her ready to devour the child as soon as it is born! In the oldest astronomy the years were reckoned by the eclipses, as it was in Egypt, China, and India. And the most ancient type of time or Kronus, as Egyptian, is Sevekh, the crocodile-headed god, that is, the dragon of eclipse who annually swallowed the moon containing the Lord of Light or his infant Image.

According to the mythical mode of representing the natural fact, three days and three nights were reckoned for the absence of the lunar light, between old and new moon, and the Lord of Light in the lunar orb was said to be swallowed by a Dragon or a monster fish and to remain for that length of time in its belly. The legend is Egyptian. The great fish is the crocodile, the dragon of the deep. This is called the fish of Horus in the Ritual. The Crocodile first denoted the earth as the swallower of the Lights before it became the Water-Dragon, and so the Manifestor, as Horus, Jonah, Tangaroa, or the Christ, could be three days in the earth or the great fish previously to his resurrection. Types and stories might be manifold; the fact signified was always the same. Hence the Jonah of the Hebrew version is identical with the Christ, not as type of him, where all is typical; and in the Roman Catacombs the Jonah of one version is the Christ of the other. Jonah issues from the great fish in the form of the Child-Christ. Thus the origin of the "three days and three nights in the heart of the earth," or in the Crocodile, is to be found in lunar phenomena.

In a later form of the Osirian legend the Twins are the double Horus, instead of the Sut-Horus of the Typhonian myth. In this we see the little dark child eyeless, soulless, maimed in his lower members, going into Tattu to meet his soul, his other self, his glorified body, the *double*, like that of Buddha, which was called his diamond body. This other self is designated the soul of the sun, and it is this which revivifies, regenerates, and transforms the child of the mother-moon into the virile Horus, the new moon horned and pubescent. There is a tradition preserved by Plutarch that the child Horus, the cripple deity, begotten in the dark, was the result of Osiris having accompanied with Isis after her decease, or with Nephthys her sister, below the horizon. Even this representation is perfectly correct according to the natural phenomena. Isis personates the moon, which dies to be again renewed. The renewal occurs in the under-world, and is out of sight or all in the dark. Osiris, as the sun below the horizon *is* the renovator of the *old*, dead orb of the moon, which he causes to re-live with his light; hence the fable of his accompanying with Isis after her demise is in accordance with the mythical mode of representing the phenomena of external nature in human imagery.

In one of its phases the moon was portrayed in the character of a thief, which was personated by the jackal, ape, or wolf, who represented

Goddess 15. Ishtar is described as ascending and descending the steps of the moon, so many days up and so many days down—of these days there would be fifteen altogether, in accordance with her name of Goddess 15. And here the Christian Mary can be identified in this lunar character by means of the Apocryphal Gospels, that contain legends of the infancy which are of primary importance, hence they have been denounced as spurious, excommunicated as heretical, and kept out of sight by Papal commands. In pseudo Matthew (ch. iv.), we learn that when the Virgin was an infant, just weaned, she ran up the fifteen steps of the temple at full speed, without once looking back. At this age she was regarded as an adult of about thirty years! The story of the fifteen steps is repeated in the Gospel of Mary's nativity (ch. vi.), where the fifteen steps are associated with the fifteen Psalms of degrees. Further, it was on the 15th day of the moon that the dark one of the twins was re-born, as the lessening, waning one of the two; and in the history of Joseph the carpenter, Jesus says that Mary gave him birth in the fifteenth year of her age, by a mystery that no creature can understand except the Trinity. The Trinity being lunar, the subject matter is identical according to the Gnosis of numbers, and Mary is also a form of the Goddess 15,—Meri, or Hathor-Meri, in the Egyptian Mythos.

It is only in lunar phenomena that we can see how the child could be born from the side of its mother, as Sut Horus was, as well as the Buddha, or the Christ. Also, the divine child, as Buddha, was said to be visible whilst in the mother's womb. The womb of the mother being the lunar orb in which the child in embryo can be seen in course of growth, it was represented as being transparent with the child on view. The child Jesus is so portrayed in the Christian pictures of the enciente Virgin Mary, as may be seen in Didron's Iconography!

The birth of the dark one of the mother-moon's two children, depends upon that part of the lunar orb which is turned away from the sun, being dimly seen through the light reflected from our earth. As the light began to lessen, and the orb became opaque, there was an obvious birth of the dark part of the moon! That was the birth of the little, dark one, of the lunar twins. So fine a point of departure from the light half to the dark, and from the dark half to the light, may be likened to a single hair—as it was in the Hindu mythos, which represents Krishna as being born from a single black hair and Balarama from a single white hair of Vishnu. This is, probably, the mythical meaning of a saying attributed to the Christ in the gospel of the Hebrews,—"And straightway," said Jesus, "the holy spirit (my mother) took me and bore me by one of the hairs of my head, to the great mountain called Thabor." The exact colour of the dark orb is slate-black, and this has been preserved in India as the complexion of the dark child, Hari or Krishna. These types of the light and dark twins were certainly continued as the two-fold Christ in Rome, one form of whom is the little black Bambino of Italy, the Christ who was black for the same reason that Sut was black in

Egypt, and Krishna was blue-black in India. He was black, because mythical, and not because the Word was humanly incarnated as a nigger! He was black because he was the child of the virgin-mother as the moon!

One type of the *twins* found in the lunar phenomena has been humanised in the story of Jesus and John; these can be traced back to Horus and Sut, who is Aan or Anup, the Egyptian John. These two appear in the Ritual as the "Precursor," and the one who is preferred to him who was first in coming. Speaking in the twin character, the Osirified deceased says, "I am Anup in the day of judgment. I am Horus, the Preferred, on the day of rising." Anup presided over the judgment; so John the Precursor proclaims the judgment; and calls the world to repentance. Jesus comes as the "preferred one" on the day of his rising up out of the waters, when John the Precursor says of Jesus, "After me cometh a man which is become before me!" John's was the voice of one crying in the wilderness, "Make ye ready the way of the Lord." "I make way," says Horus, "by what Anup (the Precursor) has done for me." The twin lunar characters of John and Jesus can be identified in the gospel where John says of Jesus " He must increase, but I must decrease." So the title of the Akkadian moon-god, Sin, as the increaser of light, is Enu-zu-na, the Lord of waxing. In the Mithraic mysteries the light one of the twins was designated the bridegroom, and in one passage we meet with the bridegroom and the bride, that is the lunar mother of the Twins and Christ as the bridegroom. John personates the dark one; like Sut-Anup, he is not the light itself, and only bears witness to the light. The Christ or Horus was consort to the mother-moon, and the reproducer of himself. John says of him, " He that hath the bride is the bridegroom; but the friend of the bridegroom which standeth and heareth him rejoiceth greatly because of the bridegroom's voice." These three, the bride, bridegroom, and John, are a perfect replica of the lunar Trinity.

John represents the dark half of the moon, the child of the mother only, and he is unmistakably identified by Jesus in or as this mythical character when he says of his fore-runner, " Among them that are born of woman there is none greater than John, yet, he that is but little in the kingdom of God is greater than he;" that is, among those who are *re-born* in the *likeness* of the *father*, as Horus *was* when the solar god re-begot him in his own image as the reflection of his hidden glory reproduced by the new moon—the least of these is greater than he who was born of the mother alone.

As we have seen, the *fox* and *jackal* were *both* of them Typhonian types of the dark power, the thief of light in the moon, and co-types, therefore, with the dragon that swallowed the moon during an eclipse. Now, the name of Herod in Syriac denotes a red dragon; and the red dragon in Revelation, which stands ready to devour the young child that is about to be born, is the mythical form of the Herod who has been made historical in our gospels. Here the legendary devourer, the dark half of the lunation. The Germans have a saying that the wolf is eating the candle when there is what is still called a thief in it. So the primitive observers saw the dark encroaching on the light, and they said the wolf, jackal, rat, or other sly animal was eating the moon as the thief of its light. This is why *Hermes* was represented as *the thief*. In two different forms of the lunar mythos the jackal and the dog-headed ape were two types of this thief of the light. And in the zodiac of Denderah, just where Horus is on the cross, or at the crossing of the vernal equinox, these two thieves, Sut-Anup and Aan, are depicted one on either side of the luni-solar god. These two mythical originals have, I think, been continued and humanised as the two thieves in the Gospel version of the crucifixion.

The character of the thief still clings to the man in the moon. In a North Frisian folk-tale the man in the moon is fabled to have stolen branches of willow, or the sallow-palms, which he has to carry in his hands forever. Here we can identify the palm-branch of the man in the moon as Egyptian. The palm-branch was a type of time and periodicity. Hor-Apollo tells us it was adopted as the symbol of a month, because it alone produces one additional branch at each renovation of the moon, so that in reckoning the year is completed in twelve branches. A form of this appears as the Tree of Life in the book of Revelation. The palm-branch is carried by Taht, the man in the moon, and scribe of the gods, who reckoned time by means of the lunations, and this evidently survives in the Frisian legend. He who once reckoned time by means of the shoots on the palm-branch became the picker-up or stealer of willow-wands or sticks, according to the later folk-lore. Also, when the moon-god was superseded by the sun as the truer reckoner of time, the character of the lunar deity suffered degradation! We find the same contention going on as there was between the number thirteen and twelve. When the year was reckoned by thirteen moons of twenty-eight days each, thirteen was then the lucky number (a charm of primroses or a sitting of eggs was thirteen), but when this was changed for the twelve months of solar time, *then* the number thirteen became unlucky or accursed. The day of rest being changed from Saturday, the old lunar god was charged with being a Sabbath-breaker. He *stole* sticks, or he *strewed* brambles and thorn-bushes on the paths of people who went to church on Sunday (the day of the Sun). He did not keep the day of rest, but would go on working, or reckoning time with his palm-branch, Sundays as well as week-days, and so he was doomed to stand in the moon for all eternity as a warning to wicked Sabbath-breakers. Taht (or Khunsu) is the Egyptian man in the moon, who in the dark half of the period was represented by the dog-headed ape; and from these came our man in the moon with his dog. The Creek Indians have the same myth. They say the inhabitants of the moon consist of a man and his dog.

The ass was another Typhonian type of the moon. In an Egyptian representation, it is by the aid of the ass-headed god Aai that the solar divinity ascends from the under-world where the dark powers have their time of triumph over him by night. The ass is portrayed in the act of hauling up the sun-god with a rope from the region below. That is one mode of expressing the fact that the moon here represented by the ass was the helper of the sun by night, in his battle against the powers of darkness—gave him a lift up, or, it may be, a ride. Again, in the Persian form of the lunar myth, it is the ass that stands on three legs in the midst of the waters, who is the assistant of Sothis, the dogstar, in keeping time. The three legs of the ass are a figure of the moon in its three phases of ten days each, like the three legs of the frog in the Chinese myth. Also, the head of the ass is an Egyptian hieroglyphic sign which has the numeral value of thirty, or a soli-lunar month. Thus we find the ass fighting on the side of the sun by night in the Egyptian mythos, and against the waters of the deluge, as a timekeeper in the Persian legend. In the Hebrew version the jaw-bone of the ass, a type of great strength, becomes the weapon of power with which Samson slays the Philistines, or fights the sun-god's battle by night against his enemies that lurk in darkness. The ass, as a lunar type, was also represented as the bearer of the solar Messiah, just as the cow carries the sun between her horns as reproducer of his light in the moon. The moon at full was the genetrix under either type. The lessening, waning moon was her colt—the foal of an ass. The new moon, as the young lord of light, came riding in his triumph on the ass, as the new moon on the dark orb of the old mother-moon! Now, in the apocryphal gospel of James, called the Protevangelium, the virgin Mary is described as riding on the ass when Joseph sees her laughing on one side of her face, and crying or being sad on the other! which corresponds to the light and dark halves of the moon. She is lifted from the ass to give birth to the child of light in the Cave. In the Greek myth Hephaistos ascends from the under-world riding on the ass, the wine-god having made him drunk before leading him up to heaven. In the Hebrew version the Shiloh is to come, binding his ass to the vine, his eyes red with wine, his garments drenched in the blood of the grape, and he is as obviously drunk as Hephaistos. This imagery was set in the planisphere, ages before our era, as the forefigure and prophecy of that which was to be fulfilled in the Christian history, according to the canonical gospels! Now it can be seen *how* the Messiah may be said to come riding on an ass, and upon a colt, the foal of an ass, although it is pitiful enough to give one the heartache, to expose the miserable pretences under which this mythical Messiah has been masked in human form, and made to put on the cast-off clothing of the pagan gods, and play their parts once more; this time to prove the real presence of a god in the world.

It was as the mother-moon that Ishtar of Akkad was designated "Goddess Fifteen,"—she being named from the full moon in a month of thirty days. The same fact is signified in the Egyptian Ritual (ch. 80), when the Woman of the moon at full orb exclaims,—" I have made the eye of Horus (the mirror of light), when it was not coming on the festival of the 15th day." She is the Egyptian form of the

the swallower of the moon, is impersonated as a Jewish ruler who commands all the innocent little ones to be murdered in order that he may include the child-Christ reborn for the overthrow of him who can only rule in the kingdom of darkness. Now, if we bear in mind that fox, jackal, wolf, and dragon are equally Typhonian types of the evil one, the destroyer, we may possibly interpret a particular epithet applied to Herod, the destroyer, by the Christ in the gospel according to Luke. When Jesus is told that Herod would fain kill him, "he said unto them, Go and say to that *fox*, behold I cast out devils and perform cures to-day and to-morrow, and the third day I am perfected." The scene is obviously in the underworld, where the moon-god descended during the three dark nights before he rose again or was perfected on the third day. It was *here* that the god as Khunsu, the caster-out of demons, or Horus, performed cures and exorcised the evil spirits that infested the departed in their underground passage where the dragon Herod, or the Typhonian reptile Herrut, lurked, and sought to kill the healer of the diseased and deliverer of the dead.

Having identified Herod, the mythical monster, with the dragon, and *as* the fox, we may carry the parallel a little farther, and perhaps identify him as the traditional murderer of John!

As already shown, in the Christian continuation of the legend, John takes the place of Taht-Aan, the dark one of the lunar twins. John and Jesus are equivalent to Aan and Horus. In the Apocryphal or Legendary Lore, John is often identified *with* and identified *as* the primary Messiah! He is so in the Apocryphal Gospel of James. In this, Herod is seeking the life of the Divine child, and he sends his servants to kill John. We read that "Herod sought after John, and sent his servant to Zachariah saying, 'Where hast thou hidden thy son?' and Herod said 'his son is going to be the King of Israel.'" Here it is *John* who is to be the infant Messiah whose life is sought by the destroyer Herod, and the fact, according to the true mythos, is that John represents the first and that one of the lunar twins whom Herod, or the Typhonian devourer, does put an end to, because he personates the dark half of the lunation, the waning, lessening moon, that darkens down and dies. In the Zodiac of Denderah we see the figure of *Anup* portrayed with his head cut off; and I doubt not that the decapitated Aan or Anup is the prototype of the Gospel John who was beheaded by Herod. In the planisphere Anup stands headless just above the river of the Waterman, the Greek Eridanus, Egyptian Iarutana, the Hebrew Jordan; and we are told that the Mandaites, who were amongst the followers of John, had a tradition that the river Jordan ran red with the blood which flowed from the headless body of John.

As I have previously pointed out, the Christ of the Gospel according to Luke has several features in common with the moon-god Khunsu, the healer of lunatics and persons possessed, who was likewise lord over the pig, a type of Typhon, the evil power. Khunsu followed Taht, as child of the sun and moon, after Taht had been, so to say, divinized into invisibility. Taht-Khunsu is the visible representative, who registers the decrees of the hidden Deity,. Amen-Ra, the god who seeth in secret. He is particularly the god of health and long life. It is said that he gives years to those whom he chooses, solicits the superior powers for an extension of the lease of life, or "asks years" for whomsoever he likes, and increases life in fulness and in length for those who do his will! "Life comes from him, health is in him, Khunsu-Taht, the reckoner of time." This is because he personated that renewal of light and time which was monthly in the moon. Khunsu is the supreme healer amongst the Egyptian gods, more especially as the caster-out of demons and exorciser of evil spirits. He is called the driver-away of obsessing influences, the great god, chaser of possessors, and is literally the lunar deity who cures what are now termed lunatics.

And it is in this character that the Christ of Luke is particularly pourtrayed. Chief of the suffering and afflicted who came to be healed by the Christ were the $\sigma\epsilon\lambda\eta\nu\iota\alpha\xi o\mu\epsilon\nu o\iota$, or those who were lunatic. Curiously enough they came to him on the mountain, where the swine were feeding—that is, where the moon-god, Khunsu, holds the typical pig in his hand, denoting the casting out of Typhon, the Egyptian devil. For it is on the mount of the moon, or in the moon at full, that Khunsu is depicted as the driver-out of demons and expeller of the powers of darkness, the enemy of Sut-Typhon, the Egyptian Satan, whose presence is represented by the pig.

In the Ute mythology, the Hero, as divine teacher of men, sits on the summit of a mountain to think. He says repeatedly,—"I sat on the top of a mountain, and did think." In the Egyptian Mythos, preserved by the Gnostics, Hermes is the divine teacher, who not only thinks, but preaches the Sermon on the Mount. The transfiguration of Osiris in the mount of the moon occurred upon the 6th day of the new moon. This ascent of the lunar moon after six days is repeated in our gospels, and can be paralleled in a myth of Buddha's transfiguration on the mount. Here, the six glories of the Buddha's head shone out with a radiance that blinded the sight of mortals and opened the spirit-vision, so that men could see spirits and spirits could see men. It was on the mount of the moon that Satan shewed Jesus all the kingdoms of the world and the glory of them, and at *that* height it may not have been necessary for him to have shewn them, as was explained by a German critic, "in a map." In Buddha's first temptation the dark Mâra causes the earth to turn round, like the potter's wheel, for him to see all the kingdoms of the world, and he promises him that he shall rule the whole four quarters! The quarters are lunar. By comparing the various myths with the Gospel versions, we find that

Sut and Horus. = Satan and Jesus.
Anup and Horus = John and Jesus.
The Double Horus = Two-fold Christ.
Khunsu - - = Christ.

The French retain a tradition that the man in the moon is Judas Iscariot, who was transported there for his treason to the Light of the World. But that story is pre-Christian, and was told at least some 6,000 years ago of Osiris and the Egyptian Judas, Sut, who was born twin with him of one mother, and who betrayed him, at the Last Supper, into the hands of the 72 Sami, or conspirators, who put him to death. Although the Mythos became solar, it was originally lunar, Osiris and Sut having been twin brothers in the moon.

The Man in the moon is often charged with bad conduct towards his mother, sister, mother-in-law, or some other near female relation, on account of the natural origin in lunar phenomena. In these the moon was one as *the* moon, which was two-fold in sex, and three-fold in character, as mother, child, and adult male. Thus the child of the moon became the consort of his own mother! It could not be *helped* if there was to be any reproduction. He was compelled to be his own father! These relationships were repudiated by later sociology, and the primitive man in the moon got tabooed. Yet, in its latest, most inexplicable phase, this has become the central doctrine of the grossest superstition the world has seen, for these lunar phenomena and their humanly represented relationships, the incestuous included, are the very foundations of the Christian Trinity in Unity. Through ignorance of the symbolism, the simple representation of early time has become the most profound religious mystery in modern Luniolatry. The Roman Church, without being in any wise ashamed of the proof, portrays the Virgin Mary arrayed with the sun, and the horned moon at her feet, holding the lunar infant in her arms—as child and consort of the mother moon! The mother, child, and adult male, are fundamental; and, as Didron shows, God the Father hardly obtains a place in the Christian Iconography for nearly 1200 years.

In this way it can be proved that our Christology is mummified mythology, and legendary lore, which have been palmed off upon us in the *Old* Testament and the *New*, as divine revelation uttered by the very voice of God. We have the same conversion of myth into history in the New Testament that there is in the Old—the one being effected in a supposed fulfilment of the other! Mythos and history have changed places once, and have to change them again before we can understand their right relationship, or real significance. In the various aspects of the divine child, born of the Virgin Mother,—the child of prophecy that Herod sought to slay,—the Christ in conflict with Satan as his natural enemy; the Christ who transforms in the waters, and is transfigured on the Mount; the Christ who is the caster-out of demons; the Christ who sends the devils into the herd of swine; the Christ who descends into Hades, or the earth, for three days, to come forth, like Jonah, or as Jonah, from the belly of Hades, or the great fish, the dragon of the waters; who breaks his way through the under-world, as the conqueror of darkness and disease, death and devil; as the saviour of souls, and leader into light; in all these, and other mythical phases, the Christ is none other than the soli-lunar hero, identical with Khunsu, with Samson, with Horus, with Heracles, with Krishna, with Jonah, or with our own familiar Jack the giant-killer. It is just as easy to *prove* that an historic Christ never existed as it is to demonstrate that the mermaid, or the moon-calf, the sphinx, or the centaur, never lived. That is, by showing how they were composed as chimeras, and what they were intended for as ideographic types that never did, and never could, have a place, in natural history. For example, Pliny in his natural history describes the *moon-calf* as a monster that is engendered by a woman only. This chimera of superstition was *originally* the amorphous child of the mother-moon, when represented by the cow that gave birth to the moon-calf. This moon-calf had the same origin and birth in phenomena as any other child of the Virgin Mother; and the mythical Christ is equally the monster, or chimera, that is engendered of the woman only. This is acknowledged when certain of the Christian Fathers *accounted* for the virgin motherhood of the historical Jesus, by *asserting* that certain females, like the vulture, could conceive without the male. For the vulture was the Egyptian type of the virgin-mother, Neith, who boasts in the inscription at Sais, that she did bring forth without the male! Hor-Apollo explains that the Egyptians delineated a vulture to signify the mother, because there is no male in this kind of creature, the female being impregnated by the wind—the wind that becomes the Holy Ghost, or *gust*, when Mary was overshadowed and insufflated.

In his Apology, Justin Martyr tells the Romans that by "declaring the Logos, the first-begotten of God, our Master Jesus Christ, to be born of a virgin mother, without any human mixture, and to be crucified and dead, and to have risen again and ascended into heaven, we say no more than what you say of those whom you style the sons of Jove." *That* was true. So far as the mythos *went* the Christians followed and repeated it after the Pagans; but being *uninitiated* A-Gnostics they continued the mythos as a human history, which made all the difference. The relative positions of those who knew and those who did not know may be illustrated by the man in the moon. That popular figure of speech did not originate in any human reality, but in telling the story without the Gnostic clue the mythos would become a human history; and Justin is in the position of a simpleton who would persuade the learned men of Rome that the man in the moon is a human being, and that the celestial virgin had brought forth Time in person, as the child of the Eternal in a cave by the road-side near Bethlehem, by which means the non-existent had become humanly extant. Naturally, the knowers assumed the mental attitude of the right forefinger laid beside the nose!

Such are the mythical bases upon which historic Christianity has reared its superstructure and built *its* Babel, with the view of reaching heaven by means of this, the loftiest monument of human folly ever raised on earth. Instead of mythology being a disease of language, it may be truly said that our theology is a disease of mythology. For myself, somehow or other, I have been deeply bitten with the desire to know and get at the very truth itself in these matters, even though it unveiled a face that looked sternly and destroyingly on some of my own dearest dreams. The other side of this desire for truth is a passionate hostility to those who are engaged in imposing this system of false teaching and swindle of salvation upon the ignorant and innocent at the national expense. As Celsus said of the Christian legends, made false to fact by an ignorant literalisation of the Gnosis,—" What nurse would not be ashamed to tell such fables to a child?" We also say with him to those who teach these old wives' fables as the Word of God,—" If you do not understand these things, be silent and conceal your ignorance." Any way, we must let go these gods of external phenomena, whether elemental, zootypological, or anthromorphic, if we would discover the divinity within, the mystical Christ of the Gnostics. And we can be none the poorer for losing that which never was a real possession, but only the shadow which deluded us with its seeming substance. To *find* the *true* we must first let go the *false*, and, to adapt a saying of Goëthe's,—until we let the half gods go, the *whole* gods *cannot* come.

APPENDIX.

GREEK MYTHOLOGY

AND THE

GOD APOLLO.

If the author of *Juventus Mundi* could but turn to Egypt, and make a first-hand acquaintanceship with its Symbolism, I think it would enlighten him more than any amount of listening round to those deluding Aryanists, respecting the origin, derivation and meaning of the Greek Mythology.

For example, let us take the case of the god Apollo, who is related to the sun, and yet is not the sun itself. The Solarites can shed no light upon the darkness of Mr. Gladstone's difficulty. Writers who talk about mythology being a "disease of language," and know nothing of the gods as Celestial Intelligencers and time-keepers for men—chief of which was the sun, when the solar year had been made out; still earlier, the moon in its various phases—can lend us no aid in penetrating the secrets of this ancient science. "Solar-worship" is good enough for them, but it will not explain mythology to us, or to itself. The child of the sun, re-born as Lord of Light in the moon, has never come within the range of their vision. Yet it is the simple fact in natural phenomena, which was represented mythically as the mode of making it known, of teaching it by means of the Gnosis or science of knowledge, as one of the mysteries, so soon as the discovery had once been made; and this is one of the most important of all the factors in mythology.

I would suggest to Mr. Gladstone that the Greek Apollo is the same soli-lunar personification as is Thoth (Taht or Tehuti), and Khunsu (or the soli-lunar Horus), that is, the child of the supreme divinity in Egypt, the solar *Ra*, as his light by night—whilst he himself is the god who is hidden from sight in the under-world—his vice-dieu of the dark. Apollo is designated Lukēgenes, or light-born. He is the image of brightness, as shown by his title of Phoibus. So the moon-god is the image of the solar deity, the reflection of his glory in the lunar disk.

Every phase of character in which Apollo appears, especially as represented by Homer, can be identified as pertaining to the male moon-god in Egypt, and the common basis of all may be found in those natural phenomena which are indicated in previous pages. In these natural phenomena, there is a common source, or foundation, to which the functions and attributes of Apollo and Taht (or the lunar Horus) can be referred, and by which the characters may be satisfactorily explained. The relationships of Apollo to Zeus, are exactly like those of Taht to Osiris, the supreme being. It is Taht who gives the Ma-Kheru, or Word of Truth, to the sun-god himself. As representative of Ra, his lunar logos, his light in the darkness, he is the Word whose promise is fulfilled and made truth by the Supreme Being, the sun that vivifies and verifies for ever. By his Word, he drives the enemies from the solar horizon, the insurgent powers of darkness which are fighting eternally against *Ra*. This is the character of Apollo as the defender of heaven against every assault. These powers of darkness, continually in revolt, ever warring with the sun, were called the giants which Taht-Khunsu, the giant-killer, slays by night, or during the lunar eclipse. Apollo also figures as the destroyer of the giants who were at war with heaven. It is said in the Egyptian texts that Ra created this god, Taht, as " a beautiful light to show the name of his evil enemy," *i.e.*, Sut-Typhon, the eternal enemy of the sun. He held up the lamp by night that made the darkness visible; showed the name, the face, the personal presence, of his lurking foe. This also is a character of Apollo, as a representative and a kind of deputy providence for Zeus.

Apollo is god of the bow! Taht carries the bow of the crescent moon upon his head! Now the hero in the folk-tales who is always successful in drawing the great bow in the trial where all his competitors fail, *is* this god of the new moon, who alone *can* bend the bow, or bring the orb to the full circle of light once more. He can be identified in the Hindu form of the Mythos as Krishna " with the Bow of Hari." The crescent on the head of Taht is the bow prepared and ready to be drawn to the full against the power of night, and every form of evil that dwells in the darkness. Thus the lunar representative of Ra, with the bow of the young moon on his head, who prepares it month after month, and draws it to the full circle night after night, may be called the preparer of bows; and in Egyptian the name Apuru signifies a preparer of bows; it also means the Guide and Herald. As the u in Egyptian stands for o, and r for l, we have Apuru=Apollo; the preparer of bows=the god of the bow as male divinity of the moon, who was the offspring of the sun and moon, the bowman of the solar god. Mr. Gladstone doubts whether the root of Apollo is Greek, and says he would not be surprised to find it Eastern. All the evidence tends to prove it Egyptian by nature and by name. Apollo is the god of knowledge, past, present, and to come; Taht is the deity of knowledge, past, present, and future—the founder of science, lord of the divine words, and secretary of the gods. Apollo is the god of poetry and music. So was Taht. He is the psalmist and singer; he is fabled to have torn out the sinews of Sut-Typhon to form the lyre—the lyre or harp with seven strings being an image of the new moon, like the bow.

Apollo was the god of healing. Taht is the supreme physician and healer; " He who is the good Saviour," as it is written on a statue in the Leyden Museum. Apollo was the bringer of death in a form that was serene and beautiful, as became the lunar Lord of light, and enlarger of the lunar light to the full,—the character and function being afterwards applied to the light of life that suffered the passing eclipse of death. One name of Taht is Tekh, which signifies to be full!

Of course the Greeks did not simply take over the Egyptian mythology intact, nor did they preserve the descent quite pure on any single line. In re-applying the legendary lore, derived from Egypt, to the same phenomena in nature, there would be considerable mixture, amalgamation, change of name, and consequent confusion. The blind Horus of Egypt reappears as the blind Orion in the Greek mythos. This is as certain as that the constellation of Orion, the star of Horus, was named Orion after Horus! His lunar relationship is shown by the recovery of his sight on exposing his eyeballs to the rays of the rising sun,—just as the eye of Horus was restored to him through the return of light at dawn. Horus in his lunar character is one with Taht and Khunsu in the other cults; that is, the lunar child may be Horus as son of Osiris, or Taht as the offspring of Ra, or Khunsu as the child of Amen; the myth being one in different religions. It follows that so far as Orion is identical with Horus he is also, or once was, identical in character with the lunar Apollo, and therefore like him of twin-birth with Artemis. Links of this lunar relationship remain. He lives and hunts along with Artemis when his sight has been recovered. He was beloved by Artemis and slain by her because he made an attempt upon her chastity—which is a common charge brought against the man in the moon by mythology!

The bringing on of the lunar mythos upon two different lines of descent, Apollo being a continuation of Taht-Khunsu, and Orion of Horus, would account for the later mixture in the relationship of the various personations—the fact in nature being represented under different names for the same character in mythology, as it had been previously in Egypt.

MAN
IN SEARCH OF HIS SOUL
During Fifty Thousand Years,

AND

HOW HE FOUND IT!

WHEN Giorgione was challenged to paint a figure in a picture so that the spectator could see all round it, he overcame the difficulty by arranging a mirror at the back to reflect the other half of his subject! In like manner, we have to get all round our present subject with the aid of a reflector. This is to be discovered in some of the symbolic customs of the pre-historic races. The records of primitive and archaic men are only to be read in the things they did, and by aid of the signs they made, from before the time of written language and literature.

The earliest human sensations, feelings, and thoughts, had to be expressed by actions long before they could be communicated in words. Gesture-language and Fetish images originated in this primitive mode of representation; and we have now to penetrate the significance of the actions, and interpret the types employed in a font indefinitely earlier than that of letters! The performers cannot tell us directly what they meant when so many mysterious things were done; they can only make signs to us on certain matters, and we have to translate their dumb show as best we can!

Sir John Lubbock says the lower forms of religion are almost independent of prayer, but he does not take into account the fact that long before prayer could be uttered verbally, it was performed and acted by means of sign-language, which we have to read in ancient customs and primitive memorials of the fact.

For example, when a crooked pin is thrown into the "Wishing Well" as an invocation to the invisible powers, the bent pin is a prayer made permanent in a visible figure, which is extant among the Egyptian hieroglyphics, as the Uten, a twisted piece of metal, signifying an offering. It was as much the sign of prayer as are the clasped hands, or the body crouching down on bended knees, or the supplication in spoken words. We have to read it as we would a gesture-sign. It is a sign in gesture-language made to the unseen powers whether for good luck or bad! So when the ear was pierced by the worshipper, as a religious rite, it was a primitive mode of appeal to the deity as the Hearer or Judge, like the god Atum, who was the first Hearer in heaven, among the Egyptian gods. Fortunately, the primitive races of the world, such as the Blacks in Africa and Australia, still continue the customs, think the thoughts, repeat the rites, employ the signs, erect the memorials, and revere the images that were the Fetishes of the human infancy. These are preserved even by those who can give no account of their origin in the past or their significance in the present, but who simply and sacredly repeat them as a matter of following the example and treading in the track of their forefathers! Now Egypt, which I look upon as the living consciousness of Africa, continued to remember, and has left a written record of what was meant by these primitive practices and fetish figures; and in one aspect of the subject, that of the burial customs, the Egyptian Bible, or Book of the Dead, becomes a living tongue in the mouth of Death itself, which enables us to interpret the earlier and most ancient typology of the bone-caves found in other parts of the world.

The Bongo, Bechuana, and other Inner African tribes of to-day, still prepare their dying relatives for the grave whilst the body is warm and flexible, by pressing the head forward upon the knees, which are bent up against the breast, with the legs flexed upon the thighs. The African customs were continued on the American continent, where they are still extant. The ancient Peruvian mummies, or preserved bodies were similarly, but more perfectly prepared for the last abode on earth. The Comanches, the Pimas of Arizona, and other Red Indian tribes, still prepare their dead for burial in this primitive way. Sometimes a net is thrown over the body of the dying, and as the hold on life is gradually relaxed, the net is drawn tighter and tighter until the body is bound up to become rigid in that shape for burial. In this position the most ancient form of the mummy is still made almost alive. And that was the most ancient mode of burial known on earth. It can be traced back in Europe to the time of the Palæolithic or first Stone Age; and there are data extant which carry that age and its customs back (in round numbers) for some 50,000 years. The custom was common amongst the most primitive races of the world, including the Blacks of the southern hemisphere, whether they committed the mummy to the earth, or, like the Tasmanians and Maori, concealed it in the hollow bole of a tree.

Next, when we learn that the primary model of the tomb was the mother's womb,—and this fact is proved by the figures of the Cairns; and by the tree, the coffin, and the vase with female breasts, being types of the mythical Great Mother of Life; and when the identity of womb and tomb is indicated, as it is, by many prehistoric names; and further, when we have compared the images interred with the corpse, we learn for certain that in burying the dead in such a fashion, Primitive Man was preparing the mummy in the likeness of the fœtal embryo, or child *in utero*. In fact, he was burying it for a future birth!

We often hear of our "Mother Earth"—and the uterine formation of certain cairns in Britain can be identified by means of Egyptian hieroglyphics and symbols, which prove that the tomb was a representative image of the maternal birthplace. Therefore, the dead, some 50,000 years ago, were buried with an idea of reproduction for another life. This mother-mould of the beginning is also shown by the "Navel-mounds" of the Red Men in America, the Nabhi-Yoni image of the Hindus, and the Nave of the Church; by the Mam-Tor, a bosom-shaped hill, and the Mamsie, a Scottish Tumulus, in which the dead were returned to the Great Mother, accompanied by various types belonging to the symbolism of rebirth. The Egyptian dead were buried in the Mam-Mesi, or Meskhen. Both names literally denote the re-birthplace of the mummy. The Meskhen is also European. The ancient Midden, in which the bones of the dead were preserved, was known as the Miskin. Miskin-Belac, in Brittany, is also called Cairn-Belac, the terms being convertible.

We now know that all descent was first traced from the Mother alone, who survived as the Virgin Mother in mythology, whose son was her own consort; and the earliest form of the burial-place was simply feminine. Later on the male type of the producer was added, and both sexes are then represented in the place of burial as the place of re-birth. In Egyptian tombs the male emblem is a sign of rising again, or of being re-erected (as they expressed it) from the female place of re-birth. And that emblem has been found in Italy, buried beneath ten feet of slowly-accreted Stalagmite—a register, probably, of 50,000 years. To this day the Chinese seek for a burial-place just where the male and female features of the ground are most perfectly pourtrayed in a natural configuration and combination of hollow and mound. It has never yet been determined by philologists whether the British word "Combe" means a hollow between two hills, or the hill itself. Many Combes are found in valleys, whereas Black Combe is a mountain. The fact is, the complete type includes both sexes. This teaches us that the cairn was double, and that the hollow below was the feminine feature, and the mound erected above was masculine. This bi-sexual type of the burial-place was continued in various forms of the grave and gravestone, the Great Pyramid of Egypt, with its Well below and conical heap above, being a Colossal stone Cairn; and the dual type culminates at last in the nave and spire of the Church, which perpetuate the same sexual symbols as the Argha-Yoni or the Nabhi-Yoni of those benighted Hindoos, who are denounced by our missionaries for their gross idolatry. It was not "Idolomania," but a primitive kind of symbolism, a natural mode of thinging their thoughts. This doubles the proof that the dead were buried with the idea of being reproduced; and this Parental imagery was employed to continue and convey such an idea to the living.

It is here, then, at the outset, that we should have to seek for the true origin of those Phallic symbols or sexual images which are found scattered the world over, the types of production having been adopted from nature and perpetuated by the primitive builders in all lands as symbols of reproduction for a future life. Such emblems were no more set up at first as objects of worship or provocation to lasciviousness than the earliest races of men went naked on purpose to display their nudity as an incentive to animal desire. Nor was there any abasement of nature in these things, the human status at the time being too primitive even for any fig-leaf kind of consciousness or shame induced by clothing. Neither were these monuments at all directly related to the religious sentiment. That only comes in here with the aspiration for another life and yearning after the second birth. The religious sentiment did not originate in procreation for this life, but in reproduction for the next; and the true sacredness was conferred on the cairns, mounds, navels, and bosom-shaped hills by the burial of the Dead. For it is certain that these types of birth, whether found in Nature or erected by Art, are associated in all lands with the places of burial, or they constitute the sepulchre itself, just as the Church is still the burial-place, or stands amid the Graves of the Dead. Hottentot or British Cairns, Indian Navel-Mounds, Hindu Dagobas, Irish Round Towers, and Egyptian Pyramids and Obelisks, with the Teba or female Ark at the base, were all erected with one meaning, and each according to the same primitive typology of a resurrection.

"*Going to the Stones*" preceded going to Church, and the people went to them because their dead were buried in or around these, the earliest Shrines. The Memorial Stones were sacred to the dead from the first, as the latest grave-stone is to-day. Some of the stones were carried from land to land and called the Bringers of Immortality. In support of my theory that the Phallic Imagery was perpetuated for symbolic uses, and not for direct worship, I would point to the Umbilicus or Navel type, which, for aught we know to the contrary, may be earlier than the Phallic or Sexual Images, because the Navel unites both sexes under one sign. Be this as it may, the primitive mode of sepulture, the formation of the earliest tomb, together with the Monuments reared above, are all founded on the natural organs of the reproductive system, and, architecturally, the so-called Phallic faith resolves itself into an objective imitation of the parts of the human body which are devoted to re-birth,—including the *bos umbilicus*. Re-birth is the ideal demonstrated by the typical use made of these burial stones in passing the bodies of persons through the various holes and apertures in them at the time of initiation into the mysteries, or the transformation of the Boy into the Man; and re-birth being the fact signified, the Serpent-shaped Mound was also a tomb, and the living Tree a Coffin, because the Tree and Serpent were natural emblems of renewal or re-birth.

This Natural Genesis will likewise account for the Mythical Great Mother, who was the earliest of all Divinities in all lands,—being pourtrayed in the image of the reproducer that unites both Father and Mother in one person, and who survives to-day as the Mother-Church.

Moreover, the emblems buried with the dead from the earliest times are ideographic symbols of perpetuation and reproduction for the life to come. The figure of an eye was common in the tombs of Egypt. The name of it, "Uta," signifies salvation; and to be saved was to be preserved as a mummy waiting to be reproduced or transformed for another life. The eye being a mirror that reflects the image, it was adopted as a type of repetition and reproduction. Thus the Eye of Horus is the Mother of Horus, and the shoot of new life in the potato comes from the " eye "—as the place of reproduction. One word serves for both eye and seed in the Ute language. The Egyptians fed the eye with oil. And filling the "Eye of Horus" is synonymous with bringing an offering of sacred oil. The eye being the lamp of light to the body, it was supplied with that which would produce and reproduce the light. Thus, by aid of Egypt, we can understand why the primitive race in Britain, and still further north, were accustomed to fill the cups and eyes carved on the cap-stones that covered their buried dead with offerings of fat. They were filling the lamp of light for the gloom of the grave, and feeding the eye as an emblem of repetition or reproduction. The symbolism still survives when candles are placed in the hands of the corpse, or left with the dead in the tomb. And in ancient Egypt the candle was synonymous with reproduction.

It is an extant custom, both with the Kaffirs and the English, to cut the hair from the tail of a calf when it is being weaned, and stuff it into the ear of its mother. The hair being a symbol of reproduction, the action denotes a desire for plenty of milk or future progeny, whilst stuffing it into the ear signifies a wish that the prayer may be heard. A drink on the morning after being intoxicated is called "a hair of the dog that bit you"! This means a repetition of the dose; and as a symbol of reproduction, hair, in one shape or another, was buried with the dead. Of course the primary type of hair is the skin—in which the dead were wrapped for preservation, transformation, and rebirth. In the Egyptian Ritual the deceased says to his God, "Thou makest for me a skin." This God is characterised as the "Lord of the numerous transformations of the skin," which had become a type of renewal, on account of its shedding and renewing the hair. The skin is needed because he has to pass the waylayers who cause annihilation to those who are enveloped. The later shoe, following the skin, is also a type of renewal and reproduction; as such it was placed on the feet of the dead, and is still thrown for good luck after the newly married pair —good luck meaning plenty of progeny. The horn of the stag or reindeer was likewise a type of renewal, coming of itself, as does the hair of the skin. Hor-Apollo tells us the stag's horn was a symbol of permanence, because of its annual self-reproduction. And when the Greenlander has suffered from an exhausting illness, and he recovers his health, he is said to have lost his former soul, and to have had it replaced by that of a young child or a reindeer. In the bone-caves of France adult skulls have been discovered which were trepanned in the life-time of the owners; and into these the bones of young children had been inserted after death—these being typical of rejuvenescence and renewal from childhood—as we learn from the hieroglyphics of Egypt.

In all likelihood the Dog was the first animal to come under the dominion of man, his earliest four-footed friend; his primary ally in the work of progress and civilisation. He hunted for the men of the Kitchen-middens; he was the guide and guard of man in the palæolithic age, and he was sacrificed to become the typical guide of the poor cave-dwellers when they got benighted in the dark of death. The bones of the dog have been found buried with the human skeleton in a very ancient cave of the Pyrenees; in Belgium; and in Britain; showing that at a period most remote the dog was looked upon as a kind of Psychopompus, an intelligent shower of the way, like Sut-Anup, the golden dog or jackal of Egypt, and Hermes in Greece,—the Dog-star in the dark of death—a guide to show the way. "I have provided myself *with a dog's head*," says the Egyptian deceased in passing through the 10th gate of Elysium. In like manner English bishops used to be buried with a dog at their feet in the coffin. They, too, were provided with a dog's head—or a dog to show them the way! Of course the dog would not have been needed as a typical guide to show them the way if it had not been believed or assumed that there *was* a way through the dark valley of the dead! This conclusion that there was a door on the other side of the grave—as proved by the types and customs—had been reached by the men of the bone-caves in all probability more than 50,000 years ago!

How, then, did primitive or archaic man attain that certainty of foothold in the dark void implied by these burial customs, and this typology of the tomb, which certainly was felt by many of the pre-historic races, including the Black Man, the Maori, and the Red Man, who has no doubt about living on in his happy hunting grounds above? whereas so many of our own race to-day are still trying mentally to take that step in the dark, and stumble, because they can find neither foothold nor stair. The question is not to be answered by supposing there was any subjective revelation made to primitive man, which showed him once for all that he was an immortal being, formed in the image of God! It has taken me many years of ceaseless research to learn for myself how lowly and limited, but *how* natural was the revelation made to primitive man; we shall have to grope on our hands and knees at times to read it. Nor can the subject be approached by any supposition that early man began by *conceiving* the existence of an immortal soul. Modern metaphysicians may talk glibly enough about "concepts of the Infinite," of the "one God," of a "soul," or of "pure spirit;" but primitive man was not a metaphysician, nor the victim of an abysmal subjectivity. That disease is comparatively modern, and the modern metaphysician will be the last man to enter into the mind of primitive men.

When we have ransacked the myths of the world, and the legends of its earliest races, we can find no such thing anywhere as a beginning with abstract conceptions! But there is absolute proof everywhere that man founded at first upon his observations of objective phenomena. Primitive man was not a theorist or dealer in Ideal notions, not the kind of man to whom Ideas are Realities, but a stubborn positivist, limited as a limpet, and holding on as hard and fast to the hard rock of his facts. The nebulosity of metaphysic is altogether a later product. My contention is that the invisible world first demonstrated its existence to the early cave-dwellers of the human mind by becoming visible to them. It did not dawn on them from any sudden illumination within, nor waken to consciousness as a memory of immortality. Conception did not precede the act of begettal. Nor did they evolve the ghost-idea without the ghost itself. The pretensions and impostures of modern theology have tended to make these simple naturalists of the past look like impostors too, although they were not; at least they are not in the eyes of those who are acquainted with the abnormal phenomena occurring in our own time, which enable us to understand the same phenomena as a factor of knowledge and religion in the past. I say knowledge, for in his way pre-historic man was a Gnostic; and the Gnostics founded their religion from the first upon knowledge. By means of knowledge they attained their truth. It appears at first sight as if the ancients, having identified the intelligence or *nous* in man, thought it could be fed forever by the knowledge accumulated in this life. The Esoteric Buddhist still expects a perpetuity of existence by means of knowledge, or the Gnosis. In the Egyptian Book of the Dead the deceased makes his way from stage to stage of his progress by what he knows. He asserts his right of way by proclaiming: "I am the one who knows," "*I am the Gnostic*," "I have come," he exclaims, "having the writing" —the proof. Certain papyri assured a passage, and "prevailing by his papyrus," like Christian with his roll, is a title of the deceased. If he knows the first chapter of the Ritual in this life the spirit of the deceased can come forth every day as he wishes, and not be turned back, *i.e.*, if he possesses the knowledge of facts, which were demonstrated by the ancient Spiritualism. He is shown in the process of creating his eternal soul, by means of the Gnosis, or books of knowledge, those of Taht-Hermes. He cries: "Let me come! Let me spiritualise myself! Let me make myself into a soul! Prevail and prepare myself by the writings of Hermes!" or the Gnosis.

The immortal nature of the Soul having been demonstrated in the Mysteries, a knowledge of those Mysteries was sufficient to ensure a safe passage through the dark of death, and a sure triumph over all opposing powers, to those who had not the Vision.

"By means of wisdom," says the wise man in the Apocrypha, "I shall attain immortality;" and "to be allied into Wisdom is immortality." To *know* was salvation. Acquiring this wisdom is described in Revelation as eating a little book on purpose to be in the spirit—or be born again in the spirit, or in the Christ, as Paul has it—or to prophesy, or to know how to be entranced, and enter spirit-world as a spirit, for that is the ultimate fact. Irenæus says of the Gnostics: "They affirm that the Inner and Spiritual man is redeemed by means of knowledge, and that they, having acquired the knowledge of all things, stand in need of nothing else, for this is the true redemption," hence they repudiated the Christian Salvation by faith. (Irenæus, B. I., chap. xxi. 4.) "The souls which possessed the saving seed of Wisdom were considered superior to all others, and the Gnostics held these to be the souls of prophets, kings, and priests, who were consequently endowed with a nature loftily transcendent. They maintain that those who have attained to perfect knowledge must of necessity be regenerated into that power which is above all." "For it is otherwise impossible to find entrance within the Pleroma." (Irenæus, B. I., chap. xxi. 2.) In our day such persons are sometimes called Mediums or Sensitives; in India they are the Adepts in the most hidden mysteries. But this Gnosis by which the deceased in the Ritual prevailed over the destroyers of form, the extinguishers of breath, eclipsers of the astral shade, or the stealers of memory—for these are among the devourers named—this gnosis of redemption and salvation, the gnosis of enduring life, was not merely information or knowledge in our modern sense. It was the gnosis of the mysteries, and all that was therein represented. The ancient wisdom (unlike the modern) included a knowledge of the trance-conditions, from which was derived the Egyptian doctrine of spiritual transformation. This passed on into the Christian doctrine of conversion, and then the fundamental facts were lost sight of, or cast out and done with. The adepts had learned how to transform themselves into spirits, and enter spirit-world as spirits among spirits, or as was sometimes said in the Totemic transformations, to enter the bodies of beasts—a survival of which we have in the Were-wolf. Hermes describes the abnormal, or trance-condition, as a divine silence, and the *rest* of all the senses! He says: "It looseth the soul from the bodily senses and motions, it draweth it from the body, and changeth it wholly into the essence of a god." Then, says Hermes, "the soul cometh to the *eighth* nature, and having its proper power, it can converse (or enter into spiritual intercourse) with the powers that are above the eighth nature." So Nirvana becomes a present possession to the Esoteric Buddhist, because in trance he can enter the eternal state.

This Gnosis included that mystery of transformation which was the change spoken of by Paul, when he exclaimed—"Behold, I tell you a mystery," "We shall not entirely sleep, we shall be transformed!" according to the mystery that was revealed to him in the state of trance. *This* was the transformation which finally established the existence of a spiritual entity that could be detached, more or less, from the bodily conditions for the time being in life, and, as was finally held, for evermore in death. This mystery of regeneration was visibly enacted in life, and taught by the transformers in the early Totemic, and later religious, mysteries.

Now, in discussing the origin of religious "ideas," writers, as a rule, know nothing whatever of this rootage in the mysteries of abnormal experience; whereas it is impossible to determine anything fundamental until this dark continent has been explored by those who have adequate knowledge of the facts that were familiar to the primitive races of men, and upon which the Gnostic religions were universally founded.

Bastian tells us how the African Cazembe, or fetish-priest, regards himself as Immortal by reason of this power of tranformation in trance. The Dacotah medicine-men can transform themselves, and enter into conscious relationship and alliance with mighty spirits, whose powers they are thus able to make their own. They can also summon spirits, and compel them to appear for others to see. The Egyptian Magi, the wise men and pure Intelligences, have the Phœnix, the bird of transformation in death, for their ideographic sign, which shows that the ultimate nature of their wisdom, as seers or magi, was based on these abnormal conditions of seership! What do you think is the use of telling the adept, whether the Hindu Buddhist, the African Seer, or the Finnic Magician, who experiences his "Tulla intoon," or supra-human ecstasy, that he must live by faith, or be saved by belief? He will reply that he lives by knowledge, and walks by the open sight; and that another life is thus demonstrated to him in this. As for death, the practical Gnostic will tell you, he sees through it, and death itself is no more for him! Such have no doubt, because they know. The Mosaic and other sacred writings contain no annunciation of a mere doctrine of immortality, and the fact has excited constant wonder amongst the uninstructed. But the subject was not taught of old, as matter of written precepts, but as matter of fact; it was a natural reality, not a manufactured idealism. It was not the promise of immortality that was set forth, or needed, when a demonstration was considered attainable in the mysteries of the abnormal human conditions, which were once common enough to be considered a known part of nature! You have got the Mosaic writings, but without the older facts that were concealed at their foundations. This is the supreme secret of all secrets in the Gnosis of the most hidden mysteries—only to be fathomed by those who could enter the abnormal conditions, and be as spirits among spirits; only to be accepted by means of knowledge. In India to-day the stage of perfect adultship includes, even if it does not absolutely consist in, the power of transformation which occurs in trance, or in the perfect blending of the normal and abnormal faculties, so that, like Swedenborg, the Adepts can live and move and have their being in two worlds at once. It was by this transformation that our predecessors of thousands of years ago discovered their immortal soul, or link of continuity, through spirit-awakenment, produced consciously by various methods of attaining the trance conditions. And in this way the dust of death was first set a-sparkle, and the gloom of the grave was brightened, and grew transparent, with the luminous form of what the Egyptians called the Osirified deceased, or the *Ka* image of the spiritual self, the glorified Eidolon of man, which was visible to their seers in this life. None but a Spiritualist can possibly comprehend the customs, practices, and beliefs of the primitive Spiritualists in times past. They were genuine interrogators of Nature, however limited their knowledge. But they made much of that which the science of to-day is inclined to make so little of, or to pooh-pooh altogether in its ignorance of the value that these abnormal conditions have for the interpretation of the pre-historic past of man, and the foundation of religious beliefs.

Did you ever read by the light of a glow-worm laid on the page of a book? I have so read in the dark. And next morning, by the clearer light of open day, found my tiny lamp had gone out; there was no glow whatever; it was nothing more than a little grey worm! My reading must surely have been hallucination, the merest illusion of the night, in the face of this common daylight fact, to which every person could testify, that the thing did not shine by day! Spiritualism is that little luminous worm, which has shone with its tiny lamp divinely lit through all the darkness of the past. Many of the earlier races learned to read a page or two in the Book of Nature by the light of it. I have read some curious leaves by means of this little night-light Yet the non-Spiritualist will take up the glow-worm in the broad day-light of our age and show the on-looker that it has no lamp, that it never did shine except as a glamour of deception and illusion in the eyes of superstition. For all that, we know it to be a glow-worm still, which goes on shining through the gloom. By the light of this we are, for the first time, able to see through many mysteries of the past, and make out the features of primitive facts, which have been almost effaced or overgrown with fable. Moreover, it has out-lived the long night of the past, and weathered all the winds of persecution; it shines on with the enlarging lustre of an ever-growing light, and at last our little glow-worm is growing luminous by day. It has had a hard struggle for life, more especially during the Christian era, but it would have been strange if that could have been put to death here which puts an end to death itself hereafter.

The earliest known form of the priest and the prophet was the medium, or seer. Professor Huxley is quite right in affirming that, although he has little use for the fact in his system of interpretation. "Beforetime in Israel, when a man went to inquire of God, thus he spake—'Come, and let us go to the seer,' for he that is called a prophet was aforetime called a seer." And the Lord might be consulted cheaply in this way for the small sum of sixpence three-farthings. They seem to have paid mediums even worse then than the world does now-a-days.

Siberian Shamanism is a survival of the most primitive kind of Spiritualism, based on mediumship and abnormal phenomena. It has no system of religion or ethics; no ritual, precepts, or dogmas; and no definite theology. The Shaman can visit spirit-world, and the spirits can come to him, speak through him, or become visible at times through his presence. That is its claim, and the sum-total of its pretentions. The Shaman of the Finns induces the supernormal ecstasy, called the "Tulla-intoon," with the ostensible object of becoming—as they phrase it—"The likeness of the spirit that is in possession of him." We now consider that such transformations do constantly occur, according to a likeness known to the observers, which was previously unknown to the medium.

The Tohunga or priest of the Maoris is their medium for spirit intercourse.

In Loango, when an adult is about to adopt a new fetish image, the Ganga or priest mesmerizes the postulant to consult him in the trance condition. He listens to the words uttered by the ecstatic, and then the choice is determined by what the somnambule says. The same practice is, or was, extant among the Acageman Indians. One of the negro methods of treatment, says Bastian, would almost appear to have been plagiarised from our animal magnetisers. In their system it is called Dorsal manipulation, and its purpose is to re-isolate the somnambulic subject after contact with the Cazembe or magician, and, as they say, for fear that the superabundance of his magical power should otherwise annihilate the victim or the subject, which looks as if they knew more than we do about matters perplexing us to-day. For this practice has the appearance of their being consciously engaged in returning some of the vitality of which the person has been deprived in producing the phenomena of the abnormal state. The West African Indians look to their mediums or magicians for protection against ghosts in general, and pay them to keep the apparitions away. The mediums, wizards, sorcerers, shamans, adepts, and others, who had the power of going out of the body in this life, were feared all the more after death by many tribes, because they had demonstrated some of the facts which created such fear and terror in the living; and had also been their exorcists and layers of the ghost. I do not suppose that Mr. Herbert Spenser will have included this fact amongst the origins of ecclesiastical institutions; yet it is a fact that the modern fiction of the ever-living one (in its secondary phase) is founded on mediumship. It is said "the king never dies." The Egyptian king, or *ank*, was the "ever-living one" on this mystical ground. So was it with the inner African medicine-man—in a sense which is only to be understood by means of the transformation and transmigration which occur in trance. We can adduce proof positive that immortality or continuity was originally demonstrated by means of these phenomena, and that in this way pre-historic man first found his enduring soul, because it was a common article of faith that only the chiefs, the seers, prophets, and kings of men, could or did obtain immortality—that is, the men who demonstrated it. These are the born immortals, the superior souls spoken of by Hermes and by the Gnostics, which possessed the saving seed of wisdom within themselves; and who were of a nature loftily transcendent.

There is a class, if not the earliest class, of chiefs or supreme beings amongst men, who were first recognised as the ever-living ones, the immortals, because they were the mediums for spirit intercourse—mediators between the two worlds. With the Tonguans to-day it is only the chiefs who have power to return after death and inspire the mediums; not the souls of the common people who had been without the abnormal power in this life. The Fijians maintain that only the few are immortal Spirits. Hence the desire to obtain such a condition, and possess that knowledge of it which was taught in the Mysteries. Here, also, we get back to the origin of conditional or potential immortality, as taught by the Gnostics.

Whatsoever secret Brotherhoods there may be of Hindu Mahatmas or Tibetan Adepts, such fraternities are known to be extant in Africa, and they are Spiritualistic. In Cabende and Loango there are secret associations of the Fetishmen or mediums. They constitute a fraternity—the brothers—and form a society apart—an Order, whose secrets are only known to the initiated, and whose mysterious faculties are the terrors of the uninitiated. Bastian describes the King of Bamba as dwelling isolated in his *banza* in an almost inaccessible mountain district, at the head of one of those systems of religious mystery which exercise an overwhelming influence amongst the natives along the West Coast of Africa. New members are admitted into these Brotherhoods only after a probation of ten years. They must prepare themselves by fasting, by drinking, by inhaling narcotics; they must give proofs of being ecstatics or mediums, by becoming frantic in the sacred dances, and by seeing in the state of trance! These are the Secret Societies of savage mediumship. The Red Men also had their brotherhoods of the adepts. The "Friendly Society of the Spirit" is mentioned by Carver. This was an association of Spiritualists who were Mediums, Magicians, or Fetish Priests. Carver saw an elderly member of this brotherhood throw a bean at a young man who was a candidate for election into the society, whereupon he instantly fell motionless, as if he had been shot, and remained for a long time in trance. One of three such societies among the American Indians is that of the *Meda* or Mediums; the chief festival of the order being that of *Medawin*. At this festival songs are sung, which are only recorded in symbolical pictures that have been preserved from time immemorial, and can only be read by the few who have been made the guardians of this secret language.

Any way, these primitive Spiritualists were terribly in earnest in their modes of over-leaping the ordinary barriers of life,—of forcing open the very door of death, and taking the other world by storm. They exhausted themselves in all manner of ways,—by starving, sweating, excessive transpiration, and internal breathing; hideous howling, partial strangulation, furious dancing, shuddering ecstasies, cutting, wounding, and bleeding, until they swooned into the coveted state of inner consciousness, which may be attained in such a variety of ways,—the crudest methods having been discovered first. An ancient Indian seer, says Mr. Tylor, would fast for seven days, to purge his vision for spiritual seeing. And he makes merry over all this light-headed business. It certainly would be a very round-about way of going to work on the theory of imposture put forth by the ignorant pretenders to knowledge in our day. And here a curious side-light may be allowed to glance on this subject. Our missionaries have recorded numerous instances in which native mediums—*i. e.*, supposed practitioners of imposture, have been converted to Christianity. The men who converted them thought they were impostors. But though they were taught to look with horror and loathing on their old practices as damnable, there is no instance of their recanting and denouncing their spirit-intercourse as trickery, or of pleading imposture, or even self-deception, which would have been so acceptable a solution to the missionaries of the mysterious manifestations. On the contrary, they have always solemnly affirmed the genuineness of the phenomena. Close observers, like Mariner, Williams, and Moerenhout, strenuously repudiate the theory of imposture. The Zulus say the continually stuffed body cannot see secret things; and the world, in general, has never shown much faith in fat prophets or poets. It evidently believes in thinness and suffering as good for them, and has always done its best to inspire them with sufficient starvation. It believes in purity by purging. Apollonius of Tyana declared that his power of prophecy was not due to magic or stimulation of the soul, but simply to his abstinence from animal food enhancing the receptive conditions. There have been many ways of reaching the other world, however, besides starving. We know the Hindus, the Chaldeans, Assyrians, Egyptians were acquainted with animal magnetism. The Egyptians and Scythians also made use of Indian Hemp for their spiritual sleepers. Indian soothsayers still prepare themselves with the sweating bath for their ecstatic condition, in which the spirits make their communications to the bystanders. The Malay retires to the desert to fast and pray, in order that he may attain the abnormal condition. The Zulu doctor fasts, suffers, castigates himself, till he swoons into the state of trance in which he carries on his spirit communication. Aristophanes wittily ridicules spirit communication in representing the cowardly character Pisander as going to a Necromancer and asking to be shown his own soul, which had long since departed and left him only a breathing body. We also find that Ælian has a gird at the Hindu mode of inducing the sacred sleep. He says the followers of Apis have a better method of getting at the spirit world. Apis is an excellent interpreter of futurity. He does not employ virgins and old women sitting on a tripod, nor require that they should be intoxicated with the sacred potion. In the Persian Bahman Yasht, the god Ahura-Mazda throws Zarathustra into the *clairvoyante* trance by giving him some magnetised water to drink.

We have been untruly taught, by those who knew no better, that this was all a delusion of the past; but the fact is that many thousands of years ago our progenitors had become sufficiently familiar with the business they were about. The African priests, says Bastian, are profoundly versed in the science of ghostly apparitions. The spirit-seers of America might get from African professors many practical rules for intercourse with spirits. Whereas the travellers and missionaries generally who report on their mysteries are entirely ignorant that spiritual manifestations and *clairvoyante* vision were natural realities in the past as they are verifiable in the present.

For example, the Serpent-Wisdom, or wisdom of the serpent, played an important part in the ancient mysteries. The "way of a serpent" and the workmanship are amongst the most amazing in universal nature. Without hands it can climb trees and catch the agile ape. Without fins it can outswim the fish. It has no legs, and the human foot cannot match it in fleetness. Death is in its coil for the bird on the wing, which the springing reptile will snatch out of its element. As a type of elemental power it has no equal; hence it was the supreme fetish in Egypt, worn as the forefront of the gods. "Wise as the serpent" is a saying; but the wisdom of the serpent has to be interpreted. It was not merely the representative of elemental power, but of mind or mental influence in the primitive sense. The serpent is the Mesmerist and magician of the animal world. With its magnetic eyes it has the power to fascinate, paralyse, and draw the prey to its deadly mouth. It probably evoked the earliest idea of magical influence, and gave to man his first lessons in animal magnetism. No disk of the Hypnotist, or navel of Vishnu, no look of the Mesmerist, has any such power as the gaze of the serpent in inducing the comatose condition. I have seen a sensitive person mesmerised by it almost instantaneously. A traveller has described his sensations as he sank deeper and deeper into the somnambulic sleep under its fatally fascinating influence. And when the shot was fired which arrested the serpent's charm and set him free, he felt the blow as if he had been struck by the bullet. In the Avesta the look of the serpent is synonymous with the most paralysing and deadly opposition. The serpent and charming are synonymous. In the Egyptian Ritual a deluding snake named Ruhak is the Great Charmer, or fascinator that draws the victim to its mouth with the magic power of its eyes. The speaker exclaims, "Go back, Ruhak, fascinating, or striking cold with the eyes." The supreme mode of exhibiting mental power is by Magic, and that is represented as charming the serpent. "These are the gods," it is said in the Texts, "who charm for Har-Khuti in the lower world—they charm Apap for him." Apap is the giant serpent of darkness, who is the eternal enemy of the sun. They cry, "Oh, impious Apap! thou art charmed by us through the means of what is in our hands." That is, by a magic wand carried in the hands of the charmers.

Primitive man must have had a long, hard wrestle for supremacy before he could have mesmerised and mastered his old subtle enemy, the serpent, or charmed his charmer, as he learned to do at last, when he became the serpent-charmer, which he ultimately did. Africans to-day will magnetise a serpent with a few passes and make it stiff as a stick. And in this character we find his figure proudly set in heaven, for the first star in Ophiuchus is known in Arabic as Ras-al-Hawwa, the head of the serpent-charmer. Ophiuchus is not merely the serpent-holder, he is the serpent-charmer. The Egyptian serpent-headed goddess Heh is called the "Maker of invisible existences apparent," which seems to characterise the serpent as the revealer of an unseen world—this it was, as the magnetiser of man —and hence the serpent type of Wisdom. Hea, the Akkadian god of Wisdom, is represented by the serpent. It was the serpent that inducted the primal pair into the secrets of the hidden wisdom when they ate of the fruit that was to open their vision and make them wise—in keeping with the character here assigned to it! In some ancient drawings the serpent and the Goddess of Wisdom are pourtrayed in the act and attitude of offering the fruit of the Tree of Knowledge to the human being. Sometimes the serpent holds the fruit in its mouth.

Africa is the primordial home of the serpent-wisdom, and the serpent was there made use of to produce the abnormal condition in Sensitives. The Africans tell of women being possessed and made insane by contact with the serpent. That is, the reptile, from the fascination of its look, fear of its touch, and use of its tongue, threw the mediums into the state of trance called the stupor of the serpent, in which they saw clairvoyantely, divined and prophesied, and so became divinely inspired, as the phenomena were interpreted. We are told that Cassandra and Helenus were prepared for seeing into the future by means of Serpents that cleansed the passages of their sense by licking them! In this way the sensitives were tested, and made frantic; thus the serpent chose its own oracle and mouthpiece and became the revealer of preternatural knowledge. The stupor caused by the serpent's sorcery created a kind of religious awe, and the extraordinary effects produced on the mediums were attributed to the supernatural power of the serpent! Those who were found to be greatly affected by it were chosen to become Fetish women, priestesses, and pythonesses. This Obea cult still survives wherever the black race has migrated, and the root of the matter, which travellers have found so difficult to get at, is unearthed at last, as a most primitive kind of Spiritualism, in which the serpent acted the part of the mesmerist or magnetizer to the natural somnambules. This I personally learned from an Initiate in the Voudou Mysteries.

In various parts of Africa, especially on the Guinea coast, the oracle of the serpent is a common institution. The reptile is kept in a small hut by an old woman, who feeds it, and who gives forth the responses when the serpent oracle is consulted. She is the medium of spirit-communication! In Hwida the fetish priests are known by a name which signifies the "mother of the serpent." In a chant of the Algonkins it is asked, "Who is the Manitu?"—or medicine man—and the reply is, "He that goeth with the serpent." The witch of Endor is called a woman who was mistress of Aub. Aub is also an Assyrian word which means the serpent. In Egyptian the serpent is Ap, to be inflated, serpent-like. In short, the witch was a pythoness, a serpent-woman inspired with the serpent wisdom of Obea or the ophite cult. In the Hebrew book of Genesis the serpent beguiles the woman to eat the fruit of the Tree of Knowledge, and is damned for doing so. But there was a sect of Gnostic Christians who paid the serpent the highest honour because it had done this thing. Being Gnostics, they were acquainted with the serpent-wisdom, and knew what the fable signified, which is what the collectors and translators of those ancient fragments never have known, and so we have a creed called Christian, founded on an impious perversion of ancient knowledge, which teaches that all mankind were likewise damned because the first pair tasted of the tree of knowledge, and all of us are additionally damned who do not accept the story as true!

The chief sacred trees of the world, the typical trees of knowledge, have always been those that produce a fruit or juice from which an alcoholic or narcotic drink could be distilled on purpose to induce the somnambulic trance. The Egyptians used the juice of the sycamore fig tree. Human beings transform into immortal spirits by drinking of its juice, which is represented as a liquid of life. In inner Africa the toddy-palm supplied the sacred potion already fermented; and what an amazing Tree of Knowledge that toddy-palm must have been! In India the Tree of Knowledge was the Pippala, or sacred fig tree. This fig tree is a meeting place for men and immortals. Under it Yama, king of the departed, and the Pitris, the protecting, fatherly spirits, quaffed the divine drink in common with human beings. From the fruit of it a drink was made, so potent that it not only exalted men to the status of immortals, and placed them on a footing of fellowship with the gods, but brought down the gods to meet with men. In other words, intoxication was a mode of spirit-communication—the mediums being inspired by strong drink to utter their revelations. This is pourtrayed on Hindoo monuments. It was the Tree of Knowledge, and the drink was divine just because it lapped the senses in Elysium, and opened the inner eyes to see in trance. In the Hindu drawings you see the medium who was intoxicated, and consulted underneath the Tree of Knowledge; she eats—or drinks—of the fruit of the tree, that her inner eyes may be opened. In the Rig-Vēda the gods are represented as obtaining immortality by constantly getting drunk with Amartyam Madam, the immortal stimulant! They drink copiously the first thing in the morning, they are drunk by mid-day, and dead drunk at night. We hear of North-American Indians who have the notion that immortality consists in being eternally dead drunk—dead drunk being a primitive mode of expressing extreme felicity in a life beyond the present—a kind of paradisaical condition. The worshippers follow the example of their gods, and drink the intoxicating soma juice to attain immortality. In this state they sing—

> "We've quaffed the Soma bright,
> And are immortal grown,
> We've entered into light,
> And all the gods have known."

Exactly as it is with the first pair of people in the book of Genesis. The Serpent informs the woman that if she will eat of the fruit of the tree their eyes shall be opened, and they shall be as gods, knowing good from evil. And when the woman saw that it was a tree to be desired to *make one wise*, she did eat of it. The Wise are the Seers in this abnormal sense. Prophets, seers, magi and wizards are the wise men. The primal pair having eaten of the Tree of Knowledge, the Elohim or celestial spirits exclaim, "Behold! the man has become as one of us," that is, as a spirit amongst spirits. This opening of the eyes means an unsealing of the interior vision. "and their eyes were opened, and they knew him," is said of those who had seen the risen Christ. So Balaam, the man who saw in vision, that is, in the trance condition, is described as the man whose eyes were opened; the Seer who saw the vision of the Almighty, falling in trance, having his eyes opened. In this aspect, eating of the Tree of Knowledge was simply partaking of the divine drink, the drink of immortality, the sacred potion or Nepenthe, which was made and administered in all the mysteries, for the purpose of producing the abnormal vision in the practice of spirit-intercourse. The Tree of Knowledge had taught them how to enter the spirit-life or spirit-world *that* way, by means of wisdom or knowledge. The Typical Tree had its *religious rootage* here, not in direct adoration, but in the mystery of fermentation, and attained its sacredness on account of the Divine drink. Hence the Trees could be very various, but the product was one. We may note that *Sophia*, the Greek word for wisdom, originally signified wine. A prior form of the word in Egyptian, as *Sefa* or *Kefa*, meant distilling and the mystery of fermentation. Alcoholic spirits were very prominent in primitive spiritism, because they produced abnormal effects! Intoxication was also a mode of illustrating the genesis of spirit—the alcoholic being a type of the human product. The facts are registered in language. In Sanskrit, *Sidhu* is distilled spirit, and *Siddha* means the spiritually perfected; the *Siddhas* being the perfect spirits. So in Egyptian, *Shethu* denotes spirits of wine; *Sheta* is the mystery of mysteries, and the *Sheta* was the coffin or sarcophagus in which the dead transformed, or were turned into Spirits. In the Bacchic Mysteries they also enacted the production of the spirit by means of fermentation; the soul assigned to Seb, who represented the sap of wood in Egypt, or, as we now see, the juice of the tree that ferments and produces the alcoholic spirit—the drink that made men wise in the Mysteries. In the book of Deuteronomy the Jews are instructed or commanded to spend their savings in drink, as an offering to the Deity, which shows that intoxication was also a religious rite with them.

It was this crude nature of these primitive practices that chiefly led to the wholesale condemnation of mediums, sorcerers, wizards, witches, and all who had familiar spirits. It was so in Egypt as in India; in the Persian writings as well as the Mosaic. And these denunciations were and still are accepted as the very word of God by those who are ignorant of the phenomena, and who could not distinguish the lower from the higher, saintly from satanic, or black magic from white. Thus, on account of certain early practices, Spiritualism was damned altogether, instead of being fathomed and explained. Our customs of drinking strong liquors, snuffing most potent powders, and smoking narcotic herbs, which are now besotting and degrading the race—so much so that our protoplasm and protozoa have to come into being half-fuddled with nicotine—so that our children are doomed by heredity to become smokers and drinkers, without being allowed the chance of making a fresh start for themselves—these very customs have been bequeathed to us as sacred survivals from the times when the trance-conditions were induced by such means!

Again, the universal customs of Transforming, of Masking and Mumming, are related to the mysteries of ancient spiritism. In Egyptian the word *mum*, whence the name of mummy, means the dead body. We have the identical word and meaning in English, applied to a beer called "mum-beer," which was not taxed because it is non-alcoholic, unfermented, spiritless, or dead beer, *i.e.*, mum-beer.

This is not so called, as some have suggested, from a man named Mummer, who was once famous for his brew of strong ale. Our mummers used to go about in masks and "mum" by making sounds with closed lips. The two sexes exchanged dresses with each other, as a part of the transformation that was being enacted by the mummers, who represented the dead come back in disguise to pay a visit to the living. The annual masking still practised by our children about the time of "All-Souls' day," is a survival of this primitive pantomime, in which the masks signify the spirits of the dead or the mummies. The institution of "All Souls" is a most ancient ceremonial festival of the dead. It is celebrated in many lands, and is common to the most diverse races of mankind. On a certain day after the Autumn equinox the spirits of all those (all souls) who had died during the year were supposed to gather together at an appointed place in the West to follow their leader, the red sun of Autumn, down through the under-world, or across the waters of the West to the land of life and light, attained upon the horizon of the resurrection. When such mysteries were performed, those who acted the part of spirits did so in masks, and therefore masks still mean the dead, the mummies or spirits. The modern pastime was an earlier religious mystery. In the genuine Christmas Pantomime we have an extant illustration of this primitive masking and mumming, which belonged to the drama of the dead, even as we find it in the Egyptian Ritual. In those subterranean scenes of the Pantomime we are really in the Egyptian Meska, the re-birthplace of the dead, where the transformations into the new life were represented; and the Meska is the original Mask as place of transformation, mode of transformation, or symbol of transformation. The pivot of the pantomime on which all turns is the principle of transformation. The transformation is from the lower world of the dead, the place of the mummies or masks—hence the giants, dwarfs, fairies, gnomes, bad spirits, and other types of the elemental powers, that were represented earlier than human spirits —to the daylight world of life, light, and liberty, now represented by fun, frolic, and lawlessness. Harlequin is the potent transformer, who wields the wonder-working wand. With his mask down he is invisible; another proof that the masks represent the dead or the spirits. The final transformation scene represents heaven; the upper world of three. The mask, then, is the face of the dead, and the death-mask of the Siberian Shaman was preserved and hung up in his late residence, just above the place where he used to sit. In New Britain the natives perform a religious ceremony called the "duk-duk," in which a spirit-messenger is represented as coming in a mask. The women and children are prohibited from seeing the mask, and they must not say that it conceals any human being. If the performer allows the mask to slip off, they kill and make a ghost of him. Masks in animal forms and fashions represent the nature-powers or the Totemic and typical ancestors, but the human mask assuredly stands for a human spirit. And the endeavour to represent this can be traced from the rudest beginnings. In some instances the human face has been flayed from the bones, and transferred to form the mask of a fetish image. The aborigines of Bolivia and Brazil used to take off the face and scalp from the skull, and reduce them to a miniature mask of humanity, supposed to possess supernatural properties, and to furnish a most potent medicine. The Maori, amongst others, learned to dessicate the head and preserve it in its own skin, on the way to complete mummifying of the corpse. Before the mummy could be embalmed entirely the skull was sacredly saved, and sometimes the flesh was imitated by coating it with a mask made of reddish matter. We are now for the first time in a position to apprehend the meaning of the mummy-image, and to appreciate the motive of the Egyptians, who practised the art of embalming the dead until it was absolutely perfected.

The Mummy or corpse was the dead mask which had been let fall from the face of life by the person who had transformed, and this was faithfully preserved, because it was the mortal likeness of the person who had transformed and become a spirit!

In the primary stage and rudest conditions of the human race, the returning ghost was naturally an object of terror and dread, the representative of all that was most fearsome in external phenomena; not in the least likely to evoke, although it helped to ultimately evolve, a feeling of reverence, which led to some kind of worship; and a long road had to be travelled from the earliest period, when the ghost was besought and propitiated *not* to appear, up to the time when the bones of the dead were kept in the house or chest, and the mask or mummy was sacredly preserved on purpose to secure the presence of the ghost as a protection for the living relatives—whence the *lares* and *penates*, and other forms of the household gods. Doubtless, it took a very long time to utilise the ghost, or fully make out its message to man. But that stage had been travelled by the Egyptians when they first come into view. It is certain that from the earliest monumental period, and, probably, ages before that, the Egyptians represented man to be what is termed an immortal spirit. The text of the 130th chapter of the "Book of the Dead" is said to have been discovered or re-discovered, in the reign of Housapti, the fifth king of the first dynasty, who lived more than 6000 years ago. At that time certain portions of the sacred books were found as antiquities, of which the very tradition had been lost. And this is the chapter of "Vivifying the soul for ever." The Egyptians were accustomed to set up two different images with the dead body in the tomb. One of these is the *Shebti*, or duplicative figure. This was one of their types of transformation; it represented the duplication of the mummy for another life, called that of the Second Breath. The other image was named the *Ka*, or second self. The 105th chapter of the Ritual is entitled the chapter of "Propitiating the *Ka* of a person in the divine nether world;" and, in the pictorial illustration, the person is represented in the act of adoring his own spiritual image, the glorified *Eidolon*, to which he relates how he abominates all filthy things, in order that his *ka*, or higher self, may be propitiated and pleased. The Egyptian title of *ka-ankh* meant the living likeness, or the likeness of the immortal, the one that lived on after death. Moreover, this *ka* was not only the reflex image of the defunct erected in the tomb; it was also pourtrayed as being born with the mortal into this life. In the scenes at Luxor, in which Amenhept III. is represented at the moment of birth, another infant, his exact likeness, is depicted as his *ka*, his genius, himself in a divine effigy. Also, it was a great joy for the spirit of the deceased to be permitted to revisit the dead body and see how carefully it was preserved, which shows us the final crowning motive for making and keeping the Mummy. In the chapter (lxxxix.) of the visit of the soul or *Ka* of the deceased to his body, it is said,—"Thou hast let my eternal soul see my body!" "He sees his body;" and "He is at peace in his Mummy!"

The chief fact with which we are now concerned, is, that the Mummy-image supplied the supreme type of transformation, and was the Egyptian *Karast*, or Christ. Various symbols of durability and rebirth were buried with the Egyptian dead, when the mummy was deposited in the *hen-ankhu*, or chest of the living. A copy of the Book of the Second Breath—*Sen-sen*—formed his pillow, and the leaves of the Book of Life were the lining of his coffin. He was accompanied by his types of protection, of duration, and renewal, the ankh-cross of life to come; the ankham-flower of life, worn at the ear, the tat-cross, or buckle of stability, the beetle of transformation, the vulture-image of victory; the green-stone (Uat) of revivification, the tablet of rosin, a type of preservation; the Level or corner-sign of *Amenu*, signifying *to come*—our "amen." And, with the eyes of the sun and moon to light him through the darkness, the Egyptian entered his tomb, called the "Good Dwelling." A number of copies of the Shebti, or double of the dead, were ranged in the Serdab to signify manifold repetition, and the Ka-image of his spiritual self was erected in the tomb, as his visible link with his dead form on earth. But, the Mummy itself was also preserved as a type, just as the mummified hawks, mice, cats, and other animals, were preserved for their typical significance. Both Herodotus and Plutarch tell us how the Egyptians ended a banquet by carrying round, in a coffin, the image of a dead body. "Look on it, they said, and drink, for when you are dead you will be like this!" That image was the mummy-type of immortality! The sentiment was not that of "Eat and drink! for to-morrow we die!" It was one of rejoicing in the assurance of immortality which the mummy-image represented. This mummy-image was the Egyptian *Corpus Christi*, the body of the Christ, or spirit which was to be reborn. We have to go a long way back to get at the origin of the types and symbols now called Christian; not one of these originated at the beginning of our era! The Christ, for instance, is a pre-Christian type, connected with the mask, the mummy, and the mysteries of transformation.

The first male type of the Christ was after the flesh, and founded on the transformation of the boy into man—the Christ who became the anointed one of puberty. This Phallic fetish associated with the rite of circumcision was the one repudiated by Paul for the spiritual Christ — not the historical Jesus. In the Gnostic sense the word made $\sigma\acute{a}\rho\xi$, or flesh, was this Phallic Logos founded on the Causative Seed; the reproductive power which transformed in this life having been made a type of transformation for the future life! In the Gospel according to Thomas, it is said—" He who seeks me will find me in children from seven years old; for there concealed I shall, in the fourteenth year, be made manifest"—that is, as the pubescent Christ or Horus. In Greek the Christ means the anointed; but the mystical or spiritual sense of the word was preceded by the physical. *Chriso* and *Chresthai* are also names for daubing over with colouring matter; and it still is a primitive practice amongst the Black men and Red men to cover the bodies or bones of the dead with red ochre. Human bones buried in the mounds of Caithness have been found coated over with red earth. This was done to preserve and save them. It was also typical of their being refleshed; and the bone, head, mask, or body so saved became the symbol of a salvation and a saviour, because it was an image of transformation. This was the mummy figure in Egypt. To "karas," in Egyptian, is to anoint, embalm, or make the mummy; and the type of preservation so made was called the Karast or Christ. Such, I maintain, is the Egyptian origin of the Christ called the Anointed in Greek. The one who transformed and rose again from the dead, designated the Karast or Christ, was represented both by the prepared and preserved mummy, and by the carven image, which was the likeness of a dead man. Moreover, this was the original Christ, whose vesture was without seam. In making the perfect mummy type of continuity or immortality the body had to be bound up in the ketu or woof, a seamless robe, or a bandage without a seam. No matter how long this might be—and some swathes have been unrolled that were 1000 yards in length—it was woven without a seam. This, I repeat, was the seamless robe of the mystical Christ, which re-appears as the coat, coating, or chiton (cf. ketu, Eg. woof) of the Christ according to John. The Assyrians also made use of a mysterious sacred image called the mamit, or mamitu. It is celebrated in their hymns as the Mamit! the Mamit! the Treasure which passeth not away! It is spoken of as a shape of salvation, descending from the midst of the heavenly abyss: a life-giving image that was placed, as is the Cross, in the hands of the dying, to drive away evil spirits. This mamit was the sign, or fetish-image, of the *one deity* who *never* fails. I have shown elsewhere that this type of eternal life was identical with the *Corpus Domini*, the mummy-krist of Egypt! The Bit-Mamiti was the house of the mummies! The Kan-Mamiti was the book of the mummy; and the Mamit I hold to have been the image of the resurrection; a type and teacher of the Eternal! So, Mammoth in Hebrew is a name of the corpse as the image of the dead.

We can trace the Karast or Mummy-Christ of Egypt a little further. When he transformed in the underworld, spiritualised or obtained a soul in the stars of heaven, he rose on the horizon as or in the constellation Orion—that is, the star of Horus, the Karast, or Christ. Hence Orion is named the Sahu, or constellation of the mummy who has transformed and ascended into heaven from the Mount of the Equinox, at the end of forty days, as the starry image of life to come, the typical Saviour of men. And Orion must have represented the risen Horus, the Karast or Christ, at least 6000 years ago! This Christ is said to come forth sound, with no limb missing and not a bone broken, because the deceased was reconstituted in accordance with the physical imagery. And by aid of this Corporeal Christ of Egypt we can understand why the risen Christ of the Gospels is made to demonstrate that he is not a spirit or bodiless ghost, as the disciples thought, but is in possession of the flesh and bones of the properly preserved corpse. They have omitted the transformation into the spiritual Christ. Thus in that character he is only the *corpus Christi*, or mummy-Christ, of Egypt—a type transferred and not a reality, either spiritual or physical. There can be no doubt of this, for the child-Christ (copied into my book) is actually pourtrayed on a Christian monument in the Roman catacombs as this very image of the Mummy-Christ of Egypt, bound up in the seamless swathe of the Karast.

Some of the Christian Fathers supposed that the Egyptians believed in the physical resurrection of the preserved body, and this false inference is frequently echoed in our own day. But it is a mistake of the ignorant. The doctrine of the resurrection of the Body is not Egyptian. There is proof extant that the Egyptians did not make the Mummy as their type of a physical resurrection. Being phenomenal and not mere theoretical Spiritualists, they had no need of a Corporeal resurrection. With them the deathless only was divine, and their dead are spirits divinized by rebirth in the likeness of their Gods. I repeat, the doctrine of the physical resurrection of the body is not Egyptian. We find in the "Book of the Dead" that the promise of all blessedness, the supreme felicity, is for the spirit not to re-enter the earthly body for evermore. In the rubric to chapter lxxxix. we read—" His soul does not enter, or is not thrust back, into his mummy forever." Their idea of the life hereafter always turned on the transformation, and not on the resurrection, of the body; and their doctrine is that of transformation in the Hades, and not of resurrection from the earth. They left the dogma of a physical resurrection to be carried off as the stolen property of the nonspiritist Christians in Rome, along with so many other dead effigies of things that never lived. Accordingly the early Christians, who were ignorant of Egyptian symbolism, did base their belief in a life hereafter upon a bodily resurrection here, derived from the Karast or Mummy-Christ. Their foothold in a future existence as spiritual entities did depend on the re-possession of an earthly physique. Without the physical possibility there was no spiritual probability hereafter for them—no life without the re-constitution of the old dead dust, which a mere whiff of science scatters forever, and so abolishes their one bit of foothold in all the universe. Modern or ancient Spiritualism has no message or meaning for such people; they are corporeally founded, and there they rest and cling to the earth with the rootage of eighteen hundred years. This was a natural result of taking over the mummy-type of Egypt without a knowledge of the typology, and the ghost-idea without the ghost in reality, or the facts upon which it was founded. The doctrines and dogmas of Christian theology are derived from Egypt and its arcanum of mystery, which the modern believers have never yet penetrated—we are only just now opening the door. And here it may be said that those Egyptologists, who are orthodox Bibliolators, first and foremost, are not going to help us much. Bibliolatry puts out the eyes of scholarship. We have to get at the facts and help ourselves!

The pre-Christian religion was founded on a knowledge of natural and verifiable Facts, the data being actual, and the method very simply scientific—whether you accept my conclusions or not,—but the Christian Cult was founded on ignorant belief, which swallowed in faith all that was impossible in fact, and unverifiable in phenomena. Current orthodoxy is based upon a deluding idealism—derived from literalised legend and misinterpreted mythology—on the idea that man fell from paradise, and was damned for ever before the first child had been born—on the idea that the world was consequently lost—on the idea that the world is to be saved and man restored by a vicarious atonement—on the idea of a miraculous physical resurrection from the dead. And all these ideas are at once non-natural, non-spiritual, unscientific, and utterly false; and year by year, day after day, their props are being knocked away. But the phenomenal Spiritualist in all ages has founded on his facts. These facts were common with the pre-historic races, and the phenomena were cultivated more intelligently in the ancient Mysteries. But they were utterly abominated and crushed or cast out by the later religion.

What has the Christian Church done with the human soul, which was an assured possession of the pre-Christian religions? It was handed over to their keeping, and they have lost it! They have acted exactly like the dog in Æsop's fable—who, seeing the likeness of the shoulder of mutton reflected in the water, dropped the substance which he held in his mouth, and plunged in to try and seize its shadow! They substituted a phantom of faith for the knowledge of phenomena! Hence their deadly enmity against the Gnostics, the men who knew. They had got hold of a faith that could stand alone independently of fact, if you only made believe hard enough, and killed out all who could not believe. They drew down the blinds of every window that looked forth into the Past, and shut out the light of nature from the blinded world in which they sought to live, and compel all other people to live, by a farthing candle of faith alone. They parted company with nature, and cut themselves adrift from the ground of phenomenal fact. They became the murderous enemies of the ancient spiritism which had demonstrated the existence and continuity of the soul and offered evidence of another life on the sole ground of fact to be found in nature. And ever since they have waged a ceaseless warfare against the phenomena and the agents—which are as live and active to-day as they were in any time past. Mediums, prophets, and seers, witches, and wizards—the Born Immortals of the early races—have always been done to death by them with horrible tortures and inhuman cruelties. They have fought all along against the most vital and valuable, the profoundest part of the knowledge of nature, the most concealed, occult, and subtle; and been at war all through against the other world. But murder will out, and the innumerable multitude of their victims are only *dead against them.* They are living on for us; they are working with us; they are fighting for the eternal truth with terrible power, against the worshippers of the gory God, the men of the "bloody faith," which has yet to pay for all the massacre and misery that the race has suffered, in order that a delusive fiction might be forced upon the world. The soul was established as a fact, and the future life was demonstrated in the mysteries of ancient Spiritism. These were the creators of a sentiment that might be called religious, for the first time, and the Christian teachers to-day are but trafficking in and beguiling the hereditary sentiment so evolved, by not only trying to do without the original factors in the past, but by seeking to efface them from Nature itself. If anything could have put an end to Spiritualism, it was the never-ceasing Christian persecution that was directed towards that end. They substituted a physical resurrection from the dead for a spiritual continuity, such as was demonstrated in the mysteries of the men who knew! As if a physical resurrection, that was alleged to have occurred once on a time, could demonstrate the continuity of spiritual existence for us! And to-day you still see their learned doctors of divinity trying to get at the other world by grave-digging—still fumbling after the spirit of man as though his essence were dust of the earth—which they say God has power to put together, every particle of it, at the Last Day; and so we shall rise again after all. They oppose, and fear Cremation, as Bishop Wordsworth admitted, because it looks as though that would destroy the physical and only foothold of their resurrection. Tombstones, tablets, and books, are still dedicated by them to the memory of those who are "no more!" The future life for them is but a desolate "perhaps." The meeting again is only a "may be." At the mouth of the gaping grave they mumble something about the "hope" of a joyful resurrection. That is the physical resurrection at the Last Day, on which the failing faith was founded at first; and that, according to John, was all the alleged Founder of the faith had to reveal when He is said to have said: "Every one that beholdeth the Son, and believeth on Him, I will *raise him up at the last day!*" The Spiritualism of the Roman Catholic Church, with its doctrine of Angels, its Purgatorial Penance, and efficacy of Prayers for the dead, is *a survival from Paganism, and was not derived from the teachings of the supposed Founder of Historic Christianity as represented in the Canonical Gospels.* Hence the rejection of that (and all other such) Spiritualism by the Protestants!

And some of our friends, who are Christians first and Spiritualists afterwards, want to convert Christianity into Spiritualism. But it will not, and cannot, be converted.

> In vain you try to engraft the living shoot
> Upon a dead tree, rotten to the root.

The Christians themselves know better than that, and they are far more logical. They apprehend truly enough that their religion did not originate in Spiritualism, but as its deadly antagonist; hence when phenomenal Spiritualism is presented in our own day as a *basis for immortality*, just as it was in the pre-Christian ages and religions of all lands, and in all the mysteries where the genuine Gnosis was unfolded, the Christians stop their ears against any such report, or take up arms to defend the faith against the alleged facts. You cannot spiritualise such a creed any more than you can make it scientific, and the reason for this must be sought, and is to be found, in its mythological and non-spiritual origin. It is of necessity at war with all the facts in nature upon which it was not founded We do not want a closer connection with a superseded system of thought, but rather a repeal of the union and the fullest freedom of complete divorce. It is for Spiritualism to join hands with Science, enlarge the boundaries of knowledge, found upon the facts in nature, not seek for an impossible alliance with a system that has always been anti-natural and at war with scientific facts, because it was falsely founded, from the first, in fable and in faith versus knowledge; the early Christians having been those who ignorantly believed, as opposed to the Gnostics, or the men who knew.

I do not propose to raise a new cry, form another sect, advertise an infallible nostrum, or pose as the founder of any fresh faith, when I say that a new and more comprehensive and inclusive kind of Gnosticism, which shall be quite free and above board and open all round, is one of the crying wants of our age. Spiritualism cannot be made to stand under or buttress the falling faith, but it may help to establish a new Gnosticism which shall found upon the facts first and let the faith follow naturally after.

THE
SEVEN SOULS OF MAN
AND THEIR
CULMINATION IN CHRIST.

WHILST the people of modern times appear to have been losing their Soul altogether, or not to have found out that they really possess one, the ancient Egyptians, Chaldeans, Hindus, Britons, and other races, reckoned that they had Seven souls, or that the one soul as permanent entity included the sum total of seven powers. The doctrine is very ancient, but it has been stated anew by the author of "*Esoteric Buddhism*," as if it were a recent revelation derived from India as the fountain-head of ancient knowledge.

Mr. Sinnett's claim is, that he has been specially appointed by the Mahatmas as their mouth-piece to the Western World, and empowered to put into print, for the first time, the oral Wisdom that has hitherto been kept all sacredly concealed. But I can assure Mr. Sinnett that the seven Souls of Man are by no means new to us, nor are they those "*transcendental conceptions of the Hindu mind*" in which he has been led devoutly to believe. To the serious student of such subjects, the system of esoteric interpretation now put forth, with its seven souls of man projected into shadowland; its races of men that go round and round the Planetarium seven by seven, like the animals entering Noah's ark; its seven planets as stages of human existence, with our earth left out of the reckoning; its seven continental cataclysms, which occur periodically; does not contain a revelation of new truth from the Orient, nor a corroboration of the old. The seven souls of man were not metaphysical "*concepts*" at any time in the past. The doctrine belongs to that primitive biology, or the physiology of the soul, which preceded the later psychology. Just as we speak of the seven senses the ancients spoke of the seven souls as principles, powers, or constituent elements of man. These were founded on facts of common perception, verifiable in nature; and we do not need those faculties of the occult adept "*which mankind at large has not yet evolved*" in order that they may be apprehended.

Mr. Sinnett is of opinion that it would be "*impossible for even the most skilful professor of occult science to exhibit each of these seven principles separate and distinct from the others."* That is, when they have been mystified by pseudo-esoteric misrepresentation, in a metaphysical phase; then they lose the distinctness of physics; and then we have to hark back once more to distinguish and identify these seven souls of man. The truth is, that when the teachings of primitive philosophy have passed into the domain of later speculations, you can make neither head, tail, nor vertebra of them—they constitute an indistinguishable mush of manufactured mystery! And the only way of exposing the pretensions of false teaching, and of destroying the superstitions, old or new, that prey upon and paralyse the human mind, is by explaining them from the root; to learn what they once meant in their primary phase is to know what they do not and cannot mean for us to-day. Nothing avails us finally, short of a first-hand acquaintanceship with the knowledge and modes of expression that were primordial.

It is quite possible, and even apparent, that the first form of the mystical SEVEN was seen to be figured in heaven by the seven large stars of the *Great Bear*, the constellation assigned by the Egyptians to the Mother of Time, and of the seven Elemental Powers. And once a type like this has been founded it becomes a mould for future use—one that cannot be got rid of or out of. The Egyptians divided the face of the sky by night into seven parts. The primary Heaven was sevenfold. The earliest forces recognised in Nature were reckoned as seven in number. These became Seven Elementals, devils, or later divinities. Seven properties were assigned to nature —as matter, cohesion, fluxion, coagulation, accumulation, station, and division—and seven elements or souls to man. A principle of *sevening*, so to say, was introduced, and the number seven supplied a sacred type that could be used for manifold future purposes. When Abraham took his oath at Beer-sheba, the Well of the Seven, we are told that he *sevened*, or did *seven*. Sevening was then a recognised mode of swearing; and Sevening is still a recognised mode of swearing with the Esoteric Buddhists, who, according to Mr. Sinnett, continue it *ad libitum*, and carry it on through thick and thin.

The seven souls of the Pharaoh are often mentioned in the Egyptian texts. The moon-god, Taht-Esmun, or the later sun-god, expressed the Seven nature-powers that were prior to himself, and were summed up in him as his seven souls, of which he was the manifestor as the Eighth One. In the Hindu drawings we see the god Agni pourtrayed with seven arms to his body. These represent *his* seven powers, principles, breaths, or souls. The seven rays of the Chaldean god Heptaktis, or Iao, on the Gnostic stones indicate the same septenary of souls. The seven stars in the hand of the Christ in Revelation have the same significance. There is a star with eight rays, which is found to be the symbol of Buddha, of Assur in Assyria, of Mithras; and of the Christ in the catacombs of Rome. *That* was the symbol of the Gnostic pleroma of the seven souls, the perfect flower or star of which was the Christ of the Gnosis; *not of any human history.* It can be traced back to Egypt as the star of Sut-Horus, a star with eight points or loops, undoubtedly meant for Orion, which was at one time the star of Annunciation, that showed the place where the young child lay, or where the God was re-born upon the horizon of the Resurrection at Easter. A very ancient form of the eight-rayed star was a sign of the Nnu, the Associate Gods of Egypt, who were the Seven Ali (Ari) or Companions (Cf. the Babylonian Ili and Gnostic Elohim), as children of the Great Mother, the Gnostic *Ogdoas.* The same type, with the same meaning, is represented in the Book of Revelation, where the son of man (who is a male with female breasts, and therefore not a human being) holds in his hand the seven stars which symbolise the seven angels or spirits who are in the service of their Lord—like the Seven Great Spirits in the 17th chapter of the Egyptian " Book of the Dead."

Seven souls, or principles in man, were identified by our British Druids. In the Hebrew Targummim, Haggadoth and Kabbala, the Rabbins sometimes recognise a threefold soul—as the Nephesh, Ruach, and Neshamah. The Nephesh is the breath of life, the anima—from the Egyptian *nef,* for the breath. This is the quickening spirit of the embryo. The Ruach is said to enter the boy at the age of thirteen years and one day. That is the soul of adultship, the reproducing spirit reproduced for reproduction at puberty. The third spirit, or Neshamah, is an intelligent soul which enters a man at twenty years of age, if the deeds of his life are right; if not, he is unworthy of the Neshamah, and the Nephesh and Ruach remain his only souls. Another Rabbi says the soul of man has *five* distinct forms and names—the Nephesh, Ruach, Neshamah, Cajiah, and the Jachida. The Cajiah is the spirit that makes to re-live; the Jachida denotes that which unifies all in one, and so establishes the permanent entity. Some persons are spoken of as being worthy to receive the Jachida in the life to come. Ben Israel teaches that the Nephesh, Ruach, and Neshamah signify nothing more than faculties, capacities, or constituent principles of the man, and that an additional soul means increase of knowledge and advancement in the study of Divine laws. The Rabbins also ran the number of souls up to seven; so likewise do the Karens of India. The Khonds of Orissa recognise four souls, or a fourfold soul. One of these dies on the dissolution of the body; one, the ancestral soul, remains attached to the Tribe on earth to be re-produced, generation after generation—in relation to which, when a child is born the priest inquires *which* member of the family has come back again? The *third* soul is able to go forth and hold spirit-intercourse, leaving the body in an inert condition. This is the soul that can assume other shapes by the art of Mleepa, or the gnosis of transformation. The fourth soul is restored to the good deity Boora, and thus attains immortality. Here, as in other instances, there is an ascending series.

Sometimes we meet with a dual soul called the *dark shadow* and the *light shadow;* at other times with a triple soul.

But we have now to do with the natural genesis of the Seven Souls and their culmination in the eighth One, the reproducer for another life, which was personified as the Pharaoh, the Repa, the Heir-Apparent, the Horus, the Buddha, Krishna or the Christ. Two sets of the seven may be tabulated in their Egyptian and Hindu shapes and compared as follows:—

INDIAN.	EGYPTIAN.
1. Rupa, body, or element of form.......	1. Kha, body.
2. Prana, or Jiva, the breath of life	2. Ba, the soul of breath.
3. Astral body..................................	3. Khaba, the shade.
4. Manus, or Intelligence...................	4. Akhu, Intelligence or Perception.
5. Khama-Rupa, or animal soul..........	5. Seb, ancestral soul.
6. Buddhi, or spiritual soul................	6. Putah, the first intellectual father.
7. Atma, pure spirit..........................	7. Atmu, a divine, or eternal soul.

Primitive man naturally observed from the first that he was brought forth by the mother, formed of flesh, made from her blood; that is the mystical water, or matter of life, and the red earth of mythology. This primal element was represented by the Great Mother of all flesh; and the first soul was accordingly derived from the blood, the mystical parent of Life. Thus, in the Mangaian account of Creation, the Great Mother, Vari, is said to make the first man from pieces of her own flesh! Flesh being blood that has taken form. " *Some, indeed,*" says Hermes, "*misled by nature, mistook the blood for the soul ;*" that is, they *took* it so, to begin with; and such was the nature of the human soul No. 1. This soul of blood is identified in Genesis ix. 4 and 5. Blood is the Adamic soul! From the Mother source came the red earth of the Adamic or primary creation, whence the Rabbins sometimes call Adam the "*Blood of the world!*" In the Semitic languages, Assyrian and Hebrew, Adam signified "*Blood*"—simply blood, as *the* red. It was thought at one time that two primal races of men were alluded to in the Cuneiform Texts, under the names of *Adamu* and *Sarku;* but it is now known that these names signify the two principles of female matter and male spirit, the Hindu perusha.

At this primitive stage begin the legends with which we have been so pitiably beguiled, or so profoundly perplexed!

In that first account of the creation of man, in the Hebrew Genesis, he is formed in the image of the Elohim, who were the seven primal elemental powers, that became celestial as the keepers of time in Heaven—in their second phase—and ultimately the seven Planetary spirits. At that early stage of sociology, man descended from the mother alone! In the second creation (for there are two), the woman is derived from the male as progenitor. The first is born of blood, the second of bone, a type of masculine substance. And these two sources, female and male, supply the two doctrinal types to Paul when he says, "*As in Adam* (the flesh-man) *all men die, even so in Christ* (the spirit-man) *shall all be made alive!*" Here the true interpretation cannot be obtained without the aid of the primitive physiology; it does not depend upon any fulfilment of fable as fact in later history, but on the adaptation of the mythical types to convey a mystical meaning in what are called "mysteries," that were very simple in their primal phase—which phase is the object of our present search.

The Psalmist refers to this Adamic man when he says, " *Put not your trust in the son of man ; his breath goeth forth, he returneth to his earth. In that very day his purposes perish.*" The antithesis to this was the Son of God, the second Adam, the man from heaven, the Christ, or immortal spirit; in short, a later type of the human soul! The first Adam represented the man, or creation of the seven souls, and the seven Elohim, whence it was said, in the Semitic Legends, that his head only *reached up to the seventh heaven.* The second Adam, or the Christ, attains the eighth heaven, as the height; or, he comes, later on, to represent the ten-fold heaven as the Adam Kadmon of the Kabbalists.

The Tahitians, whose Great Mother is named Eve (or Ivi), have the same physiological myth! They say that the first men were formed of Araea, or red earth, and on this they lived until bread was made—bread being typical of corn, corn of seed, *i.e.*, male source. All men derived from the motherhood at first—and in that mythical creation the man was really created from the woman, instead of the woman being taken from the man, which was of necessity a later creation, in keeping with the sociology. The mystery of the woman being taken from the man is mentioned in the Egyptian Ritual, or Book of the Dead. The speaker says : "*I know the mystery of the woman being taken from the man.*" The matter of such a mystery was physiological. The far earlier mystery was that of man being created by the woman from the red earth, or blood.

Next it was apprehended that the mother inspired the breath of life into her embryo. And breath, *prana, jiva,* or the *ba,* constitutes the soul No. 2. In various legends man was made from the red earth, and the Blacks of Victoria say that their creator, Pundjel, blew the breath of life, or the soul of breath, in at his navel. These were the first two souls of the seven, because blood supplied the element of flesh, or form, and breath was the primal element of life. A Yuni Indian description of death speaks of a man as having the *wind pressed out of him, so that he forgot.*

And now for a doctrinal development!

Blood and *breath* being the two primary elements or souls of life, these consequently became the two great types of sacrificial offering. Among the Amaponda Kaffirs when a new chief succeeds to the government it is a custom for him to be baptised in the blood of his brother, or some near relative, who is put to death for the purpose; and in Fiji when the canoe of a chief was launched a number of men were sacrificed, so that their souls (or Breath) might supply a wind of good luck for the sails of the vessel. It was on account of their natural genesis that these two souls of the blood and breath were typically continued in the water and the breath employed for the re-genesis, or regeneration, of the child in Christian baptism. Everyone of our religious rites and ceremonies has to be read backwards, like Hebrew, to be understood.

The observation that blood, the first factor in primitive biology, was the basis used by Nature in building up the future human being is probably the source and origin of the superstition that in building a city, fortress, bridge, or church, an enduring foundation must be laid in blood; whence the primitive practice of burying a living child, a calf, a dog, goat, or lamb—the lamb slain from the *foundation of the world* being a Mithraic and Christian survival of the same significance, with the bloody and barbarous rite of the Victim immured as a basis for the building. Sometimes, as in the legend of Vortigern, the foundation-stone was to be bathed in the blood of a child that was *born of a mother without any father;* as was the child-Horus, who was the child of the Virgin Mother only. The doctrine is Egyptian, and as such can be understood. It was applied to Horus shut up in the region of annihilation, or transformation (the Skhem), where his type was the Red Mouse.

As the breath of life was a kind of soul, so the steam of food, or the incense presented in sacrifice, was a form of the breath of life offered to the spirits of the dead or to the gods. The motive and meaning of many curious customs can only be apprehended on these physical grounds. For instance, when the Canadian Indians killed a bear they adjured the soul of the animal not to be angry with them, and then placing a pipe between its teeth blew tobacco-smoke backwards into its mouth, and thus symbolically restored that which they had just taken—its soul of breath. In the Rubric to the Egyptian Ritual it says—" *Offer ye a great quantity of incense; it makes that spirit alive.*" Drops of blood from the heart of a cow are likewise to be offered with the incense. Blood and breath (incense) were both offered by the Jews. Philo explains that the offerings of frankincense laid on the golden altar in the Inner Temple were more holy than the blood offered outside. The mystical meaning of which, he says, must be investigated by those who are eager for the truth in accordance with the Gnosis. The blood and breath survive also in the bloody wafer and incense of the Roman Ritual.

Now, we have to go back to this Soul of Breath to reach the origin of the transmigration of souls, which has been continued into the domain of later doctrines by those who were ignorant of its beginnings. To breathe and to transmigrate are synonymous in Egyptian, under the word *sen*. But the transmigration of the soul of breath is neither physical nor spiritual in the modern sense; it is an entirely different doctrine from those of the Pythagorean and the Esoteric Buddhists, both of which were derived from the same primitive original, but have been perverted until they no longer represent the early coinage of human thought, and so they can authenticate nothing in this world, for any other. With a primitive soul of breath was evolved the notion of an Ancestral soul of the race, tribe, and Totem, which of necessity was as general as the intercourse of the sexes was then common. The Commentator on the Analects of Confucius says—*" My own animal spirits are the animal spirits of my progenitors."* Another Chinese teacher says—*" Though we speak of individuals, and distinguish one from the other, yet there is in reality but one breath that animates them all. My own breath (or spirit) is the identical breath of my ancestors."* This soul of Breath, thus Pantheistically apprehended and expressed, could and did transmigrate; might be, and was, re-incarnated. It was incarnated in being individualised and discreted from the Ancestral soul; and when it went back it was merged again in the general—*qua* soul.

The king (Eg. Ank), who *never dies*, was first established upon this generic soul of the race, and not on a recurring identical personality of the reincarnated Soul. Thus reincarnation was true to the general Ancestral soul, but when continued in a later state of sociology, and applied to the Individual soul, it is a counterfeit—a false presentment of the original doctrine.

The basis of all incarnation and reincarnation has to be sought in the primitive animism of the general, Ancestral, or Pan-soul, first recognised. At that stage of thought it is *our* soul that comes, and goes, and returns again—not my soul nor yours; and afterwards the reincarnation of *soul* was continued as the reincarnation of *souls*, when souls had been individualised here on earth by the father coming to recognise his own children; but this was only through taking a false step and making a false inference.

The breath, or soul, of the dying was believed to re-enter the living. Thus, the Algonkins would bury their dead infants by the wayside to facilitate the return of their spirits, which were supposed to re-enter the future mothers as they were passing by! This was a soul of breath that could be *inhaled*, hence the practice of in-breathing souls. According to the Roman custom, it was the privilege of the nearest relative to inhale the last breath, or the passing soul, of a person dying.

But the soul that was founded on the mere breath of life, which the mother inspired to quicken the embryo, was not much to go upon for ultimate duration! The African Dinka tribe are said to reject the idea of immortality, because *their* soul is *" but a breath !"* —in which they agree with some modern secularists; because *this* sign of life visibly ceases in death! Such would be the argument of the primitive positivists, who had not got beyond their second soul —that of breath.

The third elementary is the so-called Astral shade, or shadow-soul. I once thought the *shadow* cast by the body might serve as the original type; or the image reflected in the eye. But *there is more than that in it!* There is a *shade* which is not a *shadow*. Dr. Tylor says the ghost, or phantom, seen by the dreamer, or visionary, is *like* a shadow, and thus the familiar term of the *shade* comes to express the soul! Such, however, *is not the origin*, as the Egyptian Shade, or *Khaba*, proves. The *Khaba*, or third soul, is a light, visible, but not tangible, envelope of the *Ba*, or soul of the breath. *Khab* signifies cover, to veil, to cover over. It is applied to an eclipse; and what is *shade* in a burning land but *cover?* Hence the type of the third soul is an Egyptian *sunshade!* It is so the thought is *thinged.* But they did not require, nor did they devise, a sunshade to image something like a shadow seen in sleep! In the Text, the deceased rejoices that his *shade*, cover, or *Khaba*, has not been stripped from his *Ba*, or second soul, in death. More literally, that he hasn't lost his envelope! The *Ba*, distinguished from the Shade, is said to breathe. It is pourtrayed with a human head on the body of a bird, and may be seen in the Amenti, going through the hells *accompanied by its sunshade*, for cover in a burning land! It retains form, breath and shade or covering. The Egyptian sunshade is a *fan*—actually the *shade* of *breath*. Their symbolism was so near to the natural fact!

The shadow-soul of the Khonds is one that dies when the body dissolves, which shows that the Shade with them was this corporeal soul. The Greenlanders also recognised two souls as the Shade and the Breath.

The fourth soul is an Intelligence, a form of mind, as the Power to perceive, to memorize, expressed by the Scottish "mind," to mind, or remember; the Egyptian *ment*, to memorize. In "making his transformation into the Soul" (Rit. ch. 85), the Deceased exclaims, in this character, "*I am Perception, who never perishes under the name of the Soul*" of mere breath.

The third soul being a sense-perception, or corporeal spirit, the fourth an intelligence—the intelligence developing perceptibly in the growing child — the fifth is the Animal soul that visibly descends upon the male nature at the period of puberty, and not till then. This was the first soul that was seen to have the power of perpetuating itself for this life! No child has such power; therefore at this stage it was held that the child did not possess this soul, and so, in another doctrinal development, it was taught that children who died in the pre-pubescent stage of life, had NO souls! They had the soul of blood and breath, and the Astral shade, or, as the Egyptians have it, the Envelope; they were not without intelligence; but the power of reproduction constituted a self-creative soul! It was on this ground, then, that children who died before the soul of manhood had descended on their nature to transform it at puberty, were supposed to have no substantial, or self-producing soul. This accounts for the superstition that they wandered about after death as elves, or Elementaries, on the outskirts of this life, unable to enter the other world. For the infant elementaries were believed to walk and wander as elves, fairies, and brownies, in search of a soul, or in want of a name—as the conferring of a name was one mode of constituting a personality, or communicating a soul to the child! This may be illustrated by the Scotch story,—an "*un-christened wean*" was seen wandering about at Whittingham, in Scotland, who could not obtain foothold on the threshold of the other world, being minus in the matter of an adult principle, or soul No. 5. Many saw, but none dared speak to the poor little fellow, for fear of having to give up their own soul to him. One night, however, a drunken man addressed the Elementary,—"*Hoo's a' wi' ye, the morn's morn, Short Hoggers?*" (short stockings that were *sole-less* as the child itself!) And the Elementary, having a name conferred, cried joyfully,—"*Oh! weel's me noo, I've gotten a name! They ca' me Short Hoggers o' Whittingham!*" and vanished, having obtained his soul by proxy, or through Naming. These undeveloped little spirits became the "*Wee-folk*" that peopled fairy-world. The superstitions still retain traces of this origin; those of the Brownie, for example. He is a very helpful worker, who serves freely and faithfully by night in the house, or out on the farm by day. But show him a *pair of breeks*, and he's off like Aiken-drum, the brownie of Blednock. The reason why would never be divined, apart from the natural genesis here explained. Breeches are a type of that masculine soul which the Brownie had never attained, and the poor little Elementary could not face this significant reminder of the fatal fact!

Now observe, upon this primeval constitution of a soul the rite of baptism and conferring a name (the name of the father) is founded. The doctrine of conferring a soul by proxy is very general! Hence the god-father and god-mother, or the father-god and mother-god of earlier beliefs, who represented the adult creative source. Hence, also, the power falsely claimed by the Christian Church to-day to *save* the souls of children by baptismal grace, in response to the equally false belief that children would otherwise be lost, or have to go without an eternal soul! Children that die unbaptised in Russia are not registered at all; are (or were) not reckoned in the data for the laws of mortality! What an influence such a system must exert on the pietistic, the ignorant, and feeble-minded, in forcing them into the fold of faith, out of which is supposed to open the only doorway for their little ones into everlasting life! In this manner the modern sacerdotalists employ the fetishism of the ancient medicine men in the form of religious dogmas, superstitious doctrines, and rites supposed to save.

It was at this stage of the soul that the doctrine of Salvation by means of self-emasculation had its natural genesis, and men unsexed themselves to save their souls, becoming eunuchs for the kingdom of heaven's sake; a doctrine of salvation taught by the Christ in Matthew's Gospel, which was carried out by the castrating Christians, who, like the Russian Skoptsi, looked forward to a millenium that was to come when all were self-mutilated. In the fragment of the "Egyptian Gospel," quoted both by Clement of Alexandria and Clement of Rome, we are told that the Christ, having been asked by Salome when his Kingdom was to come, answered, " *When the male with the female shall be neither male nor female.*" Now the Christ of which that could be said is of necessity the Spiritual Christ of either or of both Sexes. This is also the Christ of Paul when he says, "There is neither male nor female, for ye are all one in Christ." Christian literalisers sought to attain that type by unsexing themselves!

It follows, on the same physical basis, that the woman does not possess a soul, or, at least, not this particular soul, founded on the principle of virility, and that at this stage of thought she must derive her self-perpetuating soul from the masculine nature—if at all. In the Egyptian tale of the two brothers (in which we find the story of Joseph and Potiphar's wife), the younger one is deprived of his virile soul, whereupon he says to his consort,—"*I am a woman, even as thou art.*" Here, then, the woman is also treated as the impubescent or soulless child! Some of the Christian fathers maintained that woman has no inherent soul, which proves they could not have been Spiritualists in any practical sense! They held that woman only represented matter (our soul No. 1.) degraded and damned ever since the Fall of Man, and only to be saved by child-bearing, as Paul teaches; that is, by the grace of the male, and the addition of a later soul. The Khonds of India, who had not got beyond the general Ancestral soul of the tribe, coupled this with the masculine power, and held that Woman was *not* a producer of soul; and they actually killed off their female children, because these shared in the Ancestral soul of the tribe, without contributing to the reserved stock, and were thus robbing the males of a portion of their own proper soul. If they reserved all the virile soul to themselves, they were brave enough to capture women and wives from other tribes; and such was their argument for and defence of *female infanticide* within their own tribe! The Turks, in common with other races, hold that Woman has no soul—I am trying to show the natural ground for such belief!—and that if she is reproduced at the time of the resurrection, it will have to be in the image of the male. This doctrine was likewise maintained by Augustine, amongst other of the Christian Fathers; and it dimly survives to-day with the Mormons, whose wives are wedded to the male, in order that they who are by nature soulless may have a chance of being raised at the last day by the saving power of the husband; consequently, the more wives wedded the more souls saved. This doctrine of the masculine soul is illustrated in Egypt by the *shebti* image of the dead. Egyptologists, like Mariette, have been puzzled to know why the "*double*" of the dead, which is always *a figure of the bearded male*, should be found in the tombs, as the type of the re-arising female, as well as of the male. It was because at a certain stage of thought—in relation to the physical basis—the female had to rise again in the image of the masculine soul—the soul No. 5—if at all. Thus, the potential immortality of the female is here made dependent on the male, *through the primitive physiology dominating and determining the later doctrine.* Here, as in so many other cases, it is a survival—simply a survival—from the early physics! good for its own meaning—but unable to carry us any further—except in the way in which it will mislead us. The potential immortality of the soul is one of the oldest beliefs common to the aboriginal and barbaric races of the world. Potential, or conditional immortality, is a doctrine put forward afresh in our time by Esoteric Buddhists and certain bibliolators! But these latter never can touch bottom or determine anything whatever by wrangling over a few texts of Scripture, that have been brought on without the explanation of the oral hidden wisdom. It may be truly said of the people of one book:—"Behold! ye know not anything!" Such doctrines as conditional immortality can only be judged by their natural genesis! We shall never get at them by mistaking what we cannot understand for a divine revelation; nor by reading into them a modern mis-interpretation.

We have now to go back and learn of the primitive and uncivilised races, with whom the loss, say of Memory, is the loss of a soul. Absence of mind may be another mode of losing your soul. To lose your shadow even by having your likeness taken, may be the means of losing your soul, as is yet believed! Or it may be, that under the affliction of bronchitis or asthma, you run very great risk of losing your *prana* or soul of breath. Under such circumstances a Fijian would lie down and call upon his departing soul to come back to his bosom; or the Karen magician will run after the sick man's butterfly, as they call his wavering, wandering soul of breath, and pray it to return. And if the spirit-doctor should fail to catch the butterfly (or psyche), because it has crossed the boundary of life and death, he tries to capture the Astral Shade of a living man which may be flitting about whilst its owner is sleeping with his six other souls (or any lesser number) in the land of dreams; so that when he wakes he sickens, pines, and dies, because his other souls will besure to go in search of the missing Astral Shade—or envelope—for cover! We smile at such simplicity, but—when Plato, or any other metaphysical perverter of primitive thought, sets forth the doctrine that our knowledge is a matter of memory, and our science a mere reminiscence, that is but a sophism founded on this fourth soul of the early philosophy, which dates from the time when *the faculty of memorising was the highest recognised type of mind or a soul.*

Again, one form of the adult or masculine soul was considered to be a secretion of the marrow, the Sanskrit *mearg*, or *majja-rasa*, the sap of life—the marrow of manhood, or soul of horn and bone. An Accra saying has it that "*marrow is the father of blood*"! In the earliest biology, blood was the mother of marrow. With this change of view it was fabled that the woman was created from the man, as Eve was taken from the bone of Adam, or derived from the soul of his bone, considered to be masculine, and, as such, a form of the fifth soul. Here we can trace yet another doctrinal development. At this stage fat and oil were offered to the dead, as a type of the marrow of life, and soul of bone: the fat that was placed in the cups on the tombstones of the buried dead. To this day the Red Indians sacredly place a lump of fat in the mouth of the corpse prepared for the grave; and the Romanists anoint the dying with the oil called "*extreme unction.*" In Egypt the very divinity of Horus consisted in the preservation of the holy oil on his face; he who was the anointed or the *greased, i.e.,* the Christ (Records of the Past, 10, 164); he who was "*raised from the dead through* (and as) *the glory of the Father*"; and whose earliest advent was in the male nature, as the anointed at the time of puberty. Hence fat or oil was used as a bone-type of the primitive soul of man — the sole bone from which the first woman ever was created. This, the *fifth* soul, was at one time the *quintessence* of a man!

When the brain had been identified as the physical basis, or matter of mind, the sixth soul was then derived from this superior source of intelligence in the head. In the Egyptian Ritual (chap. lxxviii.), the Osirified deceased says,—"*Horus has come to me out of my father Osiris!*" "*He has come to me out of the brains of his head!*" That was as the *nous* of the Gnostics, the revealer of an intellectual soul, who in Egypt is the god Ptah, or *Putah,* the opener, whom I elsewhere identify with Buddha in India. The Hindu Buddhi is the sixth soul, and Putah is lord of the sixth creation: he is also known as the "*wisdom of the first intellect.*" (See "Natural Genesis," section 9.)

The Seventh soul was derived from the individualised fatherhood, which was represented by the father Atum for the first time in the Egyptian mythology — Atum being equivalent to the Buddhist *Atma,* the creative soul. Atum of the seventh creation represents the eternal—he inspires the breath of life everlasting, and is called the *one sole God without change.* At this stage of attainment the soul exults that it is created forever, and is a soul beyond time. The deceased exclaims, "*Shu causes me to shine as a living lord, and to be made the Seventh when he comes forth!*" "*I am the one born of Sevekh!*" and Sevekh means the sevenfold or seventh, the type of attainment, *as the seventh of the total series.* This "*is he who comes out sound* (in death)—*the Unknown is his name.*" The "*mystery of this soul made by the gods*" is described as being, as it were, "*self-existence*"—*i.e.* of the permanent entity attained at last. It is called the "*reserved soul,*" the "*engendered of the gods, who provided it with its shapes. Inexplicable is the genesis. It is the greatest of secrets.*" (Rit. ch. 15.)

In this way the seven souls were identified in Egypt, and may be formulated as—(1) the Soul of Blood, (2) the Soul of Breath, (3) the Shade or Covering Soul, (4) the Soul of Perception, (5) the Soul of Pubescence, (6) the Intellectual Soul, (7) the Spiritual Soul.

The first soul was *formative*.
The second soul *breathed*.
The third soul *enveloped*.
The fourth soul *perceived*.
The fifth soul *procreated*.
The sixth soul *reproduced intellectually*.
The seventh *perpetuated permanently*.

And at every one of these seven stages of development there was a fresh outgrowth of mythical legend or mystical representation—just as there might be a new efflorescence at the seven ascending knots of a bamboo cane. Much of this, however, has been shown in my "*Natural Genesis*," and cannot be repeated now.

But because the primitive and archaic man recognised and laid hold of seven elements, one after another, in the shape of form, breath, corporeal soul, perception, pubescent soul, intellectual soul, and an enduring soul, as a mode of identifying his physical elements and mental qualities—that does not make him resolvable into a number of elementary spirits after death, as is falsely imagined and maintained by the Esoteric Buddhists. There never *were* seven souls of blood, of breath, of cover, of perception, of the animal, intellectual, and spiritual nature which could have passed into another world as seven elementary spirits. These phantom likenesses of natural facts belonging to our past selves have no more power than photographs for each to become a future self. The shadows projected by the Seven did not, and could not, become spiritual beings in another world. They were only types for use in the mental world. They *were* a number of types, seven lines in an upward series, each of which served, for the time being, to denote the element at the time identified with or as *the* soul. We may look upon them as the seven lines of an ascending high-water mark. The seven elements in the nature of man never could become anything more than seven types, according to an ascertained mode of typology; whereas the Esoteric Buddhist continues them as seven potential spirits of a man, the elementaries of another life, who may either attain the immortality of a united and permanent entity there, in some far-off future, or fail for lack of power to persist, and finally die out altogether. That is not a vision of the future, human or spiritual; it is but looking in a *camera obscura* held in front, which reflects in some dim and distorting manner a picture of the past that lies behind. We shall no more deposit seven, or even two, souls in death than Oliver Cromwell could have left behind him two skulls, found in two rival museums, one of which (the smaller of the two) was said to have been his skull when he was a boy!

There is nothing in the nature of things known or prefigured to warrant us in assuming a fundamental and enduring difference in the constituent quality of beings who belong to the same species. Nature gives no hint that we can either engender a force or destroy a faculty of persisting that may be called immortal—no hint that we can commit eternal suicide, and put an end to existence, any more than we could initiate our own beginning. It is here, as so often elsewhere, that an ancient mode of expression has become the modern mould of thought. The Esoteric Buddhists, like the primitive Christians, have been beguiled by the typology which they have failed to interpret. Of course, if you only credit an undeveloped being with the human form, the life of breath, the astral shade, and a twinkle of terrestrial intelligence, you can easily establish a doctrine of conditional immortality, but I affirm that it is solely on the plan of this primitive map of man, which was only tentatively true. There never was a time when the adult male did *not* possess at least five of the seven principles or souls—those of blood, breath, shade, perception, and the animal soul—howsoever small his intellect may have been. At least four of these souls—the soul of blood, breath, intelligence, and reproduction—belong to the animal in common with man; and so we find four souls are ascribed to the Bear by the Sioux Indians. The only possible human elementary spirit is the child that died before it came of age, and that is identifiably extant—in short, the seven were not souls in the flesh that when out of it could become seven orders of spirits objective to man. Seven elements, seven principles in seven degrees of the one life's development, become seven personalities or persons solely as a mode of expression, a classification in accordance with these primitive types. And being elements, when spoken of as personages they naturally become seven elementaries; and being elementaries in this biological sense of the true Esoteric teaching, they get mixed up with the seven powers of the elements or elementals and their prototypes, which never did, and never could, have a personal existence—never were living beings. Hence the dire confusion amongst the modern echoes of the ancient wisdom, and the indefiniteness of Esoteric Buddhism, on the subject of elementals and elementaries.

In the "Natural Genesis" I have traced the seven powers of the elements to their origin in external phenomena. The seven elementaries in the nature of man may also be followed as far as they will go.

In the *Inscription of Una* (Records of the Past; 2, 8), these Seven Souls of the Pharaoh are spoken of as being invoked "*more than all the Gods.*" These were the Divine Ancestors, the Manes, who were worshipped in Egypt by the "*Shus-en-Har,*" or followers of Horus, for thirteen thousand years before the time of Menes. Being Seven in Number, they are identical with the Seven Manus, Rishis, Elohim, and other Hebdomads found elsewhere. Their origin was in this wise. The Seven, who preceded the Eighth, being looked upon as *progenitors* of the one-enduring Soul, the Horus, Christ or Buddha, became a *form of the Ancestors, or Manes; the nature of which has to be partly determined by the number Seven.* They never were the Spirits of Individual Ancestors! They originated as seven human *Elementaries,* and not as Ghosts that made their appearance in a group of seven. These seven, being correlated and combined with the seven elemental forces recognised in external nature, we have that perplexing mixture of *Elementaries* and *Elementals,* on which subject we are told the Adepts are very diffident.

The Septenary of souls can be traced from first to last by means of the Egyptian doctrine of transformation. Thus the blood source that formed the embryo was quickened and transformed into the soul that breathed. The breathing soul attained cover, and transformed into the corporeal soul of shade; this transformed into an Intelligence. The intelligent youth transformed into the adult, when the animal soul, or pro-creative spirit, manifested at puberty. The adult soul transformed into the Hebrew Neshamah, the wise soul, or the Hindu Buddhi, the soul of ascertainment, and this into the soul that makes to re-live, which was represented by the God Atum, in whom the fatherhood was individualized at last as the begetter of an eternal soul; also by the Hebrew Adam, whose head reached up to the seventh Heaven. This doctrine of transformation, and the unifying of various individualities into one personality, puts an end to the septenary, and to the diverse destinations after death of several human principles, which must have already attained totality by unity, in order that there might be a personality, or ego, in this life. Not one of the Seven Souls had obtained the permanent personality, and, as they were but seven rudimental factors in the development of an ultimate Soul, they could not become Seven Spirits as realities, or Apparitions, in another life. Each older self was merged in the new, and, therefore, the seven could neither be simultaneous nor contemporary, except when absorbed in the oneness of unity.

Hermes describes the one soul of the universe as entering into creeping things, and transforming into the soul of watery things, and this into the soul of things that live on the land; and airy ones are changed into men; and human souls that lay hold of immortality are changed into spirits, and so they ascend up to the region of the fixed stars (or gods), which is the eighth sphere; and this is the most perfect glory of the soul! But this was as the one soul of life, not as the eight, or seven individual souls. The eighth was the immortal blossom on the human branch.

The worst kind of haunting in this world is not done by the spirits of dead people, but by the phantoms of defunct ideas; the shadows cast upon the cloud-curtain of the hereafter by those things which were only types and figures of human realities here—not things in themselves from the first. And these seven, or other number of other selves, belonging to the one personality, have left their shadows in the domain of metaphysic, which is fundamentally fractured by this splitting up of the one personality into separate selves, whether sevenfold, fivefold, fourfold, threefold, or only secondary. Also, these ghosts of primitive physics are beginning to walk in our midst, and are trying to pass themselves off upon us as genuine spirit-phenomena. The Buddhist difference between personality and individuality was necessitated, and is explained by the individuality which may include a seven-fold form, or passage of the personality; seven persons in one ego, like the "Three Persons and one God" in the Trinity. In the process of doctrinal development, objective re-birth in a series of human lives, or spirits, has been substituted for the re-birth of the ego in personality at the different stages and conversions of the one being, whereas the original re-births were subjective, whether biological or psychical, and limited to the one life alone, in its successive stages of transformation.

Besides which, the Seven Souls are *all summed up in an eighth.*

This eighth to the seven is mentioned in the Book of Revelation, where the numbers of the Gnosis constitute Wisdom. The Beast, who is an Eighth, is also of the Seven! In Egypt it was the lunar Taht-Smen, the eighth, or the sun-god with the seven souls; in India, the god with seven arms. The eighth is also represented by the Buddha, who is the manifestor for the seven Buddhas, or Manus, and by the Gnostic Christ, who is called the eight-rayed star of the pleroma, or god-head, composed of seven earlier powers, of whom it is is said:—"*Then, out of gratitude for the great benefit which had been conferred on them, the whole pleroma of Æons, with one design and one desire, and with the concurrence of Christ and the holy spirit, their father also setting the seal of his approval on their conduct, brought together whatever each one had in himself of the greatest beauty and preciousness; and uniting all these contributions so as skilfully to blend the whole, they produced a being of most consummate beauty, the very star of the pleroma, and the perfect fruit* (of it), *namely, Jesus. Him they also speak of under the name of Saviour, and Christ, and, patronymically, Logos, and All Things, because he was formed from the contributions of all.*" Such is the Gnostic account of the Christ as the eighth one, in whom the Seven Souls culminated. The seven spirits were also continued in the Gnostic system as the seven angels who convey the eternal soul to the human creature. You may see them in Didron's Christian Iconography as the Seven Doves which hover round the Virgin Mary, who carries the Christ in embryo—he who, as the eighth, became superior to the angels. The dove was also said by the Gnostics to represent Christ as the eight-fold one, or the illustrious Ogdoad; the number of the Dove being 801 in Greek letters. Hence the descent of the Dove that *abode on Jesus* when he attained the Christ-hood; where the symbol proves and identifies the typical and non-historical nature of the transaction, and the Gnostic character of the cumulative Christ.

The Ass, a Typhonian type of lunar phenomena, was likewise a representative of the Word or Logos that was reproduced as the Eighth—like the repeating note in the musical scale. It is well known that the bray of the donkey is just an *octave* in its range; and this made it an utterer of the Word or Logos, who was the Eighth. We read in the Ritual (ch. 125) that "*Great words are spoken by the Ass!*" And in old Egyptian the Ass has the name of *Iu* or Iao. The Eighth was the Seventh Soul, as *first Person in the Hebdomad, the father-God afterwards reproduced as his own Son.* This was Iu-em-hept (hept=7) in Egypt; the Ass-headed Iao-Sabaoth and Iao-Chnubis of the Gnostics. When expressed by means of external phenomena it was the Solar vivifier who was reproduced monthly, or annually, by the Mother-Moon; whence the re-birth or resurrection that is still dependent on the full moon of Easter; he who became Lord of the first day, or Sunday, instead of the seventh day, or Saturday.

The divine Fatherhood being founded at last in the God, or supreme one of the seven souls, whether called Atum-Ra, or Osiris in Egypt, Vishnu in India, Adam in the Greek Mysteries, or Jehovah amongst the Jews, his manifestor was impersonated as the divine son of the father-God, in whom the octave is attained, and the God-head of all the powers or souls is reproduced just as the eighth note in music is the note of repetition, reproduction, or re-appearance. And this eighth one was the Christ, as Iu-em-hept, the son of Atum, who is designated the "Eternal Word." This eighth one, as manifestor of the seven, was also Har-Khuti, in Egypt, the Lord of Lights and of the Glorified Elect, the God whose Sign is the Pyramid-figure of 7; Krishna Agni, or Buddha in India; Assur in Assyria; Pan, of the seven pipes, in Greece; and the Gnostic Christ, called Totem, the All, who was formed from the contributions of all the Seven, identical with the Buddha, who is the outcome of the seven Buddhas, the result of their "*Collective Intelligence,*" called Adi-Buddha, or *Buddha from the beginning,* in allusion to this process of development; and whose symbol, like that of the Christ, and of Horus, is the star with eight rays! The Christ, or Mithras, or Horus, represented that height, or octave of attainment, to which the Gnostic adept aspired, and which Paul designates the full-grown Man, and the measure of the stature of the fulness of the Christ, or a sort of divine *Octavius!*

Such was the nature of the "*Wisdom*" that a Gnostic like Paul, Epopt and perfect, spoke amongst the perfected; and it would have been useless to have spoken such among A-Gnostics who were of the fleshly faith. This was the mystical Christ who came BY and AS the Holy Spirit; so Jesus is transformed into the Christ when the Holy Spirit descends upon him in his Baptism! But, after this transformation, it is said in the same Gospel that the Holy Spirit was *not yet extant* (or communicated), because Jesus was *not yet glorified.* To the genuine Gnostics this holy spirit always had been extant; but here we see its very existence made altogether dependent upon the personality and death of Jesus in the process of re-dating it and making him the author of it historically. Barnabas knew better. He identifies the Christ with the Man of the eighth Soul, who rose again on the *Eighth Day of Creation!*

Here the height was synonymous, and is identical, with the number eight! This height is represented in the Buddhist, Gnostic, and Mithraic mysteries by a ladder with eight steps, the eighth, or height, being the top of attainment, the place of the perfected; and so the octave was completed at last in Buddha-hood, in Elijah-hood, in Christ-hood, or the divine man-hood, of the pre-Christian religions; such likewise being the natural genesis of the eight ways and eight paths of Buddhism.

The Gnostics said salvation was brought by the Ogdoad; and the Saviour personified was the mystical Octavius: the superior man of the eighth creation! It is said by Peter in the Clementine Recognitions that there was an *Ideal Man* who had the right to the name of Messiah, because the Jews called their Kings the Christ, the Romans Cæsar, and the Egyptians Pharaoh. That is true. Each of these DID represent the same original type. The Roman Cæsar, the hairy, pubescent, or Anointed One, was an impersonation of this supreme soul; who happens to be the *Eighth* also by name in *Octavianus*, who was the first Emperor! (Born B.C. 63, called Augustus B.C. 27.) According to the Christianised Legends of the Sybil, the Romans wished to adore Octavianus as a divinity, but the Sybil showed him the Coming Christ in the Virgin's lap, whereupon he refused to be worshipped himself, took off his diadem, and adored the future child! Nevertheless, Octavianus was just as good an *historical* realisation of the mythical and mystical Christ as any personal Jesus could be; or, rather, both were equally impossible for those who knew.

Another Gnostic mode of illustrating this mystery may be pointed out in passing. The supreme personality was attained in the eighth degree of ascension, and the supreme sign of that personality, the pronoun I, was the ultimate outcome and representative sign of seven vowel sounds. Our letter I was the ai, ei, eta or ida of the Coptic, which has the *numeral value of eight*. Seven vowels, said the Gnostics, glorify the Word, and these were uttered in a single sound, in an O or an I. Thus the octave was completed, the height attained and expressed in a single letter sign, the I of Personality. The God Ō was also invoked with adorations in the Greek Mysteries; possibly with the "8 Adorations," which are Egyptian and Chinese. This was another sign of the Eighth Soul, Ō having the numerical value of Eight in hundreds. The sign survives as the vocative "Oh!" of religious aspiration.

According to the Gnosis, then, the Seven were only a group of phenomena which evolved the enduring entity at last, the eternal soul itself, into which they were transubstantiated in death; the re-appearing, manifesting spirit that was personified as the fully awakened Buddha, or the mystical Christ of the Mysteries. Such was the Finding of the Christ as a human product, which was first demonstrated by Spiritualism—the type having been continued by combining the mythical with the mystical! This was the "*True Logos*" which Philo and Celsus wrote about, the "*Heavenly and indestructible offspring of a Divine and Incorporeal nature*," the Gnostic "*Light which lighteth every one that cometh into the world*," not that earthly Shadow cast upon the background of ignorance called the Historical Christ. Such was the origin and mode of building up, stage by stage, the Christ of the Gnosis; the divine man, the man from heaven, described by Paul, the Christ of those who knew, the evolution of which has now been traced step by step to its culmination ; the Christ of that spiritual existence beyond the grave, which was demonstrated in the mysteries of mediumship, who was called the son of God, also the son of man, because the son as manifestor implied the father as begetter! This was in the mystical phase. In the moral aspect the Horus, Christ, or Buddha was set forth as a model to all men, the highest type of attainment for those who were climbing up the ladder of eight rounds. It was not the portrait of any one individual who could attain perfection once for all as the representative of all men. That was the fatal mistake of the Christians—the men who did not know—as it is equally the error of those Esoterists who only pretend to know. The earliest mode of attaining this Christhood, or Buddhahood, was by cultivating the trance-conditions and becoming a spirit amongst spirits. This was moralised in a second phase when attainment was made dependent upon the practice of certain saving virtues. In the final phase conversion to a belief in the Christian scheme has taken the place of both!

It is positively provable that the Christ is but a type identical with the Horus, the Iao-Heptaktis, the Buddha or Pan of the prior cultus. According to Irenæus, the Valentinian Gnostics maintained the identity of the Saviour with Pan, who is called *Christum* in the Latin text. Pan was, of course, an earlier personification of the *All*, or "All Things." The type and origin are one, under whatsoever name. Consequently Pan, or Aristæus, with the seven-fold pipe in his hand, and the sheep on his shoulders, is the Christ, the Saviour, the Good Shepherd pourtrayed in the Roman Catacombs, instead of the historic Jesus, whose picture is not there.

The Christ or Buddha of the Gnostics could not become flesh once for all, as he was the supreme outcome and consummate flower of all flesh, in the culminating stage of spiritual attainment in life, and spiritual apparition after death. The Christ being an immortal principle, and very life itself, could not be put to death; so that '*redemption by the death of Christ*" is a fundamental fallacy from the first. Here, as in other matters, the essence of all the present writer has to say is, that a *physical fulfilment is always and everywhere the doctrine of delusion.* Historic personality could not authenticate the existence of the Buddha. It had no meaning when applied to the Christ. They alone could accept such a version who were non-Gnostics and non-Spiritualists, entirely ignorant of the nature of the manifestor. It was the type of immortality, not as the mummy-image on earth, but as the starry Horus; as the *Ka* or glorified apparition that reappeared through the dark of death; as the risen Christ who rose upon the horizon of the resurrection; the Horus, whose name denotes the one who ascends as a spirit. For, the Egyptian, "*only one who comes forth from the body*" applies to the spirit in life, as well as in death. The art of leaving the body was common to the old dark races, and is practised by the rudest indigenes of many lands. The Khonds call it the art of *Mleepa* or transformation. An Egyptian artist named Iritsen (11th Dynasty) says he knows the "*mystery of the Divine Word*," and "*how to produce the mode (or form) of issuing forth and coming in.*"

Whether in this life or another, the "Wise Spirits" were all one. "*He has become as one of us*" is said of Adam when he had become a Wise or Instructed Spirit, and the Egyptians addressed their Dead as "Wise Spirits." It was this so-called Magical Art of producing abnormal conditions, and the faculty of Second Sight, that finally established the existence of a permanent individuality or soul beyond the Seven Elementaries. And it was the mystical Christ, so established, who alone could bring immortality to light; but not by a physical resurrection from the tomb. "I am the resurrection and the life" applies only to the principle or spirit—the 8th, as the one that rises again, the "*only one*," as the Ritual has it, "*who ever comes from the body*"—the typical eternal who appears as the deathless one upon the other side of the grave! This Christ cannot be made Historical or Personal FOR us,—only IN us! That is the the doctrine of Paul, of Philo, and the Gnostics, opposed to the Christian doctrine of the physical or fleshly faith.

The ultimate soul, type or phase of existence, then, was not born as a mental *concept*, nor as the result of an induction, nor as the dream-shadow made objective; it was practically demonstrated as scientific matter-of-fact! The Christ of the Gnostics, of Philo-Judæus, and of Paul, the heavenly man, or second Adam, who came from Above, was no mere doctrinal abstraction, but the spirit or ghost that could be seen,—as it was seen by Paul in visions—and made to constitute his own special mystery; and always had been seen by those who possessed the second sight! even as it continues to be seen by the abnormal seers of to-day,—which ghost, according to the evidence collected by the Society for Psychical Research, is also visible at times to ordinary vision. In pourtraying their *Ka* image of the spiritual Ego, the glorified second-self, as a type of the Eternal Being, the Egyptians represented that which their Seers saw, and you may trust them for the truth in this, as in everything else, they were so entirely truthful. Indeed, I think the mind of man has never had so profound a sense of truth and verity as in the Egyptian phase. Through life they put their trust in truth, and it was their principle of cohesion in death. The Osirified deceased says, "*I am the Lord of Truth, living it daily.* I am spiritualised, I have *become a soul!* I have *touched truth.*" Their typical Eternal is called the sole being who *lives by truth.* Before the tribunal of *eternal truth* the accused pleads that he has not even *altered a story in the telling of it!* That alone was true which is for ever; and *all along the line of progress they had groped in search of that which was ultimately true,* and *true for ever,*—the exact opposite of the Hindu *Maya,* the *untrue,* or delusion. And they vouch for the fact that the Ghost of Man is a living reality—the final reality —the Horus or Christ. In comparison with those who *know* because they *see* that there *is* a continuity of existence beyond the change called death, because they have the faculty to perceive the dead as living phantasms embodied in a rarer form, we are all of us on the blind side of things! They know because they see; and we deny because we do not know. With the savage or the civilised seeing makes all the difference, and cuts short all question of the possibility of seeing.

But to return. Esoteric Buddhism tells us the higher principles of the series which go to constitute man are not fully developed in the mankind with which we are as yet familiar. Whereas this system of thought, this mode of representation, this septenary of powers, in various aspects, had been established in Egypt at least seven thousand years ago, as we learn from certain allusions to Atum found in the inscriptions lately discovered at Sakkarah. I say in various aspects because the Gnosis of the Mysteries was at least seven-fold in its nature—it was Elemental, Biological, Elementary (human), Stellar, Lunar, Solar, and Spiritual—and nothing short of a grasp of the whole system can possibly enable us to discriminate the various parts, distinguish one from the other, and determine the which and the what, as we try to follow the symbolical Seven through their several phases of character.

The Egyptian Ritual represents the drama of the doctrinal developments relating to the passage of the Deceased, with his trials and transformations in the underworld, which furnished the matter of the later mysteries, including the Greek, Mithraic, and Christian. In this, the Deceased plays over again the whole seven characters that went to the making up of the one personality, which became permanent in the eighth nature. He is reconstructed for the other life in exact accordance with the seven principles or souls with which he was constructed in this life. On the day of reckoning souls, the seven constituents have to be collected, counted, and united in one. According to the dramatic representation, immortality depended on totality. The seven chief organs of life, or vehicles of Soul, were all preserved as types. And when put together again, according to pattern, he is as we say "*all there*," with the whole of his parts and members sound. The soul could exist independently of the heart, but there was no proper reconstruction possible without the heart being literally "*in its right place*." It was thus they acted the Mystery. The Deceased cries, "*Do not take my soul!*" (Ba.) "*Do not detain my shade!*" (Khaba.) "*Open the path to my shade, and my soul, and my intelligence* (Akhu) *to see the great God on the day of reckoning souls.*" One of the Genii says to him, "*I join together thy bones for thee. I revive thy members for thee; I bring thee thy heart, and put it in its place.*" Then the Osirified deceased exclaims, "*I am the reckoning which goes in*"—"*and the account which comes out*"—i.e., when summed up and VERIFIED. When put together and divinized as the compound image of the Seven, it is said of the Eighth Soul, "*Thy Individuality is permanent!*" Having attained his sevenfold totality, he is the Eighth one, at peace as an enduring spirit, one of the *Verified*. The deceased is thus greeted, "*Hail, Osiris! thou hast come —thy ka* (his spiritual image, or divine likeness) *with thee!*" and he is now hailed as the only one ever coming forth from the body, the foremost of those who belong to the solar race; the sun being the supreme type of the soul, as the Vivifier for ever. He has culminated in that unity which Spiritualism enables us to start with, without this prolegomena of the ancient physics. He makes the significant remark,—"*I hasten to escape the Shades!*" whose shadows have been utilised by our friends, the Theosophists, to explain away, or minimise the extant phenomena called Spiritualistic.

"*The third principle, or astral body*," says Mr. Sinnett, "*is that which is at times taken for the ghost of departed persons! Also, it may exude from the body of a spiritualistic medium, but it is no more a being than the cloud in the sky can become an animal, although it may show a spurious semblance in its form.*" This is to introduce the direst confusion, and to utterly mystify that which is sufficiently mystical! The corporeal or third soul of the series, only persists as a type, because it was once the highest representative of *the* soul. Souls that passed off into spirit-world when the soul was but a shade or covering soul, did not become sunshades in heaven nor fire-proofs in hell—nor can they issue from the medium's body as such, even though the sunshade is retained as a pictorial type of that soul! Yet the sunshade has an equal right to be classed among the Elementaries with the Astral Shade, or any other symbol of the soul. Indeed, the Siamese have the sunshade as a seven-fold type. Their sacred umbrella, that used to be the sunshade of royalty, had seven tiers to it, which represented the seven heavens in the mythical phase, and the seven souls in the mystical sense. The spirit that returned to earth when the soul was the corporeal shade, and the third was the highest in the series, would be the Shade; this being the corporeal soul, when it appeared on a visit to the living it was supposed to go back to the body in the tomb, and to pass away altogether as the body decayed. It could not go to heaven when there was no heaven made out to go to. Being third in the series, this would become a ghost that only lived up to the third generation—as we find it among the Zulu Kaffirs! But the shade never could be one of seven souls emanating from the body of a medium. In such a climate as ours it would be economical if every medium could materialise and spread out a covering in that way! Of course, if you postulate or pourtray a soul at that immature stage of development, it will be without mind or memory, language, or individuality. It will be a shadow indeed! And so it reappears amongst the ghosts of Esoteric Buddhism, but it is not one of the Intelligences known to modern Spiritualism. We may as well say that the soul of blood became a red mouse, and the soul that fed on blood became a hawk, and so on all through the series of types; *which they did according to the system of representation, although not in reality.*

The Sevens were all correlated, the seven elemental powers, with the seven elements in man; and these seven souls, or elemental parts of man, were assigned to seven creators, or gods, and considered as seven creations in mythology, each of which had its zootype, such as the red mouse, the hawk, the ape, jackal, serpent, beetle, and crocodile. Seven zootypes having been adopted to represent seven elements in external nature, these or their *equivalents* were continued to express the seven elements or souls in man. The Shrew mouse was an Egyptian type of the first formation, the soul No. 1, the "*blind Horus,*" as he was called; the hawk, of the second soul, that of breath and of sight; the monkey, of reflection (the other self); the jackal, of memory; the serpent (or goose which laid the egg), of the transformation into adultship; the frog (or beetle), of the transformation into an intellect; and the crocodile, Sevekh, which is number seven, into the Seer unseen, the soul as supreme one of the seven souls. Now, as a soul was once typified by the red mouse, it is certain that *the soul or ghost will be seen as a red mouse;* and accordingly this soul was seen as the red mouse that came out of the sleeper's mouth, in a German story. This red mouse of a soul is also mentioned by Goëthe in "Faust." That is the red mouse that typified the primary soul of blood. The German goddess Holda, the receiver of children's souls, is represented as commanding a multitude of mice. Moreover, the mouse is sure to survive in a sort of spirit-world; and here we have it. The moon was a re-birthplace for the most elementary or rudimentary souls, because it was the first step on the planetary ladder, above the sublunary sphere. And so we find the myth of souls in the moon in the shape of little mice. The Dakota Indians say the waning of the moon is caused by multitudes of mice that are nibbling at it and causing its disappearance—the mouse being an Egyptian emblem of disappearance.

The mouse was a type of the first Horus, or soul No. 1. The

hawk is a type of the soul of breath, or soul No. 2, because as Hor-Apollo explains, the hawk drinks blood, never water, and the soul is sustained by blood. As there was a soul that fed on blood in this life, the soul emaned from the body in death at that stage of thought and expression, will continue the type in another phase and sphere; so we have a soul or spirit of the dead that is supposed to come out of the corpse to suck the blood of the living; and the origin of the Vampire, that only lives by drinking human blood, has to be sought at this depth of rootage; for the blood-sucking demons of various kinds are held to be human souls, and not the elemental powers personified. If you consider (as I do) the ghost to be an objective fact in nature, the power to demonstrate, and the vision for seeing, may have existed from the earliest times, and there would be apparitions when the biology had only identified the blood with the soul of life! Now there is not only evidence of a haunting spirit at this stage—a soul of blood—a gory ghost, as the Vampire, but certain evil spirits, when conquered by a Mage like Solomon, always fled to, and were drowned in, the Red Sea, which was their fabled home and birthplace. That is the Egyptian Red Lake of Primordial Matter! In the Book of the Dead, certain undeveloped and rudimentary souls are sent back again, doomed to be resolved into the primal element, and are said in the texts to be suppressed in blood; they make their typical return to that from which they came.

Each of the Seven Principles, or Appetites, or souls, had its physical prototype, that was separately preserved by the Egyptians —the brain, tongue, heart, stomach, and other vehicles of life. Thus when the Kroo negroes hold that the *stomach* of a man ascends to heaven after death, we can understand it as a representative of one of the souls, or appetites. This soul of the stomach would need to be fed. No wonder, then, if we should hear of a demon in the shape of a stomach that goes about seeking whom it may devour. This is the *Kephu* of the Karens, a wandering wizard's stomach supposed to prey upon the souls of men.

Raw flesh and blood were offered to the uncivilised and gory ghost. But in the second phase a Soul of Breath would be more refined and not considered capable of consuming material food. At this stage we hear of the spirits snuffing the vapours and steam of victuals, inhaling the essences and smelling the aroma of food or the fragrance of flowers. In fine, we see provisions cold and hot offered—some things to eat and others to smell—the body and spirit of aliment, so to say, being presented to the Corporeal Soul of Matter and the less palpable Soul of Breath.

The shrew-mouse, or the bird, has no likeness to the human being, but the ape has a little. And at this third stage the nearest likeness to the human is adapted to express the other, or reflected, self, at the stage of the third soul; the Shade in Egypt is synonymous with the God Shu, one of whose types is the Great Ape. The Ape, as a type of the Soul, may account for the African superstition of men being changed into monkeys after death; the primitive symbol having been literalised. Now, Esoteric Buddhism professes to give some account of the seven races of man (which are founded on the seven souls) and of the evolution of the elementary into the human. In his third stage we are told that the "*Coming man had developed at first the form rather of a giant ape than of a true man, but with intelligence coming more and more into the ascendant.*" Here we can clutch the proof that the third race is a *continuation of the third soul*, and that the basis of both is to be found in Egyptian typology; for the giant ape in Egypt was the type of the third elementary, the God Shu, or shade, the monkey-man on the monuments!

The Marawi say the souls of bad men after death will become jackals; and the jackal was another of the elementaries, the one who possibly represented the fourth soul, that of memory, as he was made the remembrancer and recorder of the gods.

The soul was also reckoned to be a birth of time! Hermes alludes to every soul that is in flesh by the wonderful working of the gods in circles! In the Ritual the deceased says, "*My soul is from the beginning, from the reckoning of years*"—and he boasts that he has *time* in his body! Time is Seb, and the soul of Seb is the soul of pubescence—our soul No. 5. The goose that laid the egg was a type of this soul! The goose being a representative of the soul born of time, an equivalent for the soul according to a symbolical mode of expression, you have only to continue that type in spirit-world or fairy-world for the goose to become identical with a spirit, and you may expect to find the goose amongst the elementaries—as in fact we do. In German faeryology, or *the spiritualism of folk-lore*, we find a class of earth-spirits, or wee folk, who visit the living; and when the ground is strewn with ashes overnight the foot-prints are supposed to be visible next morning as those of the goose or duck. Here the returning spirit is identifiable with the likeness of Seb, or with his type the goose, but it does not mean that the human soul came back upon the feet of a goose! The ancient typology was continued, and remains to be interpreted. Take it literally at any stage and you must be all wrong, as are those Esoteric Buddhists who have mistaken an ancient mode of expression for a reality, and continued it into the future of the human soul, and applied it to the development of the human race, in doing which they are but wandering in a mental wilderness that is dark overhead with the shadows of the past.

The beetle was a type of our sixth soul, an emblem of transformation; and some of the primitive races held that a certain low class of spirits turn into beetles after death.

The crocodile, whose Egyptian name is Sevekh, or seventh, was a type of intelligence, as the seventh soul, the supreme one of seven, because (so Plutarch says) it could see in the water when its eyelids were closed over the eyes. It was thus the seer unseen. In the Kaffir languages the crocodile and a spirit (*i.e.*, a soul, or the intelligence) have the same name. It is said to be believed by some of the Inner Africans that when a child of their's is born the mother gives birth to a crocodile at the same time. Here the Egyptian symbolism (over which I have spent a third of my lifetime) will enable us to interpret the meaning! These poor people *intend to say their children are born with an intelligent soul*, and the fact is expressed in the African language of typology.

But the human soul in its upward ascent had not actually passed through the stages of the mouse, hawk, ape, jackal, goose, beetle, and crocodile; nor will it return to or in any such shapes; nor did it project seven such elementaries as its shadows into spirit-world; nor did any primitive race, whether savage, Egyptian, or Hindu, ever think these things. Nor were they evolutionists in the Darwinian sense. It was a mode of expression, still readable in the Ritual, where the speaker, in making his transformations of the soul, says—"*I am the mouse*," "*I am the hawk*," "*I am the ape ;*" jackal, goose, or serpent; "*I am the crocodile whose soul comes from men*"—*that is, as a type of intelligence;* "*I am the soul of the gods*," the Horus, or Christ, as the outcome of all.

Moreover, each of these souls had its representative type of Sacrifice that was eaten in eucharistic rites, and these might be traced more or less from the Shrew-mouse, that was eaten by the Hebrews, down to the body and blood of Jesus eaten by the Christians, as a mystery of transubstantiation.

It is in vain that the Pseudo-Esoterists try to saddle modern Spiritualism with this bestial set of acquaintances, elementaries, shadows, and shells as our relatives in another world. They are ignorant of the beginning, the natural genesis of this system of representation. They do not seem to know that the transformations of Buddha were of the same character, and originated in the same zoomorphic typology. The Buddha, or supreme soul, that reaches the top of attainment as the outcome of the previous seven, has in a sense been all seven, because of the one life running through them all—just as the mature man has been boy, babe, embryo. It consequently follows that whatsoever types the seven have been masked under, or represented by, may be applied to the Buddha as the ascending human soul. Hence he has various transmigrations and re-births, in which he emerges now as a bird, an ape, a frog—now as one kind of animal, now as another, because these were at first symbolic of the seven elements of body and soul that made up the totality of being—which elements in man, or in external nature, had been imaged by the zootypes of totemism that were continued as ideographs in a later phase of thought, and had no reference at all to any remote course of pre-human evolution on earth.

The Seven Races of Men that have been sublimated and made Planetary by Esoteric Buddhism, may be met with in the Bundahish as (1) the earth-men; (2) water-men; (3) breast-eared men; (4)

breast-eyed men; (5) one-legged men; (6) bat-winged men; (7) men with tails. But these were never real races of men.

These are they who were created in the likenesses of the Seven Elementals, who were represented by Zootypes, which were afterwards continued in the heraldry of Tribal Totemism. Mr. Sinnett's instructors have mistaken these shadows of the Past, for things human and spiritual. They are neither, and never were either. This mode of representation can be studied as intended typology in Egypt, whereas, in India, a land that is haunted with the phantoms of metaphysics, it has been perverted into a system of metempsychosis, and a doctrine of migration for the human soul. In the Egyptian Judgment scenes, it is common to see the wicked soul sent back as, or by means of, an unclean beast—the sow being the type of uncleanness. Such symbolical representation was made actual in India, where such souls are sent back to earth *as* beasts or reptiles. It is affirmed in the Book of Manu that "*In whatsoever disposition a man accomplishes such and such an act, he shall reap the fruit in a body endowed with such and such a quality.*" As Hor-Apollo says, the Egyptians denoted a people obedient to their king, by depicting a bee! and then the Jewish Rabbins, adopting the type, say the soul of a governor who exalts himself proudly above his people, goes into a bee! When the Jews speak of souls that migrate into beasts and birds, and Plato of souls being re-incarnated into birds and beasts, they are making unwarrantable use of the primitive typology. In the later teachings, conveyed by means of the ancient symbolism, it was threatened that the fleshly soul would be reborn as a mouse or an ass; the thief would become a rapacious rat; the coward, a reptile; the bloodthirsty tyrant a vulture, or devouring beast of prey; the lowest classes, into the vilest creatures. This is but the other side of the same mental coinage, and it is only to be understood as belonging to the same symbolism. All such primitive doctrines were indigenous to India, long ages before the latest Esoteric Buddhism was born; and here, as elsewhere, only in the earliest phases and physics, can we ever reach the root of the matter. So often the more abstract doctrines have no other foundation than this of perverted typology, the resulting metaphysical phantasmagoria being then put forth as an Esoteric revelation! That is, *the mode of representation, which was only true as fable, has been moralized and made false in fact. An ancient mode of expression has become a modern mould of thought.*

I once had a singular experience with an incipient medium, who came to me at the moment when my mind was full of Egyptian hieroglyphics. After he had entered the state of trance, these images appeared to take shape and " go for him ! " He seemed to be surrounded and pursued by the very animals I had just been copying. Because he at first mistook the mental pictures for objective realities! And this is exactly what has been done by the pseudo-Esoterists represented by Mr. Sinnett.

The natural genesis was physical and followable; the expression was typical. In the later metaphysical phase we have only the shadow, the returning *manes* of the once living meaning, trying to pass itself off as a revelation of future reality. Metamorphosis of the soul was ancestral, biological, and figurative, at first; then it was continued in the astronomical allegory—both of which are omitted by the pseudo-Esoterists. And, lastly, it was made mystical by metaphysical assumption in the later systems of Esoteric hermeneutics; and now it is pretended that the last was first, and the uppermost stratum was primary, or, in the beginning, which it IS *only* in *beginning to go back*.

In conclusion. It has been my literary lot to explore the past of human thought, and its modes of expression, somewhat thoroughly, as an evolutionary fundamentalist. The obscurity lessened by slow degrees. I began to see how the primary "*types*" of thought were originated of necessity, and for *use;* how they became the signs of expression in language and mythology; and how theology, by its perversions and misrepresentations, has instituted a reign of error throughout the whole domain of religion. But, I am not one of those who go back to rehabilitate the past, or resuscitate the religion of Osiris, or Hermes, or Buddha, any more than that assigned to Jesus by 300 sects of Christians. Neither am I at enmity with the Theosophists. I am ready to join hands with all who work for the universal brotherhood; and I am their best ally, if they only knew it.

My desire is to gain all the knowledge the past can give, and supplement it with all that is known in the present, but with face set steadfastly toward the dawn of a still more luminous day of a larger knowledge, and of loftier out-look in the future! If we turn back to the past for our revelation and authoritative teaching, we are exalting the child as father to the man. The past is a region to explore, and learn of it all we can. It is impossible to understand the present without the profoundest knowledge of the past. Without a comprehension of the laws of evolution and development in the past, and of survival in the present, we can have no opinion ourselves that is of the least value to others. And then we want to get out of it, and away from it, by growth, individual and national, as fast and as far as ever we are able. They are blind guides who seek to set up the past as superior to the present, because they may have a little more than ordinary knowledge of some special phase of it! There were no other facts or faculties in nature for the Hindu adepts or Egyptian Rekhi than there are for us, although they may have brooded for ages and ages over those of a supra-normal kind. The faculties with which the Adepts can—as Mr. Sinnett says—read the mysteries of other worlds, and of other states of existence, and trace the current of life on our globe, are identical with those of our clairvoyants and mediums, however much more developed and disciplined they may be in the narrower grooves of ancient knowledge. Much of the wisdom of the past depends on its being held secret and Esoteric—on being "kept dark," as we say. It is like the corals, that live whilst they are covered over and concealed in the waters, but die on reaching day!

Moreover, it is a delusion to suppose there is anything in the experience or wisdom of the past, the ascertained results of which can only be communicated from beneath the cloak and mask of mystery, by a teacher who personates the unknown accompanied by rites and ceremonies belonging to the pantomime and paraphernalia of the ancient medicine men. They are the cultivators of the mystery in which they seek to enshroud themselves, and live the other life as already dead men in this; whereas we are seeking to explore and pluck out the heart of the mystery. Explanation is the soul of science. They will tell you we cannot have their knowledge without living their life. But we may not all retire into a solitude to live the existence of ecstatic dreamers. Personally I do not want the knowledge for myself. These treasures I am in search of I need for others. I want to utilise both tongue and pen and printer's type; and if there are secrets of the purer and profounder life, we cannot afford them to be kept secret; they ask to be made universally known. I do not want to find out that I am a god in my inner consciousness. I do not seek the eternal soul of self. I want the ignorant to know, the benighted to become enlightened, the abject and degraded to be raised and humanized; and would have all means to that end proclaimed world-wide, not patented for the individual few, and kept strictly private from the many. That is only a survival of priestcraft, under whatsoever name. I cannot join in the new masquerade and simulation of ancient mysteries manufactured in our time by Theosophists, Hermeneutists, pseudo-Esoterists, and Occultists of various orders howsoever profound their pretensions. The very essence of all such mysteries as are got up from the refuse leavings of the past is pretence, imposition, and imposture. The only interest I take in the ancient mysteries is in ascertaining how they originated, in verifying their alleged phenomena, in knowing what they meant on purpose to publish the knowledge as soon and as widely as possible. Public experimental research, the printing press, and a free-thought platform, have abolished the need of mystery. It is no longer necessary for Science to take the veil, as she was forced to do for security in times past. Neither was the ancient gnosis kept concealed at first on account of its profundity, so much as on account of its primitive simplicity. That significance which the esoteric misinterpreters try to read into it was not in the nature of it originally — always excepting the phenomena of Spiritualism. There is a regular manufacture of the old masters carried on by impostors in Rome. The modern manufacture of ancient mysteries is just as great an imposition, and equally sure to be found out. Do not suppose I am saying this, or waging war, on behalf of the mysteries called Christian, for

I look upon them as the greatest imposition of all. Rome was the manufactory of old masters 1800 years ago. I am opposed to all man-made mystery, and all kinds of false belief. The battle of truth and error is not to be darkly fought now-a-days behind the mask of secrecy. Darkness gives all its advantage to error; day light alone is in favour of truth! Nature is full of mystery; and we are here to make out the mysteries of Nature and draw them into day-light, not to cultivate and keep veiled the mysteries made by man in the day of his need or the night of his past. We want to have done with the mask of mystery and all the devious devilries of its double-facedness, so that we may look fully and squarely into the face of Nature for ourselves, whether in the past, present, or future. Mystery has been called the mother of abominations, but the abominations themselves are the superstitions, the rites and ceremonies, the dogmas, doctrines, delusive idealisms, and unjust laws that have been falsely founded on the ancient mysteries by ignorant literalisation and esoteric misinterpretation!

NOTE TO LECTURE ON "PAUL."

In quoting evidence of the double doctrine ascribed to Paul, I omitted one of the most conclusive illustrations of the fact. We read in Galatians iii. 13—"Christ hath redeemed us from the *Curse of the Law*, being *made a Curse for us*: for it is written, *Cursed is every one that hangeth on a Tree*." The object of hanging the Condemned One on the tree was to make him Accursed. But what says the voice of Paul the Gnostic in another text (Cor. xii. 3)?—"No man speaking by the Spirit of God calleth Jesus *Accursed*, and no man can say that Jesus is the Lord *but by the Holy Spirit*." That is, the Christ of the Gnosis could not become accursed, could not be hung upon a tree, and no Gnostic would say that Jesus was the KURIOS save in the mystical or esoteric sense. Here the Historic and Gnostic doctrines are directly antipodal. This again is the teaching of Paul—"*Say not in thy heart, Who shall ascend into Heaven? (that is, to bring Christ down;) or, Who shall descend into the abyss? (that is, to bring Christ up from the Dead.) The Word is nigh thee, in thy mouth, and in thy heart*." That is, the *Word* as preached by Paul. Then follows the interpolation. Also, as an illustration of the statement made by Clement Alexander—that Paul said he would bring the Gnosis or Hidden Wisdom to the Brethren in Rome—it should have been shown by me that the teaching of the Epistle (ch. i. 23-32) is taken *almost bodily* and *repeated nearly verbatim* from ch. xiv. 12-31 of the "Wisdom of Solomon," in which the Saviour of men is *not* the Historical Jesus.

THE KARAST=CHRIST OR MUMMY-TYPE OF IMMORTALITY.

The *Karast*, which I claim to be the Egyptian original of the Greek Christ, was an image of rising again—a representative of the resurrection; and in speaking of this symbol I ought to have pointed to the fact that the alleged historic resurrection of Jesus has never yet been found pourtrayed on the so-called early Christian Monuments, including those discovered in the Roman Catacombs. But what do we find there in place of the missing fact? *The scene of Lazarus being raised from the dead*. This is depicted over and over again as the *typical* resurrection where there is no *real* one! And the Lazarus is *an Egyptian Mummy!* Thus, Lazarus IS the *Karast*, who is the Christ of Egypt reproduced in Rome like the other Mythical types perpetuated there by Gnostic Art. As the image is Egyptian, it is probable that the name is so likewise. *Las* (or ras) signifies to be raised up, and *aru* is another name for the Mummy-type; so that *Las-aru*, or Lazarus, with the Greek terminal, is the Egyptian symbol of resurrection called the *Karast*, or Christ. This typical and pictorial representation of the rising from the dead would become the story of Lazarus in the natural course of humanising the Mythos.

A RETORT.

I AM sorry to trouble my readers with a matter so personal as the present subject. It has been found out that I am not infallible. Like my fellow-mortals, I can fall into error. I have to acknowledge and regret a stupid blunder, perceived, alas! too late (p. 15 of the Historical Jesus and Mythical Christ; also p. 419, Vol. II., "Natural Genesis").

In comparing with Egyptian certain Syro-Chaldaic and Aramean words which have been left untranslated in the Greek text of the New Testament, I included the word "*sent*," entirely forgetting that it was English when I compared it with the Egyptian "*shent*," a "pool," and "*sunnt*," a healing bath. The *nature* of my inadvertence is proved in the very next lines by the remark :—"*There is no need to strain a single point for the purpose of making ends meet!*"

It was foolish, but such is the simple fact, and I will not seek to minimise my mistake. Any one engaged in attacking what he considers the supreme delusion of the European mind, and the crowning error of all time, ought to be free from the smallest errors himself. were possible! For the most is sure to be made by the enemy of the least lapse, more especially by those who have been consecrated to the service of falsification.

My error drew the attention of a Mr. Coleman, and induced him to write an article in the *Religio-Philosophical Journal* of Chicago last October, of which no copy was sent to me by the writer or publisher. To this my attention has just been called; also to a letter by the same writer which appeared in the same journal, dated February 5th, headed "*Opinions of Eminent Egyptologists regarding Mr. Massey's alleged Egypto-Christian parallels.*" Unfortunately, the letter will necessitate a reply to the previous article. In this letter the Rev. A. H. Sayce is reported to say of me to Mr. Coleman, "*Many thanks for your very thorough demolition of Mr. Massey's crudities. It is difficult to understand how a man can have the effrontery to put forward such a mass of ignorance and false quotation. You have done a real service to the cause of truth by exposing him so fully. You ask me if I can detect any errors in your essay. Errors enough on the part of Mr. Massey, but they have all been exposed impartially and mercilessly by yourself.*"

Mr Coleman continues, and quotes the following from "*one of the ablest Egyptologists in England,*" who is "*now connected with the British Museum,*" of whom he says, "*owing to the rather personal character of some of his remarks, it is thought better that his name be not published.*" The writer says to Mr. Coleman,—"*You are right in your exposure of Mr. Massey. Some people think him dishonest; and that he is quite conscious of the ridiculous blunders which he publishes. I do not think so after having examined his large book. It is a work which I should have thought could only have been written in Bedlam. No lunatic could possibly write more wild rubbish, without the least consciousness of the incredible ignorance displayed throughout. The man is AT ONCE an ignoramus of the worst kind, viz., not in the least being aware of his ignorance, and he has the pretension of explaining things which cannot be understood (except by trusting other persons) without a considerable knowledge of different languages, which he does not possess.*" If the words here used have any real relationship to known facts, it seemed to me that the Egyptologist who has taken the place of the late Dr. Samuel Birch must be the writer of the letter quoted by Mr. Coleman. I wrote to Mr. Renouf stating my inference, and asking him to favour me with a denial if he were not the writer. This is Mr. Renouf's reply. The underlining is mine :—

"SIR,—You are mistaken in thinking that the extract from Mr. Coleman's letter '*points undoubtedly*' to me. There are more persons than one at the Museum besides me, to whom it *might be supposed* to 'point.' But whatever indiscretion there may have been *till now* in this matter, I am not disposed to add to it by answering any questions as to my knowledge of the authorship of the letter to which you refer.— I am, Sir, your obedient servant, P. LE PAGE RENOUF."

That answer I look upon as eminently unsatisfactory; and I think my view will be shared by others. Only one person wrote the letter; and this explanation brings at least three under suspicion, without identifying or absolving the right one. If Mr. Renouf be the writer, instead of clearing himself he has imitated the ink-fish and taken refuge in the cloud which he has cast around his *confrères* at the Museum. I cannot think the reply is *calculated to deceive!* It contains no denial, however, and perhaps the discretion shown too late may not prove to be the better part of valour; but I leave a blank for the time being where I have not the absolute right to fill in a name.

We have heard language like this of Mr. ——— before (put in better English), when anything very upsetting has been presented to the world. *Such damnation is dirt cheap!* Also, the time has passed for *denunciation to be mistaken for disproof.* That is the kind of authority I had already counted on, and discounted, when I say, " *They must find it hard to take Truth for authority who have so long mistaken Authority for Truth.*"

By the by I may confess to Mr. ——— that I escaped from Bedlam many years ago; I would also remind him that the proper name for Bedlam is *Bethlehem;* a most ancient mad-house in which the patients have been confined for eighteen hundred years; and that our Bedlam also was once a "religious house." I am not mad myself; but I am possessed by the conviction that a good many other people are, and that no insanity is quite so virulent as that which *dates from the ancient Bedlam.* I had already warned my readers that they must expect little help from those Egyptologists and Assyriologists who are bibliolators first and scholars afterwards. Bibliolatry puts out the eyes of scholarship or causes confirmed strabismus.

I admit in the preface to my " *Natural Genesis* " that " *as a matter of course the author will have blundered in manifold details.*" At the end of three years I doubt whether I have! But of course in a work of so fundamental and pioneering a nature there will be some oversights, crudities and even graver faults that cannot be avoided in a first edition. Why, 30,000 errors have had to be corrected in the latest edition of the "Word of God." And it does seem at times to be a providential part of the scheme of things that *where the truths entirely fail to command attention first, the errors are sure to secure some sort of advertisement for the work.* In this way, even a Coleman can be turned to account.

Madness may be a matter of opinion; but whoever charges me with intended "*false quotation*" lies!

I spared no time to get at my facts, and neglected no available sources of knowledge, whether directly open to myself or derivable through the minds of those who are great linguists. As I also say in my preface I took the precaution of consulting Dr. Samuel Birch for many years after he had offered, in his own words, to "*keep me straight*" as to my facts, obtainable from Egyptian records. He answered my questions, gave me his advice, discussed variant renderings, read whatever proofs I sent him, and corrected me where he saw I was wrong. I never could understand the interest he took in me and my work. He could have had no sympathy with my real aim and ends (which are not wholly proclaimed even on my title-page), yet he was always ready to enrich my poor means with the treasures of his knowledge, so precious for my purpose; whether by letter or in person, whenever I sought him out amongst the Mummies and

"*In a corner found the toys,*
Of the old Egyptian boys,"

or got my verification direct from the monuments, including the hieroglyphic texts and pictures in his own copy of the Book of the Dead.

And now for Mr. Coleman.

He has been trying to discredit my work for over three years past. His assumption of superiority is immense, and might prove imposing if his methods of attack were not so verminously mean. His latest labour-in-vain has been to try and rear a pyramid on its apex—the sole point of a single fact—which can be sent toppling over with a single kick. Where it suits his purpose he *uses an imperfect report of a Lecture so that he may convict me of errors which are not to be found in the Book that he seeks to discredit, and industriously essays to damn.*

In the article referred to he says: "*In recent numbers of the London Medium and Daybreak there has appeared Mr. Gerald Massey's lecture on 'The Historical Jesus and the Mythical Christ,' as revised and corrected by the author, and as delivered by him in London not long since. In this lecture, which attempts to establish that the Jesus and the Disciples of the New Testament had no existence in the flesh, but were only personifications of Egyptian myths, we find a large number of asserted parallels between the life and teachings of Jesus of Nazareth and certain portions of the Osirian and other myths of Egypt.*"

The opening paragraph contains two positive, provable, falsehoods. The version of my lecture made use of by him was a reprint from an imperfect report in the New Zealand "Rationalist," which was not revised by the author. *If it had been he could only have assumed to know what he asserted without knowing.* But it is not true! It is also false that in this lecture, or in my book, I try to "*establish that Jesus and the disciples of the New Testament had no existence in the flesh, but were only personifications of ancient Egyptian myths*"—whatever *that* may mean!

On the contrary, I demonstrate the existence of the only possible historic Jesus known to Celsus, to Irenæus, to the Jews, who allow that he had twelve disciples, whom they call the "*twelve god·ess runagates.*"

What I do also demonstrate is that the mythical twelve were the followers of Har-Khuti in Egypt ages earlier.

This is a prime specimen of his mode of working, and one it is well to keep in mind all along. This is the *mode* of demolition which Professor Sayce endorses, warrants, glorifies ; and Mr. —— declares to be "quite right."

Again, I have used the Hebrew word שׁלום (Natural Genesis ii. 419), on which our learned Hebraist remarks, "*This asserted Hebrew word Shiloam is a fabrication. There is no such Hebrew word in existence as Shiloam—in unpointed Hebrew Sh, L, O, M*" ! ! "To identify Salem, or *Shalem*, with Siloam in Hebrew, the letter 'm' was required. There being no 'm' in the correct word, Shiloach, Mr. Massey manufactured a Hebrew word and printed it in Hebrew letters, as if to deceive the very elect."

Now, look at that for a lie ! with no room left for the least little wriggle-out of it !

As Mr. Coleman obviously knows nothing of Hebrew beyond the names of letters, perhaps Mr. Sayce, or Mr. —— will look it out for him in Fuerst, at page 1388, Col. 2, where the word appears with the meaning of " well " in health ; and on page 1376, Col. 1, where it means *Peace*. It is used for the Prince of peace (Is. ix. 6). And Fuerst further says " Shiloah is cognate with שׁלום (Shlom). It is quite impossible that Mr. Sayce should not have *known* this at the time he gave his sanction to Mr. Coleman's falsehoods and consummate effrontery; and it was cruel not to arrest him as he was careering round in this wild way instead of tickling the poor creature's vanity with insincere applause.

The lie and libel were so unnecessary that I am compelled to regret the wanton waste of pure malignity. When I say the " Pool of *Peace* " is Salem, or Shloam in Hebrew, I do not say that it is the Pool of Siloam ; and am only rendering the *word* " Peace." And as *Shloam* means " peace " and *salem* means peace, I used the alternative of " salem or shloam." I knew the two words were *spelt* differently, and that Shloam may be pointed Shaloam ; I also knew that they were identical in meaning. Moreover, the Pool of the waters that flow softly *is* a form of the Pool of peace. Not that either of these was involved or at all necessary to my argument. When I say " THE Pool of Peace " is in Hebrew Salem or Shloam, I am speaking of THE *mythical* pool which in Egyptian is the Pool of Hept or Peace, not the topographical pool of Siloam. I was only concerned with the identity of THE mythical original which had various localisations in different lands, Judea included.

Mr. Coleman runs a long rigmarole about the goddess " *Nu* " and the place " *Annu*," in which he flounders, in the bottomless bog of his own helpless ignorance, past all pulling out by those who have taken him by the hand—viz., Messrs. Sayce and ——.

He who enters this domain so unprepared and unequipped as Mr. Coleman, must be a fore-damned fool. I could have pitied his impotency but for his ineffable conceit and aggressive insolence.

Because I use the words " *An* " and " *Annu* " as synonyms, this great Egyptologist asserts that I identify the Lady of " *An* " with the goddess " *Nu* " to form the word *Annu*. As the monkey exclaimed when he saw the elephant taking in water at such a rate, " *To drink with the tail is immense !*" *An* and *Annu* are simply Egyptian variants of one word ; different spellings of the same word were the result of familiarity with matters upon which my corrector is so utterly ignorant that he looks upon and denounces the variants in Egyptian spelling as my *distortion* of

Egyptian names, and sapiently suggests that "*there always appears to be an object*" in my changes! He thinks the "Lady with the long hair" is *Tefnut*, and not the goddess *Nu* as I had inferred, partly because the Ritual says "*The hair of the Osiris is in the shape of that of Nu*" (Ch. xlii.), and partly because the Osiris ascends the heaven, or Nu, with his long hair down to his shoulders. Either way it matters very little.

What I do regret is that I could not have had the advantage of knowing what Mr. Coleman *thinks* about the Egyptian mythology before writing my book. The opinion of such an expert on the most profoundly allusive and problematical Sayings might have seriously modified the result. He further charges me with having got certain goddesses mixed up; it being his mission to teach me how to separate them once more and distinguish between them individually. Here he tries to turn his ignorance to account by taking advantage of the reader's and producing the impression that the ignorance is mine. He throws dust in the eyes of others and then says it was I who did it. And Mr. Sayce, in a cloud of it, swears it to me!

I may admit that this parallel of the Woman at the Well, which is but one out of fifty, is the weakest one. But it is enough for my purpose to show that the Osiris or Osirified (these being identical in character) appears at the Well or Pool of Peace; that he claims to be the Well and personates the Water; that the source of this water of life given to the Son is the Father; that a well or flow of this water comes out of Osiris to him; that the well of this water comes through him (Cf. John vii. 38, and iv. 14.); that he washes in the "*pool of Peace*," where the Osirified are made pure or healed: where the "*certain times*," as I have called them (because the seasons for healing are *dual* in the Ritual) are detailed thus—"*The Gods of the pure waters are there on the fourth hour of the night and the eighth hour of the day,*" saying, "*pass away hence*" to him who has been cured or healed.

Here it is noticeable that in the still-continued process of eliminating that which looks *too* mythical, *this passage containing the angel descending to trouble the waters and turn them into a Pool of healing has been dropped from the latest revised version of John's Gospel.*

In converting the original mythos into later history, this process of picking the owner's name or sign from stolen goods has gone on from the first, and is not yet ended!

I do *not* say or suppose anything so simple as that the writer of John's Gospel was copying from some "*variant and obscure chapter in an ancient Egyptian papyrus.*" That is Mr. Coleman's foolish way of putting it. *That* was not exactly the way in which the Osirian legend got literalized in Rome. *If it had been preserved and continued as mythos, it could not have re-appeared under the guise of historic Christianity.*

The matter had to be manipulated, converted, assimilated, in which process the original features have been somewhat defaced. This has to be allowed for in judging of my parallels, comparisons, and interpretations.

There must of necessity be a wide gulf between any one who accepts the Gospel history as pure matter of fact, and one who treats it as mainly mythical. The two can only talk to different classes of minds separated for the time being by that gulf, across which they can hardly hear each other speak.

But perhaps the most perfect of all my critic's manifold errors and monstrous blunders is this.

He writes a long essay in six columns to defend a passage in the Johannine Gospel against my mythical interpretation, with the intention of demonstrating the "stupendous display of ignorance and absurdity" which he finds in my volumes. He fights tooth and nail *on behalf of the historical interpretation* against the mythical. His one line of argument, his *raison d'être* all through, is that the events under review, the woman at the well, the Christ who drinks there, and other circumstances, *are historical!* And yet in the opening paragraph of his article he had started with saying—"*It is significant that most of these so called New Testament parallels are derived from the fourth Gospel, popularly ascribed to John. Every competent biblicist knows that the account of Jesus and his teachings given in John's Gospel differs widely from those given in the first three Gospels; and there is no reasonable doubt, in the light of historico-critical biblical science, that, while large portions of the latter are genuinely historical, the Gospel of John, as a whole,* is UNHISTORICAL, MYTHICAL."

Good God! the man is here throwing away the child with the water it was washed in! If this be so, and, as I demonstrate, the mythical gospel was first, no matter how late it appeared in the canonical gospel ascribed to John, the supposed history of the Synoptics goes to the ground! Where is the sanity in supposing that the Mythical matter of John's Gospel is the result of tattooing Egyptian fables all over the face of historic fact (as previously pourtrayed by the Synoptics), and disfiguring the human features past all recognition? The Christ of John is indefinitely divine, and that is *first:* the *final* phase looks definitely historic. That is how the Mythology was humanised. The Myth-Makers were Fabulists, but not the forgers of facts; the forgers are they who converted the fable into historic fact. Mr. Coleman says only just what I say and show on behalf of the Mythos. But what then was the sense, or where was the sanity in *labouring to prove it to be historic bit by bit, when, as a whole, it is entirely unhistorical and mythical?*

Yet Messrs. Sayce and ———— assure Mr. Coleman, with their compliments, that *he is right.*

I fancy some of my readers will suspect that he is not—*quite.*

And *this* is what it is to be *demolished!* This is doing a "*real service to the cause of truth*" So says the Rev. Mr. Sayce, and he is an authority.

Mr. Coleman charges me with *limiting my quotations* from the Egyptian Ritual to Dr. Birch's version of the "*very corrupt Turin Text,*" as if he were an authority respecting the Texts!—and then of misquoting the Texts to establish my parallel. Whereas my slight departures from the Text (in Bunsen) are the result of various emendations or corrections made by the Egyptologists, such as Renouf, including Dr. Birch himself, to whom I took them for his final opinion, and with whom I have gone over Text after Text for that purpose. I neglected no available source of knowledge, early or late. Also in reading, condensing, and connecting certain passages, I wrote with the whole matter of the Mythos in mind, and had the Ritual well-nigh by heart; which is to be at an enormous disadvantage *when judged by Mr. Coleman.*

In denouncing the "*corrupt Turin Text*" he is merely "monkeying round," by quoting the words of Mr. Renouf (Hibbert Lectures, p. 177). He consistently omits the rest of the sentence. Mr. Renouf, like M. Naville, is an expert in Textual and Verbal Criticism, and it is he who says on the same page :—

"*Dr. Birch's translation, though made about thirty years ago, before some of the most important discoveries of the full meaning of words, may still be considered extremely exact as a rendering of the corrupt Turin text; and to an Englishman gives nearly as correct an impression of the original as the text itself would do to an Egyptian who had not been carefully taught the mysteries of his religion.*"

Mr. Coleman's method, however, is the correct one for a defender of the Great Superstition to adopt; and if he were obsessed by the spirit of some fanatical Spanish monk, one of those who urged on the Mexican massacres, dead and damned ages since for his bigotry and cruelty, and re-incarnated to continue the old battle against Truth, he could not have more cleverly struck the track of the Jesuit. It is what the Christians in all ages have done to get rid of, discredit, and mystify, the pre-Christian evidences of the mythical origins; only he lacks the requisite knowledge for doing the work.

Nor is this a matter of mere Textual interpretation; and I am calmly confident that no mere verbal changes will invalidate the fundamental facts, the true doctrines, the identifiable mythology, found in the versions of Birch, Lepsius, and Naville.

On the contrary, the closer the inspection made by men of insight the more will my interpretation of the vastest number of facts ever yet collected and collated be corroborated.

Mr. Coleman has been soliciting certificates. I will give him one written on a label bound to last and stick like pitch-plaster. It is my recognition of his claims to be

THE GENUINE GNOSTIC.

He calls to Europe, high and low,
And all the Americas,—
" *That is the man who does not know;*
I am the man who does" !

The others join in Chorus; Oh!
They make his brain-bee buzz!
" *You are right, dear friend! He does not know;*
You are the man who does" !

From personal knowledge of him, and the imposture of his pretensions, I know him to be incompetent to discuss matters of Egyptology. He is not an authority in any department of literature, and has not a soul beyond the making of fly-dirts on the window to obstruct the light,—or of violating the privacy of letters so foolishly entrusted to him.

In setting himself up as a critic and corrector, mentor and censor, advocate, judge and jury, all in one, he has greatly mistaken his vocation. If he must pose as a man of letters and a symbolist, he should have been a printer's reader, allowed once a week to carry a typical banner at the tail of a Lyceum procession on Sundays. He may pass for one of the learned amongst those who know no better; in the realm of the blind the one-eyed man is a king. He shows some cleverness in writing about what he does not understand, where he is not likely to be brought to book. But he is no more capable of judging, or qualified to give a verdict, in a matter like this, than the weevil that worms its way through one of Turner's canvasses is fitted to pass an opinion on the picture.

He has an irritating itch for recognition, or notoriety, but has shown no sign of possessing, or being possessed by, the genuine passion for truth. Like an incipient Herostratus or Guiteau—the fellow who culminated as a fool gone insane with vanity—he would do anything to be talked about, or written to—even commit Massey-cre—if he were only able.*

Never did any writer known to me put forth such strenuous or futile efforts to lift himself up by his own shirt-collar and add a cubit to his stature in the eyes of the lookers on.

From the beginning to the end of his attempts, his aim and object, the total drift of all his deprecation, is to belittle my work, and make himself look large to his readers through a mist of his own making. A chief part of his criticism consists in proclaiming that he does not see! I never said he did, or could. Nelson at Copenhagen put up the glass to his one blind eye and could not perceive the signal flying. Mr. Coleman often puts his glass to two, with the same result of not seeing.

I have had to congratulate him on writing to me to set him right on the subject of astronomy, before he put his foot into it on a matter most fundamentally important to my subject; the ignorance shown by his questions being astounding.

With all his native impudence he has asserted (in the Religio-philosophical Journal), that the name of Jesus Christ was unknown until the middle of the first century A.D. (cf. the second book of Esdras—a pre-Christian book of the Secret Wisdom.)

In the same journal he classed Baring Gould as being *on my side*, in opposition to all other writers on the subject of Jehoshua Ben Pandira, and entirely overlooked the fact that although Baring Gould used the same Talmudic material as myself, his conclusions were totally antipodal to mine; and that he remains as orthodox to-day as were his conclusions then.

And now Mr. Coleman may pass with his certificates.

There is an American story of a dog who ran after a wolf, fast and furious at first, but before the race was over, the dog was seen to be flying still faster—a "*leetle bit in front of the wolf!*"

Mr. Coleman is not an authority, and has no reputation to lose. But his private backers have; and they have committed the unpardonable sin against scholarship of endorsing and justifying false statements made against me by Mr. Coleman, without taking the trouble to test the truth of his assertions or to verify the alleged facts for themselves. They were so ready to make a mountain of an underhand, underground worker's little molehill; they were so eager to have me knifed, that they have warranted a blade which was treacherously limp and leaden!

Mr. Sayce marvels at *my* effrontery in making assertions, some of which Mr. Coleman has so falsely put into my mouth; and then charges me with

---

* A literary correspondent writes of this *Sahur*:—"I know little about Egyptology, but I do know that the fellow deserves a—well, a 'serendible good drubbing' for his insolence to you. Should you reply, please give him a kick from me, if only in a *foot*-note."

"false quotation"; and he calls Mr. Coleman's puerile performance a *"very thorough demolition,"* and a *" real service to the cause of truth."* He rejoices over what he terms an impartial and merciless exposure.

To my thinking the Professor is rather Uriah-Heepishly thankful for exceedingly small mercies, and says grace to a miserable meal.

Mr. —— vouches for the fact that his correspondent is *" quite right ;"* and it appears that neither of them knows better, or else their vision was overclouded with the bile of a bitter bigotry. Either way, I warn my American friends that Mr. —— has made use of the official stamp (the Hall-mark, so to say,) of the British Museum, to pass off spurious wares upon unsuspecting people in the United States! and I fancy that, for all lovers of truth, justice, and fair play, I have so far demonstrated the congenital incompetence of my critics to sit in judgment on my work.

It really makes one ashamed of scholarship to think of two reputed great scholars backing by taking shelter behind a pretender to knowledge like Mr. Coleman to discredit me and condemn my work instead of handling the matter for themselves.

My publishers tell me they sent a copy of the "Natural Genesis" to Mr. Sayce over three years ago. I have not heard that he attempted to expose my mass of ignorance and false quotation, dispute my facts, refute my interpretation, or controvert my conclusions. True, he is not an Egyptologist nor a master of mythology. But that is no excuse nor justification for the conduct which I resent. It only serves as cause for all the severer condemnation. Of course in writing a letter he might have claimed privacy for his opinions, but cannot plead that privilege now the letter is made public.

The other writer, whom I hold to be Mr. Renouf *(pro tem.)*, is a professed Egyptologist, a good grammarian, an expert in textual criticism. I am a devoted student of his writings in common with those of other Egyptologists. But I never could think highly of his insight or range of vision. To a mind like his, in a case like mine, the profoundest acquaintanceship with the largest mass of facts—the widest and truest generalisation based on the facts, or the subtlest interpretation of them, will only look like a *departure away from* and a *going beyond the facts* as limited for him.

> I have dived deeply, and he fails to see
> The ocean hath its due profundity.

You may transcribe texts and decipher inscriptions, but with the light shut out all round by non-application of the comparative method, and from lack of illumination within, you cannot touch the Egyptian origins in mythology or language, time or space, or interpret the mystery of Egypt to her own forgetful self.

Every day discoveries are proving how limited has been the outlook, how non-evolutionary and untrue the interpretation of Egyptologists concerning the past of that people; and the latest discoveries made have swept away many of the mental landmarks, and effaced the limits of Egyptologists like Mr. Renouf, who have only just *blazed* the veriest surface of the subject. But I claim that every fresh fact made known of late years is in favour of my interpretation. In England they have been too long the victims of the Hebrew and Indo-Germanic delusions respecting the beginnings.

Mr. Renouf has declared (Hibbert Lectures, p. 243) that "*neither Hebrews nor Greeks borrowed any of their ideas from Egypt*" (see Herodotus, Plato, Plutarch, Diodorus Siculus, and others). He *thinks* the "*mythological symbolism*" of Egypt arose from "*varieties of metaphorical language*" which "*reacted upon thought*" and "*obtained the mastery*" (Ib. p. 237). Following Max Müller he says, "*Mythology, we know, is the disease which springs up at a peculiar stage of human culture*" (Ib. p. 251). Nonsense. 'Tis but a dream of the metaphysical theorist to suppose that mythology is a *Disease of language*, or anything else except his own brain. Mythology *was* a primitive mode of *thinging* the early thought; the beginnings of its sign-language being earlier than words. It *remains* the repository of man's most ancient science; and, truly interpreted once more, it is destined to be the death of all those false theologies to which it has unwittingly given birth.

He has said (Ib. p. 177) it is perhaps hopeless to expect that the Egyptian legends alluded to in the "Book of the Dead" will be recovered. My claim is to have recovered them, by application of the comparative process to a world-wide range of mythology; and it will be easier to denounce the audacity as lunatic than to disprove the right to make that claim. I do not pretend and I do explain. He is one of those critics who suspect error in what they do not understand—*e.g.* the Father-God Seb in one phase of character is the Earth. But when Seb is called the *Mother*, Mr. Renouf suspects an error in the text. It is only the mother who can bring forth. Hence we find the back of Seb opens *to* bring forth.

In his off-hand way of damning by denunciation an old friend of mine, Mr. McLennan (whose name Mr. Renouf mis-spells twice over, once as *McLellan* in the text (p. 30), and once as *McLennon* in the index), he asserts that the "*representations*" made in the zodiac of Denderah were "*not anterior to the Christian era, or Roman domination; they were borrowed from the Greeks, and were entirely unknown to the Egyptians.*" (Ib. p. 30.) Whereas the inscription found at Denderah states that the Temple had been *restored in accordance with a plan discovered in the writings of Kufu;* whilst the *chief celestial types pourtrayed all over the planisphere prove themselves to be solely Egyptian!* When I pointed out this passage to Dr. Birch, he said, "*Certainly; the types in the planisphere are not Greek. Renouf should have done as the artists did who gave the Greek on one side, the Egyptian on the other.*"

All that he was warranted in saying is that the mythological types, Typhon, Sut, Isis, Horus, Seb, Shu-and-Tefnut, and the rest of those that *never were Greek*, have been reproduced at a later period by Greco-Egyptian artists, with a few modernisations. If he intended to distinguish between the Zodiacal and extra-Zodiacal signs of the planisphere, he should have said so. But of the twelve signs the Virgin is Isis, and the Sagittarius is composed of Shu and Tefnut. He must have known, however, that when Depuis and McLennan spoke of the Zodiac of Denderah as being ancient, they *meant the planisphere*, and were *not distinguishing the one set of signs from the other.*

Rays of light from the newest dawn would bring no quickening influence to such as are mentally bound and doomed till death to remain the representatives of an expiring system of thought.

The resurrection of Egypt has brought forth a Spectre that will frighten Historic Christianity to death; or haunt the minds of men till they lose their unworthy fears and listen like truth-lovers to the message which she brings to them from the Grave.

What says Professor Mahaffy, after getting a glimpse of the ghost, and finding that the dead language has come to life again? He admits that "*every great and fruitful idea*," "*theological conception*," religious and moral doctrine, now called Christian, were also Egyptian. But, he says, "*I recoil from opening this great subject now; it is enough to have lifted the veil and shown the scene of many a future conflict.*"

I have not recoiled. The odium of opening this great subject *now* is mine. I am selected for the honour of receiving, not the civic wreath for crown of reward, but the first blows of the bludgeon on the head from those who raise the howl of insanity.

"*You will win at last,*" said Captain Burton, "*but 'at last' generally comes too late!*" Well, I do not know. The train I ride in travels with increasing speed.

For the present I have to ask my indiscriminating assailant to assume that responsibility to which he is committed by Mr. Coleman and produce the evidence for his accusations. He says he has *examined* my work; now let him cross-examine me. I am scarcely mad or Quixotic enough to think he will, but should he do so, I will undertake the printing of his exposure to the extent of fifty pages, the size of the present pamphlet.

I mean business.

I court honest criticism, and welcome genuine correction. I do not mind being misunderstood, but do resent misrepresentation. I am in search of realities myself, and have no tolerance for men or things in masks. I try to follow Truth, like the old Egyptians, my masters, with all the force of sincerity, all the fervour of faith. That is comparatively easy now-a-days when bon-fires are no longer made of man or book, and the penalties are so very slight. A loaf or two of bread the less; a greeting here or there with an offensive epithet, a rotten egg, or a dead cat, are things to be smiled at when we remember our fore-runners that were her lovers from of old, who beat out a pathway for us through all the long dark night of the past, and lit it with illimitable rows of their burning bodies, each turned into a flaming Torch for Truth.

GERALD MASSEY

A correspondent writes:—"I am reading this extraordinary '*Seven Souls*' lecture, and have been able to follow you as far as the following statement, whereat I stick. I am compelled to trouble you for an explanation. You say: '*The Roman Cæsar, the hairy, pubescent, or anointed one, was an impersonation of this supreme soul; he happens to be the eighth by name in Octavianus!*' This looks like converting history into typology. Whatever the root significance of the term '*Cæsar*' may be, was it not the historical Julius Cæsar who really *made*, i.e., signalised it, by his deeds? —the name subsequently becoming a complimentary title assumed by the Emperors who were supposed, each in turn, to reflect the lustre of the Great Julius?"

No. But *this may serve as a useful illustration of the historical versus the mythical view of the Christ*. I fear, however, that it is a failing of mine to make too many passing allusions, and use too few words where explanations may be most needed. I mean *the* Cæsar (of whom, in the case of Julius, the Roman legends related that he was born with very long hair; like the long-haired Horus, or the long-haired Christ), had a mythical origin, and bore a title that was typical. Historical rulers were invested with divinity in this way, and made into mundane representatives of the Gods. It has been my work to trace such origins on various lines of research. For these mythical origins are manifold; they can only be distinguished and determined by knowing their Genesis in natural phenomena. In the present instance, I suggest or claim that the Cæsar as well as the Ra, the Repa, the Buddha, or the Christ, was a titular representative of the eighth, the total and eternal soul—mythically the re-born Sun; mystically the re-born Spirit or glorified Ghost of Man.

THE "NATURAL GENESIS" AT THE BRITISH MUSEUM.

Many enquirers have asked me *why* the "Natural Genesis" is not in the British Museum? This question I could not understand, but a friend has verified for me the fact that my book is not to be found by means of the written catalogue in the reading-room. Doubtless it is to be got at some other way known only to the initiated, but these would-be readers during three years past were simple enough to suppose that the Second Part of one and the same work would be entered along with the First Part, it having been published in 1883.

THE COMING RELIGION.

Our "friends the enemy" cheerily assure us that certain things are settled once for all in favour of Historical Christianity, and any further kicking against the fact is all in vain. If you show them that the Mosaic Writings do not contain an original revelation to mankind, but are a Mosaic of Persian and Egyptian mythology, that the foundations of their creed are destroyed if the Fall of Man is a fable, they will tell you that does not in the least invalidate the authority of the Bible, nor imperil the Christian revelation. Oh, no! The Church has never committed itself to any particular interpretation. Let us throw up the sponge and continue the battle. Some of the Apologists (as they call themselves, without meaning it ironically) pretend to think they are so secure that they can denounce any discussion of the Mosaic legends as *intolerably tiresome*. They affect to consider the matter past discussion. But those same "certain things" were never more uncertain or unsettled than at the present time; and when they do get settled the occupation of those who preach them as God's truth to-day will be gone forever! If *they* have closed the controversy, we have just begun to open it! We have not done with the note of interrogation yet. If they have made and tied up their little bundle of old dried sticks, ours are beginning to grow, and put forth a new leaf; ours are yet green and lusty with the sap of a new life.

These people have a vision of their own, and as it was bequeathed to them they will not part with it, even though they have to close their eyes to see! They will die in the "good old faith." But that is what others of us cannot do. We have but just begun to ascertain the meaning of the good old facts that preceded the good old faith. We are finding out that names the most hallowed are spurious counterfeits of the ancient gods. We are learning that the literary fortunes of the Bible were made by Mythology, and filched from the peoples who have been spoiled as Pagans, and accursed as the spawn of Satan. There is a spirit within us that wants to see, with our eyes wide open, and will see, and must tear the bandages and blinkers off the eyes to see, each for himself, whether the traditional vision be false or true. Nature gave us eyes to see with; it was men who added the blinkers. Nature intended us to be led by our own eyes; it was men who substituted the system of leading by the nose the mass of dough-faced humanity which church and state have tried so hard and so long to knuckle and mould for the purpose of leading it by the nose. *We have found out now-a-days that even the horses pull better without than with the use of blinkers.* So ignorant are many of these men of what is being thought outside their own little world, they do not even know how the battle is going against them. They are in possession of a few crumbling out-works, and do not appear to understand that the enemy is already in the heart of the citadel itself, with the sappers and miners depositing their mental dynamite; nor care greatly, so long as the commissariat remains intact, and they can draw the usual rations! for their attitude is, "deprive us of what you please doctrinally, and resolve all our mysteries into myth, so long as you do not disestablish and disendow the Church!" So long as the out-works are standing with them inside they will not recognise defeat! And orthodox Christianity is mainly built up of out-works or scaffolding. It is not the scaffolding, however, with which the institution was built, but one that conceals the true nature of the real building inside. The ordinary worshipper stands outside and mistakes the scaffolding for the real building, and looks upon it as it rises tier above tier like so many landing-stages and resting-places on the upward way to heaven. It has been my aim to penetrate beyond this scaffolding, discover the secrets of the hiding-place, and contradict the false report concerning the builders. And what we do find is that the so-called "Revealed Religion" is simply *unrevealed mythology*, and that a spurious system of salvation was proffered to those who would accept the ancient mythology transmogrified into Historic Christianity, and be bribed into changing their old lamps for new ones! Orthodox preachers will go on asserting Sunday after Sunday, in the name of God, any number of things which their hearers do not believe, only they have heard them repeated so often—past all power of impingeing or impugning —until the sense is too out-wearied to rebel; things which they themselves do not believe, if they could once afford to question their own souls. The *Pall Mall Gazette* has lately asked the question, if you had £100,000 to spare what do you think would be the greatest charity to give it to? I should like to have replied, "Pension off a few of those poor slaves of the pulpit, who are forced to earn their living by preaching what they no longer believe." How little the orthodox world dreams of the new dawn that is rolling up the sky, glorious with its promise of the brighter, better day! Nay, it is already flaming through the cob-webbed windows, and trying to look in at the shut eyes of the sleepers, which are fast closed, or blinking at the splendour shining on their faces! They are still dreaming how to roll the world back the other way once more into the night of the past, even while they are passing, face upwards, beneath the radiant arch over their heads, alight with the dawn of a day that is not theirs; blind to the glory of its coming, deaf to the birds that soar and prophesy in song, senseless to an amazing apparition of the Eternal growing visibly present in this our world of time! Now and again the sleepers start, and you hear a troubled moan from those that dream, and know they dream, but are afraid to wake. And when they do wake they will begin shouting for the fire-engines to come and put out the flames of dawn, now reddening the sky as with a conflagration and the end of all things for them.

If these men had truly cared for religion instead of their Anthropomorphic theology, they would not have gnashed their teeth and shaken the fist at the alleged phenomena of modern Spiritualism, as they have done. They would have embraced Spiritualism as if it had held out to them the strong right hand of salvation itself. For just when scientific research is undermining and exploding the ancient beliefs that have been falsely founded on mythology—just when the Materialists think they have discovered the great secret of life in protoplasm, and we are on the verge of finding the mechanical equivalent for consciousness—just when some are assuming that force comes from the visible side of phenomena, that mind is but a property of matter, an effect rather than a cause, and thought is nothing more than a result of molecular motion—just when the scientific report is that the deeper we dive physically, the farther off recedes the heart-beat of eternal life, in breaks this revelation from a world unknown, and, as it was assumed, unknowable. And these alleged phenomena contain the sole possible, palpable, natural evidence of a future life, that men have, or ever did have, or ever can have, to go upon. But no! what they care for are the old wives' fables and the figments which have become their hereditary stock in trade; the facts may go to the devil, to whom, indeed, they generally consign them. For, if it be God himself who tries to speak with them in this way from behind the mask of matter to prove the fact, they say it cannot be our God. He is dead, and buried in a book. This must be the devil. It *is* the devil. They had succeeded in substituting the non-natural for the natural, making men believe that this sham was the supernatural. They have taught us to look for God in the wrong way. They have based religion on erroneous grounds. They have made us the victims of false beliefs, and a false belief will make despicable cowards of men who would otherwise have looked facts in the face, and been true to themselves and honest to others. They have evolved our respect and reverence by means of the whip. And now when the stick and scourge, the knout and whip, have lost their terrors, have done their worst, and had their day, it is found that religious reverence has vanished also, and the young are becoming utterly sceptical in most things, before they are old enough to be in earnest about anything; for which the false teaching is responsible. The young have been disgusted with the ancient object of reverence, the grim and gory ghost of an anthropomorphic God.

We are constantly hearing complaints respecting the want of reverence on the part of the young for the old. But if they are *old fools*, and "old women" of the wrong sex, why should they be reverenced? It is said the children of this generation have no reverence for God or man. But if the reverence was evoked by the stick, and the reign of the stick is over, what are you going to do? It is of no use complaining, and probably it is too late to think of getting a new stick.

Before condemning, however, let us look a little deeper. Why should we expect reverence for such a God as we have allowed to be set before the children? Such a God as that of the Hebrews, who cursed all mankind because one of them, and the first one, ate an apple: a God for whom David was a man after his own heart; a God who revealed himself to Moses *a posteriori*. Reverence for such a deity used to be inspired by hell-fire; and now the fires of hell are going out—in fact, as Horace Greeley said, there are not half the people damned now-a-days that ought to be, only we want these to be the proper sort. What right, what reason have we to expect intellectual reverence for the parents themselves, who pretend to believe and permit such teachings as have been imposed on their children? They are most likely to be looked upon as old fogies, hypocrites, and fools by the younger generation, as it rises up to sit in judgment on them. Reverence must ultimately depend on the object presented for reverence. The first necessity is that it shall be a reality and not a sham, not a swindle, not an imposition to be found out, whether as a father in heaven, a father in the Church, or a father in the family. Possibly the pious pretences and the pious pretenders are being found out by the younger generation. But, the veriest larrikin has no lack of respect for the cricketer Grace, the sculler Beach, or the fighter Gordon, because these, in their way and range, are living realities. And if you want to have filial respect or religious reverence, the object must be a living reality that is worthy of it! Neither men, nor women, nor children will much longer bow down to false authority, or believe blindly as they have done hitherto perforce.

> The world is waking from its phantom dreams,
> To make out that which is from that which seems.

People now demand the verification of all that is taught as true. They must see for themselves that which is set forth as the truth. They must touch it and test it to learn whether it has the ring of reality. The demand of the present is that that which is asserted by the teacher shall be verifiable by the learner in every domain of thought, all the range of nature—all that exists, being ready to supply the means of practical experiment for attaining the sure foothold of a scientific basis. It is true we are still compelled to do battle vigorously, and spend life freely in fighting against the shadows and phantoms of to-day that are thinning out, and will be seen through to-morrow—compelled to fight them and to expose their false pretensions, because so many still mistake them for solid realities. But the people, men and women, aye and little children, will ere long arise and say to these our purblind spiritual teachers—

> Begone, you foolish preachers!
> Howlers, snufflers, screechers!
> You miserable teachers!
> You God-of-blood beseechers
> You forgers of God's features!
> Who make us the devil's creatures;
> Shut up, you foolish preachers!
> Get out, you hell-fire screechers,
> Go home, you played-out preachers!

and the cry will come in sterner tones,—let the war-drums of the workers roll out with their battle-thunders now, and drown the gabble of all this foolish, fruitless war of words.

Eighteen centuries since the religion of faith, the "good old faith," began to take the place of knowledge. Its history is one long and gory record of the battles of Belief versus Knowledge, of Faith at war with Facts. What is there that men have not found compatible with faith that was all the while at war with facts? Have they not cut each other's throats, believing it to be for the glory of God? Have they not burned bodies by the thousand, believing it to be the sure way of saving souls from hell-fire? Have they not made the Cross into the hilt of the sword to give them the better grip-hold of it whilst slaughtering myriads for the faith? Men have believed that they should find God if they un-sexed themselves, and got sufficiently removed from humanity, and so have gone out as hermits into the wilderness of monkery—which was like going into pitch darkness on purpose to see your face in a looking-glass! Men have believed that their God was the natural author of the diseases and evils which they created and fostered for ages, or permitted, and are responsible for before God and man to-day. They have believed that in the field of human souls Satan was the great harvester, and God only the gleaner.

Do but think what Woman has suffered from the belief,—the foul and foolish calumny,—that *she* was the cause of the fall of the human race! She ought never to forgive it. She ought to wake up and work, and sleep no more, until that lying libel is dead and damned, and the whole system of false teaching to which it belongs is swept out of the world for ever.

Men have believed in a God who was an omnipotent fiend, a demon quite unknown to the devil-worship of the past—a curse that sat enthroned amid the universe, breathing horror all abroad, and brooding down in blackness on the souls of men. And the ascending smoke of torment was to magnify the features of his monstrous majesty. And if you were one of the chosen, elected to a front seat in the kingdom of this dreadful God, the daintiest part of your enjoyment was to be a full and perfect view of the poor tortured souls, including those of your own wee babes, a span long —the mites and midgets of hell. The inspired Mr. Spurgeon will tell you what a delectable entertainment you may expect, for he says,—"All their veins are roads for the feet of pain to travel on, and every nerve is a string on which the devil shall for ever play his diabolical tune of hell's unutterable lament!" Then, as the song of the ransomed was being sung, word would come that your father was among the damned, and you would sing all the louder,—or that several of your little ones were in hell, and your hallelujahs would be redoubled. And orthodox hearts have been warmed and hands exultingly rubbed over these pictures in the fire, which have been enjoyed with an infernal relish.

Moody, the ranter, tells a story of his God. A poor, foolish, fond mother, in Illinois, had a little child that was sick and ailing unto death. When thinking it was dying, she could not bring her rebellious mind to say "Thy will be done!" she called on God to spare her babe, she cried to him,—"Oh! God! I cannot give up my little one." And the Lord heard her prayer, and *answered* it too! He snatched the child from death, and gave it back to her—turned into *an idiot for life!* That was a smart specimen of the divine derision that is promised in the Bible,—"The Lord shall have ye in derision!" He had her there.

Such was the "good old faith!" Under such a creed the fathers were rendered unfit to beget a race of free and fearless men. Under such a creed the mother's womb has been turned into a prison-house of fear and trembling for the embryo that was wrapped and swathed in a pall of gloom before it was born, and the divine spark of soul almost extinguished by the maternal deposit of Calvinistic cloud!

The Christian scheme, if true, could only lead to eternal wretchedness all round, torments in heaven far worse than all the miseries of hell. Who could be selfishly happy in heaven with a knowledge of everlasting hell? A Hindu commentator on this creed remarks:—"One of their teachers said to me lately that all my people, about 800,000,000 every fifty years, must assuredly go to hell; and at the same time placed before me a picture of their heaven, asking me to 'flee from the wrath to come!' and escape the horrible vindictiveness of their 'God of Love!'" The profoundest appeal made by the Christian creed has ever been made to fear. The bogies of the human childhood have been continued by it and applied to prevent our growing up into women and men. Fear of eating of the Tree of Knowledge. Fear of hell-fire, or the flames of earthly martyrdom. It is fear still even when it has dwindled down to fear of *Mrs. Grundy!* From first to last the appeal has always been to fear. Whereas all the fear in the world could never get from human beings any more than the affection of a dog that licks the hand of its tyrant at feeding time, when there is no whip to be seen! Religion, for ages, has been a reign of terror, under the oppression of which it was impossible for so tender a flower as love to flourish. It did not dare to breathe forth its natural sweetness to its own maker. The deepest religious sense that myriads have ever developed all through life has been a mortal dread of death. The burden of religion in the past has been—"Prepare to die." And this is preached with damnable iteration to those who have never yet lived, have not yet begun to live, and do not know how to begin to realise the glorious possibilities of living. And what is the spiritual result of all this fearful teaching, according to the good old faith? Is it such a sense of another life, and a better world that the concerns of this world are dwarfed and rebuked in its majestic presence? Not at all! The mass of people who are called religious do not want to believe in a spirit-world, save in the abstract, as a necessary article in their creed. They are mortally afraid of the other world. Their foremost feeling is to draw down the blinds against any light breaking in on the subject from another world. They accept a second-hand belief in it on authority as a grim necessity! It's best to believe, in case it does exist after all. As the old woman said—"Ah, Sir! it's best to be polite, for you may go to the devil." But you must know that a great deal of Belief on the subject is like that of the Scotch woman who was asked how she felt when the horse ran away with her and her cart. She said she "put her trust in Providence till the breechin' broke, and then she gave up." She relied upon the visible and tangible link of connection. Her Providence was the breechin'; when that was gone, her faith collapsed altogether. For eighteen hundred years they have pretended to teach men how to die. But the first duty of men who have to die is to learn how to live, so as to leave the world, or something in it, a little better than we found it. Our future life must be the natural outcome of this; the root of the whole matter is in *this* life. The founders of Historic Christianity began with an utterly false theory of life. They mistook the anti-physical for the spiritual; the anti-natural for the divine. Life was a disease, and death the only cure. Worldly blessings were curses in disguise. Belief would work miracles, and Doubt ensure damnation. Sense was the natural enemy of the soul, and had to be suppressed. The most beautiful human body was a dungeon of sin and death in the prison-house of a doomed world. More spirit than common manifested by the youngster was the very devil in revolt against authority, and had to be put into manacles; all nature was un-hallowed, all flesh defiled, until they had pawed it over with priestly rites of regeneration. The Christian scheme of salvation is a false method of dodging the devil at last. People will no longer believe in the lying delusion when once they learn that there is nothing to be got out of it; no good to be gained by it. Its success hitherto has depended on the appeal to selfishness. Next to fear, the chief appeal has been made to the desire for gain. What are considered to be the supreme expressions of Christliness in the Gospels too often denote a low and vulgar type of morality, or they become immoral in their appeal to selfishness. "Blessed are the meek, for they shall inherit the earth." "Blessed are the merciful, for they shall obtain mercy." Blessed are the poor who are content to give up this world, their's is the promise of felicity forever in the world to come. He that giveth to the poor is making a safe investment, because he is lending to the Lord. "Be ye good bankers" is one of the most significant sayings. The appeal is continually made to the sense of personal gain, none the less selfish because it is applied to the next world instead of this; on the contrary, it is increased because the promised gain is to be eternal. You are invited to invest your capital in a bank above that offers you an eternal interest, and like all bankrupt concerns deludes the gullible by promising too much profit. Your alms are to be given secretly, and he that seeth in secret will recompense you. Isn't that calculated to fix one eye on the reward with a leer of cunning in it, as of knowing a good thing when you do see it? One almost expects to see an image of the winking Christ as well as the winking virgin. Such a promise is security for at least a profit of cent. per cent. as the *rate* of eternal interest. But we shall not catch a whale by merely offering a sprat in that way; nor receive a hundred-fold in heaven for all that we may have consciously given up and foregone on earth. All that is but a survival of primitive teachings—the doctrines of the human childhood—an inducement for the individual not to be at war with society or the Church, no matter what laws of nature may have to be sacrificed and violated. And the fact remains to be faced that the teaching is not *true*. The meek do not inherit the earth, and are not going to. We are not forgiven because we are forgiving. Nature does not keep her books of account in that way. Nor are we allowed to cook the accounts in any such fashion. Our false teachers have been monstrously mistaken. The Lord of all does not carry on the business of the Universe as an advertised system of Bribes and Fines. We cannot outset on one line of conduct that which we have done on another. No death of Jesus can save us from ourselves. It was taught that he came to abrogate certain Jewish laws, but no Jesus can upset the natural law of development. What we are now is the result of what we have been, and what we are hereafter will be an evolution from what we are here. There is no dodging the devil of cause and effect. Belief can work no cataclysmal change in death for all the false teaching in the world. No blood of the Lamb will wash out one single internal blot; no tear of pity can make the stained record white. Nothing but life can work any transformation of character here or hereafter; death does not, cannot do it.

All such teaching is entirely false. An old Scotsman, known to me, used to say, "I like Paul! puir soul, I do like Paul. But I dinna like Jesus Christ; I canna like Jesus Christ; they are aye casting it in your teeth that he dee'd for ye; and I dinna want to be dee'd for!" The old fellow's manhood rose in revolt against this salvation of the savage mind by means of blood shed in a vicarious atonement. And he was in the right. We do not want to be died for, and if we did, it would be unavailing. We can no more be died for for another life than the law will allow us to be died for in this.

Men like Jesus, or Jehoshua ben Pandira, the Jewish political and social reformer, or Bruno, or Garibaldi, or Gordon, or Garfield, are in a sense Saviours of the world. They set before us an illuminated image of immortal love. They pull down on themselves, and bear for us, the heavy burden of martyrdom, because of the wolfish selfishness of the world! But there is no salvation possible for us out of the mere act of their suffering. The only salvation is for those who range themselves on the side of these martyrs, and reformers, and forerunners, against the selfishness of the world, to work and change the crude conditions of things, which forever demand the sacrifice of the best and dearest of women and men. When Arnold von Winklereid took the double armful of the enemies' spears into his own breast, it was to make a way for his fellow-countrymen to pass on and widen the gap he had made—*not* for them to stay behind and pat him on the back, or merely subscribe to erect a statue to his memory. That the innocent *are* continually offered up on account of the besotted selfishness of the many is a fact. That they must continue to be thus offered up, until the world awakes to see this shameful sacrifice of others to save its own selfishness, is likewise a fact. But to erect this into a religious dogma, and call it the divine means of saving men, who wilfully continue and necessitate the conditions of society which cause and demand the martyrdom, is about the most immoral and damnable doctrine ever offered to humanity. Why, this doctrine of atonement is so unmanly, so cowardly, and currish, that, if put in its naked truth, the lowest rough in Whitechapel, if unperverted by orthodoxy, would be too manly to accept such an immoral mode of salvation. Any one who would consent to be saved at the expense of another, and an innocent person, ought only to escape, if at all, because he would not be worth the damning. Far nobler was the teaching of Captain George W. Pendleton of the Cleopatra, of Gloucester, Mass. His vessel was doomed and sinking fast, when the boat put off from the "Lord Gough" with a crew that volunteered to try and rescue the shipwrecked men. But with salvation in sight the American captain, by agreement with his men, hauled down his own flag of distress. He thought no boat could live in such a sea. "I said to my men, shall we let those brave fellows risk their lives to save ours? and they said 'No.' Then I hauled down the flag." And so they deliberately elected to die first. That was the gospel according to George Pendleton! But this sacrifice of the innocent to save the guilty—of others instead of self—is the religion of savages; it belongs to the most benighted conditions of the human race, and as such is doomed to die out of any state of true civilisation. The doom of Historic Christianity is sealed, because it was based upon Dogmas against which the highest instincts of the race will forever rise in insurrection, and Doctrines that are certain to be rejected by the growing moral sense of enfranchised humanity.

From what I have learned of the interior operations of natural law, such selfishness defeats its own end and aim. The only way of helping oneself is by helping others. The only true way of receiving is by giving. The fear of being lost never yet saved the soul of any man. Put aside the fable, and the foolish fraud that has been founded on it, and we are face to face with the fact that man has no power to lose his own soul or damn himself for all eternity. If man be immortal by nature, continuity is not based on morality—however much he may retard development by limiting his life to the lower self, which may be a hell to think of and struggle out of hereafter. Nor is the hereafter a heaven provided on purpose to make up for the man-made sufferings to those who have been deluded and cheated and starved out of their life in this world. If it were so, then Providence would not only be responsible for all the mal-arrangement and the misery, through not simply allowing it, but for permitting it, and *providing for* it! Whereas we see the wrong is remediable, the sufferings are unnecessary, and the Christian way out of it is a misleading *cul de sac*. It is like some of the squirrel tracks in the forest with the trail ending up a tree.

The orthodox teachings are so false that they have made the utterance of truth a blasphemy, and all the proclaimers of truth blasphemers! Oppose their savage theology, and you are denounced as an Atheist. Expose the folly of their faith, and you are an Infidel all round. Deny their miracles, and they damn your morals. *The Christian Rock*, not knowing what to say against me that was *good enough*, charged me with having published a volume of *indecent* poetry. It was a malicious lie!—a real instance of *original sin*. But that was what the ignoramus said—mistaking me, as I suppose, for Mr. Swinburne. There was something grand in the ancient martyrdom suffered by the heralds of free thought; whereas the modern reformer has to endure the prolonged torture and ignominy of being kicked to death by butterflies, or gnawed to death by gnats. The religion, founded on misunderstood and perverted mythology, has made everything wrong, and nothing short of an utter reversal, with all Nature for our guide and on our side, can set us right. Its apotheosis of sorrow, of suffering and sacrifice is entirely false, because these are on account of that which, like the "Fall of Man," never really occurred—and weeping over that which is not real is nothing more than a waste of water. Nature offers no evidence that man was meant to moan as a miserable animal. It is true that sorrow and suffering may purge and purify the life, and add a precious seeing to our sight. That which gives the wound may deposit the pearl. The iron of a steadfast soul has frequently been forged in purgatorial fires of pain. The greater the pressure from without, the more has it evoked and evolved the rebounding spirit from within. But that is because there is a power which can turn all experience to account if our life be right in its root-relationship. And human life will always have its full share of sorrow and suffering. But nothing can be falser than to try and found a religion on sorrow and suffering, by the representation of this world as *destined* to be a vale of tears, which we are bound to grow anxious to get out of as soon as we recognise that we are in it. No! *it is not in sorrow, but in joy, that we can attain the greatest unconsciousness of self, and live the larger objective life for others.* We learn as we come to a knowledge of joy, that all sorrow and suffering are but the passing shadows of things mortal, and not the enduring or eternal reality. When no longer darkened or eclipsed by the false creed which has benighted our minds and totally obscured so many natural truths, we can see to the end of these shadows—we can overlook them—in the larger intellectual light of a truer interpretation of the necessities of evolution and of the human environment. If nature has one revelation of truth to make more plainly apparent than another, it is that her creature, man, is intended for health and happiness here, in this life, and not merely hereafter— on condition of suffering here! Pleasure is the natural accompaniment of our creative or productive activities, and the human likeness of life itself is conceived and imaged in delight. Health, physical or mental, means happiness. And everywhere the pull of the natural forces and elements are on the side of health, and, therefore, of consequent or premeditated happiness; children of the blind who never saw, being born to see, and the children of the deaf mutes being born to talk. That delight in life was intended by means of health and happiness may likewise be read in the stern punishment administered by nature for every breach of natural law by which we injure our health and destroy our happiness; and, lest the personal memory of the fact for *one* generation should be too short-lived, the results and effects of the violated law are kept before us, in some cases from generation to generation, *not as gibbets* for mere vengeance, but as sign-posts pointing to the way of reformation. Health is intended, and happiness is the result. It is the happy who will be moral; not the miserable. Now, the Christian scheme would make us miserable, in order that we may be moral here and happy hereafter! Whereas Nature says, be happy here and now, by learning the laws of health—individual, social, political, universal; by getting rid of all opposing falsehood, and establishing the true conditions for evolving health and happiness everywhere for all.

"But," it has actually been urged in reply to me, and in arrest of judgment, "supposing the Christian Narrative to be entirely mythical, is not this supreme legend of divinest pity a beautiful and touching story?" Yes, and the more beautiful the deceit, the deeper the delusion. If it were only a dramatic representation, the plea would apply. But this thing has no meaning if it is not humanly true. The supreme legend of divine pity! That is pity for a fallen race on the part of a supposed deity who damned mankind for ever for the stealing of an apple! Why, our own unpaid magistracy—who are not over-lenient—would not have made more of it than a matter of fourteen days, or a month at most. Suppose you do touch the heart of the world upon false pretences, even to the extent of drawing a tear from John Morley, or getting a perfumed pastille offered up as a sweet savour in sacrificial smoke by Renan, where is the gain when once the falsehood is found out? As soon as the theological Scotsman discovers that his foundations of belief in the fall of man, in predestination, hell-fire, and eternal damnation are false, he naturally takes to whisky, and maybe for the rest of his life cannot find *a brand that is quite fiery enough!* The illusion of false ideals is always at war with reality. The Christ of the Gnostics was a true ideal, possible to all men. But an *Historic* Christ is a false ideal! Where is the sense of supposing a God sliding down to earth on a ladder with no steps to it, and then asking us to walk up minus the foothold? Also, it is in vain we set up an objective ideal for outer worship of that which can only be a reality within the soul.

The god-man of the Gnostics was not a man-god, but the god or divine nature in man, which represented the spiritual image of the Invisible God, the formless in our human form; not in *our* human form of individual personality as an historical Christ, or Horus, or Buddha. That was but the symbolical presentment of the matter. The historical realisation was meant for all men and women, not for one man Jesus, or one female Sophia. We do not want to be beguiled, or to have our children deceived any longer with the most beautiful biography of the man in the moon, who came down too soon, and whose second coming has been looked for so vainly during 1800 years. We are in search and in need of some truer illumination than moonshine. Having discovered that these beautiful legends are mythical and non-human, we do not want the little ones to be misled for life by false teachings before ever they have learned to think. The illusion of false ideals is the magical glamour with which Mephistopheles seduces the soul of Faust! A woman who sent to the lending library for a book that would make her cry, was in search of a false ideal in a world brimming over with bitter reality. A minister of the gospel had been telling his little boy a tale that was full of human interest, and the child had been deeply affected by it, but looking up, with tears in his eyes, he asked,—"Is that true, papa, or is it only preaching?" Poor child! he had heard so much from the same source that he had looked upon it as being not necessarily true, but "only preaching!" That child's position is ours. By all we know, the story is untrue. And we have done for ever with the old wives' fables and romances of mythology as a foundation for religion. We have done with a "Word of God" that is in fatal opposition to his Truth as manifested in Nature! We have done with the very God himself who, when traced to his origin, is found to be chief one of the seven devils or elementals of mythology; and who is quite worthy of that origin in many aspects of his character. We have lost the power to make believe and deceive ourselves further in this matter! It cannot be too often repeated that the foundations of the Christian faith were laid in falsehood and ignorance. The Fall of man in the beginning was *not* a fact, and consequently there could be no *curse*. It is but a fable misinterpreted; and the redemption of the New Testament is based upon the fable in the Old. There *is* no virtue nor efficacy in a vicarious atonement, and no priesthood ever had or will have the power to forgive sin, to break the sequence between cause and effect, or to evade the Nemesis of Natural law. When the great delusion comes to an end its true epitaph would be,—"This was a fraud founded on a fable." Meanwhile, the Church that continues to put forth this scheme of salvation and impose it on the public at the expense of the nation (some eight or ten millions annually!) ought not only to be disestablished and disendowed, it ought to be prosecuted for obtaining money on demonstrably false pretences!

We are often told that our civilisation is infinitely indebted to Christianity; but on the other hand it could be shown that Christianity has been infinitely indebted to civilisation, because it became the adopted religion, the official religion, of the races that happened to be in the swim and current of European progress. Indeed, our European progress has been in exact proportion as the civil law and pre-extant common law have got the upper hand of the ecclesiastical usurpation. What did Christianity do for Italy, its birthplace? If it was such a renovator of the ancient worn-out world, why did it not renew old Rome when its salvation *had been* adopted? What did it do for Greece? for Egypt? for the Mexicans? for any of the ancient races or civilisations? As Jerrold said truly, "We *owe much* to the Jews," but what do the Jews owe to Christianity? Its success has been as a parasite fed on the life of the recent races. The line of renewal was that of the races, whereas all the good results have been claimed for the Christian Creed. Thackeray was once attracted to an elderly gentleman at table who was in the habit of maintaining that everything really good or great in modern literature came directly or indirectly from Pindar. "At all events," said one of the guests, "Pindar did not write 'Vanity Fair'!" "Yes, sir," said the old gentleman with his customary assurance, "Yes, sir, he did; in the highest and noblest sense, Pindar did write 'Vanity Fair'!" In like manner it has been the custom to label every virtue as Christian that had been evolved as human, ages and ages before our own era, at which time every good thing was re-dated, christened, and re-named, as if it were the result of an historical Christ! Indeed, one expects to hear of the elements of pure air, fresh water, and clear sunlight being christened under this name, in the same way that the well-known healing by means of Mental Medicine, which was practised by the pre-Christian races, has been designated "Christian Healing." We shall probably have Christian Lunacy or Christian Idiocy! Yet the fact remains that the direst, bloodiest enemies of the human race in Europe have been the most besotted supporters of the doctrines called Christian. On the other hand if it were possible to eliminate from the factors in European civilisation the direct worth and hereditary influence of those free-thinkers who have not accepted the Historical Christian creed, what, think you, would remain of the progress that was made during many centuries? The only hold the system has ever obtained on the most intellectual of men has been the hold of the rack! the death-grip of the stake! and the embracing fires of martyrdom! Has it ever struck you how little the great minds of the past—the Shakspeares and Goëthes, those "serene creators of immortal things"—troubled themselves about Christianity? How loftily they tower and overlook it. What preacher from the pulpit ever thinks of arraigning the present social conditions as based on the rights of the stronger and the wrongs of the weaker? On the contrary, it has been accepted as a divine arrangement that suffering humanity was the cheapest thing—with a never-ending supply—for manuring the soil, for the greasing of wheels, for coining money out of. They never question whether this is the right basis of the national life. They rejoice in the scriptural assurance that the poor ye have always with you, on purpose to keep down the price of labour; or, we may add, keep up the supply of children to the brothels of the rich, at the lowest possible figure! Christian civilisation to-day is compatible with such a state of Society as was recently revealed by the *Pall Mall Gazette*. We have been assured that the one great sacrifice of the Son of God did put an end to individual human sacrifice! But Christianity has been compatible with the masses of the people of Europe being offered up for ever in one great sacrifice. And what matters the mode, if you *are* sacrificed?

> Honey and milk are sacrifice to thee,
> Kind Hermes, inexpensive Deity!
> But Heracles demands a lamb each day,
> For keeping, as he says, the wolves away.
> What matters it, meek browsers of the sod,
> Whether a *wolf* devour you or a *God?*

The pretended stewards of the mysteries of God have left it for the future to create the very consciousness of wrong in a myriad ways, that their religion has never yet taken into account. As the dogs of Dives, they have now and again given a lick to the sores of Lazarus, and promised him the healing hereafter. But when have they banded together and fought against the social system that dooms the many to poverty—that creates Lazarus as well as his sores?

When they have made large fortunes, and grown very rich, and death is drawing near, some Christians do wax charitable and grow liberal of alms. They do build large and comfortable houses for broken-down paupers to die in; they do supply hospitals for the refuge of those who are ailing and afflicted. But a good deal of the money has been donated for hell-fire insurance, and perhaps these paupers were left all through their working-life to pig together in hovels and slums, the breeding-places of pestilence, which were sure to create the diseases you treat so generously when too late. They starved, and suffered, and sickened, that wealth might accumulate for others! Peabody bequests are all very well in their way; but if the Peabody wealth had been spread in preventing the poverty and crime of the nation, instead of being wrung out of labour, and accumulating to cause these evils, how much better and more blessed would have been the prevention than the late attempt to cure, or rather to help bolster up a state of things which is forever opposed to a cure, half the life of which consists in the relief of its running sores! We do not want to become paupers, as we must ever be if we are to be forever pauperised. On reading lately that Belgravia had turned out to carry its broken victuals round in scrap-carts to the starving poor, I declare it struck a glow of shame into my face as if I had received the insult of a blow, to think of the *unnecessary necessity!* You need not wonder if the poor should damn the charity that is offered to them in the name of religion, as a bribe for them not to ask for justice; or that they should turn a deaf ear to all talk about the bread of heaven when they lack the bread of earth; or the milk of human kindness when their babes are perishing for lack of a little morning-milk from the cow! It is here that Christianity, after 1800 years, is an utter failure, and these are some of the things the Coming religion must go to the root of to be of any use for this world or any other. I knew a poor old man in England who, for 40 years, worked for one firm and its three generations of proprietors. He began at a wage of 16s. per week, and worked his way, as he grew older and older, and many necessaries of life grew dearer and dearer, down to six shillings a week, and still he kept on working, and would not give up. At six shillings a week he broke a limb, and left work at last, being pensioned off by the firm with a four-penny piece! I know whereof I speak, for that man was my father. At the same time, as you are well aware, during those 40 years any possessor of capital might have put it out to usury, and without lifting a finger himself it would have been quadrupled. Such are two of our naturalised laws of capital and labour. The one is the complement of the other; you cannot have the one without the other, and any religion that is not directed to help revolutionise this state of society is damned already, under whatsoever name!

We never can attain the stature of true manhood, or be men, so long as we will un-man ourselves by taking so unmanly an advantage as we do of our more ignorant and hitherto helpless fellow-men. No one class of men can hold another with their faces to the ground, or noses to the grindstone, without also stooping over them, in a manner that for ever hinders from attaining the perfect stature of genuine manhood. The degradation, though different, is shared in common! And, mark you, these things are done as effectually by aid of our social system, and laws of supply and demand, as if one man stood over another with the whip of the slave-driver, or sword of the executioner, in his hand. The wrong and the responsibility, the cruelty and the cowardliness are none the less because they are warranted by custom, sustained by legal enactments, and defended by the press. After the recent utterance of the Archbishop of York, who spoke of our continual doubling of the pile of the rich by halving the wages of the poor, we shall doubtless hear more from the echoists. But the redemption preached for 1800 years has failed to save the world, and it must now give way for other workers with other methods, applied to such matters as the problems of poverty, the distribution of wealth, and the ownership of land. In vain will they claim and Christen every good work of Co-operation, Communism, or Socialism, as Christian by name. The "good Lord Jesus" as an objective saviour and historical Christ *has* "had his day." Our science, applied to civilisation, will part company more and more with the found-out fraud, and will help to carry it no further! Its triumphs will not be made or allowed to support the Christian delusion in the future any more than in the past. And what is the chief cause of this novel interest in the churches on behalf of the poor to-day? Is it not for fear that the new electorate will reject the orthodox system, and that their political influence will prove fatal to the Church?

And now the question is being asked,—What is going to take the place of the cast-out faith? for it is already cast out from the minds of the men who will assuredly mould the freer thought of the future. It is not going to be re-established by law; nor by the blood and fire of the salvation army—nor by presenting our cast-off clothes to the aborigines! Nor by teaching blind Chinamen to read the Bible. Not going to be re-established even though more Bibles have been printed during the last ten years than in all the preceding centuries. *It is being rejected at home faster than you can give it away abroad!* We have *had* our religion based on belief—on belief in a God who cared an infinite deal more for a few apples than for the eternal damnation of myriads of immortal souls—a God who played fast and loose with the laws of his own nature and creation! A creed based on the divine truth of every lie that science has exploded—a belief that was in deadly opposition to all and every truth that has been established. A "good old faith" which is a fraud—so far as being saved by it goes—founded upon a legend misinterpreted. And at last the old grounds of belief are breaking up rapidly; no matter what fresh efforts may be made to deceive, delude, and secure the ignorant, the infants or the aborigines. The orthodox creed is doomed to reversal, even as a dish is wiped clean, and turned upside down. The foundations of the false, cruel, and gory faith are all afloat. It was built as the Russians reared their palace on the frozen river Neva, and the great thaw has come suddenly upon them; the ominous sounds of the final break-up are in their ears; their anchorage and place of trust is crumbling before their eyes. For they had built on the very things (or condition of things) which had sealed up the running springs, and stayed the stream of progress in its course. They have arrested for the purpose of resting. And here is the hint of Science, of Nature, of Spiritualism, of Theosophy, of Freethought, in every form—that they must move on, and get out of the way, or be moved off for ever. The orthodox religion has been dying in proportion as it lost the power to persecute! People now inquire, "what next?" As did the tad-pole when his tail dropped off. What next? as if we were going to straightway put forth a new tail! But that is not the way of Nature. She works by transformation, not by repetition; and her changes imply growth, as the out-come of a new life. It is not possible for us to swap creeds or formulate a new religion. Religion is not a set of precepts, or a mode of worship. It is not a creed that counts in the eternal court. It is not what we believe or profess, but what we are when stripped bare in the balance. Nothing avails but the life lived. Our past deeds must and will make our future fate! Some people seem to think that Spiritualism is about to give us a new tail, or at least to put a firmer tag on the old limp stay-lace of Christianity, to bind us up anew with a fresh support! They are wondering when the Spiritualists are going to open their Sunday shop for the purposes of prayer and praise. But I doubt whether that mode of procedure will ever be repeated in this world. When Sydney Smith saw his child tenderly stroking the hard shell of a tortoise to please the tortoise, he said, "you might just as well stroke the dome of St. Paul's Cathedral with the idea of pleasing the Dean and Chapter." So when we see people crowding together to worship and praise and flatter the Lord, as if they fancied they could gratify his self-esteem, or excite his benevolence, or keep his destructiveness quiet, it reminds me irresistibly of the child's stroking the tortoise to please it. The offering of words of praise which people make to show their love of God is of no more value than the cheap oblations of sham bank-notes which the Chinese burn to any amount as a sacrifice to their deities! They offer money by millions in *that* way. The only worthy way of showing love to God is in working for humanity. That is the practical test. The Lord does not want your long and loud laudations or offerings of false money!

Hermes says "there can be no religion more true or just than to know the things that are." We have *had* a religion without knowledge, and the Coming religion must be founded on knowledge. And it must be good for this world as its warrant for being good for any other. In knowledge only can we find a common ground of agreement. That which is based upon knowledge, need not be the subject of everlasting diversity and contention amongst innumerable sects. We need a first-hand acquaintanceship with the facts of Nature—not limiting Nature, however, to the little we may know of it at present. Of course, mere facts are not everything. No number of separate vertebral joints will supply a man with a back-bone. We have to collect the various joints in our scattered facts derived from a closer acquaintanceship with, and truer interpretation of Nature, but life alone can produce the unity and cohesion that will constitute a back-bone. Amongst these facts we naturally assign a foremost place to those of Spiritualistic phenomena, which the orthodox as good as prohibit to *their* followers in favour of theoretical teachings. Whereas we need a first-hand acquaintanceship here, if anywhere. Present facts are worth all the teachings of the past: by means of these we can test them. The facts in nature are the sole ground to go upon for another life, just as they are for this; facts that are scientific because they are verifiable to-day as in the past. We claim that the inner vision or second sight is a fact in nature. Pre-vision is a fact in nature. The spiritual apparition is, and always has been, a fact in nature. Conscious communication with Spiritual Intelligences is a fact in nature. But a physical resurrection from the dead is not a fact in nature, and here the Aborigines are far ahead of the orthodox Christian world in a practical knowledge of these phenomena on which the demonstration of our continuity is based. The naturalist Kircher estimated the number of intellectual proofs of the existence of God at 6561. A Spiritualist considers one actual proof of objective spiritual manifestation as worth them all. Better is one real spirit communication than a divinity put together in 6561 pieces; it is a fact that for the first time makes those figures live!— or gives a foothold for taking the first step in the unknown. As evidence of a future life, one single proof in spiritual manifestation is worth the hear-say revelation of the world. The time has not yet come for any thinker to set forth the reign of law and order in this obscure domain of Nature which, for lack of another name, we call "Spiritual," or -neo-natural; but Spiritualism is none the less real because orthodox physical science has not yet established it as one of its truths. A sufficient number of competent observers and credible witnesses testify to the occurrence and recurrence of certain phenomenal manifestations, which go to prove that we have found the sole bridge in nature that crosses the unfathomable gulf between the dead and the not-dead ; the organic and the inorganic—between mind and matter—which Science has strenuously sought elsewhere, but never yet found. A million of us know that the cable is laid between the two worlds, and the messages prove that there are intelligent operators at the other end of it, who can send us messages in human language. We know that the so-called dead are living still, however difficult it may be, and is, though not impossible, to establish their personal identity ! We know they can communicate with us and *we* with them, objectively as well as subjectively, and that the objective phenomena enable us to comprehend the true nature of the subjective—to accept and to found upon it inferentially. We know they *can* establish a rapport with us more *rare* and potent than we can with each other in the body. Some of us have felt and handled and heard that which was invisible to our sight, in the presence of those who could see and describe the forms and motions of that (or of those) which we only felt and heard. And *so* we can put our evidence together, and draw the necessary inference. Buckle has said: " The doctrine of immortality is the doctrine of doctrines. A truth compared with which it is indifferent whether anything else be true!" Anyway, Spiritualism alone offers the means of establishing it as a fact. Spiritualism *alone* offers a scientific basis for a doctrine of immortality ! The Phenomenal Spiritualist stands level-footed on the only ground of fact that is, or ever has been, offered by Nature for human foothold in the Unseen. Spiritualism alone reveals a bridge on which we can get any bit of actual foothold for crossing the gulf of death. The Spiritualist makes connection between the two worlds, and runs his trains of thought right through! Indeed, the two worlds are but one for him—they are not two, any more than the railway runs through another world by night. It is but one world after all, with two aspects. The daylight part of it is but half-revealed by day, and the dark side is but half-concealed by night. The phenomena called Spiritualistic furnish us with a means of interrogating Nature in such a way that it is sure to revolutionise all our mental science—psychology, philosophy, metaphysic, and theosophy. These phenomena show us that *we* have other and profounder facts to go upon than those hitherto included in our data. Realistic phenomena, not merely idealistic—facts in place of faith. Spiritualism opens up to our vision a Power that operates upon us, and through us, and makes use of us whether we will or no,—whether we are conscious of its presence or not—our recognition being unnecessary to its existence or operations. Spiritualism shows us how the soul of man may be fed with a sustenance drawn from the well of life within us, that is penetrated and replenished from eternal springs. And we maintain that these phenomena, called Spiritualistic (which have no relationship to the miracles of misinterpreted mythology), and these alone, do actually demonstrate the natural nexus for the continuity of life, and the next step upward in human evolution.

Some of our Free-thought Secularist friends seem to suffer from *rabies* on the subject of a future existence. The very idea of it drives them frantic; and that which is as the water of life to others only serves to aggravate their symptoms, and make them rage more furiously. The editor of the *Melbourne Liberator* says it is a swindle of the worst description to keep up the farce of a future life. Now, I think we know that there are facts in Nature which warrant the inference of another life; and simply *as facts* I would have them made known. Without the facts we cannot know the truth! Anyway, there is no warrant for those who do not know that man has a soul to dogmatise and teach that men have no souls, or that there *is* no future life. Those who do not know can have no right to pretend to know, and such pretensions of the negational dogmatists constitute a positive imposture. Whosoever owns the head, you cannot quite bring a knowledge of all things pertaining to the ultimate reality under one hat. The Agnostics show more modesty. Professor Huxley says: "Agnosticism means that a man shall not say he knows or believes that which he has no scientific grounds for professing to know and believe!" So say we. Only we claim to have scientific grounds for knowing. A crude materialistic interpretation of the Universe bottoms nothing. There is eternal motion; there is eternal life. There is a being beyond appearance. There is a Consciousness that co-ordinates the means to attain the ends, with power to turn to account all that occurs in the sphere of so-called human Free-Will. There is Intelligence involved in all that is intelligible. All who break the laws of nature do so under penalty of punishment. They learn sooner or later that there is a law-maker, whose ministers and agencies will dog the lawbreaker; however we may deny the law-maker, we cannot evade the law! False Spiritualism merely begets a craze after another life. But a true Spiritualism will turn our attention to this life, and help on the work of *this* world. Spiritualism enables us to call in the new world in our rectification and adjustment of the wrong done in the old—somewhat like calling in troops from the new world of the Colonies to fight the battle of England in the old. It has come to quicken a keener conscience in the human race; set up a loftier ideal of life and a nobler standard of appeal than fear of punishment and hope of reward. For me, Spiritualism means an aid in the certain overthrow of all false dogmas and lying legends, which have been imposed upon men, and are still imposed upon the children, in the name of God. Science has been driving in its splitting wedge with a mighty ripping and rending of the ancient beliefs. But with Spiritualism the wedge is alive, and takes root just as the seed of the Indian Bo-tree is so vital that when it is sown singly in the cleft of some lofty tower or fortress, and a drop of moisture and a smile of sunshine have caused it to quicken, it will shoot out and lay hold of the stone with its feelers and strike root to make its way down the walls to the earth outside, and laying hold of this it gathers strength and grows mightily, and sends back such force to its birth-place that the walls are rent, and the temporary resting-place betwixt earth and heaven is shattered in favour of the newer rootage and firmer foothold upon this more nutritious and life-giving ground. So will Spiritualism lay hold of the larger substance of reality, and inevitably rend the barren stone walls of the Establishments into fragments, minute enough to be ground down into the new fresh soil in which it is destined to flourish and bear fruit in the freer, larger, loftier life of a nobler human race! Spiritualism will help to break up the sacerdotal ring of priestcraft that has hemmed the people round with terrors and strangled souls with fear. It is rapidly abolishing the tyranny of death, and restoring freedom for life to those whose whole living had been turned into one long dread of death. Spiritualism will have done a great work, if only by destroying that craven dread of dying which has been instilled into us from before birth; the child in embryo having been made to feel and embody the mother's shudderings at the frightful language used by the torturers of souls, who fulminate their cruel formulas from the pulpit. If it sets us free to do our own thinking as rational men and women, who have so long and so profoundly suffered from the pretensions of the sacerdotalists, who continue to peddle, in the name of God, a system of delusion, the foundations of which are to be discovered at last in misinterpreted mythology; against which system of false teaching I, for one, am at war to the death, with any and every weapon I can lay hands on, including this most potent weapon—the sword of Spiritualism. Spiritualism is sure to be terribly iconoclastic! It means a new light of revelation in the world from the old eternal source. And you cannot have new light let in without seeing many old acquaintances with a new face. Many aspects of things will change; and some things that we mistook for live faces will turn into the sheerest masks of mockery, and whiten with the sweat of dissolution running down them. Spiritualism, as I interpret it, means a new life in the world, and new life is not brought forth without pain and parting, and the sheddings of old decay. New ideas are not born in the mind without the pangs of parturition; and to get rid of our old ingrained errors of false teaching is like having to tear up by the root the snags of one's own teeth with our own hand. But, by our own hand and will, this has to be done, for nothing else can do it. New light and new life, however, do not come to impoverish, they come to enrich, and no harm can befall the nature of that which is eternally true. It is only falsehood that fears or needs to fear the transfiguring touch of light; *that* must needs shrink and shrink until it shrivels away. Spiritualism will prove a mighty iconoclast, but the fetishes and idols it destroys will yield up their concealed treasures of innermost truth, as did the statue that was destroyed by Mahmoud, the image-breaker. The priestly defenders offered him an enormous sum to spare their God, but he resisted the bribe and smote mightily with his iron mace. Down fell the image, and as it broke there rolled out of it a river of pent-up wealth, which had been hoarded and hidden within.

Evolution, for which no place has been left in the Christian system of thought, is of itself quite capable of being the death of that system; but Spiritualism will undermine it, and dig its grave, and plant it with another nobler life. Spiritualism has already proved itself to be the greatest solvent of ancient dogmas ever known. It has acted, and is acting, like Hannibal's vinegar on the Alps, by crumbling the most stupendous obstacles of mental progress. The Spiritualistic religion is going to conquer because it is not afraid of any new facts that may be dug out of the earth, or drawn down from the heavens. It is bound to conquer, because with it free-thinking is no longer on the side of negation. Our old Free-thinkers were brave men who drew a new breath of freer life through the enlarging lungs of the world, by daring to think freely —braver men than our Spiritualists are, who are sadly in need of a fiery course of persecution to test the metal of their manhood. But on the old material plane they soon came to where their foothold ceased, and they could get no further. The freer thought of the Spiritualist gives him arms to swim the sea, and wings to mount the air, when he comes to where the earth ends,—and to the Materialist there seemed no more solid ground. I have warrant for saying that the only form of Free-thought that is feared as deadly by the Church of Rome is Spiritualistic, which cuts the ground from under it in relation to a future life. We say to them, Call it a superstition if you please. Our superstition will be the death of yours. And whenever or wherever they come fairly to the grapple we shall see, and our enemies will feel, how the old bones will crackle and crumble in the grip of its crushing power. Spiritualism, as I apprehend it, is going to be a mighty agent in carrying on the work of this world, in producing loftier souls for the life of another world, of which it gives us glimpses on the way. Let me tell you that this despised Spiritualism will put a light into the one hand and a sword into the other, that have to be flashed in on many dark places, and through many a dungeon-grating of human kind, in spite of the birds of night that may hoot at the light, and blaspheme against its brilliance.

There is a cry of womankind now going up in search of God! Sometimes accompanied with a clasping of hands—at other times with the clenched fist—and it behoves all men to know what it does really and rightly mean. It may be found to imply more than "woman suffrage," it may signify woman suffering. "Suffering from what?" do you reply. "Do we not keep her, and clothe her, and are we not prohibited, or were under the good old English law, from beating her with a stick that is thicker than your middle finger?" It may be that the brute ideal of the savage is getting to be a worn-out type here as elsewhere, and that there is a desire for a more refined and intellectual form of manhood in the intimacy of married life! So far from Woman having been the cause of any pretended Fall of man, she has been the true Saviour of humanity; or rather, the main instrument for saving because more open to the Divine influence, which I hold to be for ever working to prevent the propagation of man's worser moods, and the personification of his baser self. Often has she tried to hinder man when he was devilishly bent on defacing the coming image of the divine! And this alone, with her back to the wall, in places where there was no law on her side. How many idiots, think you, are born into the world through drunken fathers? Idiocy is an arrested development. Drunkenness is also an arrest of the soul in its brain action, which means that the idiot child is often a tiny, pitiful image of the father who was in a state of moral idiocy. The spiritual life was arrested; and there is as great a deficiency of soul as there is of blood in the brain when you swoon. It is a moral swoon made visible and permanent in a hideous effigy of Death-in-life. Lucky if the paralysis be so complete that a great criminal is not let loose on the world in active, instead of helpless, idiocy. I only dare hint at the things which are done in the world to the knowledge of women, and you need not wonder if now and again there rises the shrill, protesting shriek.

Some of my readers may have seen specimens in Greek and Italian art of what man has done to gratify the lust of the eye that he might perpetuate the lusts of the soul, and gloat over his own moral deformity, immortalised by the utmost cunning wherewith art could animate the most precious forms of inanimate nature. He has set the image of his own corruption in the shining mirror of a stainless jewel, and figured forth his moral deformity in the lustre of a gem—think of giving the worst kind of human disease to a gem! He has cut the devil of his beastlier self in the diamond, enshrined the libidinous satyr, tongue-lolling and leering from a sapphire's azure heaven, made the innocent emerald flush the face with the reflection of what was enacted in its green coolness, called up spirits of all uncleanness in the purity of a crystal. All this was very bad—very horrible—this corruption of art for the delectation of the beast with a taste in man! But what was such degradation at its wantonest and worst compared with that of a drunken man— no matter with which passion he may be aflame—furiously stamping his own hideous face, and the features of his vice, on that form of humanity which he so darkens and defiles as to well-nigh blast or blot out of it the image of God or man altogether! These jewels of life, these creations of love, to be thus brutally defaced in such a cruel way! It is horrible, most horrible! Enough to make all womankind, all motherhood, nay, all manhood, rise in revolt against it, and sicken, and spew it out. If men go reeling to the marriage-bed, reeking with the foul effluvia of drink, gross with gluttony, and stained through and through with moral disease, if the children are made from the scum of bad blood into an outer likeness of the inner corruption, what can we expect the men and women to be? If you held a tiny little bird's egg in your hand, how tenderly would you touch it! how protectingly would you fence it round and shield it from all danger! and here is an immortal soul in embryo, susceptible to every influence of the father, every feeling of the mother, looking with all its life to them for its environing conditions! Here then, instead of the ancient damnation of the flesh we need a religion of the body as well as of the soul, and a gospel of human physics. Hitherto the utmost that has been aimed at scientifically has been a better breed of horses or cattle; we ought to be at least as careful in the bringing forth of human beings. Make the tree good and its fruit will be good (barring certain "throws back" or "sports" of nature). The work has to be done from the root, and not by late trying to graft the good on a bad stock. Remember that life comes into the world according to conditions, and the first of these conditions are those of the married life. Human embryology has now to be studied religiously in the light of evolution. If I were a woman I doubt whether I should consider a smoker, or chewer of tobacco, quite good enough to father my children! The final effect—the supposed beneficial effect—of nicotine is to arrest the decay of matter that ought to be sloughed off in order that it may be renewed. No smoker is so live a man, all round, as he ought to be, or might be; and you can study them in all the various stages and degrees of dreaming, decaying, dying, poisoning the springs of future life, or bringing death into the world.

The truth is, that woman at her best and noblest must be monarch of the marriage-bed. We must begin in the creatory if we are to benefit the race, and the woman has got to rescue and take possession of herself, and consciously assume all the responsibilities of maternity, on behalf of the children. No woman has any right to part with the absolute ownership of her own body, but she has the right to be protected against all forms of brute force. No woman has any business to marry anything that is less than a man. No woman has any right to marry any man who will sow the seeds of hereditary disease in her darlings. Not for all the money in the world! No woman has any right, according to the highest law, to bear a child to a man she does not love. No mother has any right to allow her innocent little ones to be injured mentally for life by orthodox drugs and false nostrums of salvation that are vended from the pulpit by pious impostors. These—and other things as vital—will become practical so soon as womankind co-operate and insist that they shall be practised. "Women, obey your husbands," is a text that, when wrongly applied, has wrought as much human misery as that other relic of barbarism, "Spare the rod and spoil the child!" Why, the great and sole incentive with the mass of male hypocrites who support the Churches is because orthodox Christianity encourages the subjection of women, and helps to make them better—that is more spiritless—household slaves. They do not believe for themselves, but they think anything good enough for their wives and daughters to believe.

> "You cannot serve two masters, saith the Word,"
> But Satan nudges them and whispers "Gammon;"
> "You lend your Wives and Daughters to the Lord,
> You *give* yourselves to love and worship Mammon."

Our women and children are *bound* to break away from this system of fettered thought. If I could stand where stood the cock when all the world could hear him crow, *my* cry would be to the wives and mothers on behalf of the children. The women are bound to rescue the children, and to head their Exodus from the bondage of orthodoxy, even if the men are too unmanly—too cowardly to help them. No doubt, one real crux is, What are we going to teach the children? And here there is so much to be done and lived by the parents in presence of the children, and so little to be said! The life we live with them every day is the teaching that tells; and not the precepts uttered weekly that are continually belied by our own daily practices. Give the children a knowledge of natural law, especially in that domain of physical nature which has hitherto been tabooed. If we break a natural law we suffer pain in consequence, no matter whether we knew the law or not. This result is not an accident, because it always happens, and is obviously intended to happen. Punishments are not to be avoided by ignorance of effects; they can only be warded off by a knowledge of causes. Therefore *nothing but knowledge* can help them. Teach the children to become the soldiers of duty instead of the slaves of selfish desire. Show them how the sins against self reappear in the lives of others. Teach them to think of those others as the means of getting out of self. Teach them how the laws of nature work by heredity. How often has the apparently pious, God-fearing parent produced a child that seemed to the outside world the very opposite of himself, as if the devil had dropped an egg in the good man's nest. And yet this Satan of a son was but the nature of the saintly father turned inside out—only an exposure of that which had been hidden for a time beneath the cloak of hypocrisy; because in the end nature is honest, and will *out* with it. Children have ears like the very spies of nature herself; eyes that penetrate all subterfuge and pretence; and a sense of justice that, if allowed fair-play, would straightway wreck the orthodox gospel. Guide the curiosity of the little ones whilst it is yet innocent, and give them all necessary knowledge fresh and sweet from the lips of the mother and father, Mr. Ruskin.

notwithstanding. Let the children be well grounded in the doctrine of development, without which we cannot begin to think coherently. Give them the best material, the soundest method; let the spirit-world have a chance as a living influence on them, and then let them do the rest. Never forget that the faculty for seeing is worth all that is to be seen. It is good to set before the youngsters the loftiest and noblest ideals—not those that are mythical and non-natural, but those that have been lived in human reality. The best ideal of all has to be pourtrayed by the parents in the realities of life at home. The teaching that goes deepest will be indirect, and the truth will tell most on them when it is overheard. When you are not watching, and the children *are*—that is when the lessons are learned for life.

Possibly *my* Coming Religion may suggest a coming revolution? I should not wonder if it does. Anyway, we mean to do our own thinking, and to have absolute freedom of thought and expression. We mean to rescue our Sunday from the sacerdotal ring. But we do *not* mean that the day of rest and recreation shall fall into the hands of the capitalists. We mean to try and rescue this world from the clutches of those who profess to have the keys and the keeping of the other—they who hold up the other world in front of that beast of burden, the producer, as a decoying lure, like the bunch of carrots before the donkey's nose, in order that the suggestion of plenty in paradise may induce him to forego his common right to grazing-ground on earth. We mean to have a day of reckoning with the unjust stewards of the earth. We mean to have the national property restored to the people, which the churches and other bodies have withheld from the people. We mean that the land, with its inalienable right of living, its mineral wealth below the soil and its waters above, shall be open to all. We mean to have our banking done by the State, and our railways worked for the benefit of the whole people. We mean to temper the terror of rampant individualism with the principles of co-operation. We mean to show that the wages' system is a relic of barbarism and social serfdom. That under it labour must remain a slave in the prison-house of property. We mean for woman to have perfect equality with man, social, religious, and political, and her fair share in that equity which is of no sex. We mean also that the same standard of morality shall apply to the woman as to the man. In short, we intend that the redress of wrongs and the righting of inequalities, which can only be rectified in this world, shall not be put off and postponed to any future stage of existence. The religion of the future has got to include not only Spiritualism, but the salvation of humanity for this life—any other may be left to follow hereafter. It has to be a sincerity of life, in place of pretended belief. A religion of science, in place of superstition. Of joy, instead of sorrow. Of man's Ascent, instead of his Fall. A religion of fact in the present, and not of mere faith for the future. A religion in which the temple reared to God will be in human form, instead of being built of brick or stone. A religion of work, rather than worship; and, in place of the deathly creeds, with all their hungry parasites of prey, a religion of life—life actual, life here, life now, as well as the promise of life everlasting!

www.ingramcontent.com/pod-product-compliance
Lightning Source LLC
Chambersburg PA
CBHW070540160426
43199CB00014B/2303